The G
of Pac.   ....tics

The Growth and Collapse of Pacific Island Societies

Archaeological and Demographic Perspectives

Patrick V. Kirch and Jean-Louis Rallu,

EDITORS

University of Hawai'i Press | Honolulu

©2007 University of Hawai'i Press
All rights reserved
Printed in the United States of America
12 11 10 09 08 07 6 5 4 3 2 1

Library of Congress Cataloging-in-Publication Data
The growth and collapse of Pacific island societies :
archaeological and demographic perspectives /
Patrick V. Kirch and Jean-Louis Rallu, editors.
    p. cm.
  Includes bibliographical references and index.
  ISBN 978-0-8248-3134-9 (hardcover : alk. paper)
  1. Ethnology — Oceania.   2. Ethnology — Hawaii.
3. First contact of aboriginal peoples with Westerners —
Oceania.   4. First contact of aboriginal peoples with
Westerners — Hawaii.   5. Excavations (Archaeology)
— Oceania.   6. Excavations (Archaeology) — Hawaii.
7. Oceania — Population — History.   8. Hawaii —
Population — History.   9. Oceania — Antiquities.
10. Hawaii — Antiquities.   I. Kirch, Patrick Vinton.
II. Rallu, Jean-Louis.
GN662.G76   2007
306.0995 — dc22   2006034505

University of Hawai'i Press books are printed on acid-
free paper and meet the guidelines for permanence and
durability of the Council on Library Resources.

Designed by April Leidig-Higgins

Printed by The Maple Vail Book Manufacturing Group

CONTENTS

List of Tables vii

List of Figures xi

Preface xv

1   PATRICK V. KIRCH AND JEAN-LOUIS RALLU

Long-Term Demographic Evolution in the Pacific Islands

Issues, Debates, and Challenges 1

2   JEAN-LOUIS RALLU

Pre- and Post Contact Population in Island Polynesia

Can Projections Meet Retrodictions? 15

3   SHRIPAD TULJAPURKAR, CHARLOTTE LEE, AND MICHELLE FIGGS

Demography and Food in Early Polynesia 35

4   PATRICK V. KIRCH

"Like Shoals of Fish"

Archaeology and Population in Pre-Contact Hawai'i 52

5   THEGN N. LADEFOGED AND MICHAEL W. GRAVES

Modeling Agricultural Development and
Demography in Kohala, Hawai'i 70

6   PATRICK V. KIRCH

Paleodemography in Kahikinui, Maui

An Archaeological Approach 90

7   ROSS CORDY

Reconstructing Hawaiian Population at European Contact

Three Regional Case Studies 108

8   BRENDA K. HAMILTON AND JENNIFER G. KAHN

Pre-Contact Population in the 'Opunohu Valley, Mo'orea

An Integrated Archaeological and Ethnohistorical Approach 129

9 ERIC CONTE AND TAMARA MARIC

Estimating the Population of Hokatu Valley, Ua Huka Island (Marquesas, French Polynesia) According to the Archaeological Remains 160

10 DAVID V. BURLEY

Archaeological Demography and Population Growth in the Kingdom of Tonga
950 BC to the Historic Era 177

11 ROGER C. GREEN
Protohistoric Samoan Population 203

12 VALERIE J. GREEN AND ROGER C. GREEN

An Accent on Atolls in Approaches to Population Histories of Remote Oceania 232

13 J. STEPHEN ATHENS

Prehistoric Population Growth on Kosrae, Eastern Caroline Islands 257

14 MATTHEW SPRIGGS

Population in a Vegetable Kingdom
Aneityum Island (Vanuatu) at European Contact in 1830 278

15 CHRISTOPHE SAND, JACQUES BOLE, AND A. OUETCHO

What were the Real Numbers? The Question of Pre-Contact Population Densities in New Caledonia 306

16 PATRICK V. KIRCH

Concluding Remarks
Methods, Measures, and Models in Pacific Paleodemography 326

References 339
List of Contributors 375
Index 377

11   Table 1.1. Hypothesized demographic correlates of early and late populations in Polynesia.

26   Table 2.1. Death rate in epidemic years.

28   Table 2.2. Natural growth rate by islands and valleys in the Marquesas.

31   Table 2.3. Population density in the Society and Cook Islands in the nineteenth century.

82   Table 5.1. The distribution of C-shape features in relation to *makai* and *mauka* zones.

82   Table 5.2. The distribution of enclosure features in relation to *makai* and *mauka* zones.

82   Table 5.3. The distribution of platform/pavement/terrace features in relation to *makai* and *mauka* zones.

84   Table 5.4. The distribution of domestic features in relation to expansion and intensification zones.

84   Table 5.5. The distribution of C-shape features in relation to expansion and intensification zones.

84   Table 5.6. The distribution of enclosure features in relation to expansion and intensification zones.

84   Table 5.7. The distribution of platform/pavement/terrace features in relation to expansion and intensification zones.

85   Table 5.8. The distribution of domestic features in relation to areas developed during the different phases.

101   Table 6.1. Residential complexes by 100-year intervals.

101   Table 6.2. Estimated population of Kīpapa-Naka'ohu by 100-year intervals.

102   Table 6.3. Estimated population densities for Kīpapa-Naka'ohu by 100-year intervals.

118   Table 7.1. Wai'anae District, O'ahu: Population estimates for European contact.

120   Table 7.2. Populations of 'Ewa Ahupua'a in 1831 and 1835.

124   Table 7.3. Hāmākua Moku, Hawai'i Island: Population figures by parish or district.

125   Table 7.4. Hāmākua Moku, Hawai'i Island: Estimates of average *ahupua'a* populations.

131   Table 8.1. Survey of the available and most relevant ethnohistoric sources for Ma'ohi population.

140   Table 8.2. Function of space in 'Opunohu Valley excavated houses.

143   Table 8.3. Comparison of habitation-based estimates of valley population at contact.

147   Table 8.4. Some subsistence cultivars in the Ma'ohi production system.

149   Table 8.5. Staple starch productivity of arboriculture systems.

150   Table 8.6. Potential productivity of surveyed terraces.

151   Table 8.7. Available land for cultivation by soil/slope category.

152   Table 8.8. Reconstruction of subsistence cultivation system for 'Opunohu Valley and Mo'orea.

154   Table 8.9. Potential productivity of 'Opunohu Valley and Mo'orea.

169   Table 9.1. Stone structures identified in the Hokatu Valley survey.

171   Table 9.2. Low estimation of population.

172   Table 9.3. High estimation of population.

172   Table 9.4. Low estimation of population according to the method of M. Kellum-Ottino.

173   Table 9.5. High estimation of population according to the method of M. Kellum-Ottino.

181   Table 10.1. Census data for different island groups in Tonga based on numbers given in Maude (1965), Wood (1943), Walsh (1970), and Thayman (1978).

185   Table 10.2. Acres of arable land per person for each of the main island groups in Tonga.

186   Table 10.3. Projected Late Prehistoric population estimate based on 2 acres of arable land per person, with downward adjustments for Vava'u.

190   Table 10.4. Lapita site size by island group in Tonga.

209   Table 11.1. Population of Samoa in 1839.

209 Table 11.2. Population of Western Samoa in 1844 according to the LMS missionary Mills.

211 Table 11.3. Census estimates and population decline in Samoa, 1840–1853.

212 Table 11.4. Estimates of Samoan population size by island, 1840–1853.

215 Table 11.5. Cultivated land requirements in American Samoa, 1840.

217 Table 11.6. Individual cultivated land requirements in prehistoric Samoa.

237 Table 12.1. Tokelau: Vital landscape characteristics.

242 Table 12.2. Atafu: "Generations" and sibships.

245 Table 12.3. Atafu: Dwellings and population per dwelling.

249 Table 12.4. Tokelau: Calculations of modern ethnographic dwelling size and associated population numbers.

270 Table 13.1. Comparison of single population growth rates for selected time intervals, single colonizing voyage.

270 Table 13.2. Comparison of multiple population growth rates for selected time intervals, single colonizing voyage.

271 Table 13.3. Comparison of multiple population growth rates for selected time intervals, three colonizing voyages (20 people at AD 1, 20 people at AD 50, and 20 people at AD 100).

293 Table 14.1. Northern Aneityum: Land area and land use in 1830.

297 Table 14.2. Garden labor and productivity on Aneityum in 1830.

300 Table 14.3. Aneityumese age and sex structure models.

302 Table 14.4. Population of Aneityum in 1830.

303 Table 14.5. Population densities for Aneityum in 1830 using various measures.

21   Figure 2.1. Adjustment of archaeological data for Hawai'i.

30   Figure 2.2. Tahiti's population 1767–1781: Various retrodictions and a simulation.

41   Figure 3.1. Value of logits for three mortality schedules.

41   Figure 3.2. Contours of the expectation of life at birth *eo* for a range of values of A and B.

43   Figure 3.3. Expected life *e10* at age 10 for a range of values of A and B.

44   Figure 3.4. An outline of the main components for the CENTURY model of soil dynamics.

45   Figure 3.5. Increasing harvest intensity where water is limiting does not affect equilibrium plant production.

46   Figure 3.6. The equilibrium amount of mineral nitrogen and of organic nitrogen decrease linearly with increasing harvest fraction.

47   Figure 3.7. Under conditions where nitrogen is limiting at equilibrium, increasing harvest intensity lowers initially low levels of equilibrium mineral nitrogen dramatically.

47   Figure 3.8. Decreases in availability of the limiting nutrient drive proportional decreases in equilibrium production with increasing harvest intensity.

48   Figure 3.9. Changing harvest intensity can change the factor that limits production at equilibrium.

48   Figure 3.10. Production responses to water limitation in a nitrogen-limited system at two levels of rainfall.

56   Figure 4.1. Hommon's "site-population growth sequences" for leeward Hawai'i Island.

58   Figure 4.2. Cordy's time-specific population estimates for eight North Kona *ahupua'a*, from AD 1400 to 1780.

59   Figure 4.3. Site frequency histogram for west Hawai'i.

62   Figure 4.4. The Dye-Komori model of Hawaiian population growth.

72 Figure 5.1. The Kohala peninsula showing the extent of the dryland field system and the surveyed archaeological remains.

74 Figure 5.2. The location of the detailed study area (DSA) within the Kohala field system.

75 Figure 5.3. The *mauka* and *makai* zones within the DSA.

76 Figure 5.4. The domestic features within the DSA.

77 Figure 5.5. The building association groups of agricultural walls and trails.

78 Figure 5.6. Zones of initial agricultural development within the DSA.

79 Figure 5.7. Paths of agricultural development within the DSA.

80 Figure 5.8. Areas of expansion and intensification within the DSA.

86 Figure 5.9. Alternative population trends within the DSA.

87 Figure 5.10. Population growth and agricultural development in the DSA.

92 Figure 6.1. The Kahikinui region of southeastern Maui, showing areas of intensive archaeological survey.

95 Figure 6.2. Frequency distribution of conventional radiocarbon dates for Kahikinui by 100-year age intervals.

96 Figure 6.3. Frequency distribution of calibrated radiocarbon dates for Kahikinui by 100-year age intervals.

97 Figure 6.4. Radiocarbon dates respond to the "calibration stochastic distortion (CSD) effect."

99 Figure 6.5. Map of a typical pre-Contact residential cluster in Kahikinui.

100 Figure 6.6. The frequency distribution of dated habitation complexes for Kahikinui.

113 Figure 7.1. Map showing the lands *(ahupua'a)* of Wai'anae Moku, island of O'ahu.

119 Figure 7.2. Map showing the lands *(ahupua'a)* of 'Ewa Moku, island of O'ahu.

122 Figure 7.3. Map showing the lands *(ahupua'a)* of Hāmākua Moku, Island of Hawai'i.

135 Figure 8.1. Calibrated radiocarbon dates from 'Opunohu Valley.

136 Figure 8.2. 'Opunohu Valley date distribution.

138 Figure 8.3. Distribution of house sizes in 'Opunohu Valley.

155 Figure 8.4. Island-wide estimates of population for Mo'orea at contact.

161 Figure 9.1. The Marquesas Islands, showing the location of the island of Ua Huka.

162 Figure 9.2. Map of the island of Ua Huka showing the location of Hokatu Valley.

163 Figure 9.3. Survey areas within Hokatu Valley.

164 Figure 9.4. Map of stone structures in Hokatu Valley.

165 Figure 9.5. The classic form of Marquesan dwelling house.

165 Figure 9.6. Cross-section of a typical Marquesan house platform, showing the elevated sleeping area.

179 Figure 10.1. Kingdom of Tonga and other islands in Western Polynesia.

183 Figure 10.2. Principal soil types on Tongatapu and Vavaʻu.

187 Figure 10.3. Lapita phase (950–700 B.C.) sites on Tongatapu.

188 Figure 10.4. Lapita phase (950–700 B.C.) occupation sites where excavations have been conducted in the principal northern islands of the Haʻapai Group.

188 Figure 10.5. Lapita phase sites (950–700 B.C.) on the islands of the Vavaʻu Group.

192 Figure 10.6. Plainware phase (700 BC–AD 400) ceramic sites on Tongatapu adapted from Spennemann (1986).

194 Figure 10.7. Midden ridge and Plainware phase (700 BC–AD 400) settlement sites on the island of Lifuka, Haʻapai Group.

195 Figure 10.8. Plainware phase (700 BC–AD 400) ceramic sites on the islands of the Vavaʻu Group.

204 Figure 11.1a. Map of the South Pacific region showing the atolls of Atafu, Nukunonu, and Fakaofo and Olohega (Swains Island) and the islands of Samoa and American Samoa, with negotiated international maritime boundaries.

204 Figure 11.1b. Map of the South Pacific region showing New Zealand and Samoa, with the atolls of Tuvalu, Tokelau, and Pukapuka.

206 Figure 11.2. An enhanced representation of Samoan population history from AD 1790 to 1950.

219 Figure 11.3. ʻUpolu: Mid-twentieth-century land use based solely on the distinction between forest and arable land in cultivation/habitation.

220 Figure 11.4. Savai'i: Mid-twentieth-century land use based solely on the distinction between forest and arable land in cultivation/habitation, although separating from these the raw lava of late-eighteenth/ early-nineteenth-century volcanism.

221 Figure 11.5. Palauli Bay showing the two principal named coastal settlements of the 1830s.

226 Figure 11.6a. An illustrated perception of a typical structural pattern created by settlement buildings and related features, compiled from multiple text descriptions of the 1839–1840 period.

226 Figure 11.6b. The actual internal patterning found in Asaga Village (nu'u), Savai'i, in 1956.

258 Figure 13.1. Map of the western Pacific Ocean showing the location of Kosrae in the eastern Caroline Islands of Micronesia.

260 Figure 13.2. Map of Kosrae.

261 Figure 13.3. Dwelling compound of a high chief at Lelu showing houses and people as depicted in a sketch by Alexander Postels of the *Senyavin*.

268 Figure 13.4. Density plot of radiocarbon dates from archaeological sites on Kosrae's main island.

280 Figure 14.1. Map of Vanuatu and New Caledonia.

282 Figure 14.2. Dominion and district boundaries on Aneityum (Anatom) in the early Contact period.

284 Figure 14.3. Population decline and recovery on Aneityum, 1850–1990.

309 Figure 15.1. The demographic curve for New Caledonia as presented in historical publications.

313 Figure 15.2. Example of extensive dryland horticultural structures in the Tchamba Valley (east coast of Grande Terre).

315 Figure 15.3. The demographic curve of the northeast coast of Grande Terre from ca. 1840 to ca. 1945, reconstructed through historical information.

324 Figure 15.4. Poindi-Poweu in front of his dwelling at Nékipin in 1954, a mourning turban on his head.

As an archaeologist and a historical demographer, respectively, each of us has long been involved with issues of population change in the Pacific. In his early research on the evolution of the Polynesian chiefdoms, Kirch (1984) proposed a number of demographic models for pre-Contact island populations, and he argued that the growth and density of populations were key variables for understanding the *longue durée* of island societies. Rallu, for his part, wrote his doctoral thesis (Rallu 1990) on a reevaluation of the early post-Contact demography of the Marquesas Islands and other French colonial territories in the Pacific, and he has continued to make the study of Oceanic demography his main research focus. Although familiar in a general way with each other's research, we did not meet face-to-face until the late 1990s when Rallu visited the University of California at Berkeley. Naturally enough, our discussions turned to the topic of long-term demographic evolution in the Pacific Islands. In particular, we were both interested in the question of whether certain orthodox views on the size of Contact-era populations in the Pacific — views such as those of Norma McArthur (1967), for example — needed to be reconsidered.

After several such meetings and discussions, these problems of Pacific paleodemography seemed to us to warrant the possibility of an international workshop of scholars who could help to focus on the complex set of problems — methodological and theoretical — surrounding long-term demographic evolution in the Pacific. In particular, we wanted to bring together both demographers and archaeologists for a multidisciplinary collaboration. The France-Berkeley Fund, jointly administered by the French Ministry of Education and the University of California, reviewed our proposal and agreed to underwrite the basic costs of such a conference, which was hosted in December 2003 at the Richard Gump Research Station on the island of Moʻorea, French Polynesia. Over several days, in the relaxed atmosphere of the shores of Paopao Bay, the twenty-five participants presented papers, discussed ideas, and held informal conversations, often extending deep into the tropical night. By week's end, there was enthusiasm for the idea of bringing together a revised and edited set of these contributions, with this volume as the result.

We first and foremost express our gratitude to the France-Berkeley Fund for the financial grant that enabled this project. The Richard Gump Research Station, headed by its research director Neil Davies and facilities manager Frank Murphy, along with their dedicated staff, went out of their way to make our stay productive and enjoyable. Eric Conte of the Université de Polynésie Française, along with Neil Davies, comprised the local organizing committee and greatly assisted with arrangements in Tahiti and Moʻorea, including publicity. We also thank the Ministry of Culture, Territory of French Polynesia, and its former minister of culture, Professor Louise Peltzer, for lending their support to our project. Finally, we thank all of the participants for the time and insights they have given to the workshop and to the revised papers.

Patrick Vinton Kirch
Jean-Louis Rallu

PATRICK V. KIRCH AND JEAN-LOUIS RALLU

Long-Term Demographic Evolution in the Pacific Islands

Issues, Debates, and Challenges

The final decades of the eighteenth century were a time like no other in the history of the Pacific Islands. Although the Manila galleons had been crossing the Pacific with their cargoes of gold, silver, and the diverse riches of the East for some two centuries, and while a few other voyagers (among them Tasman and Schouten and Le Maire) had ventured beyond the narrowly defined Spanish routes, the vast majority of islands in the Pacific had yet to experience "first contact" between indigene and European. The "discovery" of Otaheite (Tahiti) by Captain Wallis of the *Dolphin* in June of 1767 — and the reports soon to follow from Louis de Bougainville — set the intellectual salons of Europe buzzing with accounts of Polynesian isles. Exploration of the Great South Sea suddenly became a centerpiece of the Enlightenment project, forever linked with the Herculean voyages of James Cook, who literally created the modern cartographic representation of the Pacific (Thomas 2003; Salmond 2003).

The voyages of Cook, Vancouver, Bougainville, Bligh, La Pérouse, D'Entrecasteaux, Wilson, and others in the final decades of the eighteenth century brought island after island into their first contacts with Europeans. With their long isolation from the West broken, the pace of change in island societies quickened dramatically. Perhaps the most immediate — and often devastating — consequence of such first contact was the introduction of a host of diseases previously unknown to the islanders for which they had no prior exposure and lacked resistence. Cook himself was famously aware of this problem, although his issuing of orders to prohibit sexual contacts between his ships' crews and the Hawaiians failed to halt the spread of sexually transmitted disease during the initial encounters between the British and Hawaiians at Kaua'i and Ni'ihau in 1778 (Bushnell 1993). The impact of "virgin soil epidemics" is now understood as a critical part of the larger process of "ecological imperialism" (Crosby 1986) by which the West was able to so rapidly and aggressively expand from the Old to the New Worlds, including the Pacific.

Yet the question remains: How severe were the effects of depopulation in the first few decades following European contact with individual island societies? Any answer depends upon having accurate estimates of indigenous population sizes and densities at the moment of first contact. Two possible sources of information may inform us of these populations: the firsthand accounts of the European voyagers and direct archaeological evidence for population and settlement density in the late pre-Contact period. In the debates that have swirled around the question of Pacific populations over the past few decades, it is almost exclusively the first source that has been drawn upon, critiqued, and typically rejected as unreliable. Our aim in this book is to explore the second avenue: the possibilities of a paleodemography of the Pacific as opened by recent advances in archaeological research. Moreover, the questions we seek to address are not limited to the sizes of Pacific populations at the moment of fatal encounter at "first contact" but extend to the longer, deep-time evolution of island populations.

Otaheite: Johann Forster versus Norma McArthur

We will not attempt to canvas the entire field of Pacific historical demography here, but we will spotlight the core issues through a brief consideration of how historians, demographers, and anthropologists have viewed the population of that quintessential Pacific locale: Tahiti. Robertson, master of the *Dolphin* — among those who first laid European eyes upon the island — was greatly impressed by the density of its population:

> from the shore side one two and three miles Back there is a fine Leavel country that appears to be all laid out in plantations, and the regular built Houses seems to be without number, all along the Coast. . . . This appears to be the most populoss country I ever saw, the whole shore side was lined with men women and children all the way that we saild along. . . . (Robertson 1948, 139)

On the eve of his departure, after time for exploration and reflection, Robertson would pen in his journal: "I dare venter to say there is upward of a hundred thousant Men Women and Children on it" (1948, 234).

Cook, in May 1774, was even more impressed by the multitude of the Tahitian populace, stating that "the whole Island cannot contain less than two hundred and four thousand inhabitants" (Beaglehole 1961, 409). But it was Johann Reinhold Forster, naturalist on the same second voyage, who wrote the most detailed exposition, "On the Numbers of Inhabitants in the South-Sea-Isles, and their Population," as part of his famous *Observations* (1996 [1778], 145–152). His estimate for all of Tahiti was 121,500 persons. Forster drew upon two empirical sources of data to derive his population estimate: (1) a review of a "great naval expedition" assembled at Pare, which allowed an estimate of the number of fighting men; and (2) a detailed estimation of the numbers of breadfruit trees and the population these could, in principle, support. The latter, interestingly, prefigures modern efforts at estimating populations through the "carrying capacity" approach (see chapter 8). Forster used these two methods to cross-check each other, finding that the potential for breadfruit production surpassed the actual numbers estimated by the first method: "Having thus fairly stated the possibility of so great a population, we shall certainly not be thought unreasonable in our estimate" (150).

Yet "thought unreasonable" he would be by twentieth-century demographers and anthropologists. The dean of Society Islands' ethnohistory, Douglas Oliver, would write that Forster's efforts were "pure fantasy" (1974, 34). Oliver was heavily influenced by the work of Norma McArthur (1967), a historical demographer whose key book *Island Populations of the Pacific* epitomizes a mid-twentieth-century perspective that the early voyagers had routinely and consistently overestimated the populations they encountered at first contact. McArthur reduced the population of Tahiti, at the advent of Europeans, to a mere 30,000, barely a quarter of Forster's estimate. Oliver (1974, 33) elevates this estimate slightly to 35,000.

Why this rejection of the much higher estimates of those who actually witnessed first contact? Although the arguments presented by historical demographers including McArthur (1967) are complex and nuanced, the answer fundamentally comes down to two points: (1) a decision to privilege the historical "head counts" and later censuses undertaken some decades after first contact, usually by missionaries; and (2) a judgment that the effects of "virgin soil" epidemics in the critical first few decades of contact were not nearly so severe as would be implied by acceptance of the early voyagers' estimates. The first London Missionary Society (LMS) contingent arrived in 1797, three decades after Wilson and the *Dolphin,* and upon reconnoitering Tahiti found that "the accounts of former navigators as to the populousness of the country are greatly exaggerated" (Wilson 1799, 166). Wilson ventured a district-by-district count, arriving at an islandwide total of 16,050 (215). By 1829, an LMS head count reduced this number to a mere 8,658 (Rallu 1990, 227).

Beyond her claim that epidemics reported by natives — whom she asserted were unable to count numbers greater than ten or twenty — were meaningless, McArthur did not explicitly discuss why she thought it impossible that Tahiti or other Pacific islands could have undergone massive population declines in the first three or four decades following contact with Europeans as a result of virgin soil epidemics. But this viewpoint is implicit throughout her work, as she consistently rejected early voyagers' estimates of high populations, preferring to take missionary counts as far closer to the mark and only slightly elevating those later numbers to arrive at values for Contact-era populations. Most historical demographers of the Pacific have followed her lead.

David Stannard's Challenge

The staid field of Pacific historical demography, with McArthur's work setting the tone, was precipitously challenged twenty-two years after the publication of her major tome by David Stannard (1989), a historian and professor of American studies, who addressed the question of how many inhabitants had first met Captain Cook — not at Tahiti, but at another of his famous landfalls, the Hawaiian Islands.[1] In chapter 4, Kirch reviews in some detail Stannard's argument and the reactions it provoked. For the moment, suffice it to say that Stannard took serious issue with the accepted orthodoxy of Hawaiian historical demography, that — in a case very parallel to that of Tahiti — the estimate by Lt. King of Cook's company of some 400,000 Hawaiians was a considerable overestimate. Applying the same kinds of assumptions as McArthur, scholars of Hawai'i (most notably Schmitt 1971, 1973, 1977) had reduced their estimates of the population at first contact to 200,000 or so for the entire archipelago.

Referring to the revolution in historical demography that had shaken up notions of the pre-Columbian population of the New World (e.g., Dobyns 1966), Stannard argued with great passion that "Pacific island historical demography remains largely in an arrested state similar to that of such scholarship in the Americas several decades ago" (1989, xvii). For Hawai'i specifically, Stannard adduced a variety of evidence to argue that rather than revise Lt. King's 1778 estimate downward, the truth lay in the other direction. "In 1778 . . . the population of Hawai'i was probably almost as large as it is today," on the order of 800,000 to perhaps 1 million people (see chapter 4). Notably, some of this evidence was *archaeological* in nature, such as archaeological surveys of vast agricultural field systems and terrace complexes (19–21) and of extensive areas of inland settlement that would have escaped the notice of early voyagers (123–124). Indeed, in an exchange with demographer Eleanor Nordyke, the critical importance of archaeological data to help resolve the debate over the size of the Contact-period Hawaiian population came to the fore, with both Nordyke and Stannard seeming to agree about nothing except the fact that "archaeological assessments" could perhaps offer key evidence (112–113, 122–123).

Archaeologists in the Pacific had themselves not been uninterested in questions of pre-Contact populations and long-term demographic histories. For Hawai'i, there had been considerable writing and debate about population growth in prehistory, primarily with respect to rates of growth and the shape of the overall population growth curve (e.g., Cordy 1981; Hommon 1976; Kirch 1984, 1985; Clark 1988; Sutton and Mulloy 1989). In direct response to Stannard, Dye (1994) even attempted an estimation of the total Contact-era population based on a radio-carbon-date proxy model (see chapter 4 for further discussion). In other regions of the Pacific, archaeologists had used various methods to estimate local populations using settlement data or estimates of agricultural productivity (e.g., Bellwood 1972 and Kellum-Ottino 1971 for the Marquesas; Green 1973 for Tonga).

Moreover, the frequent discovery of often dense settlement distributions in the interior reaches of islands was leading at least some archaeologists to question the historical demographic orthodoxy epitomized by Norma McArthur. Christophe Sand, synthesizing the emerging archaeological record of New Caledonia, strongly questioned the validity of historically based estimates as low as 40,000 persons for this large high island, where abandoned terrace and field systems blanket vast stretches of the now-abandoned interior valleys (Sand 1995, 281–309; see also chapter 15, this volume). Spriggs echoes this view for Melanesia as a whole, writing of the "archaeological evidence of massive population disruption and decline attendant upon European contact" as seen in abandoned village sites, agricultural systems, and discontinuities in settlement patterns (1997, 253–254).

Stannard's challenge to the received orthodoxy of Pacific historical demography has not gone unheeded by the archaeologists. In his synthesis of Oceanic prehistory, Kirch (2000, 313) opined that "the ball is now in the archaeologists' court; it is up to us to seize the challenge and apply all of the lines of material evidence at our command to break out of the old debates." However, demographic archaeology is not necessarily a straightforward endeavor; there are numerous methodological and theoretical obstacles to tackle. The contributions to this volume represent one step in that direction.

Archaeology and Paleodemography

Efforts to develop a "demographic archaeology" have a long history, with specific examples in various parts of the world (Cook 1972; Hassan 1979, 1981; Paine 1997). Throughout his influential writings, V. Gordon Childe (e.g., 1951 [1936]) stressed the role of population growth as a key thread in understanding the development of human societies. Later, the provocative theory of Ester Boserup (1965) spurred archaeologists to examine aspects of the archaeological record for evidence of population growth and decline as these might be indexed to sequences of intensification (Spooner 1972). More recently, archaeologists have struggled to develop detailed demographic histories for specific regions and time periods, as in the Maya lowlands (Culbert and Rice 1990).

Essential to an archaeological approach to demography is the development of specific methods for accurately estimating prehistoric populations. Recognizing that it is impossible to conduct a "prehistoric census," archaeologists must rely upon some form(s) of proxy measure of past population. Although many specific variants have been put forward and elaborated for use in specific contexts, such proxy measures can be grouped into four major categories, based upon the kinds of data utilized: (1) osteological demography; (2) settlement demography; (3) dating curves as proxy models; and (4) productivity or carrying capacity approaches. We briefly review each of these approaches, with specific reference to their prior and potential application in the Pacific.

Osteological Demography

While we cannot go back in time to carry out a census of prehistoric people, skeletal remains — especially when these are concentrated in cemeteries or other specialized burial facilities — do provide direct evidence of past populations. Physical anthropologists and paleodemographers have expended much effort on developing techniques for reconstructing key demographic parameters from such skeletal series, especially through the construction and interpretation of *life tables* (Angel 1969; Weiss 1973; Moore et al. 1975). In theory, such life tables allow one to infer such parameters as survivorship, age-specific mortality, and life expectancy. Nonetheless, the use of life tables derived from skeletal remains is very much affected by issues of sampling and representativeness (such as the frequent underrepresentation of infants or other subgroups within a population). Moreover, the interpretation of such tables typically requires an assumption that the population in question was stable and stationary. Skeletal series are often accumulations representing long periods, often hundreds of years, during which times the population in question may have undergone significant changes in patterns of fertility and mortality. These are assumptions that cannot always be made for prehistoric groups, leading to various critiques of osteological demography (e.g., Bocquet-Appel and Masset 1982; Sattenspiel and Harpending 1983).

Some use has been made in the Pacific of life table analysis of pre-Contact populations, where sufficiently large skeletal assemblages have been recovered through archaeological excavations, such as at Mōkapu, Puʻu Aliʻi, or Keōpū in the Hawaiian Islands (Snow 1974; Underwood 1969; Collins 1986), the Hane dune site in the Marquesas (Pietrusewsky 1976), the ʻAtele burial mounds on Tongatapu (Pietrusewsky 1969), or the Taumako cemetery in the Duff Islands (Houghton 1996). Kirch (1984, 111–116) drew upon four of these cases from Hawaiʻi, the Marquesas, and Tonga to suggest some demographic responses to density. However, given the problems noted above, such interpretations are open to question.

While osteological demography can tell us much about the health and mortality patterns of populations, it cannot provide data on growth rates or on absolute population numbers. For this reason we did not attempt to include the life table approach within the scope of our workshop. Moreover, recent sociopolitical trends in the Pacific, as elsewhere, have rendered the study of prehistoric skeletal remains problematic or impossible. In Hawai'i, for example, all significant collections of human remains have now been reburied under the terms of the Native American Graves Protection and Repatriation Act (NAGPRA), and newly discovered remains are typically subject to immediate reinterment without analysis.

Settlement Demography

Certainly the most widely used, if methodologically varied, approaches to estimating past populations on the basis of archaeological data have involved some form of "settlement demography" (Paine 1997, 4–6). Under this rubric we may include any methods that attempt to count past populations through some proxy measure of human settlement, whether this be numbers of settlements, areas of settlements, rooms per settlement, "packed house volumes," individual houses, house floor area, or other measures (Cook 1972; Ammerman et al. 1976; Hassan 1981, 63–92). Essentially, these methods are a form of archaeological census taking involving the quantification of some aspect of human settlement or residence, with an assumption that material remains in evidence — in a quantifiable unit — are related to some mean number of persons. Perhaps the best-known example is Naroll's (1962) application of cross-cultural comparative ethnographic data to establish a mean value for floor area in relation to population. A rigorous example from the Maya lowlands is Turner's (1990) use of house counts.

Settlement demography is not without its own problems and issues (e.g., Santley 1990), some of which derive from the particular culture-specific ways in which people house themselves, frustrating any attempt at a "one-size-fits-all" archaeodemography. Other problems concern the importance of dating control and contemporaneity of structures, reoccupation of houses, and the range of variation in average family or household size. In theory, however, many of these problems are resolvable or at least amenable to parameterization within an acceptable error range, thus permitting archaeological census taking to proceed.

Settlement demography is the most important approach used by the contributors to this volume. In the Pacific, despite wide variation in the nature of residential housing and settlement patterns (see Oliver 1989 for a review of these), there is a strong tendency toward permanent residential structures, each associated with a household group — often an extended family unit. Moreover, such household residences often (but not always!) left archaeological traces — such as stone-walled enclosures, curbstone outlines, or stone-faced platforms and terraces — that are readily identifiable through archaeological survey and excavation. In the chapters to follow, specific examples of settlement demography are presented for the Hawaiian Islands, the Society Islands (Moʻorea), and the Marquesas.

Dating Curves

John Rick (1987) suggested that the cumulative record of radiocarbon dates available from the preceramic period of Peru might be taken as a proxy measure of population, introducing the notion of "dates as data." The basic assumption here is that the amount of cultural burning in a specific region — given consistent cultural practices in cooking, hearth making, and so on over time — will be proportional to the overall population. Given a large enough sample of radiocarbon dates from cultural contexts — and again assuming that there is no bias in the selection of samples from any particular time period (an important assumption) — the total sample of dates should provide a proxy measure of population. However, this can only be a *relative* measure, not a basis for estimating absolute population sizes. Thus a sample of dates, when plotted over time, should in theory be able to tell us something about relative *rates* of population growth, stability, or decline over that time period.

In the Pacific, this approach has been used by Dye and Komori (1992b) to derive the historical trajectory of population growth in the Hawaiian Islands. Using a further modification of this method that linked the recent end of the dating curve to historic-period census data, Dye (1994) also attempted to generate an absolute estimate of the pre-Contact Hawaiian population, but this requires making a number of questionable assumptions, as discussed in detail in chapter 4. In this volume, we not only reevaluate the Dye-Komori dating curve model for Hawaiʻi, but we look at the application of the method to Moʻorea in the Society Islands (Hamilton and Kahn, chapter 8), and to Kosrae in Micronesia (Athens, chapter 11).

Carrying Capacity Approaches

The fourth and final approach to archaeological demography involves some form of estimating the resource potential (or agricultural production capacity) of a specific environment or region and thus the total number of persons who might, in theory, be supported by this environment. Such approaches may be referred to as "carrying capacity" estimates, taking the term from population biology for the theoretical maximum population (K) that can be sustained in a given environment. The literature on carrying capacity and the various assumptions and problems associated with its use, especially for human populations, is vast and cannot be reviewed here (but see Hassan 1981, 164–173; Glassow 1978; Dewar 1984). A fundamental problem with this approach, however, is that human populations rarely if ever achieve such maximal levels of K, and they certainly do not sustain them over long periods. Thus estimates of K provide only a theoretical upper limit for population, given some specified technology and environmental conditions. Nonetheless, such estimates may be useful as a cross-check on population estimates derived from settlement demography or other methods.

In the Pacific, there have been attempts to estimate the carrying capacity of particular islands or sections of islands, such as Bellwood's (1972) attempt for Hanatekua Valley in the Marquesas. More useful, however, has been the application not of total carrying capacity but of the estimated production or yield of specific agricultural systems, especially when these systems have been documented through archaeological survey. Spriggs (1981), applying Bayliss-Smith's (1978) methods for estimating "standard populations," pioneered this approach in Aneityum. Similarly, Spriggs and Kirch (1992) used such a model to estimate the potential agricultural production of the irrigation systems of Anahulu Valley, O'ahu, in the early post-Contact era. As population numbers were known independently from census data, these estimates could be used to evaluate the potential levels of surplus production.

In this volume, several contributors apply variations of the carrying capacity approach — or more specifically, agricultural production models — in order to estimate potential population sizes (see chapters 6, 8, 11, and 12). Often such estimates are used in conjunction with some method of settlement demography to provide independent cross-checks on population estimates, and in our view this is the best application of the carrying capacity approach.

Long-Term Demographic Evolution in Pacific Societies

Resolving the uncertainties surrounding the sizes of Contact-era populations in various island societies — attempting to develop some new, independent criteria on which to evaluate the competing claims of Forster and McArthur and to address Stannard's challenge — is certainly one goal of archaeological demography in the Pacific. But it is by no means the only objective. Equally important is understanding the long-term demographic evolution of island populations. Many questions arise when we begin to ask what were the historical trajectories of Pacific populations over the hundreds and thousands of years that people occupied various islands. Were founding populations typically small and potentially vulnerable to extinction? How fast did populations grow under "pristine" conditions, in the eastern Pacific at least, without the constraint of most Old World diseases? Had island populations typically stabilized by the time of their encounter with Europeans, or were they still increasing? What are the correlates of the recent findings that initial settlement dates for Eastern Polynesia appear to be later than originally estimated: number of settlers, subsequent immigration, and their cultural implications? Given human reproductive potential and pristine environment, growth rates were certainly much higher among Polynesian settlers with developed agricultural techniques than in Neolithic communities or even sixteenth- and seventeenth-century Europe, and even the largest islands and archipelagoes could have been populated right up to their theoretical carrying capacity levels long before European contact (see Rallu, chapter 2). Did this happen, or were populations regulated and stabilized well below maximal density levels?

In his 1984 book on the evolution of Polynesian societies, Kirch laid out six different theoretical models for long-term population growth on remote Oceanic islands. These included (1) extinction, (2) exponential, (3) logistic, (4) overshoot or "crash," (5) oscillating, and (6) step models for population growth on islands (Kirch 1984, 101–104, fig. 27). He suggested that it was possible that any of these different models might apply in a particular historical case, but that in general some form of a modified logistic model might be the most common. The Hawaiian case, tested on settlement data from west Hawai'i Island, seemed to validate at least one instance of a logistic growth model (104–111). This led Kirch to suggest a more general set of propositions concerning early (colonizing) versus late (pre-Contact) populations in Polynesia (table 16), which can be summarized in Table 1.1. In part, this set of hypothesized correlates reflects the *cultural* equivalent of the r/K selection continuum proposed by MacArthur and Wilson (1967) as a general process in island biogeography (Kirch 1984, 86–87).

Whether such a general model, from density-independent to density-dependent conditions, accurately or adequately accounts for long-term demographic change on islands is a matter that requires empirical testing. Moreover, whether such a transition would be best modeled as a logistic process or as some more abrupt and nonlinear type of transition (such as the rapid onset of stability after a phase of exponential growth) needs to be determined through the acquisition of fine-grained temporal data on population sizes and growth rates for particular islands. There was much discussion and debate surrounding this problem at the Mo'orea workshop, and it is probably premature to attempt any synthesis at this stage in our research. Nonetheless, there was general agreement that understanding the underlying sequences of population growth and regulation is key to broader efforts at interpreting the *longue durée* of sociopolitical evolution in island societies.

The Collapse of Contact-Era Populations

Assessing population trends from initial settlement to reach high pre-Contact densities is only part of the problem. The collapse that followed European arrival still remains to be explained. Such tremendous decline has rarely been studied in depth and remains controversial in the pre-Columbian Americas and the Pa-

Table 1.1. Hypothesized demographic correlates of early and late populations in Polynesia (modified after Kirch 1984: table 16).

Parameter	Early, colonizing populations	Late, precontact populations
Size	Small (<100)	Large
Density	Low (<10/km^2)	High (range 50–250/km^2)
Intrinsic growth rate (r)	Relatively high	Low
Mortality	Density independent	Density dependent
Cultural regulation	Limited; relaxation of incest taboo in Eastern Polynesia	Important: abortion, warfare, celibacy, infanticide, other controls

cific as well. A reduction of population to around 5 percent of its contact size is something that must be scrutinized and cannot be accepted without question. It was probably the main reason for rejecting Cook's and other explorers' figures. With some legitimate reasons, historians recently intended to revise the virgin soil hypothesis. However, there are well-documented cases of extremely high epidemic death rates in the nineteenth and early twentieth centuries, as well as year-to-year rapid decline over decades. But the poor health situation in the first decades of colonization, with almost no medical services to combat introduced diseases — respiratory, digestive, and sexually transmitted — and the effect of new ways of life with immoderate consumption of alcohol (often adulterated or locally brewed from coconuts) certainly played a role that may be more important than the virgin soil factor. Given the new evidence of high densities, the collapse can no longer be put in question, in some islands at least. But was it a general phenomenon, or were some islands or archipelagoes spared the devastation? These new findings in the direction of early estimates raise more questions on the process and causes of population decline that followed. Such collapse also bears strong consequences for native communities with respect to their cultures and social structures and the rapid changes they had undergone in the nineteenth century.

Whereas population modeling applies to the pre-Contact period, with a need to constrain models with data on archaeology and other sciences such as biology when more information will be available on environmental change, the post-Contact era is certainly a field for historical demographers. But as data on the first decades are critically missing, once again, densities provided by other sciences will remain the only measure of the adequacy of retrodictions. In other words, if it is accepted that only about 5 percent of the Marquesan population at contact remained in the early twentieth century, does this also apply to other islands or archipelagoes? Multidisciplinary work will be more necessary than ever to bring answers to the questions of the size and density of Polynesian populations at contact, their various phases of growth, and the magnitude of decline and its various forms. In the vast Pacific, answers from multidisciplinary research will be local and any generalization will be dangerous. However, these answers will have the strength of observation against the wide range of uncertainty offered by models.

Précis of this Volume

The fifteen chapters to follow address, through a variety of approaches and case studies, the various themes outlined above. Most but not all of the contributions are by archaeologists who are attempting to bring the data of prehistory to bear on questions of pre-Contact demography and long-term population growth. Chapters 2 and 3, however, set the stage for these archaeological case studies by raising more general issues from the standpoint of historical demography and population ecology. Rallu looks at the potential for reproduction and growth rates in island settings and compares these to what archaeologists think they see in the pre-Contact record. In addition, he turns his analytical lens around and reassesses the potential rate of post-Contact population collapse, raising new questions about the impact of "first contact." In chapter 3, Shripad Tuljapurkar, Charlotte Lee, and Michelle Figgs look at the problem of population regulation in island environments, with special reference to limits on agricultural production and how these may have contributed to population control and stabilization.

Chapters 4 through 7 all focus on the Hawaiian Islands. Although one of the last island groups to be settled by Polynesians and thus with a relatively short time depth (at least compared with islands in the western Pacific), Hawai'i is of great interest to Pacific paleodemography for several reasons. First of all, we have the controversy over the size of the Hawaiian population at first contact, which epitomizes the larger debate about historical demographic reconstructions. Second, archaeological approaches to pre-Contact demography have a longer and more intense research history than in most other Pacific islands. If there is real potential for archaeology to contribute to the problems of long-term demographic history, then Hawai'i will be a key proving ground. In chapter 4, Kirch reviews prior efforts along these lines, assessing what we have learned and what still needs to be done. This is followed in chapters 5 through 7 by three specific case studies, all using some variant of the settlement demography approach. Chapter 5, by Thegn Ladefoged and Michael Graves, models agricultural development and demography in Kohala, Hawai'i Island, and in chapter 6 Kirch considers the paleodemography of Kahikinui, Maui. Ross Cordy, in chapter 7, also brings the post-Contact documentary record of the Mahele land records and censuses to bear as a cross-check on his archaeological survey data.

In chapters 8 and 9, we look at two valley case studies from French Polynesia. Hamilton and Kahn (chapter 8) apply a multidisciplinary approach to the large valley of 'Opunohu on Mo'orea in the Society Islands. Ethnohistoric documents, house counts, and estimates of agricultural productivity are all used to try to constrain a range of possible maximal population estimates for the valley. For Hokatu Valley on the island of Ua Huka, Eric Conte and Tamara Maric (chapter 9) use a Marquesas-specific variant of the house count approach, made possible by the ethnohistoric record of culture-specific sleeping practices.

We then turn to Western Polynesia, where David Burley (chapter 10) evaluates the archaeological record for long-term population trends in the Kingdom of Tonga over nearly three millennia. In Tonga, the particulars of the archaeological record do not favor a house count approach, but some form of settlement demography is still possible, as he demonstrates. Chapter 11 is by Roger C. Green, who originally wrote it some decades ago as he was completing the first systematic archaeological work in Western Samoa; it addresses discrepancies between the historical demographic estimates of McArthur (1967) and what is implied by the density of surface archaeological remains. This is followed by a close look at the Tokelau Islands of Western Polynesia by Roger and Valerie Green (chapter 12), who draw upon a rich set of ethnohistoric records to reconstruct the demographic processes on these small atolls within the past several centuries. The Tokelau case provides an excellent model for various demographic parameters under traditional Polynesian economic and social conditions.

Moving farther west, J. Stephen Athens (chapter 13) looks at the Micronesian high island of Kosrae, noted for its intensive arboricultural system dominated by breadfruit production. Athens uses a radiocarbon dating proxy model to assess long-term demographic trends and also assess the question of maximal population of Kosrae through an agricultural productivity model. For Aneityum in southern Melanesia, Matthew Spriggs (chapter 14) applies estimates of agricultural production to estimate population levels in the late pre-Contact era and compares these to the historical demographic record of the early missionaries. And Christophe Sand, Jacques Bole, and A. Ouetcho (chapter 15) turn to the vast, near-continental island of New Caledonia, for which the historical record had suggested extremely low population densities in the later nineteenth century. Based on the extensive archaeological evidence for dense inland settlement, they question the validity of these historical estimates, hinting that the impact of first contact in La Grande Terre may have been far more severe than previously reckoned. In a concluding commentary, Kirch (chapter 16) canvasses the fundamental problems of "methods, measures, and models" in Pacific paleodemography.

Notes

1. Norma McArthur had died before Stannard's book was published, eliminating the possibility of what surely would have been a lively and contentious debate between them. Stannard, citing a personal communication from historian Gavan Daws (1989, xvi, 82), says that McArthur herself was working on the question of Hawaiian Contact-era population at the time of her death and was inclined toward reducing the estimated population to less than 100,000.

Pre- and Post-Contact Population in Island Polynesia

Can Projections Meet Retrodictions?

 From the "rediscovery" of the Pacific Islands by Europeans, the debate has been constant — and sometimes raging — about the size of island populations at the time of contact. These controversies are based on the imprecision of first estimates of large populations by European navigators and on ideological aspects influencing reinterpretation of the numbers given by the only witnesses of contact, in comparison with much smaller populations enumerated in the nineteenth century. Initially, the debate was purely between historians and social anthropologists; demographers later entered the scene, followed by archaeologists. Recently other sciences — mostly biology and environmental science — have brought new evidence of high densities and profound environmental changes following population pressure in the Pacific Islands in prehistoric times.

After a brief review of the ideologies that supported Pacific Island population estimates and reestimates, this chapter deals with two ways of estimating Polynesian populations at European contact. The first uses demographic projections to simulate population development from initial Polynesian settlement using information given by archaeology and social anthropology. The second is a retrodiction, using reliable statistical information of the late nineteenth century.

Some Ideological Aspects and Common Errors

Tahiti is at the origin of many ideologies about the Pacific — among others, the "noble savage." Several early European visitors estimated its population: Robertson (second mate of Wallis), Boenechea, Forster (botanist of Cook's first voyage), and Cook.[1] However, the size of islands was not well known; navigators anchored in a given place and rarely circumnavigated the island or did so briefly, and they knew nothing of the interior, a common cause of underestimates. These estimates, based on a few local impressions, were influenced by important gatherings that were a cause of overestimation. But we must not forget limits of those gatherings due to the existence of property conflicts and even wars in "paradise." Cook reported that chiefs of other districts were allowed to visit him only several days after his ship had anchored.

Culpability for spoiling a pristine environment was rapidly felt and suppressed by many Europeans. It is surprising to see how quickly some administrators, navy officers, and even sometimes missionaries denied the introduction of diseases, even rejecting that the 1699 (or 1700) smallpox epidemic in Guam could have caused any death: "Father Palomo (in 'Continuation . . .' to Corte) vehemently denied that any loss of life resulted from the event" (Underwood 1973, 18). Very high infanticide reported by missionaries—for example, "women give birth to 8 to 10 children and raise only 2 or 3" (Wilson 1799) more than thirty years after contact, at a time of frequent epidemics and widespread diseases—is also suspicious (see below) and may be among the self-justifications of Christianization or a way to limit the role of contact on population decline.

Several historians, anthropologists, and demographers have written in favor of a relatively small population for Tahiti at contact. McArthur (1967) gave an estimate of 30,000. Although she was a demographer, she did not give much statistical basis for her estimate, except for Tupaia's list of warriors totaling 6,780. McArthur sees this figure as accounting for most of the adult male population, whereas Banks clearly reported that Tupaia had stressed it was only *"taatatoa"*—the warrior caste. She dismisses the fact that, in the review of part of the fleet of Tahiti preparing to attack Eimeo (Mo'orea) in Faaa on April 26, 1774, Cook saw a larger adult male population that he estimated at 7,760—including rowers and other staff. McArthur's figure certainly influenced Oliver's estimate of 35,000 (Oliver 1974). Oliver considers the fleet seen by Cook on April 26, 1774, as slightly over-enumerated, attributing it to all of Tahiti and dismissing Cook's report that the fleet came from and returned to the west and southwest part of the island. Actually, the eastern districts did not agree to attack Eimeo; the Teva I Tai (Taiarapu) were still in conflict with the Teva I Uta and probably did not participate (Adams 1964). This attitude to revise steeply downward the estimates of the only witnesses of Polynesian population at contact may stem from a mixture of feelings of self-esteem and consciousness of responsibility that could be named the "colonizer's complex."

My personal experience of this was during my Ph.D. defense, when I was criticized for more than doubling McArthur's estimates—a tremendous revision by demographers' standards. Demographers, from European examples, said that populations recover after an epidemic. But there were no examples in Europe of as rapid back-to-back epidemics as in the Pacific. Finally, the jury requested that I publish only my lower estimate "just above 70,000" (Rallu 1990, 222).

Low estimates at the time of contact may be based on two kinds of errors. Many historians saw negative growth curves not like curves but more like straight lines: as arithmetical rather than exponential negative growth. Moreover, and this is the second error, one could assume growth rates to be more negative in the first decades after contact — when Polynesians were not at all immunized against the new diseases, resulting in catastrophic epidemics — than in the second half of the nineteenth century, when negative growth was still widely observed.

Pre-Contact Population Development

Data and Hypothesis

The necessary information to include in a model of pre-Contact population development consists of date of first settlement, number of settlers, date of stabilization, average growth rate prior to stabilization, and type of growth (exponential or logistic). Uncertainty is very large for all these parameters. A ±100 years bracket typically pertains to archaeological dates, and in 100 years a population experiencing probable growth rates of prehistoric Polynesian populations can double.[2] It should be noted that reexcavation of sites in Eastern Polynesia has frequently yielded dates several centuries later than earlier results (Kirch 2000), changing the time span of population growth, a problem that we shall have to address. The date of stabilization is estimated by other methods, taken from a large set of dated dwelling sites, and it is probably also affected by an uncertainty of about 100 years. Assumptions on the number of settlers can also strongly affect results; for instance, there is no reason to choose 25 rather than 50 or 100 settlers, doubling or quadrupling estimates at any later date. But the main uncertainty is growth rates in prehistorical times. Under the exponential law that is the more likely to apply, a slight difference in growth rate can change results manyfold after ten or more centuries.

An important factor of the level of growth is migration. It is possible that a few years after settlement on a new island, settlers depleted in numbers after the long sea trip return to their islands to bring a few more people to ease constraints on marriage opportunities or just to ensure the survival of the settlement. Given the time scale, this is about the same as assuming a larger number of settlers. We know also that movements, such as visits for cultural or religious ceremonies, occurred frequently. Did these involve migration on a large scale? To avoid migration uncertainties, we can define "closed" areas. For instance, if the Marquesas were closed from Central Polynesia and open to the south (Tahiti — and from there east to Easter Island) and north (Hawaiʻi), then we can consider such a large area as closed. This would work on the condition that Tahiti did not receive migrants from Central Polynesia via the Cook Islands and, in turn, send migrants to the above area.

We use population projections by age and sex, with age-specific fertility and mortality rates, and we include exceptional events such as disasters and other factors including gender-selective infanticide and male-excess mortality. To run this model, demographers would usually assume low life expectancy (around thirty years) and low growth (0.1 to 0.2 percent yearly). These parameters are those observed in the earliest historical demographic data available for sixteenth- or seventeenth-century Europe, and much lower rates (<0.01 percent) are found for prehistoric times (Hammel 1996). The situation was probably very different in the Pacific Islands, where the many diseases and pests found on continents were absent and where Polynesians arrived with agricultural and other techniques. Indeed, much higher growth was not uncommon on continents as well. China experienced yearly growth rates around 1 percent in the late seventeenth and early eighteenth centuries, in 1750–1850, and perhaps also around the turn of the first millennium.

Due to its isolation, the second settlement of Pitcairn Island by the *Bounty* mutineers and a few Polynesians in 1790 offers a unique case of a nineteenth-century Pacific island whose population was not affected by epidemics.[3] It also did not benefit from much import of Western goods, besides those taken from the *Bounty*. Thus, the Pitcairn case could almost represent a pre-Contact Polynesian situation. We ignore the first decade, characterized by strife and many murders. In nineteenth-century Pitcairn, growth rates were very high, often above 3 percent yearly (Lummis 1997).[4] However, the age structure was typical of an immigrant population with a high proportion of adults of reproductive age. What is mainly apparent from Pitcairn data is low mortality: 15.6 per 1,000 in 1864–1893, including low infant mortality of 50 per 1,000 in 1800–1825. But numbers of births in 1800–1825 were well below an expected total fertility rate (TFR) of 6. This was due to a childless rate of 40 percent among settler women, probably linked with sexually transmitted diseases (STDs) they acquired in Tahiti, although some women obviously avoided giving birth with a given partner but became pregnant from another one, their previous partner having children either from a previous wife or in a later union.

To calculate a pre-Contact stable population close to the Pitcairn parameters, we input TFR (6) with a very young fertility age pattern (mode at 20–24, teen-age rate of 250 per 1,000), as observed in the Marquesas in 1921–1925 (Rallu 1990, 78) and typical of Eastern Polynesian fertility, linked with permissive sexual behavior. Sexual behavior in Polynesia certainly resulted in higher fertility than in premodern Europe, where fertility occurred mostly after marriage and all women did not marry. Moreover, life expectancy was probably higher than in premodern Europe due to the absence of various diseases in the islands, although most probably lower than inferred from the Pitcairn data. Life tables from large archaeological data sets of estimated age at death could provide this information, but they are affected by various biases, such as infant, children, commoners, and perhaps women being less often found due to burial with lighter structures to protect them. Although Pitcairn data would lead to life expectancy above fifty years, we may start with forty years. This choice seems generous considering that it is only seven years less than life expectancy observed in Polynesia in the early 1950s. In a stable population, this model gives a growth rate of 2.3 percent. This rate could not have occurred for long periods in pre-Contact Polynesia. With a founding population of fifty settlers, it would result in 4.33 million persons after five hundred years and 42.1 million a century later!

Exceptional events such as natural disasters (drought, hurricanes, tsunamis) and wars reduced growth significantly. Average long-term growth was probably below 1 percent. Introducing five disasters every century, each one killing 30 percent of the population, would reduce growth in our model to 0.8 percent.[5] This seems to be a high frequency of large disasters, but minor disasters also occurred. Yearly hurricanes cause more or less severe food shortage that, associated with higher incidence of parasitic diseases, result in weakening a population's health and increasing the premature deaths of children and the elderly. It would be difficult to account for all these events in a model; however, it appears that a basic high growth can be drastically reduced by reference to recurring disasters. In a second model, we use the more common prehistoric life expectancy of thirty years and fertility of 4.86. The resulting yearly growth rate is 0.5 percent. This could be assumed to be a kind of average for long periods, including the effects of major and minor disasters.

When densities became high, it was even necessary to contain growth to almost nil. Various human interventions were used for that purpose: infanticide, human sacrifice, more frequent wars, eventually followed by massacres. Infanticide of 10 percent of boys and 15 percent of girls and an excess mortality[6] of young adult males (warriors), associated with a reduction by 2 percent of fertility due to brief union disruptions following deaths, would reduce growth in our first model from 0.8 to 0.1 percent. In the second model, infanticide of 5 percent of boys and 8 percent of girls, and the effect of wars accounted as above, also reduces growth from 0.5 to 0.1 percent. Thus, infanticide and losses due to warfare did not need to be very high to stabilize a population.

Some Observed Data on Growth

Archaeological datasets for dated habitation sites are now large enough to provide an estimate of population trends in the Hawaiian Islands (Kirch 2000, 295). These data for Hawai'i show exponential growth followed by sudden stabilization or even decline after AD 1700. The first part of the curve, until AD 1300, fits a 0.35 percent exponential growth rate (Figure 2.1). Then, growth rates increase to nearly 0.5 percent. From AD 1600, growth stops and is immediately followed by decline. This evolution is typical of human populations: increases in growth rates due to improved agricultural and other techniques followed by sudden stabilization when carrying capacity, given a certain level of techniques, is reached. Stabilization is achieved through human intervention, such as birth control or various customs.

A Few Applications and Questions They Raise

We shall now illustrate how slightly different growth rates can have huge effects on population size in the long term and the need to constrain models on a probable range of population densities. We shall also consider later dates of initial settlement. Given the lack of data, it is nearly impossible to choose growth rates to input to our model — 0.35 percent, 0.40 percent, 0.50 percent, or even 0.90 percent — but after ten, twelve, or fifteen centuries, population size can differ manyfold. With a yearly growth of 0.5 percent, fifty settlers yield a population of 19,872 after 1,200 years; with a growth rate of 0.6 percent, the figure is 65,546 — more than three times as much. Therefore, we will assume a priori population density to estimate growth, rather than the contrary. Using the exponential law, a probable density and associated population size, and duration of growth from archaeological data, we calculate growth rates for various Polynesian archipelagoes. We assume that the settler population consisted of fifty persons; a smaller number would raise problems of interbreeding. This also seems a likely number for a small fleet launched to discover new lands or escaped from wars.[7] In a first step, we assume that migration after settlement is negligible and shall consider archipelagoes to avoid dealing with short-distance migration that may have been frequent.

The Marquesas would have seen increasing population for 900 years, from first settlement around AD 700 to stabilization around 1600.[8] Assuming a density of 150 persons per square kilometer (p/km^2), it is associated with a population of 157,000. The yearly growth rate to reach this figure over this period of time is just slightly under 0.9 percent. With a slightly lower rate of 0.8 percent, the population would be 65,000 and the density 62 p/km^2. Rates between 1.0 and 1.1 percent yield populations between 387,000 and 944,000 respectively — more than enough to people all of Eastern Polynesia, just from fifty settlers in AD 700 in the Marquesas.

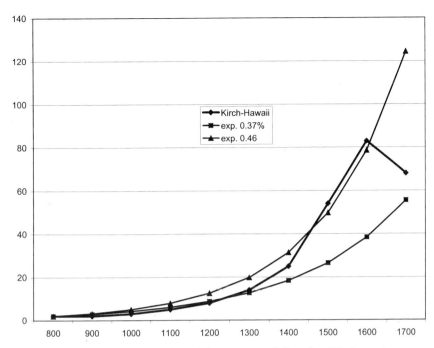

Figure 2.1. Adjustment of archaeological data for Hawaiʻi (based on Kirch 2000).

With an earlier date of initial settlement of AD 200, for instance, 157,000 inhabitants are reached in AD 1600 with a growth rate of 0.577 percent. This is still much higher than in European historical demography.

No precise data on the date of stabilization are available for Tahiti and the Society Islands, but the fact that many customs were used to reduce growth and density was acknowledged by Tahitians and early visitors. An a priori time span of growth of 900 years and a growth rate of 0.9 percent (as for the Marquesas) yields 159,000 inhabitants and a density of 151 p/km² for Tahiti, or 99 p/km² for the Society Islands as a whole. A slightly higher rate of 0.95 percent yields 248,000 people and a density of 155 p/km² for the Society Islands archipelago. This area being open to the east and south, this population was probably scattered as far as the Australs, Mangareva, and even Pitcairn and other archipelagoes that have been populated from the Society Islands.

Now, let us apply the same reasoning to the more recently settled islands. The Gambier Archipelago, with its main island of Mangareva, was settled in about AD 900 (Conte and Kirch 2004). With fifty settlers and the same growth rate as the Society Islands (0.9 percent), Mangareva would have had 26,500 inhabitants in AD 1600. A density of 150 is associated with only 6,900 inhabitants. The origin of the

Rapa Nui (Easter Island) population and of extinct populations in Pitcairn and other minor islands to the east can probably be traced to Mangareva. Mangarevans also eventually emigrated to atolls of the Tuamotus, so that the above 26,500 people would cover a much larger area than the Gambier Archipelago, including Rapa Nui. Mangareva and the margins of this area, Pitcairn and the Tuamotus, did not offer much in the way of resources and may have seen stabilization earlier or been deserted (Pitcairn, Henderson, and some atolls).

Rapa Nui was settled around AD 900, probably from Mangareva, with stabilization around AD 1600. With our baseline density of 150 p/km^2, the island would carry 25,650 inhabitants. This population can be achieved from fifty settlers with a similar growth rate of 0.9 percent. Population pressure on the environment lasted long enough for some resources such as forests to be put under stress and finally exhausted. But, given the facility of voyaging to the west, it is surprising that no return migration occurred to Mangareva or the Society Islands. This would suggest that large-scale migration was not so easy in pre-Contact Polynesia, especially to islands in the west with already relatively high population pressure.[9]

The Hawaiian and New Zealand cases lead to further questioning. With 900 years of growth (from AD 700 to 1600) and a growth rate of 0.5 percent (see Figure 2.1), fifty settlers in Hawai'i would yield 4,500 inhabitants. A growth rate of 0.9 percent yields 159,000 inhabitants and a slightly higher rate (0.95 percent) yields 248,000, a figure closer to the usual estimates of Hawaiian population at contact but still associated with a low density of 15 p/km^2. The Hawaiian Islands have higher altitudes and hence a lower precentage of usable land than the smaller Polynesian islands. After accounting for high altitude (>900 meters above sea level) and other uninhabitable land (lava flows, barren lands, steep slopes, and swamps — most of Kaua'i's West lowlands in prehistoric times), roughly half the total land area of the islands, the density remains at 30 p/km^2. One would need about 450,000 inhabitants to reach 54 p/km^2, a figure closer to Eastern Polynesian densities suggested by other contributors to this volume. There may also have been significant immigration after settlement, either from the Marquesas at any given period or from Tahiti after AD 1400, resulting in higher growth rates. The latter would be consistent with increased growth from that date (see Figure 2.1), but such increase can also be a result of new agricultural techniques or simply imperfect data. In the opposite direction, the introduction of customs from Tahiti, such as human sacrifice and intensive warfare, may also have reduced or stopped growth before high densities were reached. This shows that densities measured on limited areas by archaeologists, with information on the nature of soils, climate, and environment, are the most useful and that extrapolation for rather large islands — as well as comparison between islands — will be difficult.

With settlement around AD 1000, fifty settlers with a growth rate of 0.9 percent yield a population of 65,000 for New Zealand at contact. If we assume 200 settlers (to account for a hypothetical "Great Fleet"), the figure would be 260,000, with a density of 2.25 p/km².[10] Growth rates of between 1.0 and 1.1 percent (for fifty settlers) yield populations between 143,000 and 316,000. In any event, stabilization of the Maori population at such a low density (Davidson 1984) probably reflects the situation in some areas and, actually, population growth continued through expansion to new settlement areas. There are reports of densities as high as 60 p/km², with one fortified *pa* (a defended settlement) per km² in some regions of the North Island. It is clear that some kind of clustering effect occurs in archaeological sites and is responsible for the stabilization of New Zealand data. Dates of initial settlement as late as AD 1200 (Anderson 2003) imply either higher growth, larger numbers of settlers, or periodic immigration (see below). For instance, after 600 years, fifty settlers with growth rates between 1.3 and 1.4 percent yield populations between 116,000 and 210,000. Two hundred settlers with growth rates between 1.0 and 1.1 percent yield 78,000 and 142,000 people. The New Zealand Maori came from Eastern Polynesia and shared similar sexual behavior. Early-twentieth-century data show very high teenage fertility rates for New Zealand Maori. On these vast islands, with fewer tropical disasters, natural growth may have been higher than in the smaller islands of Eastern Polynesia.

Introducing Migration

What would be the effect of important migration and what settlement scenario would it imply for Polynesian population development? Let us keep our model of fifty settlers and a 0.5 percent growth rate. Limited emigration of 5 percent of the population every century reduces the yearly growth rate from 0.5 percent to 0.45 percent. If our model population experiences this emigration from the time it reaches 10,000 persons (1,100 years after settlement) until 1400, it would become 44,000 instead of 54,000 without migration. Assuming these migrants reach an uninhabited island and keep the same growth rate, 10,000 people would be found there (or a surplus of 10,000 if they reach an inhabited island). Three hundred years later (600 years after the new settlement), the population would reach 72,600. This represents a rather short and atypical developmental period. Assuming emigration started when population at origin was just above 1,000, the new population would be only 19,900 some 800 years after settlement, and it would reach 63,000 after 1,000 years — still a rather short developmental period, despite slower growth at the beginning due to smaller emigration. However, this can fit with later settlement dates.

Let us now imagine what could be "stabilization emigration": emigration starts when density reaches 30 p/km² (31,500 inhabitants in the Marquesas, for instance). In our second model, this occurs 1,300 years after settlement. A century later, the population would be 54,000, meaning that 22,500 have to leave to stabilize the population over a century. Unless emigration was accepted as a large collective suicide in Polynesia, descendants of these emigrants would be found on a newly discovered island, numbering 56,000 after 200 years and 113,000 a century later. This sudden and rapid population buildup is totally inconsistent with evidence of long developmental periods found by archaeologists, and the large-scale stabilization migration hypothesis has to be rejected.

Actually, the discovery of Hawai'i and Tahiti occurred when densities were still low in the Marquesas, invalidating again models inferring discoveries of new islands when high density is reached. However, small constant immigration cannot be ruled out, but it would mean a shorter developmental period. Such a pattern could fit with New Zealand population development, although 200 settlers with growth rates of 1 percent do the same. It could also help adjust with later dates of first settlement.

The various immigration hypotheses also raise a few questions regarding development of cultures. As regards the hypothesis of stabilization migration, how would Polynesians keep knowledge of navigation if they waited for centuries for high densities to push them on to discover new lands? High emigration, however, does not mean large immigration if most people died at sea. But would they leave if tens of thousands were to die? And even if discovery voyages may have been much more risky, such massive migration would have found islands the position of which would soon have become well known. In the case of constant immigration, how would distinct languages and cultures evolve in the context of important continuous arrivals? How would land conflicts be avoided with new immigrants?

What Did We Learn from this Exercise?

Even if this exercise comes up short on providing a method to estimate the population in the pre-Contact period, it does demonstrate the importance of levels of growth rates. Very low growth rates (0.1 percent to 0.2 percent) and small settler populations — from 50 to 500 people — are not compatible with the peopling of Eastern Polynesia without continuous significant migration; such large-scale movements from Central Polynesia are questionable. The sequence of island settlement and the pattern of long developmental periods, as they are known now, are not consistent with high migration triggered by high density. Finally, growth was probably much higher on isolated islands of the Pacific than on continents at the same time due to an epidemic- and pest-free environment and different behavior as regards sexuality and fertility. However, such basic normal-year high growth was drastically reduced by natural disasters. Human intervention, through customs and wars, further reduced growth to stabilize populations. Finally, a long period of time is not necessary to people islands in Polynesia, and more recent dates of settlement need only minor adjustments of growth rates, eventually through limited immigration.

In short, the most probable pattern of the peopling of Polynesia is fortuitous discovery of new lands by small numbers of settlers, well before high densities were reached. This does not exclude occasional and limited migration such as from Mangareva to Rapa Nui or from Tahiti to Hawai'i, leading to minority populations that intermarried or became large enough to create conflicts. Altogether, population development was rather simultaneous in Eastern Polynesia, and most islands reached the stabilization phase between AD 1500 and 1700. Stabilization was not due to emigration — at that time sea voyages were frequent and emigrants would have reached other islands — but to new behavioral patterns that limited growth.

As with models that are run for long time periods, growth rates have to be adjusted to reflect expected population density, data on the latter being provided by archaeology, biology, and environmental science as necessary to constrain the models. Although archaeological data seem to be easily affected by bias linked with the localization of fieldwork, such data can provide valuable information on densities in various islands and environment, as shown in other chapters of this book.

Post-Contact Population Trends

In order to retrodict mid- or late-nineteenth-century data to the time of contact, we need to know the number and type of epidemics, death rates by type of epidemics, the geographical extension of epidemics, and yearly birth and death rates (normal years); we shall see that the latter can vary with time. This information is missing for all islands. We do not even have an accurate count of all epidemics from reports of navigators hearing of the consequences of their predecessors' visits by surviving natives. Cook reported the following about Boenechea's legacy: "[T]hey say that it affected the head, throat and stomach and finally made them die . . . they call it assa no pepe" (Beaglehole 1968). Benign diseases could be fatal to people with no immunity to them after centuries of isolation. Most of the early visits of ships brought epidemics — most often influenza, but also measles, dysentery, whooping cough, and smallpox. Missionaries could sometimes tell the nature of epidemics and reported huge numbers of deaths, often killing a quarter or a third of the population.

Impact of Epidemics

It is well acknowledged by modern medicine, and it is now noted by the threat of bioterrorism, that smallpox kills about 300 per 1,000 of a nonimmu-

Table 2.1. Death rate (per 1,000) in epidemic years.

Epidemic Type	Year	Place	Rate per 1,000
1918 flu	1918	Society Islands	191
1918 flu	1918	Samoa	196
1918 flu	1918	Nauru	180
Measles	1854	Tahiti	97
Flu	1849	Guam	25[1] (b)
Whooping cough	1898	Guam	141[1,2]
Smallpox[3]			300
Unspecified	1914	South Marquesas	126

1. Deaths due to epidemic only
2. Rate for children 0–4 in Agana (from data in Underwood 1973)
3. Estimated to be fatal to 30 percent of nonimmunized people
Sources: Underwood 1973, Rallu 1990.

nized population. Death rates observed during years of epidemics in the mid-nineteenth century — although part of the population was already immunized at that time — are extremely high, often killing 100 per 1,000 of the population or up to 200 per 1,000 for the 1918 flu (Table 2.1). But data for New Zealand show rates of "only" 80 per 1,000 in 1918 for the most affected regions and often around 40 per 1,000; frequent contact with a large European population probably immunized the Maoris more rapidly (Pool 1983b; Rice 1983). This is still an extremely high mortality, given that rates between 40 per 1,000 and 50 per 1,000 were considered very high for developing countries in the mid-twentieth century. Actually, the impact of the epidemic itself is still more impressive. The 1918 flu deaths represent a death rate of 5 per 1,000 in mainland France, but it was 155 per 1,000 in the Society Islands, meaning that the disease was thirty times more fatal in the latter. The excess death rate during measles epidemics fell from 70 per 1,000 in 1854 to only 7 per 1,000 in 1951. Thus it was ten times higher than a century later, when medical facilities existed and the population was more immunized.

Nothing is known about age-specific death rates of epidemics before the twentieth century. In the Society Islands, death rates of the 1918 flu were 150 per 1,000 for males and 220 per 1,000 for females aged 35–39. But the rate rose dramatically after age 60 to 400–500 per 1,000, meaning that almost one out of two persons died from the epidemic (Rallu 1990, 256), whereas local Europeans and Chinese were not much affected. Thus, 150 years after contact, older generations in Polynesia were still much more sensitive to the flu virus than Europeans and Chinese.

We use population projections to account for age-specific death rates of various types of epidemics and resulting age structures that are a very important factor for recovery. In our model, all types of epidemics have a total death rate of 180 per 1,000, and an epidemic year growth rate is –14 percent; only the age pattern of mortality changes. After an epidemic such as the 1918 flu, mostly affecting adults and the elderly, the recovery time of our second model population is seventeen years. Actually, the age pattern of the 1918 flu epidemic is favorable to recovery, because mostly older people not involved in reproduction die. Successive epidemics of this type cause less and less decline; four such epidemics in twenty years reduce the population by 22 percent, because the first occurrences have already taken their toll on the most targeted elderly population. Other types of epidemics such as dysentery and smallpox take a toll on all ages of the population, whereas measles, whooping cough, and scarlet fever are children's diseases. In Europe, infancy diseases affect mostly newborn children (under a year) and secondarily the 1–4 and 5–9 age-groups. Polynesians were not immunized against diseases they did not get in childhood, and deaths of adults occurred as well as those of children; this was most recently seen in the 1951 measles epidemic in Tahiti (Rallu 1990). Epidemics more specifically affecting children than adults have pernicious effects on population. In the first ten or fifteen years, growth rates increase rapidly because reproductive ages are less affected. But recovery is not yet complete when the depleted cohorts arrive at reproductive ages. Then the number of births falls again and growth is sluggish or even negative again. It takes thirty years instead of the seventeen years noted above for the population to return to the pre-epidemic figure. Four epidemics of this type in twenty years will reduce the population by 42 percent.

Constant Year-to-Year Population Decline

The impact of epidemics has been discussed at length, but it is less well known why, after two or three decades of increasingly frequent contact, a continuously high mortality occurs, consisting mostly of respiratory diseases (tuberculosis) and diseases related to alcohol consumption.

Constant high death rates were first witnessed by missionaries in the 1820s in Taiarapu: "[O]n the small peninsula, people died very quickly, there was not there half the inhabitants of 10 years ago and their number is quickly declining" (Wilson 1799). This clearly leaves the impression of constantly high mortality.[11] Strictly speaking, a decline by 50 percent in ten years implies negative annual growth rates of 67 per 1,000. Although very imprecise and incredibly high, it is on the order of magnitude observed in the Marquesas from civil registration data.[12] The situation varied considerably from the northern Marquesas—where the administration and a doctor were located—to the southern group, still almost uncontrolled in the 1880s and without a doctor until 1924. The average yearly

Table 2.2. Natural growth rate (%) by islands and valleys in the Marquesas.

	1886–1895	1896–1905	1906–1915	1916–1925
Nuku Hiva	−3.0	−1.3	−0.5	−0.2
Ua Pou	−1.4	−1.2	0.8	−0.6
Ua Huka	−4.0	−1.8	0.5	−1.1
Northwest	−2.6	−1.3	0.1	−0.4
Hiva Oa	−2.3	−2.4	−4.1	−5.9
–Atuona	−1.8	−2.2	−5.3	−4.8
–Hanaiapa	−3.2	−3.5	−5.8	−8.3
–Puamau	−2.5	−2.8	−2.2	−6.4
–Hekeani	−2.0	−1.2	−2.7	−5.7
Tahuata	−1.5	−2.4	−0.8	−3.2
Fatu Hiva	−1.8	−2.4	−3.2	−2.5
Southeast	−2.1	−2.4	−3.8	−4.6

growth rate was −2.2 percent in 1886–1905 in the latter, declining to −4.6 percent in 1916–1925, without epidemics (Table 2.2). But the situation was worse still in Hiva Oa, where it was −5.9 percent, and in the Puamau and Hanaiapa Valleys, record rates of −6.4 percent and −8.3 percent, respectively, were reached. This extreme negative growth was the result of high mortality and low fertility due to STDs. Death rates reached above 80 per 1,000 and the birthrate was around 25 per 1,000, with less regional variation than for mortality. Such extreme conditions were limited to a decade, fortunately, because after thirty or forty years of such rates, population would have almost completely disappeared. Nevertheless, in the 1886–1924 period, the average natural growth rate in the southern group was −3.2 percent, meaning a halving of the population in twenty-one years;[13] in those forty years, the population declined by 74 percent. Important local variations show that the situation could be very different over short distances. Thus, the situation in Tahiti Nui and Taiarapu was certainly different, as Wilson's remarks are specifically attributed to Taiarapu and probably limited to a decade or so. With such large variations over small distances, it is difficult to base estimates for large islands as well as for different islands. It is also noticeable that the lack of health services played an important role. Several decades after contact, the virgin soil factor was no longer the main reason for decline, but it was still present as shown by abnormally high epidemic death rates in the late nineteenth and early twentieth centuries.

Tahiti. With no complete information on the number of epidemics in Tahiti in the first half of nineteenth century, we shall project a –2.5 percent rate from 1848 backward, assuming that, in the decades between contact and 1800, epidemics translate to such average yearly growth. This assumption seems a minimum, given that with –2.5 percent, population decline over thirty years is 53.2 percent, accounting for five epidemics with a growth rate of –14 percent (or just two severe epidemics with a growth rate of about –30 percent), and a yearly decline afterward to 1840 remains in the smaller range of the Marquesas (above). This exercise leads to a population of 72,750 in 1767 (Figure 2.2).[14] This can be considered a conservative estimate. An average yearly decline of 3.0 percent yields 110,400 people at contact.[15] A higher estimate of 167,800 can be linked to the 1848 population with a rate of –3.5 percent. Similar rates were observed in the southern group of the Marquesas, although not over such a long period, but the impact of early epidemics is also roughly accounted for. This exercise shows that it is possible, from observed data in the region, to connect a population of 150,000 in Tahiti at contact with figures of first censuses. Then the ratio of population decline to mid-nineteenth century would be 1 to 16, or only 6.2 percent of the initial population remaining. Small declines continued until 1881, with 5,960 Polynesians in Tahiti, and the overall decline results in just 4 percent (or 1 to 25) remaining. It appears that using an estimation of the proportion of population remaining after a long period can lead to very different and uncertain estimates. For instance, assuming 4 percent of the population remained instead of 5 percent leads to an estimate of the original population larger by 25 percent. On this basis, Stannard's estimate of Hawai'i's population should be considered as questionable.

It is also noteworthy that McArthur's estimate for Tahiti appears simply unacceptable, translating into an average yearly growth rate in 1767–1848 of –1.4 percent.[16] This is not only lower than in the Marquesas one century later and inconsistent with the many epidemics and missionaries' observations of constant decline, but it is also lower than in 1848–1863 (–1.7 percent), a period affected by only one rather mild epidemic of measles in 1854 (death rate of 97 per 1,000). The missionary census of 1829–1830 gives a figure of 8,568, which is also unacceptable. Even without accounting for underenumeration in the 1848 census, the decline in 1830–1848 (from 8,568 to 8,082, or –0.3 percent yearly) is smaller than in 1855–1863 (–1.0 percent), whereas the first period witnessed three epidemics. The 1841 smallpox epidemic resulted in the disappearance of the anti-Christian movement Mamaia, whose members refused to be vaccinated. The 1843 dysentery epidemic could also have caused many deaths, and scarlet fever in 1847 had an

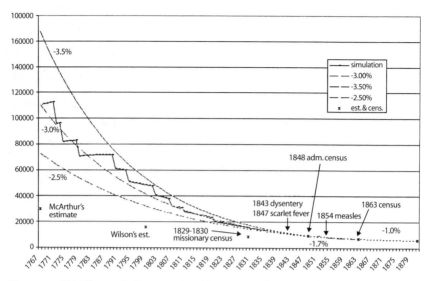

Figure 2.2. Tahiti's population 1767–1781: Various retrodictions and a simulation.

impact on children and perhaps also on adults. Finally, missionary estimates or "censuses," as well as McArthur's estimate that they influenced, imply growth rates that are not consistent with events observed in the 1840s and do not match trends thereafter; they should be rejected as far too low.

Marquesas. For the Marquesas, the period of frequent contact is later than in Tahiti. Limiting the retrodiction from the 1887 census (5,246 people) to 1,800 with a rate of −2.5 percent yields a population of 46,100, a rate of −3.0 percent yields 70,200, and a rate of −3.5 percent yields 107,300. Reports of epidemics are still more lacking for the Marquesas than for Tahiti due to reduced missionary presence and less frequent administrative visits. However, the 1804 famine killed one-third of the population in some islands (Dening 1974). Famine also occurred in 1797–1798, 1820, and 1862 (or 1867) (Kellum-Ottino 1971), the latter followed by a smallpox epidemic brought by returnees from the Peru slave trade. In 1844, Lesson ([1844] 1981) witnessed an epidemic — following consumption of adulterated alcohol brought by a ship — that killed hundreds of people on Nuku Hiva. There were no epidemics from 1886 to 1914, when the southern group was hit by an unspecified epidemic resulting in a death rate of 126 per 1,000. Fortunately, a quarantine prevented the 1918 flu from reaching the Marquesas. Most remarkably, the yearly decline lasted until 1924, about forty years longer than in Tahiti, with a low point in the population of 2,255. Thus, to retain our previous and tentative estimate of 45,000 at contact (Rallu 1990, 49), the overall decline leaves just 5 per-

Table 2.3. Population density in the Society and Cook Islands in the nineteenth century.

	1828	1840	1846	1881	1897
Tahiti			8.9[4]	5.7	
Mo'orea			11.2*	7.1	
Huahine					17
Tahaa					12
Raiatea					12
Bora-Bora	45				32
Maupiti					47
Rarotonga	89**	65			
Mangaia			69		

 * 1848, from 1848 census after author's correction.
** 1830, from N. McArthur's estimate of 6,000 inhabitants.

cent of the initial population, or a ratio of 1 to 20.[17] A contact population of 63,000 translates into decline to 3.6 percent, or a ratio of 1 to 28, reaching very high values in this particular case. Still, we have a feeling that repeated famines, smallpox, and unreported epidemics would point to an even higher average decline than 3.5 percent for the first half of the nineteenth century; but famines and epidemics probably did not affect all islands.

Other Islands. Smaller islands were less frequently visited because they could not provide abundant supplies to ships, and they were therefore less exposed to introduced epidemics, tuberculosis, STDs, and alcohol consumption. It is remarkable that early censuses in the middle or late nineteenth century show higher densities as we move west from Tahiti to the less visited western Leeward Islands and the Cook Islands. Density was still 32 p/km^2 in Bora-Bora in 1897, 47 p/km^2 in Maupiti, and 65 p/km^2 in Rarotonga in 1840. Obviously, a ratio of overall population decline of 1 to 20 or even 1 to 5 cannot be assumed for the westernmost islands in Eastern Polynesia without reaching improbable densities. Even assuming a rather high density of 150 p/km^2, the low point is still 21 percent of initial population in Bora-Bora and 43 percent in Rarotonga, allowing for some additional decline in the second half of the nineteenth century. Some of the Hawaiian Islands were frequently visited by whalers and traders and could have witnessed a decline similar to Tahiti. In large islands such as New Zealand and New Caledonia, epidemics could have affected limited areas, with lower overall decline than in Tahiti or the Marquesas.

Finally, we may return to our previous estimate of 66,000 inhabitants in Tahiti (Rallu 1990, 222) and to the original version of my Ph.D. dissertation. If we assume that there was only one (Boenechea's) epidemic between 1767 and 1774 and that it was as severe as the 1918 flu (–15 percent growth), the population at contact would have been 78,000. Two similar epidemics would lead to 91,500. There were also wars in Taiarapu and Tiraoou in the period. Thus a population close to 100,000 — a figure similar to early estimates and to Cook's second estimate after correction — seems quite plausible. But based on the above development, we tend to consider this estimate conservative.

Conclusions

Although such exercises are always artificial, they show that it is possible to match projections from Polynesian settlement and retrodictions from late-nineteenth-century censuses to rather high densities in a few islands of Polynesia at contact. Such densities have even been observed in the mid-nineteenth century in some of the Cook Islands. In the case of Tahiti, it also matches estimates based on the observations of first visitors.

It seems probable that natural growth was much higher in prehistoric Polynesia than in Western historical demography due to an epidemic-free environment. Thus, starting from small numbers of settlers and limited migration, Polynesians covered island landscapes to the point that new customs, such as infanticide and human sacrifice, were adopted to limit growth. Given the probable levels of growth rates in pre-Contact Polynesia, later dates of first settlement are compatible with only minor adjustment of growth rates or small-scale migration.

European contact resulted in steep declines of population. Decline was certainly higher in the late eighteenth and first half of the nineteenth centuries, when epidemics and new diseases ravaged nonimmunized Polynesian populations, than after 1850 when the first statistical data are available for Tahiti, invalidating various low reestimates in the mid-twentieth century. Tahiti, the Marquesas, Aneityum in Melanesia, and a few other small islands testify to such incredibly high declines, leaving around 5 percent of the initial population, but in other islands (Bora-Bora, Maupiti, Rarotonga) decline was limited to remaining populations of 20 percent or even 40 percent. Given the large local variations observed in the Marquesas and the Society Islands, it will remain difficult to assess the path of population after contact and, therefore, density at contact for large islands and different small islands and valleys, not to speak of the Pacific as a whole. While there is a wide range of figures that are "demographically" acceptable, more information is needed on dates of first settlement, length of growth periods, densities, and trends. Such additional archaeological data are necessary to input to models so that we can attain a more precise knowledge of population development in the highly varied islands of the Pacific.

Notes

1. We will not consider Boenechea's estimate (10,000) because he did not circumnavigate the island and because he based his estimate on that of missionaries (8,000 to 12,000) who did not travel far from the village where they landed in Taiarapu. The king of Peru — from reports of Rodriguez, who visited most of the island and reported that it was densely populated — lifted Beonechea's estimate to 15,000. Rodriguez gives only one figure: 1,000 people seen in the small district of Mataoae in Taiarapu, evidence that his compatriots' figures are unreliable.

2. In 100 years, with a 0.7 percent yearly growth rate, a population grows by 100 percent; with 0.5 percent, it grows by 65 percent.

3. Pitcairn was inhabited by Polynesians before the arrival of the *Bounty* mutineers, but the island had been deserted for some time before that.

4. Adams recorded all births and deaths in the *Bounty*'s Bible and in his diary. This and such high growth are a strong advocacy in favor of completeness of data. Data for Pitcairn used in this section are from Lummis (1997) and Shapiro (1968).

5. In the Marquesas in the mid-nineteenth century, Robarts reports of drought and famine killing a third of the population of some islands (Dening 1974). A drought and famine in 1943 in Truk reduced the Nauruan population displaced there by about a third, including a small number of deaths due to war (Underwood 1973).

6. Death rates in the ranges of 15–19, 20–24, 25–29, 30–34, and 35–39 are increased by 50 percent, 80 percent, 70 percent, 50 percent, and 20 percent, respectively, already a high impact of warfare.

7. Double-hulled canoes leaving for discovery voyages or fleeing conflicts were not the big war canoes but smaller ones. They were loaded with food, animals, and plants to eat during the trip and to plant and breed in a newly discovered land. Due to this heavy load, they probably did not carry many people (Eric Conte, personal communication).

8. Suggs (1961) suggests population stabilization as early as AD 1400, but we discount this now outdated study.

9. It could be argued that Rapa Nui no longer had large trees to build seagoing canoes, but possible links with Mangareva could have provided these.

10. We assume all of them live on North Island.

11. Another example of the exceptionally poor health situation in Tahiti at that time is the heavy toll on Pitcairn Islanders during their six-month stay in 1831: seventeen deaths out of a population of eighty-six, or death rate of 219 per 1,000, just in half a year of exposure.

12. Emigration from the Marquesas, as well as internal migration, were negligible before 1930 and barely affect the trends.

13. In this, the 1914 epidemic in the southern group is responsible for less than 5 percent of the decline.

14. Note that for 1848 we use a census figure corrected for underenumeration: 9,360

inhabitants in Tahiti instead of 8,082 (Rallu 1990, 232–233). With the uncorrected figure, results would be 16 percent lower.

15. In a more refined estimation, with an average yearly decline of 3 percent (Figure 2.2), we use seven epidemics causing declines of 15 percent each in 1767–1810; until 1790, population still increases between epidemics, but less and less and yearly decline reaches 1.5 percent in 1803–1810. In 1810–1840, we use four smaller epidemics: two with decline rates of 10 percent and two with 8 percent; yearly decline is 2 percent until 1820 and 2.5 percent in 1820–1830, returning to 2 percent afterward. The three epidemics in 1841, 1843, and 1847 cause a 5 percent decline each, and the 1854 epidemic causes a 9 percent decline, as estimated after correction of civil registration for underreporting of events (Rallu 1990, 229–230). Yearly decline decreases from 1840 to observed values of 1.3 percent in 1848–1853 and 1.0 percent until 1880. This is just an exercise to illustrate a possible trend of Tahiti's population from contact to 1881.

16. Using our corrected figure for 1848, without correction the rate would be –1.6 percent.

17. To illustrate again the danger of using the proportion of the population remaining for estimates of other islands, if the decline had ceased by 1886 as in Tahiti, 11 percent of the population would have remained (a ratio of 1 to 9).

3   SHRIPAD TULJAPURKAR, CHARLOTTE LEE, AND MICHELLE FIGGS

Demography and Food in Early Polynesia

 The study of prehistoric populations relies on heterogeneous and incomplete data—archeological, ethnographic, ecological, historical—that need to be interpreted and integrated using conceptual and analytical models. For the island populations of Polynesia, Kirch (1984, 1994) provides a synthetic summary and model of demographic and cultural evolution over a millennium. This synthesis frames history in a temporal demographic sequence: Founding immigrants begin a period of exponential numerical increase in time and of spatial spread; then follows a confrontation with Malthusian limits that is manifest in expansion into marginal areas and in the slowing or cessation of population increase; the latter period is marked by the evolution of sociocultural hierarchies in the form of chiefdoms. This temporal story rests on assumptions concerning the relationship between agriculture and long-run population dynamics, including the productivity of agriculture in prehistory, the nature of marginal areas, Malthusian limits, and carrying capacity. This chapter examines these and related concepts from demographic, ecological, and comparative perspectives. First, we examine briefly and critically Malthusian limits and carrying capacity, followed by the concepts of marginal areas and sustainability. Second, we consider the problem of demographic reconstruction based on the limited data available for prehistoric populations. We present a new data-driven method that uses data tabulated by Weiss (1973) on various prehistoric populations to generate a new family of model life tables. The success of this approach suggests that we may be able to reduce reliance on mortality models for contemporary populations. Finally, we discuss an ecologically based approach to the interaction between agricultural practices and soil dynamics. Sowing, fertilizing, and cropping alter the cycle of nutrient flow from the atmosphere and the soil into plants and back again. We propose a quantitative model of this cycle and its dynamics and discuss its use in studying the relationship between agriculture and demography in prehistory. We argue that such an approach can provide robust insights into the dynamic processes that underlie population change and population-environment relationships in prehistory.

Malthusian Limits and Carrying Capacity

Population change results from an arithmetic difference between birthrates, death rates, and immigration. Assuming no net long-run immigration (probably appropriate for early Hawai'i but not necessarily for other islands) and initially exponential growth, a transition to population limitation requires either a decrease in birthrates or an increase in death rates. Malthus (see, e.g., Lee 1987; Cohen 1995) argued for increased mortality as a result of declining per capita resources; a less likely alternative was a decrease in birthrates. The Malthusian view has been grafted onto the ecological model of logistic population growth, in which the rate of population change (i.e., of the difference between birthrates and death rates) is assumed to decrease when a population increases toward a number called the "carrying capacity." The time trajectory of a population that follows an upward logistic is a saturating S-shaped curve that flattens at the carrying capacity.

We say a real population's dynamics are "Malthusian" if we can demonstrate that birthrates or death rates are negatively affected by the population number (Lee 1987) — a more measured view than one that equates Malthusian dynamics with catastrophic checks. Lee reviews evidence of Malthusian feedback in human and animal populations. Direct density feedback is hard to demonstrate in human populations, so analyses usually focus on intermediate variables such as harvests and wages. Historically, shifts in such variables are likely driven by variation in weather, with vital rates changing in response to per capita availability of food (driven by changes in supply and/or purchasing power). Long time series of English population data, ca. AD 1400 to 1700, provide some of the best evidence, and there is weaker evidence from other studies of early humans. Fertility appears to respond negatively to density; there is weaker evidence for a response in mortality. While these effects serve to reduce long-run population growth rates toward zero, historical populations often show both short-term and long-term cycles. Other studies of European demographic history (e.g., the studies of Scandinavian countries reported in Bengtsson and Saito 2000) show that demographic responses to changes in food supply and weather are complex and vary with local factors. For example, geography and topography make a difference to the impacts of weather on local areas, connectedness between populations can serve to link areas with relatively high food production to those with low production, and so on. Negative feedbacks of the Malthusian sort may also be countered by positive feedbacks (e.g., the general ideas in Boserup 1981 or the complex adaptations discussed in Kirch 1994), which may complicate efforts to estimate population feedback effects. The estimates in Lee (1987) provide a basis for considering population dynamics over time in early Polynesia, using density-dependent stochastic models, but such an analysis has not been done as far as we know.

A different approach to density limitation is in terms of the intuitively appealing if slippery concept of "carrying capacity," which is thought of as estimating either the limits of population or the "logistic" carrying capacity (an equilibrium level sustainable indefinitely). An operational assessment of carrying capacity is more problematic than an effort to establish Malthusian feedbacks. As discussed by Cohen (1995), any estimate of carrying capacity depends on contextual factors (e.g., technology and individual and social tastes and preferences) and the temporal and spatial scale at which one seeks to specify sustainability. It is difficult to go from general principles to an estimate of carrying capacity for a prehistoric population, given the limited data available; efforts to make such estimates even in data-rich situations have often been useless. Cohen gives many examples of estimates of carrying capacity for human populations based on a priori arguments about limiting factors such as land or water. These estimates have been very different and are rarely consistent with observed changes of population over time.

But two other approaches to carrying capacity have been used for early Polynesian populations. The first is illustrated by Kirch (1984) and estimates the largest sustained population numbers observed in a given area over a given time period based on archeological data. Ideally, this method requires population sizes to be estimated over at least a few generations (say 75 to 100 years) and that the estimates be stable over that time (e.g., the variation in numbers between years is small in some specified sense). Direct estimates are difficult (perhaps impossible) from archeological data alone, but indirect estimates based on habitation density can be made. Results from this method are clearly valuable in estimating a carrying capacity as a population level that was sustained for some time, but they do not explain why that particular level was an equilibrium. The second approach, illustrated by Hamilton and Kahn (chapter 8 in this volume), takes a different view of carrying capacity as the largest potential population size that could be supported in a specified area in a specified time period. Here the area and period of study define the technology — choice of crops, farming methods, use of animals, output per area per time of various types of soil — and geographical data are used to assess the maximum productivity of soil and the area of soil that is worked. Several chapters in this volume use some variant of this analysis. This approach is valuable in providing a geographical inventory but appears to lead to quite large estimates of potential food production. These approaches are probably limited in their ability to evaluate long-run changes in food supply or soil condition. A dynamic approach (below) may help in this regard.

Marginal Areas and Sustainability in Agricultural History

The concept of the margin has played an important role in historical discussions of population change. For Polynesia, Kirch (1994) discusses the establishment and expansion of settlements in island areas that appear to be poor in rainfall or water storage, soil quality, and access to marine resources. For medieval England in the early part of the last millennium, Postan (1966) argued a similar interpretation of the expansion of population into the boundaries of established arable land in England during the period AD 1100–1200, followed by a retreat from the margins when population collapsed during the 1300s. In both cases, the movement into marginal areas is thought to be a reflection of population increase and Malthusian limits in more fertile areas, and marginal areas are thought to be of poor agricultural potential and susceptible to degradation of soil and natural resources. Over the years, there has been a reevaluation of the concept of a "margin" in the literature on medieval England that ties in to our earlier discussion of Malthusian limits and carrying capacity.

Bailey (1989) and Hatcher and Bailey (2001) show that the notion of a marginal area in the English setting was tied (at least implicitly) to the concept of economic rent, which Ricardo (1817) defined as "a return due to the land alone as a factor of production." Thus a marginal area was one where this rent was low for one or more of a variety of factors: poor soil quality, the need for high labor inputs to create or maintain production, or the distance from markets or other places of exchange. These authors point out that an area may seem marginal if viewed purely in terms of the potential productivity of soil per unit of labor, but that the economic rent depends on other factors. These include institutional factors (e.g., a marginal area may provide freedom from communal or institutional restrictions on individual behavior, crop selection, or farming practice; or a marginal area may remove or reduce burdens of taxation) and specialization (e.g., marginal areas may benefit from specialization in cloth making, collection of shells, quarrying, or other activity). Such factors would seem relevant in Polynesian societies, especially as they underwent a transition to complex societies with hierarchical controls (Kirch 1994). Our point here is that the role of "marginal" areas needs to be evaluated in a broader context of the relationships between people and institutions.

Sustainability of agriculture is another concept that plays a role in the discussion of Malthusian limits and of marginal areas. The notion that soil fertility is an exhaustible stored component of soil is often used in discussions, but it needs critical examination. Indirect evidence for soil degradation can be found in historical reports (e.g., of declining tree cover and the production and imports of food; Angel 1972 reviews such evidence for the Eastern Mediterranean over a long span of prehistory). But in other cases, as with medieval England (e.g., Postan 1966), records of agricultural output can be misleading. Whitney (1923) provides an early reassessment of a suggested decline in English wheat harvests from AD 1200 to 1600, showing that statistical evidence for a decline is weak. Long (1979) returns to this question, arguing that technology (implements and methods used to work the soil) rather than soil quality was probably the limiting factor on production over this period. Long notes the famous Rothamsted experiment on long-term (over a century) wheat cultivation on a plot with no manuring where annual yields were maintained at a constant level with no sign of exhaustion. We believe that the exhaustion or degradation of soils and environment are not inevitable consequences of long-term habitation and population growth — they need to be demonstrated. We return to this question following our discussion of soil nutrient dynamics.

Demographic Reconstruction in Prehistory

The reconstruction of Polynesian demographic history faces the problem of estimating or assuming appropriate vital rates for mortality, fertility, and migration (e.g., Rallu 1990; Pool 1991). The crux of the problem is that we know much about modern human demography but relatively little about prehistory, so there is a tension between borrowing methods based on modern data and a reliance on the sparse and potentially inaccurate data on early populations such as those that come from skeletal series. Wood et al. (1992) and Meindl and Russell (1998) provide good reviews of the difficulties involved, and both discuss in detail models of the age pattern of mortality. Although these authors advocate some newer methods, many scholars still go back to the seminal work by Weiss (1973), who developed the first systematic model life tables based on prehistoric data. Weiss relied on the Gompertz model of mortality, which works well for modern human adults, and to that extent his models are perhaps biased. We show that it is possible to rely entirely on data from prehistoric populations to generate a family of model schedules of mortality. Our approach avoids some (but certainly not all) of the criticisms that have been leveled at mortality models in paleodemography.

We selected from the life tables collected in Weiss (1973) a subset of thirty-six tables that included data on ages under 10 years. We focused on this subset because infant and child mortality is a key element of the overall life table; a separate analysis, not reported here, was conducted using the other tables and leads to similar results for adult ages. We used a simple smoothing procedure to generate life tables for age groups in five-year-wide intervals for ages 0 to 70, giving us a set of life tables $l(a,s)$ for ages a and samples s. The first step is to transform the data to a logit scale; that is, we compute logits $n(a,s)$ such that

$$l(a,s) = exp[n(a,s)] / [1 + exp[n(a,s)]].$$

This is a standard transformation in mortality analysis that essentially puts the life table values on a more useful logarithmic scale. Defining the average logit over all samples to be $k(a)$, we then performed a singular value decomposition (SVD) of the deviations from this average (for the SVD, see Thisted 1988). An SVD will yield a set of age "patterns" that are an orthogonal decomposition of the data, and each pattern has an associated positive weight called a singular value. These weights tell us what fraction of the variation in the set is described by the corresponding patterns. In our case, we find that the first pattern explains 79 percent and the second pattern another 15 percent of the variation, for a total of 94 percent. Thus we conclude that the pattern in any sample is effectively described by a model of the form

$$n(a, sample) = k(a) + A\,h(a) + B\,g(a),$$

where $k(a)$ is the observed mean, $h(a)$ and $g(a)$ are the first and second SVD patterns, and A and B are constants. Figure 3.1 displays the values of the logits for these three schedules; observe that $h(a)$ shifts the entire schedule downward (if A is positive), whereas $g(a)$ shifts young ages down and old ages up (if B is positive). To find a model life table for any particular sample, we must choose A and B to fit some overall parameters of the data, such as the expectation of life at different ages. To illustrate the procedure, Figure 3.2 shows contours of the expectation of life at birth $e0$ for a range of values of A and B, and Figure 3.3 shows the expected life $e10$ at age 10 for the same parameter ranges. To fix A and B, one must specify the values of both $e0$ and $e10$. Alternatively, one could use different computations to specify how A and B can be fixed in terms of other measures of mortality (e.g., survival to age 10, and e10).

We find it striking that a two-parameter relational model describes so much of the variation in the data we used. We note that the data sets in Weiss come from a diverse array of places and times. Our finding surely reflects strong underlying regularities in early mortality patterns, even if they are not the same as in modern human data. These results suggest that further analysis along these lines should be fruitful. We have found this modeling approach useful in a study of demographic reconstruction for the Hawaiian Islands.

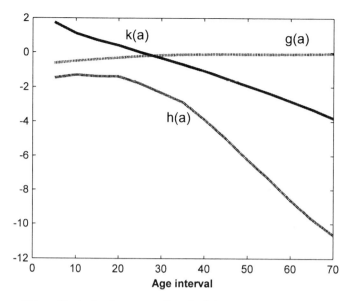

Figure 3.1. Value of logits for three mortality schedules.

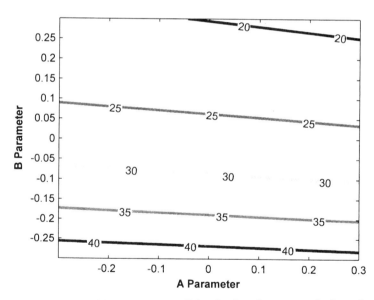

Figure 3.2. Contours of the expectation of life at birth *eo* for a range of values of A and B.

Agriculture and Soil Nutrient Dynamics

Understanding the properties of the soils that prehistoric humans farmed may provide important insights into the challenges they faced and the choices they made (Vitousek et al. 2004; Kirch et al. 2004). Just as much as human populations, however, crop growth and soil nutrient status are dynamic entities. Models describing the interaction between plants and soils are a subject of active interest in ecosystem ecology because of their utility for addressing questions about how natural systems may respond to global climate change. These models, including CENTURY, RothC, G'DAY, and many others, generally take the form of parameter-rich computer simulations that vary in some details and in their ability to accurately describe different natural communities (Smith et al. 1997). Mathematical formulations of such models attempt to capture the broad similarities between the different simulations and to reveal essential characteristics that hold across ecosystems (Jenkinson 1990; Agren and Bosatta 1996; McMurtrie and Comins 1996; Bolker et al. 1998; Baisden and Amundson 2003). The insights gained from analytical descriptions of ecosystem dynamics provide a framework in which to approach ideas and questions important to agroecosystems, such as the notion of sustainability and the importance of observed spatial or temporal environmental variability in terms of yields of food crops.

We know of at least one study that pairs a simulation model with its analytical counterpart to explore questions about agricultural systems (Baisden and Amundson 2003), but we are not aware of any work that is appropriate to subsistence agriculture. Here we describe the essential features of nutrient cycling and present an analytic model derived from the well-validated CENTURY simulation model. We use the models to explore the effects of harvesting on sustainable plant production under water and nitrogen limitation. We vary the effective amounts of the limiting factor to determine what strategies might increase production. We also investigate the dynamics of cropping and interpret our findings in terms of subsistence agriculture.

Our goal is to show how this mechanistic approach can play an important role in models of population and agriculture and to illuminate our understanding of early agricultural populations.

A Model of Plant-Soil Dynamics

Nutrients in all ecosystems cycle between the soil and the atmosphere. Plants take up water and inorganic nutrients such as nitrogen from the soil and obtain inorganic carbon from the air. When plants die, they return carbon and nitrogen to the soil in organic forms. Soil microbes digest organic matter, releasing carbon dioxide back into the air as a byproduct of respiration and leaving behind

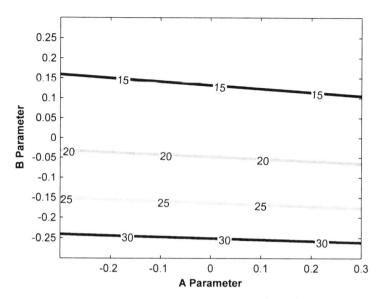

Figure 3.3. Expected life *e10* at age 10 for a range of values of A and B.

more recalcitrant organic material. They may incorporate nitrogen into their own tissues or release nitrogen in inorganic forms that are again available for plant uptake or escape in gaseous form to the atmosphere. Nitrogen from the atmosphere returns to the soil via biological fixation of nitrogen gas or by atmospheric deposition of mineral nitrogen (Brady and Weil 2002).

Soil organic matter (SOM), like radioactive material, decays linearly (Jenkinson 1990; Townsend et al. 1995), but not all organic material decays at the same rate. Compartment models treat SOM as made up of discrete fractions, each of which has a unique exponential decay rate. Perhaps the most successful compartment model is CENTURY (Parton et al. 1987, 1988), which has been successfully applied to a wide variety of natural systems (see, e.g., Schimel et al. 1997; Raich et al. 2000). An outline of CENTURY's compartments is shown schematically in Figure 3.4. From that figure it will come as no surprise that CENTURY is a parameter-rich simulation model, which makes it difficult to set up and run in situations with limited data; simulation results from the full model can also be hard to interpret. What we seek are robust insights into the relationships between agricultural practice, soils, and climate. To obtain these, we follow Parton et al. (1987) and Bolker et al. (1998) and develop a compact system of equations that represent the model's core of exponential organic matter decays and coupled nitrogen flows. Below we present a description of the model's general behavior (the equations, code, and other technical material are available from the authors on request).

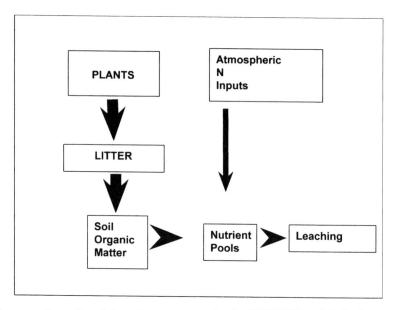

Figure 3.4. An outline of the main components for the CENTURY model of soil dynamics.

Plant growth (or productivity), which provides the inputs of organic material to the soil, is a function of light, water, carbon dioxide, and nutrient availability. The component that is in shortest supply relative to plant needs limits plant growth (Sterner and Elser 2002). In this chapter, we assume for simplicity that the only factors that can be limiting are the water and nitrogen available in the soil for plant uptake. Monthly rainfall, temperature, and soil texture, all model parameters, combine to determine soil moisture. Plant-available mineral nitrogen is a model variable, and its abundance therefore depends on external inputs and removals as well as on its cycling through the system. In CENTURY, a fixed parameter specifying the maximum carbon-to-nitrogen ratio of new plant tissue and fixed functions for the maximum production per unit of water define plant needs. For a given set of parameter values, we can compare available water and nitrogen to the amount needed by plants to find out which factor limits the system. The identity of the limiting factor has important consequences for nutrient cycling in the model ecosystem, as we discuss in more detail below.

Once we understand the general behavior of the model, we can ask and answer questions about the effects of human participation in the nutrient cycle. For instance, we can discuss sustainable ecosystem states in terms of model equilibria, since we know that the latter are indefinitely sustainable system configurations. Next, we explore the effects of adding harvesting to the model, which we represent by removing a fraction of new plant growth from the system rather

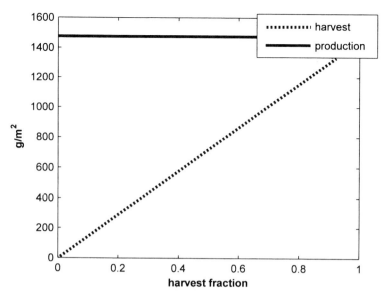

Figure 3.5. Increasing harvest intensity where water is limiting does not affect equilibrium plant production, and therefore harvesting larger fractions of production yields larger harvests.

than returning it to the soil. We determine how increasing harvest intensity affects model equilibria and dynamics under varying levels of nutrient and water availability, and we interpret our results in terms of food supply to subsistence agriculturalists.

Impact of Human Harvesting Activity

The effect of harvesting on plant production and harvest size depends on what factor limits production at equilibrium. Other parameters affect the numerical values of the model results, but the patterns we describe here are robust. Increasing harvest intensity where water is limiting does not affect equilibrium plant production, and therefore harvesting larger fractions of production yields larger harvests (Figure 3.5). Even though only water is limiting here, the equilibrium amount of mineral nitrogen and of organic nitrogen decrease linearly with increasing harvest fraction (Figure 3.6).

Under conditions where nitrogen is limiting at equilibrium, increasing harvest intensity lowers initially low levels of equilibrium mineral nitrogen dramatically (Figure 3.7). Organic soil nitrogen decreases similarly and is 0 at 100 percent harvest. These decreases in availability of the limiting nutrient drive proportional decreases in equilibrium production with increasing harvest intensity. The result is a very slow increase in equilibrium harvest size with increasing harvest fraction

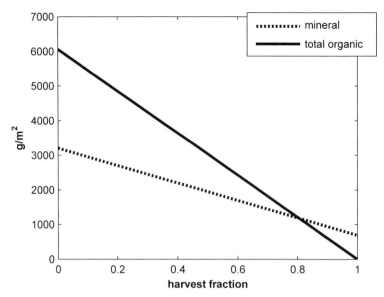

Figure 3.6. The equilibrium amounts of mineral nitrogen and of organic nitrogen decrease linearly with increasing harvest fraction.

over about 30 percent (Figure 3.8). The maximum sustainable harvest, less than 20 percent of the production in the uncropped system, occurs at 100 percent harvest. Increasing N inputs while remaining in the nitrogen-limited regime results in proportional increases in production and harvest levels, but increasing N inputs enough can switch the system to water limitation.

Even without changes in inputs of water or nitrogen, changing harvest intensity can itself change the factor that limits production at equilibrium. Figure 3.9 shows such a situation, where water is limiting for harvest fraction less than 0.4 and nitrogen is limiting for harvest fraction 0.4 and above.

We examine the impact of harvesting on system dynamics by simulating the system without harvest until it reaches equilibrium. We then impose 30 percent harvest, allow the system to equilibrate again, and return to 0 percent harvest to examine recovery. When water is the limiting factor, harvesting does not affect plant production, so this procedure does not actually result in any dynamics in production or harvest. Figure 3.10 shows how production responds to this treatment in a nitrogen-limited system at two levels of rainfall. Both runs show the same qualitative behavior: Production plummets under harvest and then returns after cropping stops. The equilibrium levels of production and the temporal scale of system responses depend on soil moisture. Just 20 cm of monthly rainfall will

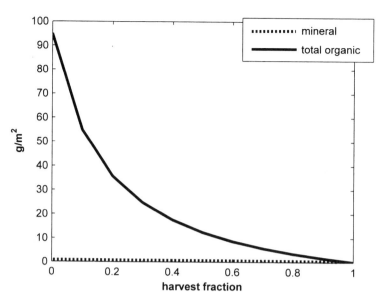

Figure 3.7. Under conditions where nitrogen is limiting at equilibrium, increasing harvest intensity lowers initially low levels of equilibrium mineral nitrogen dramatically.

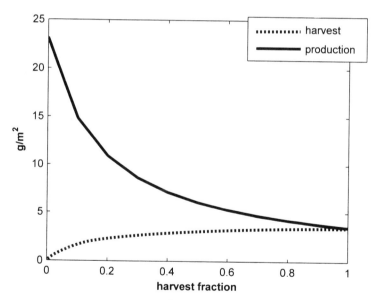

Figure 3.8. Decreases in availability of the limiting nutrient drive proportional decreases in equilibrium production with increasing harvest intensity, resulting in a slow increase in equilibrium harvest size.

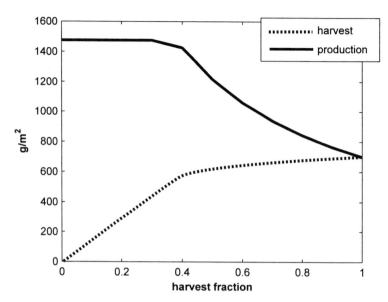

Figure 3.9. Changing harvest intensity can change the factor that limits production at equilibrium. Here water is limiting for harvest fraction less than 0.4, and nitrogen is limiting for harvest fraction 0.4 and above.

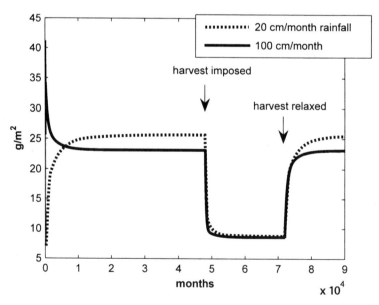

Figure 3.10. Production responses to water limitation in a nitrogen-limited system at two levels of rainfall.

lead to higher production equilibria than 100 cm with cropping as well as without. All system responses are faster in the high-rainfall case. The dramatic drop in productivity occurs over roughly eighty years with low rainfall and about fifty years in the high-rainfall case. Recovery to precropping equilibrium levels takes about 2,000 years and 800 years, respectively.

Implications for Food Supply

Harvesting does not affect equilibrium plant production when water is the limiting factor because plant growth in that case depends on rainfall levels and not on any factor that cycles through the plants. Only at the point where losses of organic matter change soil water-holding properties could harvesting change water availability. In contrast, harvest lowers steady-state production under nitrogen limitation because removing plant material imposes an additional loss of the limiting factor on the system. One implication of this difference is that, under water limitation, cropping a larger fraction of plant production increases the size of the sustainable harvest; whereas if nitrogen is limiting, equilibrium harvest sizes are small compared to productivity in an equivalent uncropped system, no matter what level of harvest effort is applied. In both situations, however, harvest constitutes a loss of nitrogen from the soil. Therefore, the possibility exists for intense enough cropping in a water-limited system to drive nitrogen levels low enough to become limiting (see Figure 3.9). Aside from its impact on plant production, reducing system nitrogen to the point where it becomes limiting would lower the nutrient quality of the harvested material, whether or not a switch in limitation is possible and the precise level of harvest intensity where it would occur is a function of plant needs and of inputs and losses of water and nitrogen.

How relevant are equilibrium results to subsistence agriculture? We examined the dynamics of applying harvest to an uncropped system with two very different moisture inputs and found that harvest sizes decline to equilibrium levels over just a few decades in both cases. Larger harvests might be possible if expansion of agriculture to new areas is possible before old ones suffer declines in productivity. Alternatively, landscape-level strategies that set aside portions of land in fallow may provide a way to increase harvests. Given that the time needed to recover soil nutrient status after relaxing harvesting is so much longer than the time needed to draw nutrients down, however, equilibrium levels of harvest are likely to be the relevant standard for agricultural systems.

One way to increase equilibrium harvest size without collecting a larger fraction of plant production is to add nutrients or water. Model behavior demonstrates that increases in the limiting factor increase plant production (and therefore harvest size) proportionally. Modern industrialized agriculture takes advantage of this fact in the forms of extensive irrigation and intensive fertilization. The activities that subsistence populations may undertake to improve their agricultural fields deserve careful attention if we are to understand their potential food supply.

Soil moisture affects nutrient cycling dynamics via its effect on decay rates as well as via water limitation. The analysis shown in Figure 3.10 demonstrates that spatial heterogeneity in soil moisture may have important implications for subsistence agriculture. The most important question is what is limiting in each place. If low-moisture areas are limited by water and high-moisture areas are limited by nitrogen, harvesting will affect the two locales very differently. Even if the same factor is limiting in both places, different levels of moisture can result in different levels of equilibrium productivity and different rates of responses to change. Additionally, as it affects the balance between weathering and leaching, abundant rainfall can induce enrichment of or limitation by rock-derived nutrients such as phosphorus (Vitousek et al. 1997), which is a process we have not considered here. Phosphorus can be included in the model, however, and analysis of its effects using the approaches illustrated here is an important avenue for future research.

Applications and Implications for Understanding Prehistory

We have shown how an understanding of plant-soil nutrient cycling dynamics as a linear dynamical system can illuminate the ways in which agricultural practice and natural conditions influence food production. The approach described here allows for much future work. One direction would be to introduce seasonality to the model, in harvesting as well as in environmental conditions and plant growth, to allow representation of processes that occur over annual or multiyear time scales. Another major issue is the effect of temporal stochasticity — for example, to study the effect on agriculturalists of droughts or climatic regime shifts. Tillage effects are also potentially important, as mechanical disturbance of soil can result in the conversion of organic nitrogen to plant-available mineral forms (Baisden and Amundson 2003). An exploration of these factors using a combination of simulation and analytical modeling will contribute much to our understanding of how subsistence agriculturalists interacted with the natural world.

Discussion

We began this chapter by discussing the limitations of our understanding of the feedbacks between demographic change and subsequent population growth and between populations and their agricultural resources. We also pointed to the problems of using demographic methods based on modern data to model prehistoric populations. We suggest two strategies to advance our understanding. For demographic analysis, we believe that data on early humans do contain useful regularities that can be exposed by data-driven analyses; we illustrated this approach by developing a new model mortality schedule for early humans. For the study of resources, food, and agriculture, we suggest a systematic analysis of dynamic models that couple agriculture explicitly to the nutrient status and dynamics of soil. This approach matches well with modern approaches to defining and assessing the resilience, sustainability, and degradation of soils (Lal 1997). These threads — demographics and agriculture — provide the elements that need to be combined into a coupled dynamical picture of human-environment dynamics in prehistory.

4

"Like Shoals of Fish"

Archaeology and Population in Pre-Contact Hawai'i

 Just before noon on Sunday, January 17, 1779, Captain James Cook brought the HMS *Resolution* and *Discovery* into Kealakekua Bay on the southwestern coast of Hawai'i Island.[1] Now on his third voyage of discovery in the Pacific and well acquainted with most of the major Polynesian archipelagoes and islands, Cook penned this remark in his journal:

> The Ships very much Crouded with Indians and surrounded by a multitude of Canoes. *I have no where in this Sea seen such a number of people assembled at one place*, besides those in the Canoes all the Shore of the bay was covered with people and hundreds were swimming about the Ships like shoals of fish. (Cook in Beaglehole 1967, 490–491, emphasis added)

Other members of the ships' company were similarly impressed by the large indigenous populace come to greet them, Lt. Rickman reinforcing his captain's opinion that this was "the greatest multitude of Indian spectators in canoes and on shore, that we had ever seen assembled together in any part of our voyage" (1966, 296). Lt. King estimated some 800 canoes carrying about 9,000 people (Beaglehole 1967, 502–503), while Corporal of Marines John Ledyard pushed this estimate of waterborne Hawaiians to 15,000, not counting the crowds on shore, which in his view were even more numerous (Munford 1963, 203).

Whatever the real numbers may have been, the scene described that fateful day left no doubt in the minds of any European observers present that the archipelago they had newly descended upon was thickly populated. Indeed, no matter what position one takes on the sizes of indigenous Pacific populations at first contact—whether conservative (McArthur 1967) or radical (Stannard 1989)—it is certain that the Hawaiian Islands were home to the largest single population of Polynesians anywhere within the vast triangle. Yet more than two centuries after Cook's arrival in Kealakekua, the question of exactly how many Hawaiians inhabited the archipelago not only remains unanswered, it has recently become the subject of increased disagreement and controversy. The reasons for this uncertainty have been rehearsed in the literature many times, and I will give only a brief synopsis here.

An Unresolved Debate:
Hawaiian Population on the Eve of Contact

As Cook himself was killed in Kealakekua and did not discuss population numbers in his surviving journal, the only firsthand attempt at anything like an empirically based estimate was that of Lt. King. In his shipboard journal, King gave a figure of 500,000 for the entire archipelago, but candidly qualified that "it is mere guesswork, founded principally upon the Numbers given to Otaheite, & the comparative size & Cultivation of these Islands with that" (Beaglehole 1967, 620). In the later official Admiralty publication of the voyage, King reduced his estimate to 400,000 and gave a rationale based on the observed population of Kealakekua in proportion to its length of coastline, then generalizing this ratio to the islands at large (see Stannard 1989, 3–4). But not all who were present agreed; the *Resolution*'s master, William Bligh, a careful observer who also drafted the first map of the islands, penned a note in his copy of the *Voyage* reducing King's estimate to 242,200, but he regrettably gave no details justifying this rather precise count (Beaglehole 1967, 620, fn. 1).

Two major problems confront any effort to assess the reliability of King's estimate: (1) the absence of other empirically based population estimates within the first few decades after Contact;[2] and (2) the impact of foreign diseases during this same crucial time period. The first population figures that can be considered as reliable do not appear until after the arrival of the Protestant missionaries in 1820, with rough head counts beginning in 1823 (142,050 persons) and a reasonably accurate census by 1832 (130,393 persons) (Schmitt 1973). Thus for forty-five years, during which cultural and biological contacts between Hawaiians and the outside world became increasingly frequent, the historical demographic record is effectively mute.

There is no question that diseases for which the Hawaiians had little or no immunity were introduced (beginning with Cook's first contact at Kaua'i in 1778) and that they had negative effects on both fertility and mortality during this forty-five-year period (and after) (Bushnell 1993). What is unknown — and, perhaps, unknowable at least from the documentary sources — is their quantitative impact on the overall Hawaiian population. Was this, as David Stannard (1989) passionately argues, a true decimation on the order of a 90 percent reduction, similar to what has been proposed for the "virgin soil epidemics" that are now felt to have wreaked havoc throughout the New World (Dobyns 1983; Ramenofsky 1987; Stannard 1992)? Or was the rate of population reduction somewhat less, as suggested by a retrodiction of the historically documented logarithmic rate of Hawaiian population decline between 1830 and the end of the nineteenth century (Bushnell 1993, 269, fig. 1)?

In the face of these problems, most scholars throughout the twentieth century have tended to regard King's estimate as being on the high side and have reduced the estimated Contact-period population to between 250,000 and 300,000, a figure favored by Schmitt (1968, 22) and Nordyke (1989, 17–18), two of the most respected authorities on Hawaiian demography. Others, however, have not hesitated to advance even lower estimates, such as Peter Buck's 100,000–150,000 (Schmitt 1968, 21).

In a short monograph published in 1989, David Stannard took aim at the scholarship of Schmitt, Nordyke, and other historical demographers, claiming that their reductions of the 1779 King estimate of 400,000 were not merely intellectually unjustified but amounted to a form of "historical amnesia" with respect to a veritable "holocaust" (Stannard 1989, 143). Stannard adduced a variety of evidence to argue that, if anything, King's estimate was too low, and that the real numbers at first contact were at least 800,000 and possibly much higher. For Stannard, knowing the "real numbers" is a matter that makes "an enormous difference . . . because the larger the population on the eve of Western contact, the greater the subsequent horror" (143).

Stannard's monograph includes commentaries from both Nordyke and Schmitt; the latter concluded that "the true number is ultimately unknowable" (Schmitt in Stannard 1989, 120).[3] Nordyke, however, rejected Stannard's proposal "until an . . . archaeological assessment verifies increased population density in the highlands of the islands or until other conclusive scientific data is presented" (Nordyke in Stannard 1989, 113). Stannard himself invoked the results of archaeological surveys (e.g., 1989, 19–21, 30, 33, 123, 125) in arguing for the presence of large inland populations not accounted for in King's estimation. Thus, in addition to shaking up the field of Pacific historical demography, Stannard's work suddenly made the question of prehistoric Hawaiian population an *archaeological* problem.

Archaeology and Hawaiian Paleodemography

Not that archaeologists had been uninterested in questions of population size, growth rates, and other issues of paleodemography in pre-Contact Hawai'i. In the early 1920s, Kenneth Emory used an inventory of archaeologically observed house sites on Lāna'i to estimate that island's maximum pre-Contact population;[4] and during his subsequent study of the isolated island of Nīhoa, he used a combination of house-terrace counts and an estimation of possible agricultural production from dryland terraces to derive a possible population estimate (Emory 1924, 50–51, 122 and 1928, 12).[5] After Emory's pioneering efforts, however, archaeologists working in Hawai'i lost interest in such questions until the advent of a "processualist" approach in the late 1960s (see Kirch 2000, 37–41). With the archaeological paradigm shift from "culture history" to "processualism," a host of new research questions came to the fore, among them considerations of pre-Contact subsistence economies, ecological adaptations to differing environmental zones, and the nature of settlement patterns and sociopolitical organization. All of these topics are intimately linked to population and demographic variables, particularly from the "cultural systems" theoretical perspective, which guided much archaeological research in the 1960s and 1970s. At the same time, the advent of large-scale research projects (largely funded through "contract" or CRM agreements) began to provide the kinds of data that could potentially be used to model pre-Contact population sizes and trajectories. These data included intensive surface surveys of stone structural remains, including habitation sites and increasingly large sets of "absolute" dates for such sites.[6] It was the availability of such data sets, stimulated by the new theoretical and research perspectives, that allowed questions of Hawaiian paleodemography to be addressed anew.

It is important to note that archaeologists have been focused on two rather different kinds of questions with respect to Hawaiian paleodemography. The first question concerns not the absolute size of the Hawaiian population (or regional subpopulations) but rather the long-term demographic trends that led to the growth, over roughly a millennium, of a large population from what is generally presumed to have been a very small founding propagule.[7] Here the specific subquestions become (1) What was the intrinsic rate (r) of growth? (2) Was this rate constant or varying over time? and (3) What was the overall shape of the population growth curve? The second major question concerns actual population sizes: What was the numerical population at a given time period, either of the islands as a whole or of specific regions? and ultimately, What was the final population of Hawaiians on the eve of contact with the West?

The Hommon/Cordy/Kirch Models

One of the first to make use of the relevant new data sets was Robert Hommon (1976, 1986) in his model for the formation of "primitive states" in Hawai'i. Hommon is not explicit about the role played by population in his theoretical model, but from his writings one can infer that he views population largely as an *independent* variable; population growth spurs other changes in the cultural system, particularly the need to expand and intensify agricultural production. For example,

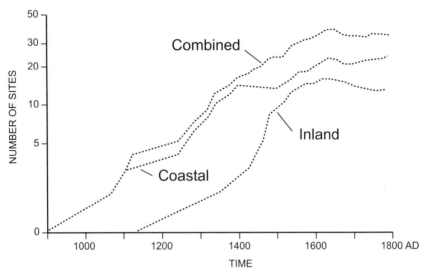

Figure 4.1. Hommon's "site-population growth sequences" for leeward Hawai'i Island (redrawn from Hommon 1976). Note that the y-axis is on a logarithmic scale.

he writes that "the need for additional food for *a continually growing population* appears to be the simplest explanation for the inland expansion initiated about A.D. 1400" (1986, 64, emphasis added). To track population growth over time, Hommon drew upon a data set of fifty-one dated habitation sites from several areas along the western side of Hawai'i Island (1976, 189–224). The aim was to generate a proxy population growth curve, or what Hommon called "site-population growth sequences"; several alternative sequences were generated, depending upon differing assumptions regarding site establishment and abandonment. As can be seen in Figure 4.1, while the curves vary somewhat, especially in the final stages (after ca. AD 1600), they are all fairly consistent in suggesting a *nonlinear* rate of population increase. In all scenarios, population grew relatively rapidly before ca. AD 1400, then began to taper off, and in the period from AD 1600 to contact either leveled off or declined.

Hommon drew upon these population growth curves to suggest that beginning around AD 1400 there was a major phase of "inland expansion," as most of the new sites at this time began to appear in inland or upland areas, away from the coast where the oldest sites are located. This inland expansion was seen to be linked with the development of extensive agricultural field systems (such as were investigated by Newman [1970] and Rosendahl [1994] at Lapakahi): "As the first two centuries of inland expansion drew to a close, an increase of at least four-fold in the Hawaiian population had accompanied the development of large, productive agricultural complexes in the salubrious core regions of the districts" (1986, 65). Although his argument is more elaborate and nuanced than can be briefly summarized here, in essence Hommon saw these demographic and economic changes as underpinning other major transformations in Hawaiian sociopolitical organization, including changes in kinship, land tenure, and tribute exactation.

In contrast with Hommon, Cordy was theoretically explicit about the role of population growth in Hawaiian cultural change, seeing it not only as an *independent* variable, but as "the initiating independent input" to change (1974, 97). Thus "population pressure" was the key variable (or "prime mover" in the jargon of 1960s processual archaeology) that led to a series of cultural "readjustments." In his original formulation, Cordy noted that it was not yet possible to empirically "validate" population pressure in the Hawaiian case (1974, 99); thus in his subsequent study of prehistoric social change in North Kona, Hawai'i Island, a major objective was to generate quantitative data on population size and change over time (Cordy 1981). Here Cordy focused on the second major kind of question: the estimation of actual population sizes for local subpopulations at specific periods in time.

In developing a "Hawaiian-specific model" for estimating pre-Contact population, Cordy reviewed the methods of Naroll (1962) and LeBlanc (1971) based on house-floor area, rejecting these in favor of a method of counting the archaeological remains of "contemporary sleeping houses" and multiplying this number "by 6 [persons] to gain an absolute population estimate" (Cordy 1981, 91). The mean per-house figure of six persons was based on an observation by Lt. King on Cook's voyage,[8] and the problem of assessing contemporaneity of houses was addressed through the use of hydration-rind dating of volcanic glass artifacts surface collected or excavated from these structures. Applying these methods to several areas (*ahupua'a* territories) in North Kona, Cordy was able to derive time-specific population estimates by fifty-year periods. In aggregate, his North Kona data from eight *ahupua'a* show the regional population beginning with eighteen persons at AD 1400–1450, rising to a maximum of 240 at AD 1650–1700 and falling off slightly to 216 at AD 1750–1780 (Cordy 1981, table 58). When Cordy's data are plotted as a curve, they reveal a pattern not unlike Hommon's sequences, with a major phase of growth from AD 1400 to 1600 and then leveling off and declining (Figure 4.2). Cordy rightly commented, however, that his estimates — which were based entirely on a sample of coastal sites — might not be representative: "[T]he communities that have been analyzed are in arid areas and communities in fertile areas may have had higher populations" (192).

In my early writings on the evolution of Hawaiian and other Polynesian societies, like Hommon and Cordy, I also pointed to a key role for "population dynamics" (Kirch 1980, 41–43 and 1982), drawing explicitly upon a cultural analogue to

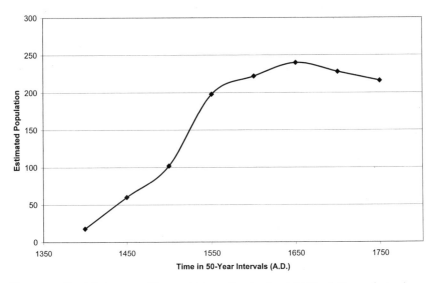

Cordy's Population Estimates for North Kona

Figure 4.2. Cordy's time-specific population estimates for eight North Kona *ahupua'a*, from AD 1400 to 1780 (based on Cordy 1981, table 58).

the *r*/K selection theory of island biogeography (MacArthur and Wilson 1967). I summarized my hypothesis as follows:

> In general, we would expect the colonizing populations of the Polynesian islands to follow the *r*-selection pattern — with rapid population growth, generalizing and broad-based subsistence practices, and only weakly developed sociopolitical controls on production. In contrast, later populations that have achieved high levels of density would be expected to follow K-selection patterns — conscious regulation of population growth, economic specialization, well-developed sociopolitical controls on production, and intense competition. This shift from density-independent to density-dependent adaptations should take place both on individual islands and over whole archipelagoes. (Kirch 1980, 42)

In short, I viewed — and continue to view — human population not as a strictly independent or dependent variable in cultural evolution, but as part of complex biocultural systems in which feedback loops can produce significant changes in fertility or mortality patterns over time.

Following this hypothesis of a cultural *r*/K selection continuum, I further suggested that some form of *logistic population growth* would be predictable for island populations. To test this hypothesis, I initially drew upon the data sets newly developed by Hommon and Cordy, which in my view provided "empiri-

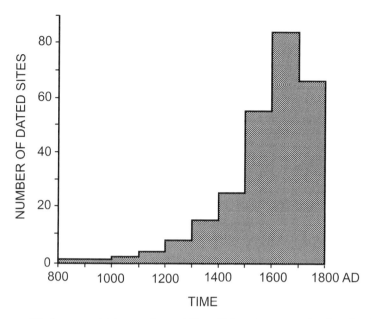

Figure 4.3. Site frequency histogram for west Hawai'i, based on a sample of 170 dated habitation sites (redrawn from Kirch 1982).

cal validation for a logistic model of prehistoric population growth" in Hawai'i (Kirch 1980:42). In a second paper (Kirch 1982), I applied an expanded data set of 170 dated habitation sites, which were plotted as a site-frequency histogram, clearly showing a logistic (sigmoidal) curve (Figure 4.3). That this curve had a pronounced negative inflection in the final time period led me to speculate that the pre-Contact Hawaiians might have significantly overshot the archipelago's carrying capacity, an interpretation which in hindsight was insufficiently supported and too-hastily advanced.[9]

My views on the dynamic role of population change in pre-Contact Hawai'i were developed more fully in two books published in the mid-1980s (Kirch 1984, 1985). In *The Evolution of the Polynesian Chiefdoms,* I devoted an entire chapter to demographic change as one of several key variables underlying Polynesian cultural evolution, and I turned again to the Hawaiian case as one in which the archaeological evidence was sufficiently robust to provide a compelling demonstration of the logistic growth model.[10] Here I used two data sets: (1) a western Hawai'i Island sample of 113 dated residential sites;[11] and (2) a sample of 655 features from the arid leeward island of Kaho'olawe, dated by the hydration-rind volcanic glass method. Both data sets confirmed a modified logistic curve, although the Kaho'olawe sample evidenced a more pronounced negative inflection, again suggesting the possibility of an "overshoot" scenario in which overly intensive land use resulted in a reduction in carrying capacity.[12] In *Feathered Gods and Fishhooks*, I reviewed the emerging archaeological evidence for pre-Contact population growth in the Islands, again drawing attention to the overall sigmoidal or logistic pattern seen in the data. I cautioned, however, that "we are just beginning to develop the empirical methods to chart demographic change, ... and the questions loom larger than the answers." Nonetheless, I felt that it was clear from the west Hawai'i data that "the period from about AD 1250 to 1650 was critical and, in this region at least, may have been a major era of technical, social, and political change in which demography played a significant role" (Kirch 1985, 289). Thus, rapid population growth and concomitant geographic expansion of population into both inland and ecologically marginal regions were key characteristics of what I called the "Expansion Period" (AD 1100–1650) in my four-period cultural historical sequence for the archipelago (303–304). I noted, however, that while the period as a whole probably saw a tenfold increase in total population, the *rate* of increase changed from early to late phases of the Expansion Period. For the Proto-Historic period (AD 1650–1795) just prior to European contact, the data seemed to indicate that "growth rates had declined substantially and that local populations may have been oscillating around a 'plateau'" (307).

Another voice weighing in on these efforts at paleodemographic reconstruction was that of Jeffrey Clark (1988), who offered a critique of some methodological problems in the work of Hommon, Cordy, and Kirch. In particular, Clark drew attention to flaws in the technique of volcanic-glass dating that affected the "degree of accuracy" in the various dated samples (a problem that soon led to the abandonment of this technique in Hawaiian archaeology). He pointed out that Hommon had restricted his sample to prehistoric sites, and thus "an accurate picture of population growth into the critical early historic period is not available" (23); and he raised statistical problems in Cordy's method of calculation of site occupation spans (25). Although offering no new data of his own, Clark concluded on a cautionary note, suggesting that "detailed regional models of population size and growth are premature" and calling for refinements in method and better data sets (29). Nonetheless, Clark did aver that the data sets in hand were sufficiently in accord that prehistorians could "agree that the growth in population can be depicted by a modified logistic curve" (29).

One additional field project of the 1980s addressed demographic issues from a significantly different perspective — the Anahulu Valley study of Kirch and Sahlins (1992), which concentrated on the post-Contact archaeology and ethnohistory of a rural valley on O'ahu, remarkable for its well-preserved taro irrigation systems. In this case a large archive of historical documents (including mission registers, government censuses, and other records) provided precise numerical data on population numbers in the early nineteenth century. Drawing upon these documentary sources, one of our objectives was to "compare actual resident population to the theoretical population levels of the taro irrigation systems" (2:28). Since the calculation of theoretical agricultural production levels and attendant "carrying capacity" had been one method used extensively by archaeologists in various parts of the world (Hassan 1981), we saw in the Anahulu Valley case (where the population was independently known) an opportunity to test this approach. Moreover, we were interested in using the Anahulu case to test models of "social production" (Brookfield 1972, 1984) — that is to say, the levels of potential surplus exactation by chiefly elites — within early post-Contact Hawaiian society. Our results were highly instructive, indicating that in the Anahulu Valley the level of surplus extraction from the irrigation systems was probably around 50 percent of total production (2:161, 172), a figure that is validated by extensive archival documentation of regular tribute prestations.[13] The Anahulu case thus raises an important caveat on use of the "carrying capacity" method of population estimation, especially with respect to highly stratified, complex societies in which tribute exactation and other forms of "social production" must be figured in to any quantitative models.

The Dye/Komori Model

The most recent attempts by Hawaiian archaeologists to address paleodemographic questions have been by Tom Dye and Eric Komori (Dye and Komori 1992a, 1992b; Dye 1994; see also Allen 1992; Williams 1992; Spear 1992), who proposed a method for using cumulative probability distributions of series of radiocarbon dates as a proxy measure of population, based on an approach originally developed by John Rick (1987) for Peru. Rather than using radiocarbon dates to temporally order a series of habitation sites that are then counted, this method takes the dates themselves as a proxy for population numbers. The underlying premise is that "changes in population are reflected in changes in the abundance of wood charcoal recovered from archaeological contexts associated with everyday domestic activities of cooking, lighting, and heating" (Dye 1994, 2). Furthermore, rather than treat a ^{14}C determination as a single "date" or even a statistical age range, the Dye-Komori method uses the probability distributions generated by one of the statistical programs (CALIB) for the calibration of radiocarbon years to calendar years and sums all of the individual probability distributions for a sample of dates into a single cumulative distribution. Dye and Komori used a database of 598 radiocarbon dates — much larger than what had been available a decade earlier — that had been accumulated largely as a result of numerous contract archaeology projects throughout the Islands. The result, as seen in Figure 4.4, is a graph that is taken by Dye and Komori to be a reasonably accurate proxy for actual population numbers over time. The shape of this graph is noteworthy:

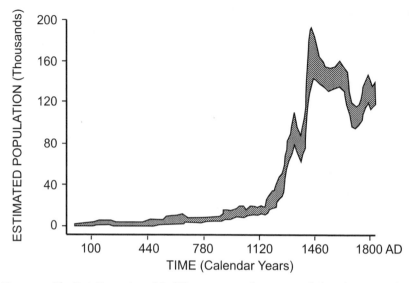

Figure 4.4. The Dye-Komori model of Hawaiian population growth, based on an analysis of 598 radiocarbon dates (redrawn from Dye and Komori 1992b). The shaded area indicates the zone between 95 percent confidence intervals.

(1) It reaffirms a modified logistical growth model; (2) it shows a phase of rapid population increase between ca. AD 1120 and 1440; and, (3) it indicates a late pre-Contact decline in overall population from a peak at ca. AD 1441. In key respects, then, this curve supports the models generated earlier by Hommon, Cordy, and Kirch.[14]

Dye and Komori, however, were interested not only in generating a graph that could be used to track changing rates of growth over time but in estimating actual population numbers. In particular, they wished to address the recent claim put forward by Stannard (1989) that archaeological evidence would show that reductions of King's 1779 estimate of 400,000 Hawaiians were mistaken. The problem was to convert a graph in which the *y* axis was a cumulative probability distribution (on a scale of 0 to unity) into a graph where the *y* axis was numbers of people. Dye and Komori did this by anchoring the right-hand end of the graph to the size of the Hawaiian population as documented by the missionary census of 1832 (130,313 persons), thus allowing the *y* axis to be converted to a scale of population numbers (N). Interpolating from the graph, the maximum population ever achieved, around AD 1440, would have been 163,293. Bracketing the graph with 95 percent statistical confidence limits, the range of possible population numbers at this maximum would be between 141,787 and 192,606. Thus, rather than validate Stannard's claim, the Dye-Komori model did just the opposite, lending apparent support to Schmitt's and Nordyke's reductions of the King estimate; in fact, it pushed their estimates even lower.

While the Dye-Komori model has much to recommend it, it is not without methodological problems, some of which are ignored or glossed over by the authors and many of which have to do with the technical and statistical peculiarities of radiocarbon dating. Since the Dye-Komori model has not to my knowledge been explicitly examined from this perspective, I list four potential problems below.

1. *Isotopic fractionation error.* Only 347 of the 598 dates used had associated $\delta^{13}C$ determinations, necessary to correct initial ^{14}C ages for isotopic fractionation and convert them to "conventional radiocarbon ages" (Stuiver and Polach 1977). This is a significant problem, because many Hawaiian dryland wood species (C4 pathway taxa) have $\delta^{13}C$ values averaging around –12 °/oo, whereas C_3 pathway woods typically have values around –25 °/oo. Dye and Komori were aware of this problem but suggested that only 8 percent of the total sample was so affected. However, in recent work at Kahikinui, Maui, where we have run 170 radiocarbon samples (see chapter 6), fully 27 percent of samples yielded $\delta^{13}C$ values significantly lower than the –25 °/oo, which is automatically used by radiocarbon labs to calculate sample age when the actual $\delta^{13}C$ has not been determined. The implication is that as many as a quarter or more of the 251 dates in the Dye-Komori sample, or perhaps 11 percent of the total sample, are represented in the cumulative distribution curve by probability values that significantly *underrepresent* the true age of the samples (on average by about 200 years). Since most of the dates fall at the late end of the Dye-Komori graph, the effect would be to artificially elevate that portion of the curve.

2. *Modern ages and probability distributions.* A second problem glossed over by Dye and Komori concerns the fact that some 103 out of the sample of 598 dates were reported by the radiocarbon laboratories as "modern" ages, rather than as B.P. dates (i.e., the measured age did not significantly differ from the modern standard). For these dates, it is not possible to generate a relative probability distribution (because these dates cannot be calibrated), and Gaussian distribution curves (normal probability distributions) were substituted. This is like mixing apples and oranges from a statistical point of view, although the net effect will probably not overly alter the final result.

3. *Multiple calibration intercepts.* As most archaeologists who deal with radiocarbon data are well aware, the relationship between radiocarbon years and calendar years is not 1:1, due to temporal variation in the production

of ^{14}C in the atmosphere — the so-called Suess effect (Taylor 1987, 24). This problem has been resolved by developing high-precision bidecadal calibration curves that convert a radiocarbon age into a calendar age (e.g., Stuiver and Pearson 1993). However, such curves are not smooth but have many "wriggles" or "kinks" — the so-called de Vries effect (Taylor 1987, 30). Unfortunately for Hawaiian archaeologists, the period between ca. AD 1500 and 1800 has several of these kinks, with the result that when radiocarbon dates for this late time period are calibrated, the resulting probability distributions are strongly bimodal or trimodal. A cumulative plot of such distributions is therefore inherently bound to produce a strongly "wavy" curve, which is exactly the shape of the Dye-Komori curve in the period from AD 1450 to 1800. One must be clear in interpreting such a graph that the "waves" or undulations are an artifact of the calibration curve and not a direct reflection of fluctuating population numbers.

4. *Archaeological sample collection bias.* Dye and Komori consider two kinds of potential archaeological collection bias (geographic bias and site-temporal bias), but they do not mention a potentially significant third kind of sample bias: systematic exclusion of samples from sites bearing Euro-American artifacts. Radiocarbon dates are expensive and can rapidly consume an archaeologist's research budget; moreover, they are not very precise for the recent end of the time scale (due to problems discussed above). Therefore, when archaeologists in Hawai'i excavate or test a site that proves to contain imported artifacts of Euro-American manufacture (e.g., beads, glass, metal, ceramics), they typically assign such a site to the post-Contact period (and often can use the artifacts to fairly precisely date the site, much more accurately than they could by using the radiocarbon method). In my experience, archaeologists almost never submit charcoal samples from such sites for radiocarbon dating. What this means is that the aggregate sample used by Dye and Komori comes exclusively from sites containing *only* pre-Contact (traditional) Hawaiian artifacts. Yet their graph purports to extend well into the post-Contact period, where they anchor it to the 1832 census. But, in fact, they have not included any dates from sites actually occupied during the final fifty-three years of their study period, and the shape of the probability distribution curve for this period is derived merely from the cumulative "tails" of individual probability distributions for dates from pre-Contact sites.

Problems 1 and 2 above could readily be resolved by rerunning the calculation of a cumulative probability curve using a new and expanded set of radiocarbon dates that includes only "conventional ages" that have had δ^{13}C determinations and that have been properly calibrated (i.e., excluding so-called modern age determinations). Problem 3 is to my knowledge not resolvable, as it is an artifact of the calibration procedure itself. Problem 4 could be resolved, but only if Hawaiian archaeologists begin to submit radiocarbon dates from sites containing post-Contact period artifacts; this is unlikely to happen anytime soon, given the costs involved.

These problems by no means render the Dye-Komori model useless, but they do constrain the ways it may be interpreted. As a smoothed curve, it once again strongly validates a phase of rapid growth in the overall Hawaiian population beginning around AD 1100 and peaking around AD 1400–1500, reinforcing the Hommon/Cordy/Kirch models. However, it would be an overinterpretation to take the "waves" in the recent, right-hand portion of the curve as direct reflections of population trends in the late pre-Contact period. And, given the problems of nonrepresentation of post-Contact sites, whether one can justify anchoring the curve to the 1832 census—and thereby convert the graph to a numerical population curve—is questionable.

Current Problems and Issues in Hawaiian Paleodemography

Where have we come in nearly three decades of thinking about and trying to model population dynamics in the Hawaiian Islands? I will attempt to sum up what I think we have learned—and what we still don't know.

What We Have Learned About Hawaiian Paleodemography

1. Extensive surface surveys on all of the major islands except Ni'ihau leave no doubt that by ca. AD 1600 there was widespread human use and occupation of virtually all of the lowland zones (i.e., areas below about 800 m elevation, excepting where there are steep slopes), even into regions considered fairly marginal from an ecological and agricultural viewpoint. Although population density clearly varied over this lowland landscape, there were no significant "empty zones" into which new settlements could have expanded.

2. All attempts to model population growth, whether locally or archipelago-wide, and whether using site-based or date-based data sets, concur in demonstrating a major phase of population growth in the middle part of the cultural sequence. As shown by Rallu (chapter 2), the curves for this phase of growth are best fitted to an *exponential* rate of increase. The time spans associated with this phase differ slightly between models, but in general the period of rapid (approximating exponential) growth can be bracketed between about AD 1100 to 1500, and this corresponds with what has been

termed the Expansion Period (Kirch 1985). During this period, the Hawaiian population probably increased about tenfold, whatever the absolute numbers.

3. Between around AD 1500 and contact at 1778, the rate of population growth dropped off significantly, producing a kind of "plateau" on the various graphs. None of the varied data sets provide any support whatsoever for Stannard's view that the Hawaiian population continued to "increase at a rapid pace until Cook's arrival in 1778" (1989, 67; cf. Dye 1994, 16).

4. Taken as a whole, all of the work on Hawaiian paleodemography points to an earlier period of exponential growth, followed by a rapid onset of stabilization after about AD 1450–1500. Earlier discussions of this trend interpreted it as a "modified logistical" curve (e.g., Kirch 1984), but it may more properly be interpreted as strictly exponential from the period of initial settlement up through the late Expansion Period, followed by a rapid shift to stability. In any event, all of the work to date supports a theoretical model of a long-term shift in population growth from density independent to density dependent, as I first argued (Kirch 1980, 1984).

Unanswered Questions

1. The size of the total archipelago-wide population at the time of initial contact with Europeans remains insufficiently resolved. The Dye-Komori model gives some support to the earlier estimates of historical demographers such as Schmitt and Nordyke that the total population was perhaps in the 200,000 range, and it fails to support Stannard's contentions. However, there are sufficient technical problems with the Dye-Komori model that in my view it cannot yet be unequivocally accepted.

2. Population density levels for representative ecological and economic zones (e.g., leeward slopes, windward valleys, transitional valleys, etc.), as well as for individual islands, have not been determined, either for the immediate pre-Contact period or for earlier time periods. Archaeological settlement survey data suggest that density levels varied significantly across the Hawaiian landscape, and these data should provide the basis for working out such density figures (see chapter 6 for the Kahikinui case). For example, there are reasons to suspect that density levels may have varied sharply between the geologically young landscapes of Maui and Hawai'i and the older islands to the northwest — Moloka'i, O'ahu, and Kaua'i — but this needs to be tested on empirical grounds.

3. Population dynamics in the critical two to three centuries prior to European contact (AD 1500–1778) remain hazy. This is the period for which

various models suggest either a leveling off of population and achievement of stability or possibly even local or regional reductions in population size. Moreover, it is during this Proto-Historic period that cultural controls on fertility and mortality patterns are expected to have been most influential (given a theoretical shift to a density-dependent situation). Other likely influences are significant population movements or dislocations caused by chiefly mandate and commoner migration in response to excessive chiefly tribute, labor exactation, or warfare. Such local or regional migration patterns are indeed hinted at in late-period Hawaiian oral traditions.

Conclusion

Archaeologists working in Hawai'i have made real progress toward understanding the long-term demographic history of one of Polynesia's largest and most noteworthy archipelagoes. However, much remains to be accomplished, especially resolving — if possible — the question of just how many people inhabited the island chain at the moment of Cook's arrival in 1778–1779. One of the most important steps that can now be taken to move forward on resolving these problems is to attempt to construct robust and fine-grained paleodemographic models for a variety of local-scale areas and regions throughout the archipelago. This does not preclude further attempts to rework islandwide data such as the Dye-Komori model, and indeed, this would also be worthwhile since the radiocarbon database continues to expand every year. However, fine-grained work at the local scale is more likely to give us insights into such matters as population density levels and their changes over time, to allow us to reconstruct accurate population sizes for specific areas or territories, and to trace the temporal associations between phases of population growth (or decline) and other major trends in the archaeological record, such as the construction of ceremonial structures (heiau) and the intensification of agricultural systems. In chapters 5 through 7, various investigators present just such detailed local-scale studies for several regions within the Hawaiian Islands.

Notes

1. Unlike some writers, in this volume we use the glottal stop in Hawai'i both for the island and the archipelago.

2. Captain George Dixon, one of the first traders on the Northwest coast–Canton circuit, is the only other relatively early observer to estimate population. During his visit in 1787, he found King's figure "greatly exaggerated" and suggested that a 1779 population of 200,000 would be "much nearer the truth" (quoted in Schmitt 1968, 20).

3. In a more recent review of Hawaiian population, Schmitt (1998, 183) writes: "Without

definitive archaeological evidence to resolve the conflicting estimates, pre-Contact population levels are likely to remain a controversial subject."

4. Emory (1924, 50) says he saw 489 houses and estimated that with areas not surveyed, 630 would be a reasonable total. However, it is clear that Emory regarded only formal structures with clear stone alignments and formal hearths as "house sites." I suspect that by the standards of modern intensive survey methods his counts would be found to be substantial underestimates.

5. Assuming that all of the house terraces and "bluff shelters" on Nīhoa were occupied contemporaneously, Emory estimated a maximum population of between 170 and 220 persons. He then calculated that an annual crop of about 48 tons of sweet potatoes might be grown on the 12 acres of terraces revealed by his survey, observing that "a little less than 1,000 pounds a year could be supplied to each of a hundred individuals, and this amount would be only a meager supply" (1928, 50). Although brief, Emory's Nīhoa estimate prefigures the use of two of the main approaches developed more recently in archaeological demography: house counts and agricultural carrying capacity estimates (Hassan 1981).

6. Most commonly, such "absolute" dates (as opposed to "relative" dates based on artifact seriation) are radiocarbon age determinations, but for a period during the 1970s to the early 1980s there was also extensive use of hydration-rind dating of volcanic glass flakes. Unfortunately, a variety of technical and calibration problems with volcanic glass dating were never resolved, and this method has subsequently been abandoned.

7. It should be noted that there is still no firm agreement on the date of first Polynesian colonization of the archipelago. Anthropogenic effects reflected in sediment cores from several localities on Oʻahu (Athens 1997) indicate an established population by at least AD 800, but earlier radiocarbon dates from several other sites, while contested, suggest the possibility of slightly earlier settlement. Likewise, the size of the founding propagule(s) remains unknown, although the loading limitations on Polynesian voyaging canoes make it unlikely that this exceeded 100–200 persons, even if several canoes were involved.

8. King's comment was, "From the frequent opportunities I have had of informing myself of this head, I am convinced, that six persons to a house is a very moderate allowance" (in Cordy 1981, 91).

9. This proposal was made in the context of an article that dealt with the impact of the prehistoric Polynesians on their natural environment, in which I adduced a range of evidence showing that the island ecosystem had been heavily modified prior to European contact. That there was significant natural resource reduction and in some cases land degradation as well has been validated by numerous subsequent studies. What I would now retract from my 1982 article is the implication of an overall significant reduction in carrying capacity.

10. In this book, I also devoted a section to the analysis of skeletal populations from three archipelagoes, generating life tables and inferring aspects of paleodemography (Kirch 1984, 111–116). This aspect of my work inspired a critical response from Sutton and Mulloy (1989). Skeletal populations do provide another potential source of information on prehistoric population dynamics in the Pacific, but I defer discussion of these data and the problems associated with their interpretation to another occasion.

11. This sample incorporated the Hommon and Cordy data sets, with two additional data sets from Kalāhuipuaʻa and Waimea-Kawaihae.

12. Unfortunately, the Kahoʻolawe sample was based entirely on hydration-rind dating of volcanic glass. It will be instructive to see how this site-frequency curve compares with a curve generated exclusively on the basis of radiocarbon-dated sites, something that may be possible in the future given the continued massive CRM archaeological work on the island.

13. These records include the infamous "Aloha Gidiona" letters written by Paulo Kanoa, secretary to the high chiefess Kaʻahumanu, to the local land steward Gidiona Laʻanui of Anahulu, making seemingly endless demands for taro, poi, pigs, fish, and other foodstuffs (Kirch and Sahlins 1992, 2:172–173).

14. In the same issue of the *New Zealand Journal of Archaeology,* Allen (1992), Williams (1992), and Spear (1992) also applied the Dye-Komori technique to regional — or context-specific — sets of radiocarbon dates, primarily from Oʻahu. The various graphs generated display a variety of permutations on the overall growth curve of Dye and Komori (1992).

5

Modeling Agricultural Development and Demography in Kohala, Hawai'i

 Population size, density, and changes are often invoked in anthropological interpretations of cultural organization and change (Boserup 1965; Hill et al. 2004; Read and LeBlanc 2003). For archaeologists, measuring prehistoric populations on the basis of archaeological materials represents something of a methodological challenge, since we cannot directly census individuals but must rely upon proxy measures (Hassan 1981; Peterson 1975). Archaeologists have also debated the specific role of population parameters in cultural change—that is, whether they are independent or dependent variables relative to other domains such as subsistence, warfare, and complex social organizations (Cowgill 1975; Read and LeBlanc 2003).

In Hawai'i, measurements of prehistoric population have traditionally relied upon ^{14}C dates, in some cases regardless of context but usually associated with archaeological features that are identified as "residential" or "habitation" in terms of former use (Kirch 1984; Hommon 1986). This is an approach that is employed elsewhere by archaeologists, but in Hawai'i the main problem lies in tracking population changes during the latest phase of prehistory (i.e., including part of the seventeenth and most of the eighteenth centuries) and the early Proto-Historic period, typically defined as the period after the arrival of Captain James Cook in 1778 and prior to the arrival of the first Christian missionaries in 1821 (Clark 1988). Carbon 14 dates are notoriously unreliable during this interval, and yet it was a period of considerable cultural and population change in Hawai'i. Still, most researchers (Kirch et al. 2001) believe that Hawaiian populations experienced a phase of exponential growth, followed by a phase of declining rates of increase, which in turn was followed by population collapse occurring soon after Cook's arrival. With the exception of the last phase of population collapse, we still lack exact dating of these phases and the points of inflection change. Furthermore, linking population measures to some other variable of interest—for example, agricultural development—requires archaeologists to have independent dates on agricultural features or deposits. The research reported here represents one attempt to resolve the issue of relying on ^{14}C dates by employing relative dating of both habitation features and agricultural field constructions from the northwestern portion of the island of Hawai'i. While not without related measurement and reliability issues, this analysis points the way to new methods of tracking both prehistoric population and agricultural development simultaneously.

The leeward Kohala landscape is a palimpsest of archaeological features. The area is noted for one of the most extensive dryland agricultural field systems in the Hawaiian archipelago (Figure 5.1). It also contains a rich archaeological record relating to residential, religious, and other subsistence activities. Rosendahl (1972, 1994) suggests that the coastal region of leeward Kohala was first permanently occupied around AD 1300. He notes that with an increase in population over the next two centuries, people began exploiting the uplands for slash-and-burn cultivation, residing in seasonally occupied, dispersed habitation sites. According to Rosendahl, the extensive system of bound field plots was constructed in the uplands from AD 1500 to 1800, a period of time when upland residential patterns gradually changed from seasonally shifting to permanent dispersed occupation. He suggests that the "peak of agricultural development and population growth" occurred between AD 1800 and 1850, a time of increasing European contact (Rosendahl 1994, 22). While the notion that the period of peak population in the area lasts almost seventy years after initial European contact is contentious (see Stannard 1989), Rosendahl's general outline of the pre-Contact demographic sequence seems plausible.

Rosendahl (1972, 1994) based many of his general propositions on the excavation and mapping of 201 residential features found in a 61.2-hectare study area of upland Lapakahi. He divided the residential features into "C-shaped structures" (a category that included L-shaped and other structures with similar morphology), "platform structures," and "square/rectangular structures" consisting of enclosures. Rosendahl suggests that C-shapes and platforms were the primary domestic features during the pre-Contact era, while enclosures were used only for residential purposes during the historic period. Rosendahl's statements about population change appear to be based on the relative frequencies of domestic features dating to the different periods. He also notes the correlation between the level of agricultural development in the area with assumed population levels and sociopolitical complexity. While this facet is underdeveloped in his work, the implicit assumption is that the amount of land under production at any one time should directly correlate with population levels. Indeed, these two methods for reconstructing demographic trends — that is, changes in the frequency and distribution of domestic features on the one hand and the extent and trajectory of agricultural development on the other — are two of the most commonly em-

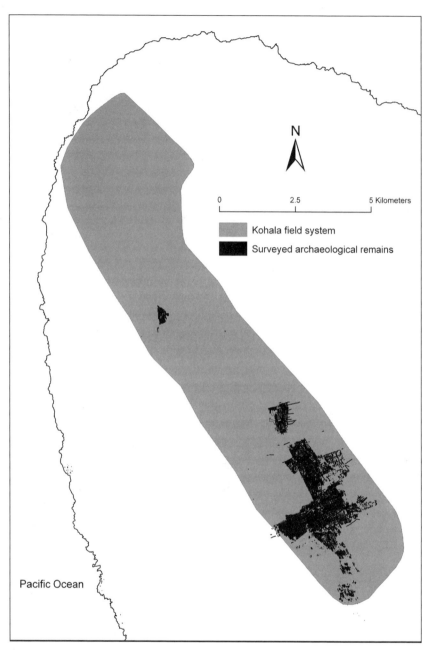

N

0   2.5   5 Kilometers

Kohala field system

Surveyed archaeological remains

Pacific Ocean

Figure 5.1. The Kohala peninsula showing the extent of the dryland field system and the surveyed archaeological remains.

ployed. Recent archaeological work in the Kohala field system provides a fine-grained data set to evaluate and refine some of these basic methods and demographic proposals.

Establishing the Relative Chronology of Domestic Features and Agricultural Development

During the past ten years, we have directed a project that has intensively surveyed over 7.75 km^2 of the upland Kohala field system.[1] Recently we have joined a team of researchers (Kirch et al. 2001) investigating human ecodynamics in Hawai'i. We have now recorded 3,028 agricultural walls with a total length of 179.6 km, 417 segments of trails with a total length of 58.3 km, and 3,656 architectural features (not including several hundred small mounds) in the uplands of Kohala (see Figure 5.1). While we are beginning to understand the variation in this dataset, the analysis presented in this chapter focuses on a detailed study area (DSA) of 111.9 hectares in the southern *ahupua'a* of the field system (Figure 5.2). The DSA extends *mauka* (inland) from the *makai* (seaward) edge of the field system and can be divided into two adjacent zones: the *makai* zone and the *mauka* zone (Figure 5.3). The *makai* zone in the southern *ahupua'a* of the field system extends from the lower elevation of the field system at 600 m to a topographic break in the landscape at ca. 680 m. The *mauka* zone extends inland from an elevation of 680 m on a less steeply sloped landscape to an elevation of ca. 790 m. The *makai* zone is 46.3 ha in size and the *mauka* zone is 65.6 ha Within the 111.9 ha DSA we have recorded 689 agricultural walls, 69 segments of trails, and 1,185 architectural features. Of these 1,185 architectural features, we have classified 196 as "domestic features" (Figure 5.4). Our criteria for inclusion in this category follows the work of Rosendahl in that we have defined three basic classes of domestic features: "C-shapes," "platforms/pavements/terraces," and "residential enclosures."

Our ability to model population change in the DSA relies on establishing changes in the frequency of domestic features and changes in the area under agricultural production. Ideally, each of the 196 domestic features would be securely dated through a series of radiocarbon dates. We have excavated fifty-three domestic features and now have radiocarbon dates from eight of them. All of these dates suggest that the eight features were occupied after ca. AD 1650 (Ladefoged and Graves forthcoming). Radiocarbon dates from sweet potato remains found within the field system (Ladefoged et al. 2005) and in association with agricultural walls and trails (Ladefoged and Graves forthcoming) suggest that the area was initially used as early as AD 1290 to 1410, with agricultural development taking place from ca. AD 1500 onward. In lieu of secure absolute dates from a large

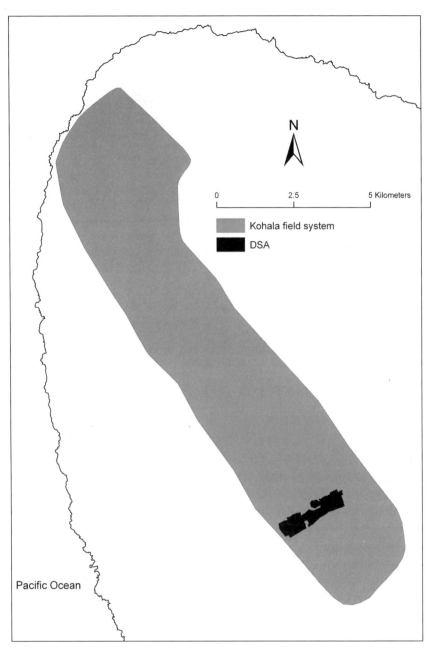

Figure 5.2. The location of the detailed study area (DSA) within the Kohala field system.

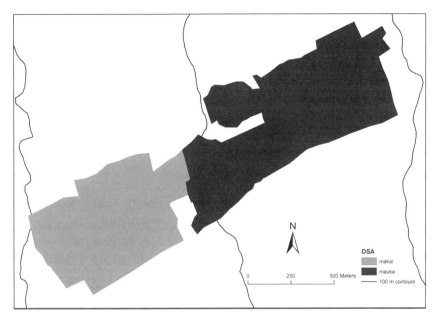

Figure 5.3. The *mauka* and *makai* zones within the DSA.

sample of domestic features, we can estimate the relative chronology of these features by considering their association with agricultural walls and trails.

Recently we (Ladefoged et al. 2003; McCoy 2000) established a method for determining the relative chronology of agricultural development in the field system by considering the abutment and intersection of walls and trails. Rosendahl (1972) first recognized that agricultural plots could be chronologically ordered based on the matching and mismatching terminations and intersections of walls and trails. We developed this observation into an explicit set of rules for temporally ordering walls and trails. Given this methodology, it is possible to document agricultural development in Kohala and to distinguish between the two processes of expansion (utilization of a previously unoccupied area) and intensification (expenditure of more energy in a fixed area of land to increase production). We would suggest that it is possible, with caution (and some caveats), to extend the relative chronological determinations for the walls and trails to spatially associated domestic features. Thus, while we currently have only a limited number of absolute dates for the domestic and agricultural features in the DSA, we have devised a method for establishing their relative chronology that enables us to address issues of past demographic changes. We first consider the method for establishing the relative chronology of agricultural development and then investigate the spatial and

Figure 5.4. The domestic features within the DSA.

temporal patterning in agricultural development and the distribution of domestic features.

Tracking Agricultural Development

Ladefoged et al. (2003) describe a procedure for determining the relative chronology of agricultural development. We have built on those principles, and in the current analysis we determine the relative chronology of wall and trail construction in the DSA by analyzing the relationships of walls abutting trails and walls intersecting trails. The first step in deriving the relative chronology of agricultural development is to identify building associations, or "groups," between sets of walls and trails. This is done by identifying the walls that abut on specific trails. The assumption is that if a wall abuts a trail, the wall was built at the same time or later than that trail and can therefore be assigned to the same building association or group. We assign the 689 walls and 69 trails in the DSA to five broad groups of building associations (Figure 5.5).

The relative order of construction of these groupings is determined by a second step: We consider how the walls assigned to each grouping intersect with other trails that are not part of that grouping. We assume that younger walls were often

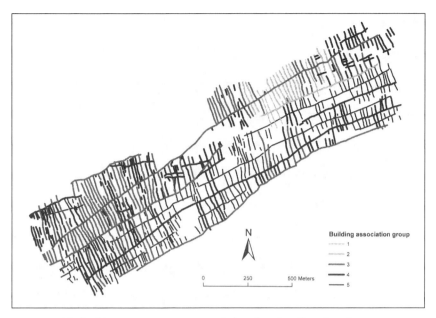

Figure 5.5. The building association groups of agricultural walls and trails.

built to abut trails that were already in place and older walls were more likely to be intersected by the construction of younger trails. Successively younger trails formed a grid between which later walls were constructed and which abutted them. The relative ages of building groups are determined by identifying the group that has more walls intersected by the trails associated with another group. For example, the walls associated with group 2 (shown as thick light gray lines in Figure 5.5) are intersected at a much higher frequency by the trails assigned to group 3 (shown as thick medium gray lines) than the walls assigned to group 3 (shown as thick medium gray lines) are intersected by the trail assigned to group 2 (shown as thick light gray lines). This would suggest that group 2 walls and trails predate those assigned to group 3. Similarly, the walls assigned to group 3 (shown as thick medium gray lines) are intersected at a much higher frequency by the trails assigned to group 4 (shown as thick black lines) than the walls assigned to group 4 (shown as thick black lines) are intersected by the trails assigned to group 3 (shown as thick medium gray lines). Finally, the walls assigned to group 4 (shown as thick black lines) are intersected at a higher frequency by the trails assigned to group 5 (shown as thin black lines) than the walls assigned to group 5 (shown as thin black lines) are intersected by the trails assigned to group 4 (shown as thick black lines). It should be noted that the walls assigned to group 1 (shown

Figure 5.6. Zones of initial agricultural development within the DSA.

as thin light gray lines) are not associated with any trails. These walls, however, are intersected by the trails assigned to groups 2 (shown as thick light gray lines) and 3 (shown as thick medium gray lines) and are therefore assumed to predate the group 2 and 3 constructions.

The walls and phases assigned to the five groups of building associations are classified into four temporal phases of agricultural development. For analytical purposes, we have combined groups 1 and 2 into a single phase of development (phase 1). We have done this because the area of group 1 walls is very small. Subsequent groups of walls and trails are classified as subsequent phases of development (i.e., group 3 = phase 2, group 4 = phase 3, and group 5 = phase 4).

The distribution of the walls and trails associated with these four broad temporal phases suggests that agricultural development began at different times in different parts of the DSA (Figure 5.6). Approximately 6.5 percent (7.3 ha) of the DSA was developed — that is, expanded into for the first time — during the earliest phase. Approximately 33 percent (36.9 ha) of the DSA was initially developed during the second relative phase, approximately 32.9 percent (36.7 ha) during the third relative phase, and ca. 27.6 percent (30.9 ha) during the final interval.

As noted, the process of agricultural development can involve both expansion into previously unoccupied zones and the further intensification of a zone

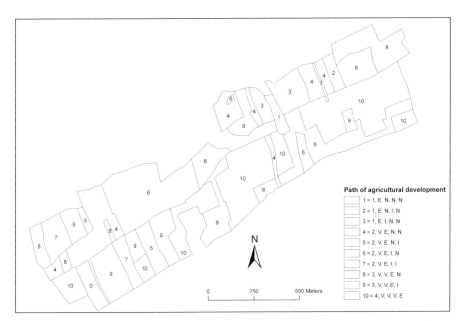

Figure 5.7. Paths of agricultural development within the DSA. The different "pathways" are numbered 1 through 10 in the figure. The coding refers to when the land was initially developed and what took place in each of the four temporal units. "V" refers to vacant; "E" refers to expansion; "I" refers to intensification; and "N" refers to no development. Thus a code of "5 = 2, V, E, N, I" can be read as the fifth pathway of agricultural development, where the land was vacant during the first phase, expanded into during the second phase, underwent no further intensification during the third phase, and was intensified during the fourth phase.

through the construction of additional walls and trails (see Ladefoged et al. 2003 for a discussion of this distinction). Establishing the relative chronology of the walls and trails by considering the relationship between wall and trail abutments and intersections provides a means of determining which regions of the field system were initially used and which regions were subsequently intensified. In this way we can distinguish a number of different pathways for agricultural development in the DSA. These paths are defined by the period within which the process of initial expansion into an area took place and if and when any subsequent intensification occurred.

Ten alternative pathways of agricultural development are documented in the DSA (Figure 5.7). The DSA covers 111.9 ha, and of this area, approximately 7.3 ha were initially occupied during the first phase. Out of these 7.3 ha, 1.3 ha were further intensified only during the second phase, 1.2 ha were further intensified only during the third phase, and 4.8 ha were never intensified. Of the 111.9 ha of

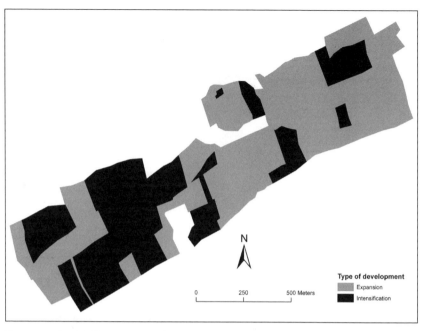

Figure 5.8. Areas of expansion and intensification within the DSA.

the DSA, 36.9 ha were first occupied during the second phase, and of these 36.9 ha, 4.5 ha were further intensified during the subsequent third and fourth intervals, whereas 16.5 ha were intensified only during the third interval, 2.7 ha were intensified only during the fourth interval, and 13.2 ha were never intensified. Approximately 36.7 ha were first occupied during the third interval, and of this area, 15.7 ha were intensified during the fourth phase and 21 ha were never further intensified. Finally, 30.9 ha of the DSA were occupied only during the fourth and last temporal phase.

What these figures clearly show is that some portions of the DSA were intensified at some point in time, whereas others were not. Regions that underwent intensification at any time are classified as "intensification areas," and regions that were used but never intensified are classified as "expansion areas" (Figure 5.8). Of the 111.9 ha in the DSA, 43.7 ha (or 39 percent) were intensified at some point, whereas 68.2 ha (or 61 percent) were developed solely through expansion. This would suggest that this southern portion of the Kohala field system was based somewhat around expansion as opposed to intensification, a conclusion that substantiates the initial analysis of Ladefoged and Graves (2000).

The Distribution of Domestic Features

There are distinct patterns in the distribution of domestic archaeological features in relation to the different zones of agricultural development. The frequency of domestic features associated with each phase of development can be used to create simplistic estimates of population trends. In order to do this, however, two conditions must be considered.

The first is the extent to which the different classes of domestic features (C-shapes, platforms/pavements/terraces, and enclosures) are functionally equivalent. A considerable amount of research in Hawai'i suggests that these classes are not equivalent, with the class of C-shapes being functionally distinct from the classes of platform/pavement/terrace and enclosures (Tuggle and Griffin 1973; Kirch 1985; Clark 1987). C-shapes are often interpreted as being either temporary field shelters (Rosendahl 1994) or elements (e.g., cooking houses, lithic activity areas, sleeping houses) of permanent household complexes (Weisler and Kirch 1985; Ladefoged 1991). C-shapes were therefore multipurpose structures that could reflect either permanent occupation or more temporary intermittent (daily or for multiple days) use in agricultural fields.

The spatial distribution of C-shapes in the DSA provides some indication of these multiple uses. As noted, there is an environmental gradient within the DSA from the drier and lower altitude *makai* portion of the study area to the wetter and higher altitude *mauka* portion. The distribution of C-shapes is markedly different in each of these zones. Taking into account the different sizes of the *mauka* (65.6 ha) and *makai* (46.3) areas, there is an unequal distribution of C-shapes in the two sections of the DSA. There are far more C-shapes than expected in the *makai* section and far fewer in the *mauka* section (Table 5.1). A similar pattern holds true for enclosures (Table 5.2) but not for platform/pavement/terrace features (Table 5.3).

Platform/pavement/terrace features are distributed somewhat evenly throughout the *mauka* and *makai* zones of the DSA. This would suggest that platform/pavement/terrace features were elements of permanently occupied households, whereas a proportion of the C-shapes were used as temporary field shelters in the drier, lower elevation, more marginal zones of the DSA. The high concentration of C-shapes in these areas might reflect intermittent use of the *makai* area during wetter years. Without extensive excavations it is difficult to determine the proportion of C-shapes that functioned as intermittent field shelters and the proportion that were elements of permanently occupied household complexes. Our estimate is that ca. 50 percent of the C-shapes were elements of permanent households and 50 percent were temporary field shelters.

Table 5.1. The distribution of C-shape features in relation to *makai* and *mauka* zones (chi-square = 123.1, df = 1, Asymp.Sig. = 0.00).

Zone	Observed N	Expected N
Makai	120	56.3
Mauka	16	.7
Total	136	

Table 5.2. The distribution of enclosure features in relation to *makai* and *mauka* zones (chi-square = 12.3, df = 1, Asymp.Sig. = 0.00).

Zone	Observed N	Expected N	Residual
Makai	16	8.3	7.7
Mauka	4	11.7	−7.7
Total	20		

Table 5.3. The distribution of platform/pavement/terrace features in relation to *makai* and *mauka* zones (chi-square = 1.2, df = 1, Asymp.Sig. = 268).

Zone	Observed N	Expected N	Residual
Makai	20	16.6	3.4
Mauka	20	23.4	−3.4
Total	40		

The second condition that must be considered before deriving dynamic population estimates is the extent to which archaeological features were reused through time. It is conceivable that features were only occupied during the phase in which they were initially constructed. Alternatively features could have been built during earlier phases and subsequently reused and reoccupied during later phases. The distribution of domestic features in the DSA provides some insight into the likelihood of these two alternatives. The analysis of the agricultural walls and trails suggests that some areas of the DSA were occupied more intensively and for longer periods of time than others. Approximately 43.7 ha of the DSA have undergone intensification at some point and therefore were presumably occupied for more extended periods of time. In contrast, 68.2 ha of the DSA were developed solely through the process of expansion and were therefore probably occupied for more limited periods of time. If there was little reuse of domestic features, then the additive effect of constructing new features would result in areas that had been intensified through time containing more features than expansion areas that were occupied for more limited periods of time. This is indeed the case, with there being significantly more domestic features than expected in areas that have been intensified and significantly fewer domestic features than expected in areas that were only expanded into and never intensified (Table 5.4). However, when the different classes of domestic features are distinguished, this pattern holds true only for C-shapes and enclosures and not for platform/pavement/terrace features (Tables 5.5, 5.6, and 5.7). Platform/pavement/terrace features are equitably distributed in expansion and intensification areas. This would suggest that some of these features were reused in subsequent periods. Our excavations at fifty-three domestic features shed further light and suggest that there was reuse of some features, particularly of C-shapes in the *makai* portion of the field system. While accepting a low level of reuse as indicated by the distribution of all domestic features in different zones is a conservative approach (in that it will underestimate population numbers) and somewhat justified, the patterning in the individual classes of domestic features and the archaeological evidence suggests that reuse did take place. In our analysis below we examine some alternative ranges for the proportion of feature reuse.

Paleodemographic Trends in the Southern *Ahupua'a* of the Kohala Field System

Incorporating the extent to which different classes of domestic features were reused through time allows us to propose a model of population change for the southern *ahupua'a* of the Kohala field system. As a basis, 4 domestic features are located in areas initially developed during the first phase, 106 features are in areas initially developed during the second phase, 46 are in areas initially developed during the third phase, and 40 features are in areas initially developed during the fourth phase. It should be noted that given the relative areas of development during each phase, there are significantly more features associated with the phase 2 areas than expected and significantly fewer features associated with the other phase areas (Table 5.8).

These numbers can be used to construct a number of alternative population trajectories, and these are shown in Figure 5.9. The first series in the chart depicts the frequency of domestic features associated with each phase of agricultural development, assuming that all domestic features associated with a preceding phase were reused in subsequent phases. This curve obviously depicts the maximum number of domestic features in use during the final phase of occupation. An alternative is to assume that no features were reused, and population levels at each phase should be represented by only the number of domestic features in the regions developed during that phase (Figure 5.9, series 2). The two conditions

Table 5.4. The distribution of domestic features in relation to expansion and intensification zones (chi-square = 18.6, df = 1, Asymp. Sig. = 0.00).

Zone	Observed N	Expected N	Residual
Expansion	90	119.5	−29.5
Intensification	106	76.5	29.5
Total	196		

Table 5.5. The distribution of C-shape features in relation to expansion and intensification zones (chi-square = 13.5, df = 1, Asymp. Sig. = 0.00).

Zone	Observed N	Expected N	Residual
Expansion	62	82.9	−20.9
Intensification	74	53.1	20.9
Total	136		

Table 5.6. The distribution of enclosure features in relation to expansion and intensification zones (chi-square = 5.7, df = 1, Asymp. Sig. = 0.017).

Zone	Observed N	Expected N	Residual
Expansion	7	12.2	−5.2
Intensification	13	7.8	5.2
Total	20		

Table 5.7. The distribution of platform/pavement/terrace features in relation to expansion and intensification zones (chi-square = 1.2, df = 1, Asymp. Sig. = 0.273).

Zone	Observed N	Expected N	Residual
Expansion	21	24.4	−3.4
Intensification	19	15.6	3.4
Total	40		

previously discussed — that is, the extent of reuse and the degree to which domestic features were functionally differentiated — can be included in the estimates. It was noted that some domestic features (i.e., some C-shapes) should be considered temporary field shelters and not permanent residences. The third series of the graph represents the population trajectory if only half of the C-shapes are considered permanent residences and all features were thought to be reused in

Table 5.8. The distribution of domestic features in relation to areas developed during the different phases (chi-square = 41.479, df = 3, Asymp. Sig. = 0.00).

Zone	Observed N	Expected N	Residual
1	4	12.8	−8.8
2	106	64.6	41.4
3	46	64.3	−18.3
4	40	54.3	−14.3
Total	196		

subsequent phases. Series 4, 5, and 6 of Figure 5.9 depict three additional alternatives. In each of these series, only half of the recorded C-shapes are considered permanent residences and included in the frequencies. Furthermore, the relative rate of feature reuse varies in series 4, 5, and 6, with values of 75 percent, 50 percent, and 25 percent being used, respectively.

The difference between accepting a cumulative frequency of domestic features (series 1) and counting only the domestic features associated with each particular phase (series 2) is marked. The assumption of 100 percent reuse results in an increasing growth curve, and the assumption of no reuse produces a curve with a peak and a subsequent sharp decline. The first series is probably an overestimate of population numbers, whereas the second is probably an underestimate. Considering the extent of feature reuse and functional differentiation further refines the estimates of population trends. Halving the number of C-shapes but allowing for total reuse between phases lowers the overall frequencies but maintains the general shape of the series 1 curve. Altering the value of reuse drastically affects the curve. With a reuse value of 75 percent, population continues to increase between all phases, but with a reuse value of 50 percent, the frequency of domestic features actually declines between phases 2 and 3 before rebounding slightly in phase 4. Accepting a reuse value of 50 percent of domestic features in subsequent phases and half of the C-shapes being classified as permanent residences indicates that there were approximately 3.5 domestic features in the first phase, 70 in the second, 64 in the third, and 78 in the fourth (Figure 5.9, series 5). A reuse value of 25 percent (Figure 5.9, series 6) produces a similar curve to the 50 percent reuse curve (series 5), with correspondingly lower numbers.

It is possible to derive population estimates from the changing frequencies of domestic features using a "house count" method (Hassan 1981; see also Kirch, chapter 6, this volume). The Hawaiian ethnohistorical literature (Malo 1951; Handy and Pukui 1958) suggests that households *(kauhale)* usually consisted of four or five structures. Further archaeological and ethnohistorical accounts suggest that there were six to eight people per household (see Cordy 1981; Kirch 1985;

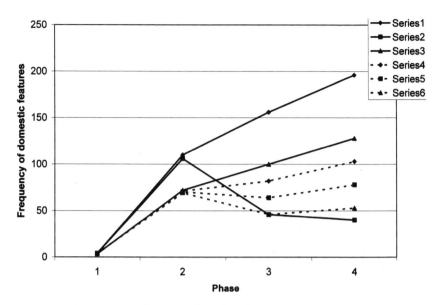

Figure 5.9. Alternative population trends within the DSA.

Weisler and Kirch 1985; Ladefoged 1991; Kirch this volume). Using an estimate of eight people occupying four structures in a household provides a rough estimate of two people per domestic feature. Assigning two people per domestic feature with a reuse value of 50 percent and half of the C-shapes being classified as temporary features (i.e., Figure 5.9, series 5) would suggest that there were approximately seven people living in the DSA during the first phase, 140 during the second, 128 during the third, and upwards of 156 people by the fourth phase. Given a DSA area of 111.9 ha, that is a density of 139.4 p/km² during the fourth phase. Extrapolating this density to the entire Kohala field system, which has an approximate area of 59.4 km², provides a rough estimate of 8,280 people in the uplands of the field system just prior to European contact.

Relative changes in production values can also provide an indication of changing population levels. This, however, is a complicated relationship, as undoubtedly a considerable portion of production during the later periods of Hawaiian prehistory was a surplus being used to fund elites, military, and religious activities. The cumulative percent of areas under production during each phase of initial development provides one means of tracking changing rates of production. This measure would not, however, account for the process of intensification and increased production within some areas in subsequent phases. If regions of intensification during phases 2 through 4 are adjusted by a factor of 1.5 in relation to areas of nonintensified regions (i.e., zones of expansion), the relative cumula-

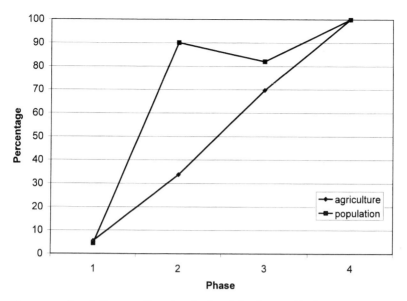

Figure 5.10. Population growth and agricultural development in the DSA.

tive percentages shown in Figure 5.10 series 1 are obtained. Series 2 of this figure depicts population growth as a percentage of phase 4 population levels, assuming 50 percent reuse of domestic features and only half the C-shapes being included. The difference between the two curves is interesting because it suggests that the rate of production increased linearly from phase 1 to phase 4, whereas population increased dramatically between phase 1 and phase 2, dipping slightly in phase 3, and then reaching a peak in phase 4. This suggests that while agricultural production in the southern *ahupuaʻa* continued to increase, the actual number of people in the area declined at one point and then increased only marginally from phase 2 levels. It would appear that a far greater surplus of agriculture was being produced during the latter phases of development in the DSA.

Conclusion

The palimpsest landscape of the Kohala field system provides clues for documenting population trends. A major problem with using these undated surface remains for temporal analyses is determining their relative chronology. Fortunately the fine-grain relationship between the abutment and intersection of agricultural walls and trails makes it possible to derive a chronology for agricultural development. An analysis of the distribution of domestic features in relation to both agricultural zones that were initially developed during different phases and agricultural zones exhibiting alternative developmental pathways indicates the differential use and reuse of various classes of domestic features. Specifically, the distribution of C-shape structures suggests that they were used as both permanent residential features and temporary field shelters. The distribution of C-shapes in relation to zones of agricultural development and excavation data suggests that some features were being reused over extended periods. By adjusting the frequencies of domestic features to account for these processes, it is possible to derive estimates of population trends and levels. It is suggested that the largest increase in population occurred between the first and second phase, with a maximum population in the DSA being reached during the fourth phase of approximately 156 people. In contrast, agricultural production increased almost linearly throughout the four phases of development. The discrepancy between these two trajectories suggests that the amount of agricultural surplus relative to farmers' needs that was being produced during the later phases was probably more than during the earlier phases.

It would seem that the early and dramatic increase in population within the southern portion of the Kohala field system represents a combination of population growth and influx in what was a previously underutilized area for dryland agriculture. In subsequent temporal phases, fewer people were added to the upland population, although agricultural expansion continued, with about 60.4 percent of the DSA land converted to fixed fields during the last two temporal intervals. Another 23.4 percent of the total area was intensified at this same time. This raises the possibility that during the latter phases of agricultural development, a sufficient population was already occupying this upland zone to provide the labor for agricultural production. While this area and dryland agriculture generally is subject to year-to-year variation in output due to unpredictable rainfall, years of average or better rainfall would have produced substantial surpluses for the local population. Some of this may have been banked (e.g., fed to pigs) or stored (for future consumption), but a portion of these surpluses were undoubtedly given as tribute to the Kohala chiefs. Our analysis of archaeological measures of population and dryland agriculture provides an empirically based indication of agricultural surplus production, a resource that was undoubtedly used to fund the religious and military activities of competing factions in the area.

Notes

We thank Patrick Kirch for the invitation to the conference on Moʻorea and all the participants for their helpful comments and discussion. The research was funded by NSF biocomplexity grant BCS-0119819 (Principal Investigator Patrick Kirch), grants from the University of Auckland, grants from the University of Hawaiʻi, and a grant from the

Wenner-Gren Foundation for Anthropological Research. We thank our colleagues on the NSF grant (Oliver Chadwick, Sara Hotchkiss, Patrick Kirch, Peter Vitousek, James Coil, Marjeta Jeraj, and Shripad Tuljapurkar) for their collaborations. Permission to conduct fieldwork was provided by the State of Hawai'i, Division of Land and Natural Resources, and by Monty Richards and Pono Van Holt.

1. For a review of our work in Kohala, see Ladefoged and Graves (2005); our analysis of agricultural development in the area is presented in Ladefoged et al. (1996), Ladefoged and Graves (2000), Ladefoged et al. (2003), Vitousek et al. (2004), and Ladefoged et al. (2005); our initial work on residential features is presented in Graves et al. (2002) and on religious features in Mulrooney and Ladefoged (2005) and Mulrooney et al. (2005); we have examined issues of territoriality in Ladefoged and Graves (2006) and sociopolitical transformations in Ladefoged and Graves (2000).

Paleodemography in Kahikinui, Maui

An Archaeological Approach

When Captain James Cook arrived at Kealakekua on Hawai'i Island in January 1779, he and his companions were struck by the multitudes of Hawaiians who filled the bay with their canoes and lined the shores (see Kirch, chapter 4 in this volume). Seven years later, the French explorer Jean-François de Galaup de la Pérouse, in command of the frigates *Boussole* and *Astrolabe,* was the next European explorer to arrive in the archipelago. His initial experience was quite unlike that of Cook. Deciding to visit Maui rather than Hawai'i, La Pérouse first passed Hāmoa Point in Hāna and coasted about one league offshore of Kīpahulu District. The scenery was lush and verdant, with "waterfalls tumbling down the mountainside into the sea" (Dunmore 1994, 80). Shortly, however, the ships' crews began to witness an entirely different landscape:

> We saw no more waterfalls, the trees were fairly sparsely planted along the plain, and the villages, consisting only of 10 or 12 huts, were quite distant from each other. Every moment made us regret the country which we were leaving behind, and we only found shelter when we were faced with a frightful shore, where the lava had once run down as waterfalls do today in the other part of the island. (Dunmore 1994, 82)

La Pérouse had just sailed past the district of Kahikinui, situated on the southern flank of the great volcanic dome of Haleakalā. Clearly, this was no Kealakekua Bay, with fertile and vast plantations extending inland. Kahikinui was arid, the land streaked by black and reddish brown lava flows descending from Haleakalā's rift zone, and as La Pérouse observed, the population was sparse. A few canoes put to sea and followed the ships until they dropped anchor at Keone'ō'io Bay, west of Kahikinui in Honua'ula District, bringing "pigs, sweet potatoes, bananas, arum roots [taro]," and other articles to trade with the French.[1] These agricultural products hint at what La Pérouse could not have readily observed from his marine vantage point a league or so offshore: that the population of Kahikinui resided largely in the uplands — 2 or more kilometers from the coast — where environmental conditions were suitable to Polynesian horticulture.

Kahikinui offers a particular kind of window on the Hawaiian past, including questions of paleodemography. Though not completely unique in this aspect, Kahikinui is marked by its aridity, in large measure due to its topographic position in the rain shadow created by the looming hulk of Haleakalā, rising 3,055 meters from the sea. It is what the Hawaiians called an 'āina malo'o (Malo 1951, 204) — a dry land where irrigation was not possible and where the sweet potato (Ipomoea batatas) took primacy in the local agricultural regime (Handy 1940, 161; Coil and Kirch 2005).[2] Consequently, the archaeological record of Kahikinui reveals a great deal about the ability of pre-Contact Hawaiians to adapt to what can only be described as an "ecologically marginal" landscape (Kirch et al. 2004).[3] For the archaeologist interested in paleodemography, Kahikinui may tell something about population numbers and demographic processes "at the margin," in contrast to what Rob Hommon once called the "salubrious core regions" of the islands. Here we can hope to gain some idea of what the low end of the range of population densities was in pre-Contact Hawai'i.

The Kahikinui Archaeological Project

The Kahikinui Archaeological Project (KAP), now entering its twelfth year, is oriented around several major objectives, one of which is to reconstruct the long-term population history of the district (Kirch, ed., 1997, 1998). Taking advantage of the fact that Kahikinui is one of the last remaining regions in the archipelago where — thanks to the lack of modern development — one may investigate settlement patterns at the level of an entire traditional district (moku), our research has been based on intensive survey of large sample zones (Figure 6.1). To date these have included all or significant parts of four of the district's eight ahupua'a territories (Kīpapa, Naka'ohu, Mahamenui, and Manawainui), along with nearly complete coverage of the entire coastal zone. This survey work has thus far resulted in the accumulation of a site database (now running in ArcGIS) with >3,000 individual archaeological features — primarily freestanding stone architectural components — the vast majority of which consist of traditional Hawaiian house clusters (kauhale). These data provide the critical raw material for estimating population on the basis of a "house-count" method (Hassan 1981; Turner 1990).

In addition to extensive survey, we have also undertaken both areal and test excavations in more than 100 individual structures, totaling about 400 m² of sample area. These include ritual (heiau) and agricultural features as well as habitation sites, although the majority of our excavated sample derives from residential contexts. Most importantly for paleodemographic reconstruction, we now have

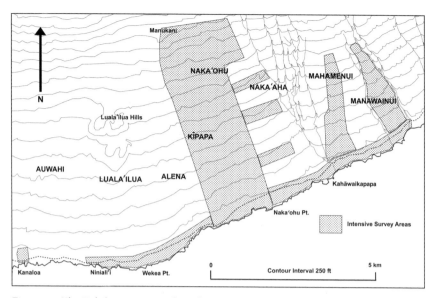

Figure 6.1. The Kahikinui region of southeastern Maui, showing areas of intensive archaeological survey.

available a database of 169 radiocarbon age determinations from these excavations, one of the largest such samples of well-dated sites in the Hawaiian Islands (Kirch unpublished data). These dates provide the opportunity to establish reasonably good temporal controls for the survey data, thus constraining our house-count estimations of population size in a way not possible for many other areas that have been archaeologically surveyed.

In 2002–2004, KAP entered a new phase as part of a multidisciplinary "biocomplexity" project funded by the National Science Foundation (Kirch et al. 2001). This has allowed us to greatly expand our efforts at understanding the environmental constraints and correlates of human settlement and production in this environment and also brings new expertise at dynamic population and resource modeling to the project.

Kahikinui: Environmental Constraints on Population

Before turning to paleodemographic estimates per se, it may be instructive to review in more detail the environmental factors that were likely to have imposed constraints on human population growth and density within Kahikinui. Chief among these are (1) availability of potable water, (2) limitations on wild food resources, and (3) constraints on the ability to cultivate Polynesian crops and on horticultural yields.

Water

The abundant rainfall found throughout the windward and intermediate zones of the archipelago is orographically induced, as moisture-laden trade winds are forced to rise rapidly over the islands' mountainous interiors. However, in the lee of 3,055-m high Haleakalā, Kahikinui almost totally lacks such orographic precipitation. Instead, rainfall is restricted to short periods of southerly wind reversals (*kona* storms), which typically occur during the winter and spring months (from November to April) (Carlquist 1970, 66). Modern rain gauges indicate that along a gradient running up the mountain slope from the shoreline, average annual precipitation in Kahikinui ranges from a low of <300 mm at the coast to perhaps 1,000–1,500 mm in the main upland farming and residential zone (ca. 450–900 masl). Given the young lava and tephra substrates, this limited rain sinks rapidly into the surface, and while there are incipient drainage channels, these have flowing water only for a few hours during the most severe *kona* storms. Most of the time, surface water is totally lacking in Kahikinui.[4]

Aside from the serious problem of whether this limited winter rainfall regime is sufficient to meet the growing requirements of Hawaiian crop plants, it poses the further problem of potable water for direct human consumption and other needs (cooking, washing, food processing). Slightly brackish but potable water is available along the coast in small wells and seeps at the tide line, and these were certainly utilized. However, carrying water from sea level to the main upland residential zone some 1–2 km inland would have been extremely demanding on labor resources. Most likely, however, limited water supplies were available from small seeps and springs within the upland zone, as suggested by Stock et al. (2003). These water sources were presumably fed by a higher water table resulting from more extensive upland forest cover in pre-Contact times, which was able to capture significant amounts of fog-drip precipitation from the cloud layer that forms diurnally along the Haleakalā mountain flank between 800 and 1,900 masl. In spite of the likely presence of such upland seeps and springs, a limited potable water supply was surely one major constraint on population in Kahikinui.

Wild Food Resources

Terrestrial food resources in the Hawaiian Islands were largely limited to a diversity of birds, and the dryland forests of Kahikinui were probably as well stocked in this regard as other regions. Far more important, however, were littoral and in-shore marine resources (shellfish, fish, turtles, and seaweeds), for these comprised a major proportion of the protein intake. In this regard, Kahikinui is indeed marginal when compared with other areas of the archipelago, for it wholly lacks a fringing reef, and most of the coastline consists of sea cliffs that are difficult and dangerous to access. Our own survey of biotic resources (O'Day 2004) reveals a limited array of shellfish and fish taxa, these occurring in much lower densities than elsewhere, where coral and algal growth on fringing reefs contribute a large herbivore base to the trophic pyramid. Moreover, there are few good canoe landings, and the offshore 'Alenuihāhā Channel (the name translates literally as "great billows smashing") is notoriously rough throughout most of the year, making pelagic fishing difficult. In short, while marine food resources are not wholly lacking, they are much less abundant and more difficult to obtain than elsewhere in the Islands. This too must have constrained potential population levels.

Constraints on Agricultural Production

Thirdly, and certainly most important, were environmental constraints on agricultural production, since this is the most critical parameter defining overall "carrying capacity." The estimated annual 1,000–1,500 mm rainfall received on the upland slopes of Kahikinui would be sufficient for cultivation of sweet potatoes and yams *(Dioscorea alata)*, both of which have varieties with short growing seasons that can be accommodated within a winter cropping regime. However, such scant rainfall is on the low end for taro *(Colocasia esculenta)* and probably bananas *(Eumusa* hybrids) and is certainly not adequate for breadfruit *(Artocarpus altilis)*. As secondary crops, both sugarcane *(Saccharum officinarum)* and ti *(Cordyline fruticosum)* would have been able to grow in Kahikinui.

Further agronomic constraints were posed by the regional geologic and edaphic substrates, which are dominated by relatively young and unweathered lava flow slopes (Kirch et al. 2004). The Kahikinui landscape is thus markedly "mosaic-like" in character, with individual substrate patches varying widely in their nutrient availability and workability (stoniness). Our pedological investigations along a dual chrono-sequence and climo-sequence indicate that some of the older and higher substrates have lowered nutrient status, whereas very young substrates are too rocky and lack sufficient fine-grained sediments for adequate cultivation. This leaves a group of substrates, largely tephra covered, with ages between ca. 30,000 and 90,000 years BP, which appear to have been the primary foci of agricultural efforts. Thus, as population increased, there could have been considerable competition for access to and control of the limited areas in which growing crop plants would have been most productive.

The Kahikinui Radiocarbon Corpus and Population Dynamics

As noted, we have now accumulated a corpus of 169 radiocarbon dates from residential (N = 126, open sites and rock shelters), agricultural (N = 15), and ceremonial (N = 28) contexts. As these radiocarbon data underlie our efforts

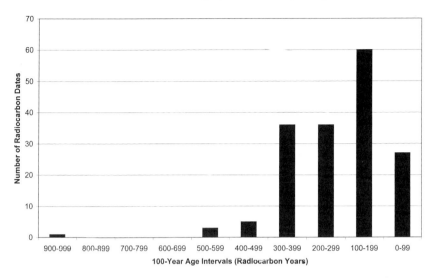

Conventional 14C Ages, Uncalibrated (N=168)

Figure 6.2. Frequency distribution of conventional radiocarbon dates (N = 168) for Kahikinui by 100-year age intervals.

to understand either relative population dynamics (growth rates) or specific population numbers and densities, we need to briefly consider the nature of the dating corpus, keeping in mind that radiocarbon dates are fundamentally statistical estimations of the probability of a particular sample of carbonized wood (or other material) dating to a given range of calendar years. Figure 6.2 shows a histogram frequency distribution by 100-year intervals of "conventional ^{14}C ages" for Kahikinui in *radiocarbon years* before present (i.e., not calibrated to calendar years);[5] these are effectively the "raw data" for chronological control in Kahikinui. The sample is unimodal but strongly skewed to the recent end of the time scale, especially the period 100–199 ^{14}C years BP. Note that the 0–99 year interval is made up primarily of dates with low $\delta^{13}C$ values (derived from C4 pathway woods), which will calibrate on average about 200 years older than they appear here. When this sample of dates is calibrated, using the bidecadal atmospheric calibration curve established by radiocarbon dating of known-age (dendrochronologically dated) bristlecone pinewood samples (Stuiver and Pearson 1993), the distribution changes to that shown in Figure 6.3. Here we can see that about one-half of the dates fall into the period from AD 1700 to 1799, and that one could potentially smooth these data to form an exponential growth curve (but not a logistic curve).

In Figures 6.2 and 6.3, the corpus of dates is graphed by 100-year intervals;

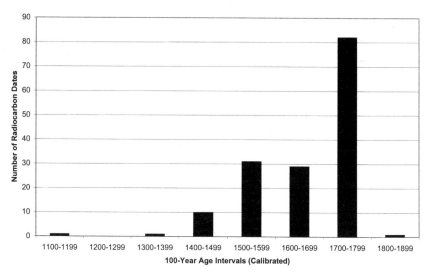

Kahikinui Calibrated 14C Dates, 100-Year Intervals (N=162)

Figure 6.3. Frequency distribution of calibrated radiocarbon dates (N = 162) for Kahikinui by 100-year age intervals.

what happens if we try to break the time scale down into smaller intervals? The results are shown in Figure 6.4, a histogram frequency distribution at fifty-year intervals, in which the data show marked peaks and troughs. This tendency for dates to group together is *not*—and this must be stressed—a reflection of "real" temporal periodicity in the true ages of the samples, but rather an artifact of the calibration curve itself. As McFadgen et al. (1994) have demonstrated, because the ^{14}C calibration curve is not uniform but has areas both with steep slopes and with wiggles, a series of what they call "ambiguous regions" results, where a single ^{14}C age can have multiple corresponding calendar year ages. Calibration of a series of dates results in what McFadgen et al. call the "calibration stochastic distortion (CSD) effect," which is the "systematic increase or depletion of the number of calibrated dates on the calendar scale, related to the slope of the calibration curve" (223–224). It is critical to understand that a set of calibrated radiocarbon dates such as those from Kahikinui cannot be interpreted on too fine a temporal scale. Clearly, the distribution by fifty-year intervals shown in Figure 6.4 responds to this CSD effect. However, the CSD effect is largely smoothed out by the 100-year intervals used in Figure 6.3. For the purposes of estimating population dynamics, then, the best we can hope for is temporal resolution on the order of about one century or more, not less.

Two further points emerge from these basic radiocarbon data. First, taken as

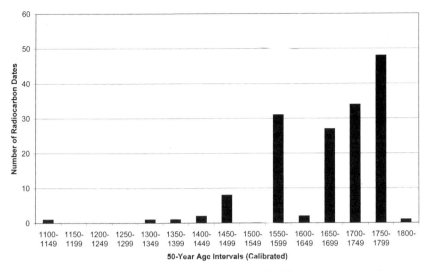

Kahikinui Calibrated 14C Dates (N=162)

Figure 6.4. Radiocarbon dates (N = 162) respond to the "calibration stochastic distortion (CSD) effect" (see text for discussion).

a crude index of human activity on the landscape (and keeping in mind that the total sample reviewed thus far includes ritual and agricultural context samples as well as residential sites), the total sample of ^{14}C dates from Kahikinui is best interpreted as reflecting an exponential growth process. There is no indication of a significant reduction in the frequency of samples for the later time intervals, and thus no basis for inferring a logistic progress. This contrasts with prior evidence for both west Hawai'i Island and for the archipelago as a whole (Hommon 1976; Cordy 1981; Kirch 1984, 1985; Dye and Komori 1992b; Dye 1994), which indicate an exponential curve until ca. AD 1400–1500, followed by stability, for the Hawaiian population as a whole (see Kirch, chapter 4 this volume).

Second, the chronology for human activity on the Kahikinui landscape effectively begins in the fifteenth century AD, with only the slightest trace of activity prior to AD 1400. This means that people began to settle and utilize the Kahikinui lands *at the same time that the archipelago-wide growth curve reached its peak* (see Dye and Komori 1992b). In other words, Kahikinui did not partake of the process of "inland expansion" first discussed by Hommon (1976), which seems to have commenced between AD 1100 and 1200. Rather, the occupation of Kahikinui appears to be a population "overflow" effect from other regions, beginning only as the main period of "inland expansion" was coming to a close. Presumably this is a reflection of the marginality of Kahikinui in terms of water, resources, and agricultural potential, as noted earlier. As Dixon et al. (1999) have suggested, Kahikinui is a high-risk environment, one that people tackled only when other options had become closed to them.

Estimating Population Levels: House Counts

To move from the estimation of general growth trends to projections of actual population numbers over time and space requires more than radiocarbon data alone. Probably the most successful methods used by archaeologists in various parts of the world to achieve such projections make use of some variant of the "house-count" method (e.g., Hassan 1981; Turner 1990). In essence, one wants to be able to count individual housing or residential units, controlling these by time period, thereby achieving a proxy census. Assuming (1) that the nature of such housing units is stable over time so that the mean number of occupants can be presumed as a constant, (2) that such housing units are readily visible in the archaeological record, and (3) that they can be dated with some confidence, this method is without doubt the most reliable.

Fortunately, the archaeological landscape of Kahikinui lends itself well to this approach. Habitation sites occur as clusters of individual stone structures, grouped together into discrete complexes (often situated on ridgelines or on the crests of knolls) where each structure was functionally distinctive. The Hawaiian ethnohistoric literature (Malo 1951; Kamakau 1964; Handy and Pukui 1958) identifies such residential clusters by the term *"kauhale"* (literally, "group of houses") and informs us that among the key functional types to be found in a cluster were the following: (1) the common dwelling and sleeping house, *hale noa;* (2) a men's eating house, *mua;* (3) an oven or cookhouse, *hale kāhumu;* (4) various storage structures; and (5) a women's menstrual house, *hale pe'a.* These sources also indicate that such clusters were occupied by single nucleated households, which might count from one to three generations among its members. An archaeological example of such a residential cluster from Kahikinui is shown in Figure 6.5.

Over the course of our decade-long archaeological survey in Kahikinui, as already noted, we have recorded more than 3,000 stone structures, the majority of which are components of such residential complexes. For the purpose of this chapter, I have focused on our largest contiguous sample area — the adjacent *ahupua'a* units of Kīpapa and Naka'ohu in the central part of the *moku.* Within this sample area, which comprises approximately 6.75 km², some 544 individual stone structures can be grouped into 117 residential complexes. This total of residential complexes should be taken as a minimal count, since a number of isolated or small structures have been regarded as "temporary" sites or sites with special functions and have been excluded from the overall count.

Figure 6.5. Map of a typical pre-Contact residential cluster in Kahikinui, with functionally discrete structures.

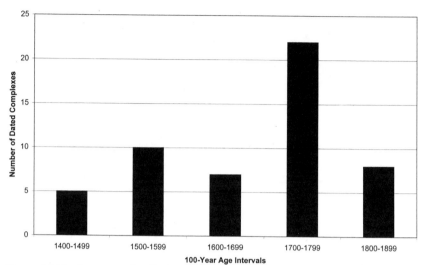

Kipapa-Nakaohu Habitation Complexes (N=51)

Figure 6.6. The frequency distribution of dated habitation complexes for Kahikinui (N = 51), based on the sample of excavated and dated residential features.

Given that we know from the radiocarbon database (and from post-Contact historic sources) that Kahikinui was occupied over a period of about five centuries (AD 1400–1900), it is evident that we cannot assume contemporaneity for all of these 117 residential complexes. Here our large sample of radiocarbon dates derived from habitation contexts is critical, for this allows us to place temporal constraints on the house-count data. Figure 6.6 shows the frequency distribution of dated habitation complexes for Kahikinui (N = 51), based on our sample of excavated and dated residential features. Included in this sample are eight habitation complexes with post-Contact European artifacts; although not radiocarbon dated, these sites can be put into the time series, and it is indeed important to do so, as Native Hawaiian occupation in Kahikinui continued throughout most of the nineteenth century.

If we now assume that the proportion of residential sites by 100-year time intervals in our sample of fifty-one dated complexes is representative for the district as a whole, we can use the frequency distribution given in Figure 6.6 to model the numbers of households in the Kīpapa-Naka'ohu sample area based on a total house count of 117, as shown in Table 6.1.

To convert the data in Table 6.1 to an actual estimate of population sizes over time requires a knowledge of the average number of persons who occupied a residential complex. Lt. King, on Cook's voyage in 1778–1779, reported that "six persons to a house is a very moderate allowance," and this figure was adopted by

Table 6.1. Residential complexes by 100-year intervals.

Temporal period (AD)	Percent of residential complexes/period	Number of complexes in Kīpapa-Nakaʻohu
1400–1499	10	12
1500–1599	20	23
1600–1699	14	16
1700–1799	41	48
1800–1899	16	19

Table 6.2. Estimated population of Kīpapa-Nakaʻohu by 100-year intervals.

Temporal period (AD)	No. of complexes	Est. population (6 persons/complex)	Est. population (8 persons/complex)
1400–1499	12	72	96
1500–1599	23	138	184
1600–1699	16	96	128
1700–1799	48	288	384
1800–1899	19	114	152

Cordy (1981, 91) in his study of North Kona. If anything, this figure may be a slight underestimate, given the ethnographic data reported by Beaglehole and Beaglehole (1941, 69) for average household size in six Polynesian societies, with a low of 6.5 (Pukapuka and Pangai, Tonga) and a high of 8.77 (ʻUvea). The Beagleholes concluded that "the Polynesian household ranges between six and eight persons," and we can use both values to set probable upper and lower limits to the Kīpapa-Nakaʻohu population by 100-year age intervals, as in Table 6.2.

We can further translate these population estimates into densities, as in Table 6.3. Densities have been calculated as a range (based on the six to eight persons/ complex range) for both the primary zone of human habitation and land use (<900 masl, 6.75 km²) and for the entire *ahupuaʻa* up to the summit of Haleakalā (ca. 15 km²). As can be seen, for the period just prior to European contact when Kahikinui population was clearly at its peak, the maximum density achieved in the lowland zone would have been between about 43 and 57 persons/km², depending on average household size. The figures for the *ahupuaʻa* territory as a whole are between about 19 and 25 persons/km². These values are on the low end of ethnographically documented population densities in Polynesia and are probably realistic in view of the environmental marginality of Kahikinui.

Table 6.3. Estimated population densities for Kīpapa-Nakaʻohu by 100-year intervals.

Temporal period (AD)	Persons/km² in zone <900 m asl	Persons/km² in entire *ahupuaʻa*
1400–1499	10.7–14.2	4.8–6.4
1500–1599	20.4–27.2	9.2–12.3
1600–1699	14.2–18.9	6.4–8.5
1700–1799	42.7–56.9	19.2–25.6
1800–1899	16.9–22.5	7.6–10.1

We can also use these data to make a rough approximation of the total population of Kahikinui District, on the assumption that the population density for Kīpapa-Nakaʻohu was consistent across the other *ahupuaʻa*.[6] Within the entire *moku* of Kahikinui, there are approximately 72 km² of land <900 m elevation, which at the same density levels for Kīpapa-Nakaʻohu during its period of maximum population would suggest a total *moku*-wide population of between 3,074 and 4,096 persons.

Population Limits of Kahikinui

How large a population could the Kahikinui agricultural environment support? An alternative approach often used by archaeologists in their efforts to estimate ancient populations is to calculate the theoretical "carrying capacity" of a particular region or landscape, whether through the hunting-and-gathering of wild resources or through a supposed level of agricultural production (Hassan 1981; Glassow 1978). This approach has been used before in Polynesia, such as by Bellwood (1972) for the Marquesas, and it is essayed with respect to the ʻOpunohu Valley by Hamilton and Kahn (chapter 8, this volume). There are, of course, many assumptions that must be made when estimating levels of potential agricultural production (amount of arable land, crop types and average yields, labor inputs, the effects of short-term perturbations such as drought, and long-term perturbations such as nutrient depletion), all of which result in very large standard errors on the ensuing estimates (see Tuljapurkar et al., chapter 3, this volume). My own view is that the house-count method, when possible, yields a far more accurate and precise estimate of actual population numbers. Nonetheless, it may be instructive to consider a potential agricultural carrying capacity model for Kahikinui, to contrast with the numbers derived from the method of house-count census.

For present purposes, I will keep this model particularly simple, with only a single dominant crop, sweet potato *(Ipomoea batatas),* for which we have good ethnohistoric (Handy 1940) and archaeobotanical evidence (Coil and Kirch 2005). In reality, the Kahikinui agricultural system certainly also included other crops, such as *Cordyline* (for which we also have archaeobotanical remains), bananas, and probably some amount of taro *(Colocasia esculenta)* grown in upland plots, possibly extending into the forest zone. To keep our model as simple as possible, however, we shall simply assume that the daily caloric needs of the resident population were met entirely by sweet potato production, supplemented by protein obtained largely from marine gathering and fishing, and to a more limited degree by animal husbandry of dogs and pigs. (These protein sources are also evidenced by the zooarchaeological record; see Kirch and O'Day 2003.) For purposes of calculation, an average daily intake of 2 kg of sweet potato tubers (approximately 2,000 cal) will be assumed.

With the 6.75 km² survey zone of Kīpapa-Nakaʻohu, for which we have estimated the population on the basis of house counts, we have no evidence for sustained gardening below about 300 masl (due to insufficient rainfall), which eliminates some 2.25 km² of barren zone. However, it is possible that gardens extended into the forest zone above the uppermost residential complexes, adding perhaps 0.75 km² of arable land. In all, this totals about 5.25 km² of potentially arable land. But this potentially arable area is broken up into patches of different substrate ages with differential workability and nutrient status (Kirch et al. 2004), and considerable allowance must also be made for (1) areas of lava outcrop and (2) areas taken up with houses, ceremonial structures, and other uses. A very rough estimate is that, at most, perhaps one-third of the total potentially arable land area could have been under cultivation at any given time. This gives a total of 1.75 km² of garden land for the former occupants of the Kīpapa-Nakaʻohu area.

A second key variable is sweet potato yields. Given the winter rainfall regime of Kahikinui, it is unreasonable to assume more than a single crop per year. Although Yen (1974, 50) remarks on the ability of the sweet potato to give relatively high yields—clearly a major reason it was adopted as a key crop in various parts of Eastern Polynesia—these cannot be expected to have reached the levels of modern experimental trials. Massal and Barrau (1956, 24–26) suggest that yields on the order of 3–6 tons/acre are likely for indigenous cultivation regimes in the Pacific, a range validated by Yen's references to Oceanic ethnography (1974, 50). Chung (1923), in an early paper on Hawaiian yields, estimated 4 tons/acre. Again, given the marginal status of Kahikinui, it may be best to assume yields on the low end of the scale. For present purposes, we will assume an average yield of about 2 tons/acre (or 4.9 metric tons/hectare), with a single crop per year.

Using these values for area of land (175 ha) and yield (4.9 mt/ha), an admittedly coarse-grained estimate of the potential annual agricultural production of the Kīpapa-Nakaʻohu area would be 857.5 mt/yr. Consuming 2 kg per day, an inhabitant of the *ahupuaʻa* would need 0.73 mt/yr for basic sustenance. If every last tuber were consumed, leaving nothing for tribute, "social production" (such as feeding pigs and dogs), or exchange and assuming no wastage, rotting, or other depredations to the crop, in theory a population of 1,175 persons could be sustained on this annual yield. This figure is roughly three times greater than the maximum population estimated by the house-count method.

Does this mean that the population figures derived from the house counts are significant underestimates? I do not think so, because the house-count estimates are based on intensive archaeological survey combined with extensive temporal controls from a large ^{14}C database. Rather, this exercise reinforces the view that carrying capacity–based estimates typically tend to *overinflate* the actual population. What such an estimate of agricultural production does tell us, however, is that it certainly was economically feasible for the Kahikinui landscape to sustain a population at the density levels of ca. 43–57 persons/km^2 of occupied zone suggested by the house-count method. Moreover, this density could have been achieved while still allowing for considerable "excess" production to be diverted to animal husbandry, tribute exactation, and exchange, all of which are abundantly attested in the ethnohistoric literature for Hawaiʻi (see Brookfield 1972, 1984 on "social production"). Finally, we must keep in mind that an estimate of "average annual production" makes no account for the vagaries of the natural environment, particularly the likely effects of drought, which in an arid region such as Kahikinui could at times have been devastating (see Tuljapurkar et al., chapter 3 in this volume, for further discussion of agricultural limitations on population).

Post-Contact Population Decline in Kahikinui

Finally, what can we say concerning the rate of population decline in Kahikinui following European contact? The larger question of the impact of European contact — and especially of communicable diseases — on the indigenous Hawaiian population is at the heart of Stannard's (1989) arguments for a "Hawaiian holocaust." The missionary census of 1831–1832, considered the first reasonably accurate count, gave the following figures for Kahikinui (Schmitt 1973, 18):

Kane (males)	154
Wahine (females)	129
Keikikane (male children)	119
Keikiwahine (female children)	115
Pau loa (totals)	517

With a ratio of only 0.82 child/adult, this clearly was a population already in decline, some fifty-three years after first contact with the West. If our estimates of the probable maximum population of the entire *moku* are correct, the 1831–1832 population was roughly between one-sixth and one-eighth of its pre-Contact maximum. This is indeed a veritable population collapse, even if short of a true decimation in the literal sense. By 1836, the population had declined still further to 447, although no age or sex breakdown is provided (Schmitt 1973, 38).

These historical data from the 1830s provide an opportunity to cross-check the accuracy of our house-count method of population estimation, as our archaeological survey of residential sites also includes complexes with known historic-period occupation components. Within the Kīpapa-Nakaʻohu survey zone, we have identified seven complexes with material culture assemblages that would indicate occupation in the 1830s or slightly later. At six persons/house (and by post-Contact times this number may have been lower), the population of Kīpapa-Nakaʻohu would have stood at around forty-two persons. Kīpapa-Nakaʻohu represents about 9.3 percent of the total land area within Kahikinui, so the estimated total population of the district, based on our archaeological house-counting method, would be 445. This is almost exactly the number given by the census of 1836, confirming that the archaeological and historical data are in good accord.

Conclusions

Elsewhere in this volume (chapter 4), I argue that in order to advance our understanding of Hawaiian paleodemography, both in the pre-Contact but also early post-Contact periods, we need a number of data-rich empirical studies undertaken at the local or regional scale. Here I have endeavored to put forward just such a case study, based on a long-term archaeological project in which both the survey and chronological data are intensive and well controlled. The particular value of the Kahikinui case is that it shows the probable levels of population as well as the temporal dynamics of population growth and decline in a region that was on one end of the spectrum of human landscapes within the Hawaiian archipelago. Thus the long-term population history of Kahikinui does not stand for or represent the demographic story of the entire archipelago. Rather, it illuminates what happened at the margins, even as that marginal history was inescapably linked to and interacted with the more productive and (presumably) populated "salubrious cores."

Thus we see that the history of population growth in Kahikinui took a somewhat divergent course from what has been evidenced elsewhere in the Islands. Rather than being a participant in the phase of "inland expansion" of population that began around the twelfth century AD, Kahikinui remained virtually unoccupied up until the early fifteenth century. Only then did small numbers of settlers begin to move into this vast tract on the leeward slopes of Haleakalā, establishing residences and gardens primarily in the uplands where rainfall was sufficient for cropping. The most plausible interpretation is that Kahikinui had been deemed too arid, too marginal, until most other parts of Maui had been territorially claimed and occupied.

Once settled in the fifteenth century, population in Kahikinui began to increase slowly through the sixteenth and seventeenth centuries, but then it effectively tripled in size between the late seventeenth and early eighteenth centuries. This century just prior to European contact was the period of highest human population density within the *moku* of Kahikinui, and we must therefore imagine that the pressures on land and resources were concomitantly greater than ever. There is no indication, however, insofar as we can temporally resolve our data, of a decline in population prior to European contact. In this sense the population history of Kahikinui also diverges from the aggregate history reconstructed for the archipelago at large, which we have seen to be marked by a sequence of exponential growth followed by a rapid shift to population stability after ca. AD 1450–1500. In Kahikinui, growth also appears to have been exponential, but this continues after the apparent demographic stability reached elsewhere, and it had not shifted to a stable situation by the time of the fateful encounter with Cook and the West.

Finally, the Kahikinui data tell us something of the aftermath of that contact, with a six- to eightfold population decline in just under five decades. And this statistic leaves us with a tantalizing hint toward the answer to that largest of questions in Hawaiian paleodemography: What was the total population of the archipelago at contact? If—*and this is a very big if*—the post-Contact rate of decline indicated for Kahikinui were to hold true for the archipelago as a whole, then a retrodiction of the 1836 census would suggest a pre-Contact maximum in the range of 650,000 to 860,000 people. Stannard's claim that King's 1779 estimate of 400,000 was an underestimate would be vindicated.

But it would be premature to make this leap, for too many assumptions intervene. The local population decline in Kahikinui may well have resulted from substantial out-migration to port towns and other parts of the island and thus not be representative of the actual effects of disease on mortality and fertility rates. We need several more detailed case studies from other regions around the archipelago before we can definitively test the veracity of Stannard's claim. But I do believe that Stannard and Nordyke were both correct in pointing to archaeology for the answer to this ultimate question. The generations who populated the Hawaiian Islands from initial Polynesian discovery until the fateful encounter with Cook left their sedimented traces over the Hawaiian landscape; it is those traces that hold the clues to the archipelago's pre-Contact demographic history.

Notes

The research reported here has been supported in part under the following grants from the National Science Foundation: BCS-0119819 and SBR-9805754.

1. It may have been one of these Kahikinui people who, having traded successfully for the Frenchmen's "old metal hoops" (Dunmore 1994, 83), returned to Naka'ohu Ahupua'a to carefully incise, using a metal implement, the outline of a square-rigged ship on the basalt overhang of his rockshelter residence (Millerstrom and Kirch 2005).

2. Edward S. C. Handy, who made a study of traditional Hawaiian agricultural practices as they survived into the 1930s, called the region from Kaupō "through Kahikinui, Honuaula, and Kula . . . the greatest continuous dry planting area [for sweet potatoes] in the Hawaiian Islands" (1940, 161).

3. The term "ecologically marginal" is clearly relative and must be understood from the perspective of Polynesian economic systems, which over several millennia had been adapted to tropical island ecosystems whose climatic, edaphic, hydrologic, and biotic conditions and resources are very different from that of arid Kahikinui.

4. This is the main problem that beset attempts at cattle ranching in Kahikinui over the past century (P. Erdman, pers. comm., 1996) and that was only partly solved by bringing a pipeline in from 'Ulupalakua to supply a chain of watering troughs.

5. The term "conventional ^{14}C age" follows the definition of Stuiver and Polach (1977) and means that these dates have been corrected for isotopic fractionation (δ^{13}C values) but not calibrated to calendar years.

6. This assumption may not in fact hold up, given that at least two *ahupua'a* (Luala'ilua and Alena) have relatively young geological substrates that probably restricted their agricultural production more severely than Kīpapa-Naka'ohu.

7

Reconstructing Hawaiian Population at European Contact

Three Regional Case Studies

 My research interests have long focused on the development of complex societies in Polynesia and Micronesia (Cordy 1981, 1985b, 1986, 1993, 1996a, 2000), by investigating relevant related variables such as polity territorial size, polity population size, population density, amount of food cultivated and amounts in intensive cultivation vs. extensive cultivation, amount of livestock produced, size of temples, offerings at temples, and so on. Demographic variables are clearly important. A key demographic measurement needed in such research is an estimate of population sizes at European contact. This chapter looks at three regional datasets within the Hawaiian Islands: the districts of Waiʻanae and ʻEwa on Oʻahu and Hāmākua on Hawaiʻi Island.

Methods and Assumptions Used for Archaeological Estimates of Population

Three main archaeological approaches have been used to estimate actual population numbers in the Hawaiian Islands: (1) frequency distributions of radiocarbon dates, (2) carrying capacity estimates, and (3) house counts. The first method has considerable potential (e.g., Dye and Komori 1992), but limited dating of upper deposits in sites (Cordy 1996a, 605) and possible calibration problems (Hommon 1992, 156) suggest there is not yet an accurate archipelago population curve for the late pre-Contact era (AD 1600s–1700s). (See Kirch, chapter 4 this volume, for further discussion of problems with this approach.) The use of this method to suggest a contact population number lower than 200,000 persons seems untenable at present. The second approach of estimating carrying capacity has yielded figures that appear much too high for contact times (see chapter 4), indicating that most populations were not near their subsistence carrying capacity.

House counts are the primary method that has been used in the relatively few archaeological studies of Hawaiian demography. This approach also requires considerable methodological building blocks, especially deciding what type of house to count. I have argued that permanent houses are the primary house type useful in reconstructing population numbers (Cordy 1981). Hawaiian households at European contact used many types of temporary houses, for varying lengths of time, and with some recurrently used and some not. Thus, counts including temporary houses do not give a one-to-one count of households, while permanent habitation counts generally do.[1]

The Hawaiian land records from the 1840s and 1850s (commonly called the Mahele land records) clearly show that Hawaiians at contact identified a *pā hale* (house lot) or *kahuahale* (house foundation, house site) where their household resided. In other words, a permanent house site was a Hawaiian concept. This pattern of a "permanent house site" is also clear in the early historical records (e.g., Malo 1951; Kamakau 1976; Beaglehole 1967; Campbell 1967). But essentially, these are all terms for the same pattern.[2]

A problem with permanent house site counts is how to identify the permanent house site archaeologically. This is an issue that I tried to address some years ago (Cordy 1981; Cordy et al. 1991). It has been portrayed as a size-based approach, which is incorrect. I look at several variables, including number of structures, size ranges of these structures, labor expenditure (well-made corners, facings, walls, etc. vs. more expedient, informal construction), and associations. This approach has application problems when no surface architecture exists, such as in coastal areas where house posts often were placed directly into sand without stone architectural foundations. In these contexts, it has been difficult to assign postholes to specific structures. Thus, identifying separate structures is extremely difficult, even before attempting to distinguish between permanent and temporary houses. Problems with this approach once arose where large walled house enclosures were the housing remnant, with no visible architectural remnants of houses within the house lots. However, it has proven possible to distinguish whether these house-lots are permanent houses by comparison with similar, nearby house lots that do contain house structures and by labor expenditure variables (Cordy 2001b). In general, I believe that when surface architecture is present it is possible to identify permanent housing, and in most archaeological settings in Hawai'i dating to the 1700s, surface architecture dominates the landscape. Archaeologists need to identify houses in a replicable manner so that others can evaluate the analytical approach and the data and judge for themselves if an interpretive match occurs.

A final problem with archaeological house counts concerns chronology. Simply dating a house site has problems. The span of use of the house site needs to be established — and with some accuracy — if one is going to determine a count of how many houses (or people) were present at any point in time (Cordy 1981; Clark 1988). Fine chronological control is required. In the 1970s, volcanic glass hydration dating seemed to provide the answer, but the method proved to have unresolved problems. Individual radiocarbon dates with error ranges of 150–200 years do not provide precise ages, only gross chronological control. For estimating Contact-era population, this means that the Contact era effectively becomes a time span on the order of AD 1650–1800. Such dating is not sufficient for accurately reconstructing population from house counts at different time periods, much less truly understanding the chronological sequencing of demographic, political organization, and food production variables. This is a serious problem (Tuggle 2004). It is imperative that better chronological approaches be developed in Hawai'i. Until then, we can discern only gross chronological patterns of population based on house counts. Accurate reconstruction of population sizes and other dimensions of culture on a fine temporal scale is not yet possible.

Methods Used Here

Counts of permanent house sites as a measure of the household are used in the Wai'anae archeological examples given below. In historical cases, households are associated with claimants or occupiers of house lots (*pā hale* or *kahuahale*) in the Mahele land records (Native Register; Native Testimony; Awards Books) or are represented by a taxpayer (a household) in the tax records (Barrère 1971, 18). In the 'Ewa and Hāmākua cases, actual census counts are used (Schmitt 1973).

Population counts for households are computed using Lt. James King's estimate of six people per household (Cook and King 1784, 128).[3] King's estimate was based on his 1779 observations at Kealekekua, where he spent much time ashore; King is regarded as one of the best observers of the third Cook expedition (e.g., Beaglehole 1967). An alternative estimate that is sometimes used is Rev. William Ellis' 1823 estimate of five people per household (Ellis 1963, 76). Ellis had spent several years in the Society Islands and was fluent in that language and thus quickly understood Hawaiian. His estimate was based on two months' travel around Hawai'i Island and may be reasonable, but it was made well after contact, so King's earlier estimate is used here.[4]

When using archaeological data to compute house counts, an assumption must be made on the percentage of house sites in use at contact (the 1700s being the Contact era, given radiocarbon dating accuracy problems). This is difficult, for even in projects with extensive dating, only a few house sites are dated and probably not their spans of occupation. Recent, large-scale projects have shown that most surface ruins of house sites were in use in the 1700s (Cordy et al. forthcoming; Burtchard 1996; Kolb et al. 1997; Bishop Museum, forthcoming; Dixon et al. 2000). Thus, my calculations make the assumption that 100 percent of the surface permanent house sites recorded were in use in the 1700s; this may inflate the archaeological estimates.

The community land *(ahupua'a)* is used here as the unit of analysis within the region. *Ahupua'a* tend to be inland-heading rectangular-shaped lands on slopes or pie slice–shaped units where communities are valley based. Historic documents (tax records, censuses, etc.) clearly reference data to *ahupua'a,* and archaeological sites can be placed within *ahupua'a.* Indeed, the *ahupua'a* has been a basic unit of archaeological analysis in Hawai'i since the Mākaha, Hālawa, and Lapakahi studies of the late 1960s and early 1970s.

One archaeological limitation to estimating *ahupua'a* populations is that we rarely obtain a sample of all (or nearly all) of the households occupied at European contact. Continued occupation and urbanization of shorelines and intensive modern cultivation have destroyed sizable parts of the archaeological record in many *ahupua'a,* especially for many former high population areas. Urban O'ahu covers the former high population areas of Waikīkī, Honolulu, and Nu'uanu in Kona District, Kailua and Kāne'ohe Bay in Ko'olaupoko, and the lands around Pearl Harbor in 'Ewa. It is extremely rare to encounter entire archaeological records surviving in fertile, high population *ahupua'a* (e.g., Hālawa Valley on Moloka'i, Waipi'o and Waimanu Valleys on Hawai'i).[5] The areas with intact settlement patterns surviving tend to be the more remote, less fertile areas that were largely abandoned in the middle to late 1800s and that were not favorable for land-altering modern cultivation (e.g., Kaho'olawe; Lapakahi and parts of dry North Kohala, Kalāhuipua'a and 'Anaeho'omalu in arid South Kohala, and arid North Kona on Hawai'i Island; Kahikinui on East Maui). Consequently, methods need to be developed to estimate *ahupua'a* populations from incomplete archaeological records.

Problems with estimating Contact-era *ahupua'a* population also exist for the historical data. Early historical censuses and tax records and Mahele-era land records date to the 1830s–1850s, after sizable population decline. Censuses and tax records could be extrapolated back if one knew the contact population and could determine the percentage of decline by the date of the census information. Prior to 1989, we fairly confidently used Schmitt's (1968; 1971) population estimates of 250,000 to 300,000. In 1989, however, Stannard proposed vastly higher estimates of 800,000 to 1 million.

Stannard (1989) used a baseline figure of people per shoreline mile from King's findings at Kealakekua Bay in 1779 (six persons per household) and a series of assumptions that raised the estimate: (1) using eight people per household; (2) 100 percent of all coastlines inhabited; (3) a ratio of population of 3:2 for windward vs. leeward areas; and (4) interior regions being heavily occupied. Problems exist with each of these assumptions. Kealakekua, with 2,400 people, was a royal center, and such areas had much higher populations (e.g., Cordy 1994). Using a royal center as a baseline average is likely to yield an estimate that is too high — perhaps much too high. Windward areas do not seem to have had populations any larger than leeward areas based on archaeological, oral historical, and historical data (e.g., the size of irrigated *kalo* [taro] systems on Oʻahu, dryland systems on Hawaiʻi, and distributions of large *luakini heiau*, royal centers, and general population). Also, archaeology clearly shows that, generally, relatively few houses were present in inland areas (upper valleys or upland slopes several kilometers from the shore). These points suggest that Stannard's upward adjustments may have serious problems.

Yet Stannard's work still raises important questions about Schmitt's estimate. Stannard (1989) argues that the magnitude of the population drop between Cook's arrival in 1778 and the 1830s was much greater (such as 20:1) than that suggested by Schmitt's work. This implies high death rates and low birthrates and/or high infant mortality. The Hawaiian accounts indicate that the first large number of deaths of chiefs was in the 1804 *ʻokuʻu* epidemic, and they suggest this was the start of the epidemics (Malo 1839; ʻĪʻī 1959; Kamakau 1961; see also Bushnell 1993), so a 20:1 decline may be too large. But clearly, venereal disease arrived with Cook and spread quickly. Population replacement rates should have begun to decline dramatically due to sterility and venereal disease–related infant deaths (Bushnell 1993; Cartwright and Biddis 1972, 54–63).

In sum, there is no accepted contact estimate for the archipelago with which to extend back the census data (censuses, tax records, etc.). The evidence does not yet support vastly higher archipelago and island estimates based on the assumptions proposed; but there are also reasons to suggest the 250,000–300,000 estimates might be too low.[6] The best that seems possible is to estimate a population of 300,000 and above. For purposes of example in this chapter, I use 300,000 as a contact estimate for the archipelago to calculate the percentage decline for years of census and taxpayer data and thereby extrapolate contact estimates from these records. With these above methodological issues discussed, the rest of this chapter looks at three regional studies — entire *moku* (districts) of Contact-era times. These *moku*, as already noted, are Waiʻanae and ʻEwa on Oʻahu and Hāmākua on Hawaiʻi.

Waiʻanae District, Oʻahu

Waiʻanae Moku is one of the six traditional districts on Oʻahu that were part of the Kingdom of Oʻahu in the 1700s. Figure 7.1 shows the lands *(ahupuaʻa)* within the *moku:* Nānākuli, Lualualei, Waiʻanae, Mākaha, Keaʻau, ʻŌhikilolo, Mākua, Kahanahāiki, and Keawaʻula.[7]

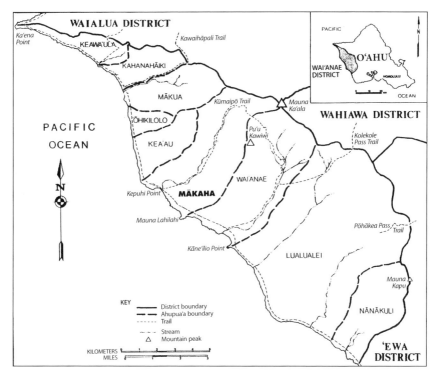

Figure 7.1. Map showing the lands *(ahupua'a)* of Wai'anae Moku, island of O'ahu (Cordy 2002, adapted from Green 1980).

Wai'anae Moku stretches for 32 km along the western leeward shore of the island and back up to the crest of the Wai'anae Range, the western of two mountain ranges on O'ahu.[8] This *moku* is characterized by older, wide, flat-bottomed, amphitheater valleys. The largest is Lualualei, 7.4 km wide along the coast and extending 8 km inland. Wai'anae and Mākaha are also large valleys, although not nearly as large as Lualualei. Wai'anae is extremely dry, with rainfall at the shore and in the lower valleys averaging ≤508–762 mm, while the upper valleys have 762–1,270 mm. Along the back ridgelines of Wai'anae and Mākaha Valleys and on Ka'ala, the highest peak on the island, rainfall is 1,524–2,540 mm. Only Wai'anae Valley had a perennial stream that reached the sea. (It also had Kamaile—a large, spring-fed coastal marshland.) The other valleys have intermittent streams, with Mākaha and two Lualualei streams flowing in their uppermost reaches.

Wai'anae Moku has been extensively studied archaeologically, including multiyear research projects in Mākaha by the Bishop Museum in the late 1960s and early 1970s (e.g., Green 1980), in Nānākuli by the State Historic Preservation Division in 1988–1991 (e.g., Cordy 2002a), and in Wai'anae from 1997 to the present by the Historic Preservation Division, Wai'anae High School's Hawaiian Studies Program, and the University of Hawai'i–West O'ahu (Cordy 2002b; 2003). Additionally, months of intensive survey were done across the back of Lualualei by AMEC (Dixon et al. 2003).

Most of Wai'anae Moku's surviving archaeological landscape is in middle and upper valleys, because modern housing has generally been confined to coastal areas, while sugarcane cultivation was restricted to the mid-lower valleys of Mākaha, Wai'anae, and Lualualei. Surprisingly, more of the coastal archaeological landscape survives than in many other urbanized areas due to the older age of much of the housing in this area (lacking the substantial bulldozing of modern house lots) and to the existence of undeveloped beach parks.[9] The archaeological landscapes in the interior of these valleys are the largest surviving on the island of O'ahu today.

Archaeological work in Nānākuli has identified an extensive dryland agricultural system in the upper valley consisting of approximately 120–140 ha of simple mounds, clearings, and short irregular terraces on slopes and short terraces across intermittent streams. Scattered among these fields were twenty-seven house sites (twenty-five of these with one to three structures, two with five structures), each interpreted as a household. There is one associated temple of minimal labor expenditure. It is estimated from reconnaissance survey that a few more house sites are slightly upslope in a small area of unsurveyed forest reserve land (three such sites have been briefly recorded). Thus, with thirty households in the upper valley, it is estimated that 180 people resided in the upper valley. This number is derived assuming that 100 percent of these households were occupied in the 1700s, multiplied by the household estimate of six people.[10] A small coastal scattering of houses is described in the historical records with an associated small temple recorded. Impressionistically, the historical sources suggest a population equal to the interior or twice its size. Agricultural fields had associated permanent houses, but also a large number of walled field areas had only temporary housing, suggesting that those farming the land lived elsewhere — probably near the shore. In 1855, ten taxpayers lived along the shore, yielding an estimate of forty households at contact and 240 people on the shore. An estimate of 420 people for Nānākuli Valley in the 1700s results from the archaeological and historical estimates.

In the adjacent large valley of Lualualei, archaeological and historical research shows permanent habitations only near the shore and 7–8 km inland at the base of the mountains. The inland housing is associated with dryland farming remains in most areas (where rainfall reaches and exceeds 1,016 mm) and with small sets of irrigated *kalo* in two stream tributaries at the northern end of the valley where spring-fed stream flow existed. The parts of the valley between the mountains and the shore have minimal agricultural remains (due to aridity) and scattered temporary housing. Lualualei has two coastal areas known through historic records and limited archaeology to have had small numbers of houses: Ulehawa and Māʻili (Cordy 2002a). Historic records suggest that five inland areas at the base of the Waiʻanae Range were other identified sub-*ahupuaʻa* land units at European contact: Pūhāwai, Mikilua, Pāhoa, Kauhiuhi, and Hālona. Recent archaeological work has identified at least 141 house sites across the back of the valley, clustered within the five inland land units (Dixon et al. 2003; Dixon 2002, pers. comm.).

Crude population estimates can be produced for Lualualei from historic records. In 1855, Māʻili (on the shore) had nine taxpayers (each representing a household). If Ulehawa had the same, eighteen households may have been along the shore in Lualualei. With 1855 populations considered to be 25 percent of those at contact, a coastal estimate of seventy-two households and 432 people would result for the 1700s. Of the five inland areas, Pūhāwai is one area where both Mahele land records and taxpayer census records seem complete. Pūhāwai had eleven taxpayers in 1855. This can be adjusted to forty-four households and 220 people at European contact. (This seems high for the small Pūhāwai area.) If the five inland areas had similar sized populations, 220 households result in an estimate of 1,100 people (again possibly too high if the Pūhāwai estimate is too high). This would yield a total crude estimate of 1,532 people for Lualualei.[11]

This historic-based estimate for inland Lualualei (1,100) is somewhat similar to the archaeological-based estimate for the back of the valley, where 141 households have been identified (with a small area yet to undergo intensive survey). Multiplied by six, with the assumption that all were occupied in the 1700s, we derive an estimate of 846 for the upper valley.

The next land to the north in the *moku* is Waiʻanae Valley, the only valley with a perennial stream flowing to the sea and with a large coastal spring-fed marshland. The marshland, Kamaile, was divided into sections *(moʻo)* of irrigated *kalo* land at European contact, covering 55 ha. The main stream had irrigated *kalo* from behind the sandy coast and a back-dune fishpond all the way up its length to the upper valley. Within the upper valley, additional irrigated *kalo* fields were present along tributary stream flats, descending as terraces down steep slopes (fed by springs and draining into the streams), and across gradual slopes between tributaries (with water from streams by canals). Some form of irrigated *kalo* cultivation was present in the intermittent Kawiwi drainage at its seaward end, where swampy land existed and drained into the perennial stream. Besides these fields, a large area was under intensive dryland cultivation and covered the slopes of the north side of the valley, next to the upper valley. This entire area contains descending rectangular fields with low terrace facings.[12]

We have not yet completely surveyed the upper-middle and upper valley of Waiʻanae. However, controlled sampling within the intensive dryland field system area found thirty-five house sites of one to five structures each (thirty of these have one to three structures)(Cordy 2001b). A common house type here is a low-walled, 200–300 m² rectangular enclosure (a house yard) with internal structures. (Very few temporary habitations are present in the upper valley, indicating that the farmers in this area were likely those that were living there.) Given the percentage of our survey coverage in the intensive dryland field area, we estimate that fifty-five house sites are present in this area. This accounts for 330 people. More houses are present up-valley around the irrigated *kalo* fields, and we estimate that altogether there were 500 people in residence in the upper-middle and upper valley. The lower-middle part of the valley and the shore are well recorded in the Mahele land records, identifying houses and fields, and archaeological projects here and there confirm the extent of the fields. The evidence indicates that two-thirds to three-quarters of the fields and population was in the lower valley at European contact. Thus, the archaeological estimate in the back of the valley can be used to yield a crude estimate for the entire valley of 1,500 to 2,000. This archaeological estimate is close to estimates derived from historic records. In 1855, Wai'anae had 106 taxpayers (households). Computing this as 25 percent of the contact population, 424 households would be estimated for the valley, in turn leading to an estimate of 2,544 persons (at six per household).

A slightly different approach can be used to estimate Wai'anae's population. The Mahele land records for Kamaile — the area with the large coastal *kalo* marsh — indicate that all strips of irrigated *kalo* fields *(mo'o)* were in use in the 1840s (Cordy 2001a). This is reasonable, despite the archipelago's population decline. By the 1840s, valleywide population decline from disease and emigration would have created vacant land, and it was the upper valleys that were substantially abandoned. But another likely form of emigration for upper valley residents was down to the vacant plots in the prime lands of the lower valley, with easier access to marine resources. Some of these areas remained fully used. The full-land situation in coastal Kamaile is of interest for contact population concerns. A thorough review of the Kamaile records identified thirty-four households with claimed awards in Kamaile and twenty-one other named householders who held land or houses (Cordy 2001a). Possibly fifty-five households were present, a likely close approximation of maximum population at European contact. Multiplied by six, this yields an estimate of 330 for Kamaile. The coastal lands along the stream behind Pōka'i Bay were of similar area and likely held as many people, as did the seaward end of the Kawiwi drainage and the areas extending up to the upper valley along the main stream. From this perspective, these areas may have held 1,320 people. When added to the archaeological estimate for the back of the valley, this yields an estimate of 1,820.

Mākaha is the next valley up the Wai'anae coast. This valley had a stream that flowed much of the year in the upper valley but that was intermittent in the lower valley. Irrigated *kalo* fields were identified archaeologically in the narrow stream flats of the upper valley. Dryland fields were found along the base of the slopes of the lower valley. The Bishop Museum's multiyear work here identified a number of house sites, mostly at the interface of the upper and lower valley. Historical documents describe a small coastal settlement and an associated small temple. Using the archaeological house counts and estimating the percentage of the settlement along the shore, there may have been 100 households in this valley (Green 1980, 79). This yields an estimate of 600 people — lower than the estimate from the 1855 tax records. Forty-two taxpayers (households) were present in 1855, which computes to 168 households and a population of 1,008 in the 1700s.

Kea'au and 'Ōhikilolo share the next valley to the north. This smaller valley is primarily a broad coastal plain with tiny, narrow intermittent tributaries descending to the plain. No population estimate has been calculated for this area, and I have no information on taxpayer counts at this time.

To the north, the next valley contains two lands: Mākua and Kahanahāiki. This is a larger valley, similar in size to Mākaha, with a broad lower valley. The Mākua side has several narrow side streams flowing from its upper valley. Kahanahāiki consists of the flat lower valley and gradual slopes at the base of the northern valley wall. These lands are only partially surveyed archaeologically (Cordy 2002a; Williams 2003), and no archaeological estimates of population have been computed at this time. In 1855 this area had twenty-one taxpayers (households), which yields a contact estimate of eighty-four households and 504 people.

The last *ahupua'a* of Wai'anae is Keawa'ula, a narrow strip of land along the base of the Wai'anae Range extending out to Ka'ena Point, the northwestern extremity of O'ahu. Archaeological survey found permanent dwellings and associated dryland fields only at one location: a small coastal flat not far from the Kahanahāiki border (Cordy 2002a). The actual number of house sites could not be determined due to post-Contact alteration, but the archaeologists estimated a population of 50–100 persons. In the 1820s missionaries had twenty-four students here, perhaps representing six families (four children/students and two adults/family) (Chamberlain 1826). Using six per family, an estimate of thirty-six people results. Using the 1823 missionary estimate of 142,000 (Schmitt 1973, 8), the 1820s population was 47 percent of that at contact. A contact population estimate of seventy-six people results. It seems unlikely that this land ever had more than 100 people in residence.

The Wai'anae Moku data are summarized in Table 7.1. There was a wide range of populations among this *moku*'s *ahupua'a:* large (Wai'anae), moderate (Mākaha and Lualualei), smaller, and one with a very small population. Wai'anae Ahupua'a (the largest population) is the only one noted in the oral histories and historical

Table 7.1. Waiʻanae District, Oʻahu: Population estimates for European contact.

Ahupuaʻa	Taxpayer-based estimates	Archaeological estimates	Combined estimates	Possible totals
Nānākuli			420	420
Lualualei			1,532	1,532
[Inland area]	[1,100]	[846]		
Waiʻanae	*2,544	1,500–2,000		1,500–2,544
Mākaha	1,008	600		600–1,008
Keaʻau ʻŌhikilolo	—	—		—
Mākua Kahanahāiki	504			504
Keawaʻula	**76	50–100		50–100

* Another estimate for Waiʻanae, based on Mahele land records (lower valley) and archaeology (upper valley), is 1,820.

** This estimate is derived from 1820s student counts.

sources to have been the residence of a high chief (Cordy 2002a). This land also had the only extensive irrigated *kalo* lands. It further contained nine of the twelve major temples *(heiau)* of the *moku* (those greater than 500 m² in size) (Cordy et al. 2003). The estimates for Waiʻanae Valley's population are similar to those of royal centers, such as King's estimate for Kealakekua and the estimate for Waipiʻo (to be seen shortly).

ʻEwa District, Oʻahu

ʻEwa was another of the six traditional *moku* on the island of Oʻahu at European contact (Figure 7.2). The data for this region are primarily historical, as relatively little archaeology has been done in this district. The archaeological landscape has been extensively altered by urbanization (expansion of urban Honolulu), military base construction (Pearl Harbor), and modern sugarcane cultivation.[13] ʻEwa is located in the center of the leeward, south shore of Oʻahu, around the three-fingered embayment of Puʻuloa (Pearl Harbor), and extends up to the center of the island. It is bounded inland to the east by the ridgeline of the Koʻolau Range and to the west by the ridgeline of the Waiʻanae Range. ʻEwa includes flowing streams that emerge out of the Koʻolau and Waiʻanae Ranges, cut through the descending central plateau, and empty into small floodplains along the edges of Puʻuloa. These floodplains are also watered by small natural springs. ʻEwa also includes an extensive, raised limestone plain to the west of the harbor (the ʻEwa Plains), an area of low rainfall and minimal, patchy soils.

At contact, the agricultural lands of ʻEwa were focused on the small floodplains

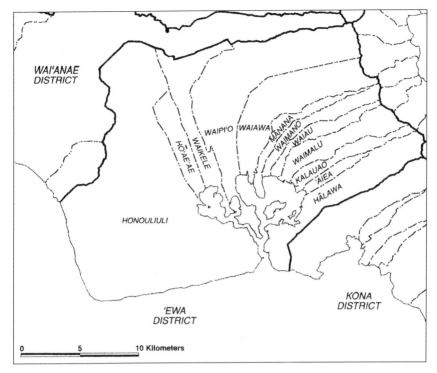

Figure 7.2. Map showing the lands *(ahupua'a)* of 'Ewa Moku, island of O'ahu (prepared by Eric Komori, Hawai'i Historic Preservation Division).

and adjacent slopes. *Kalo* was planted in the marshlands, watered by the streams and springs. Water drained from the taro fields into numerous nearshore fishponds of various sizes. Dryland crops and tree crops (notably bananas) were on the adjacent slopes. Some irrigated *kalo* cultivation is expected on stream flats in narrow upper valleys or gulches. In the one upper valley that has been surveyed, Hālawa, cultivation was solely dryland cultivation on small gradual slopes at the base of valley walls (Bishop Museum, forthcoming). On the lower central plateau, slopes between streams had dryland cultivation (often reported as sweet potato cultivation), but it is uncertain how far inland this prevailed. The 'Ewa Plains had very small patches of dryland cultivation (Tuggle and Tomonari-Tuggle 1997).

There were twelve *ahupua'a* lands in 'Ewa at contact (Table 7.2). Each had fisheries in the harbor, floodplains with irrigated *kalo* and fishponds, and interior lands (lower *kula*, upper valley stream/gulch drainages, and mountain forest). Honouliuli and Hālawa had larger coastal areas, with Honouliuli including the 'Ewa Plains and Hālawa the coastal flats at the eastern mouth of the harbor.

Permanent habitation was primarily around the edges of the floodplains, with

Table 7.2. Populations of ʻEwa Ahupuaʻa in 1831 and 1835.

Ahupuaʻa	1831 Total*	% District	1835 Total	% District	European contact estimate
East Loch					
Ahupuaʻa	27%		27%		
Hālawa	400	10	283	8	786
ʻAiea			51	1	142
Kalauao	440	11	186	5	517
Waimalu			230	7	639
Waiau	253	6	63	2	175
Waimano			132	4	367
Middle Loch					
Ahupuaʻa	29%		29%		
Mānana	256	6	214	6	594
Waiawa	913	23	263	8	731
Waipiʻo			513	15	1,425
West Loch					
Ahupuaʻa	44%		44%		
Waikele	723	18	464	14	1,289
Hōʻaeʻae			154	5	428
Honouliuli	1,026	26	870	25	2,417

*The 1831 census presents population for pairs of *ahupuaʻa* (Hālawa-ʻAiea, Kalauao-Waimalo, Waiau-Waimano, Waiawa-Waipiʻo, Waikele-Hōʻaeʻae). Only Mānana and Honouliuli have 1831 population figures just for their *ahupuaʻa*.

small scatterings/clusters of houses up narrow upper valleys/gulches, on the lower *kula* slopes, and in a few locations on the ʻEwa Plains. The Mahele land records document hundreds of house lots overlooking the irrigated *kalo* fields on the floodplains of ʻEwa. Archaeological survey in upper Hālawa Valley—the only upper valley yet surveyed in ʻEwa—shows small numbers of permanent habitations scattered up the north and south valleys. Also, the Mahele records show a small set of far inland awards along a gulch in Waipiʻo Ahupuaʻa. Archaeological work in Honouliuli has found a very few permanent house clusters on the Ewa Plains (Tuggle and Tomonari-Tuggle 1997), and small housing clusters up the inland-heading base of the Waiʻanae Range are suggested by the presence of small *heiau* (perhaps similar to the pattern found farther inland in the Schofield area of Waiʻanae Moku: Robins and Spear 1997). Historical and oral historical documents also mention a few scattered houses on the lower *kula* lands of the central plateau. The picture that results for the 1700s is of a high percentage of housing about the Puʻuloa floodplains.

ʻEwa is renowned in indigenous oral accounts (dynastic histories) for its population and for the taro cultivation and fishponds on its floodplains at Pearl Harbor (Kamakau 1991). The ruler of the Kingdom of Oʻahu occasionally resided here along the shore — perhaps at Māʻilikūkahi in Honouliuli in 1520–1540, and definitely at Piliwale in Waipiʻo in 1560–1580, Kalanimanuia in Kalauao in 1600–1620, and in later Kingdom of Hawaiʻi times, Kamehameha briefly resided in Waipiʻo (Cordy 1996; dates based on ruling genealogies with twenty years/generation). High chiefs also resided in these lands; for example, in 1620–1640 at Haʻo in Waikele and Kaʻihikapu, possibly in the Hālawa area (Cordy 1996).

Table 7.2 shows the distribution of population among the *ahupuaʻa* of ʻEwa Moku in the 1831 and 1835 censuses. In the 1831 census, in some cases pairs of *ahupuaʻa* were lumped together. In the 1835 census, figures are available for each *ahupuaʻa*. Several patterns are noticeable. In 1831, three areas had large populations: Honouliuli (1,026), Waikele-Hōʻaeʻae (723), and Waiawa-Waipiʻo (723). The 1835 data show the same pattern, with clarification of the status of the pairs. Honouliuli (870), Waipiʻo (513), and Waikele (464) stand out as the population centers of the 1830s, with 25, 15, and 14 percent of the district's population, respectively. These *ahupuaʻa* had the larger floodplains. At the other end of the spectrum, ʻAiea (51) and Waiau (63) had much smaller populations and also the smallest floodplains. Based on the Mahele land records on the size of floodplains (amount of irrigated *kalo* land), this 1830s distribution of population seems likely to match the 1700s pattern. Table 7.2 also presents estimated contact populations for this *moku,* extrapolating back from the 1835 census (36 percent of 300,000). These estimates are purely heuristic and are meant only to suggest what might be possible numbers. They do show a number of *ahupuaʻa* with larger populations — notably Honouliuli (2,417), Waikele (1,289), and Waipiʻo (1,425) — where high chiefs and rulers did reside.

Hāmākua District, Hawaiʻi Island

The last regional dataset to be examined is Hāmākua Moku (Figure 7.3), one of the six districts *(moku)* on Hawaiʻi Island. This information comes primarily from historic data sources, as part of a synthesis of settlement patterns for this district (Cordy 1994). Modern intensive sugarcane cultivation formerly took up the eastern two-thirds of the district, and most archaeological sites in this area are gone. The western one-third consists of larger valleys and marine benches that still contain much of their archaeological resources.

Hāmākua lies entirely within the windward area of the island. It is a well-

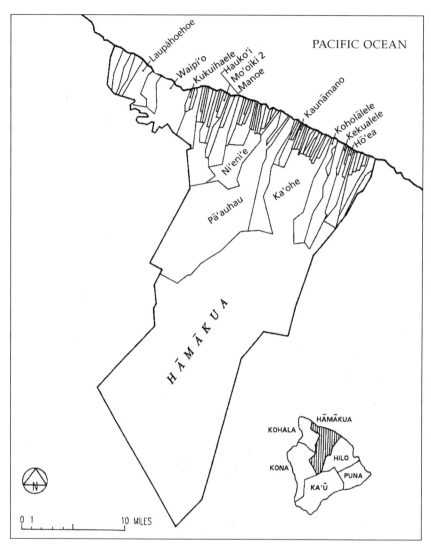

Figure 7.3. Map showing the lands *(ahupuaʻa)* of Hāmākua Moku, island of Hawaiʻi (Cordy 1994).

watered land, receiving >2,540 mm of rainfall annually, and it has numerous permanent streams. Hāmākua has 45 km of shoreline, consisting of larger valleys in the west on the older, eroding Kohala Mountains and gradual slopes cut by steep, narrow gulches in the eastern two-thirds of the *moku*. There are no coastal plains, and the slopes terminate in cliffs 100 m high. The larger valleys' bounding ridges end in sea cliffs 300 m high, with each valley having a separate embayment. The two large valleys of Waipiʻo and Waimanu have larger lower valley floors and narrow upper valley tributaries. Both have sizable streams that flow to the sea, fed in part by overflow from waterfall pools at the base of the lower valley walls. The eastern slope areas extend from the seacliff edge up through the lower, forested slopes of Mauna Kea, up and over Mauna Kea, and across a high interior plateau, terminating in the saddle between Mauna Loa and Hualalai at the 1,524 m elevation, overlooking Kona Moku and the calm, western leeward coast.

At European contact, Hāmākua was divided into approximately a hundred *ahupua'a* (community) land units. Seven of these *ahupua'a* were in the large valley region to the west. The two largest *ahupua'a* were those of Waimanu and Waipi'o, the large fertile valleys. Waimanu's land consisted only of its valley and valley walls, while Waipi'o Ahupua'a included its valley and tracts of adjacent uplands on both sides of the valley. The remaining ninety-odd *ahupua'a* of the eastern areas of Hāmākua were narrow rectangular strips of land, running from the cliff up the slopes (across house and farmland) and into the *'ohi'a-koa* rain forest. Most averaged 0.2–0.6 km wide and extended only 4.0–6.3 km inland. Some stretched farther inland, however, and one particularly vast *ahupua'a* — Ka'ohe — encompassed Mauna Kea and the interior plateau region.

The valleys were dominated by irrigated *kalo* systems on their valley floors. Waipi'o is renowned in the oral histories as the economic center of Hāmākua from at least the AD 1400s on. Its lower valley floor (1.2 km wide and 4.4–4.8 km long) was covered in irrigated *kalo* fields at European contact; the Hi'ilawe side valley had descending irrigated taro terraces, and the narrower upper valleys had extensive, descending irrigated terraces along stream flats. In contrast, in the eastern slope lands nearly all the *ahupua'a* had dryland fields located between the top of the sea cliffs and the edge of the *'ohi'a-koa* forest. With very high rainfall, dryland *kalo* was the staple here, planted in small fields, with bananas and sweet potatoes commonly mentioned in the records.

These Hāmākua lands — and more specifically, Waipi'o Ahupua'a — are renowned in the oral dynastic histories (e.g., Kamakau 1961; Fornander 1880; Cordy 2000). Waipi'o was the early ruling center of the Kingdom of Hawai'i, dating back to ca AD 1400 (using ruling genealogies and twenty years per generation). Indeed, from 1400 to 1600, Waipi'o was the sole ruling center of the kingdom. After AD 1600, Waipi'o was one of many ruling centers of the kingdom, where the ruler periodically resided. Not surprisingly, Waipi'o also had numerous major *luakini heiau* (national-level temples) and was the religious center of this district.

Housing was in a fringe along the coastal edge of the slopes and along the floors of the large valleys, mostly in the lower valleys. None of the records indicate inland populations on the eastern slopes. Historical data indicate no inland permanent populations in the forest, on Mauna Kea, or on the interior plateau, a finding supported by archaeological research (Cordy 1994). Waipi'o was by far

Table 7.3. Hāmākua Moku, Hawai'i Island: Population figures by parish or district.

Parish or district (# inhabited *ahupua'a*)	Est. at contact	1831–1832*	1842	1845	1849
Honopue (1)	128	59	47	30	
Lapāhoehoe (1)	220	101	81	80	**254
Waimanu (1)	591	272	218	199	
Waipi'o (1)	2,609	1,200	921	824	736
Eleio (7)	922	424	339	320	208
Kaupulena (11)	828	381	305	260	221
Kawela (10)	1,252	576	461	340	244
Honoka'a (10)	678	312	250	220	197
Pa'auhau (7)	917	422	338	270	264
Hanakamali'i (16)	1,152	530	424	280	233
Ka'ohe (10)	598	275	220	170	139
Ka'ala (12)	613	282	226	190	136
Totals	10,508	4,786	3,830	3,183	2,632

*Only Waipi'o's and the total district's populations are available for 1831–1832. The remaining 1831–1832 figures are estimates, calculated on the percentage of overall total population declines within Hāmākua from 1831–1832 to 1842. The 1831–1832 population figure for Waipi'o comes from Waimea Station Reports (1833, 2–3), and the 1831–1832 district total comes from Schmitt (1977, 12–13). 1842–1849 figures come from Lyons' (1842) Statisticks Book.

**This count is a combination of Honopue, Lapāhoehoe, and Waimanu.

the largest population center of this region in the 1700s, and oral histories indicate that it had been for many centuries (Kamakau 1961). This can be seen vividly in Rev. Ellis' journal of his trip around Hawai'i Island in 1823 (Ellis 1963); his party counted houses in Waipi'o, specifically focusing on this effort. They counted 265 houses and multiplied them by five people per household, yielding an estimate of 1,325 (using my figure of six per household, this estimate would be 1,590).

Table 7.3 shows the *moku* patterns for the 1831–1832 census and the 1842 census. Population of individual *ahupua'a* in the eastern two-thirds of the *moku* (the slope lands) was not recorded in the censuses; rather, populations were collected for sets of *ahupua'a* labeled as internal parishes (districts) by the missionaries. These sets include seven to twelve *ahupua'a* each. Table 7.4 present the average *ahupua'a* size for each set (total divided by number of *ahupua'a*). Both tables also include estimates for European contact. When originally studying the Hāmākua censuses in the early 1990s, I used Schmitt's (1977) estimate of 100,000 for Hawai'i Island, and the 45,792 census count for Hawai'i in 1832 is a 54 percent decline.

Table 7.4. Hāmākua Moku, Hawai'i Island: Estimates of average *ahupua'a* populations.

District or parish	No. of inhabited *ahupua'a*	European contact	1831–1832	1842
Honopue	1	128	59	47
Laupāhoehoe	1	220	101	81
Waimanu	1	591	272	218
Waipi'o	1	2,609	1,200	921
Eleio	7	132	61	48
Kaupulena	11	75	35	28
Kawela	10	125	58	46
Honoka'a	10	68	31	25
Pa'auhau	7	131	60	48
Hanakamali'i	16	72	33	27
Ka'ohe	10	60	28	22
Ka'ala	12	51	24	19

See Table 7.3 for district totals.These totals were divided by the number of *ahupua'a* per district to yield these *ahupua'a* estimates.

The figures document significantly that population was not evenly divided among the *ahupua'a* of Hāmākua. Waipi'o had about 25 percent of the population, with its contact estimate of 2,609 as a royal center compatible with that of Kealakekua and with *ahupua'a* having resident high chiefs in 'Ewa and Wai'anae. Individual *ahupua'a* in the eastern two-thirds of Hāmākua had quite small populations, ranging from 51 to 132 people per *ahupua'a*.

Conclusions

I believe that the regional cases discussed above do indicate that we can estimate (crudely) district or *moku* populations and population distributions at European contact using archaeological and historical data—or a combination of both kinds. The Wai'anae Moku case presented here shows that archaeological estimates of middle-upper valleys can be combined with estimates for the lower valleys derived from historical land and tax records to produce *ahupua'a* estimates. Care needs to be used with a thorough database and knowledge of the land records and places, and we are still refining the Wai'anae Valley estimates. If we compile enough of these regional studies from different sources, I believe that we will eventually be able to get a more realistic picture of island and polity population sizes at European contact.

The Waiʻanae, Hāmākua, and ʻEwa examples all show that populations varied considerably among the constituent *ahupuaʻa* of each *moku*. These internal differences seem to reflect patterns of the 1700s, seen in the area of their cultivated lands and the distribution of large *heiau*. Waiʻanae Valley's estimate (1,500–2,000 archaeological, 2,544 taxpayer), Waipiʻo's (2,609), and the lands of Honouliuli (2,417), Waikele (1,289), and Waipiʻo (1,425) in ʻEwa all show high populations consistent with King's estimate from the Kealekekua royal center (2,400). Yet other *ahupuaʻa* with much smaller populations were present. This pattern indicates that use of *ahupuaʻa* with the highest population estimates for calculating *moku* and archipelago estimates will likely highly inflate population estimates.

Interestingly, in the Waiʻanae Moku data — where we do have archaeological and later taxpayer-derived data — the latter estimates (based on a contact total of 300,000) are similar to and actually slightly higher than the archaeological estimates. These are interior Lualualei (846 from archaeology versus 1,100 from taxpayer records), Waiʻanae (1,500–2,000 archaeology versus 2,544 taxpayer; 1,820 Mahele land–based estimate), Mākaha (600 archaeology vs. 1,008 taxpayer), and Keawaʻula (50–100 archaeology versus 76 student records). This suggests a lower post-Contact *moku* decline in Waiʻanae than in Kirch's Kahikinui (see chapter 6, this volume). This may mean different rates of decline occurred among *moku*. Kahikinui and similar marginal lands may have had a greater exodus by the mid-1800s. In turn, some ruling centers and port towns (such as Lahaina and Honolulu) had considerable arrivals. These variations need consideration.

Also, the similarity of Waiʻanae's estimates derived from a 300,000 contact estimate to archaeological estimates may suggest support for the 300,000 estimate. The ʻEwa and Hāmākua cases with similarly derived census extrapolations show the main population centers — royal centers and those of high chiefs — consistent in size with King's Kealakekua Bay estimate. If higher contact estimates were used to extrapolate back the census data, populations for these centers would vastly exceed the Kealakekua Bay and the Waiʻanae Valley archaeological estimates, which seems suspect, as one would expect Kealakekua (as an active, important center) to be equally as large. Perhaps the 300,000 figure is not that far off.

Clearly, these are all only crude estimates, built on methodological building blocks (often assumptions) stacked one upon another. The extrapolations back from the census and taxpayer figures are purely illustrative examples. We are working on refining our Waiʻanae Valley estimates with additional work — more thorough archaeological survey and more archival work with the land records. While archaeologists and historians cannot yet produce highly accurate estimates, regional analyses involving archaeological information — as well as historical and oral historical information — can start to give us better views of population distributions, enable useful crude estimates, and help us refine assumptions for making population estimates. They point in directions where more research is needed.

As Kamakau noted in 1867, "In ancient times the land was covered with people" (1961, 235). Many people indeed resided in the Hawaiian Islands in the late 1700s. The Islands appear to have had the largest population in Polynesia. By the 1830s, the decline was dramatic and horrific, deeply worrying Hawaiians and outsiders alike. But just how many Hawaiians there were at contact remains to be seen. This question can be resolved only with continued research on these demographic issues.

Notes

1. There are cases of households with several *pā hale* (house lots), primarily for chiefs. The Mahele records identify a few lesser chiefs with a house lot in the land that they administered and another at the ruling center. The ruler, high chiefs, and retainers likely had multiple *pā hale*—one at each ruling center. Polity reconstructions using house counts from multiple royal centers need to address double counting issues. Most of the population had one *pā hale*.

2. Clark (1988, 25) suggests that some people lived only in "seasonal" houses in a shifting residential pattern. He argues that estimates need to add in these houses (count and divide by 2, assuming 2/household). He notes such housing is interpreted archaeologically in Lapakahi (Rosendahl 1972) and in Waimea (Clark 1987). I seriously question these conclusions, at least for the contact era. The 1820–1840 land records for Waimea and for dry Kohala clearly show people claiming permanent house lots, with no mention of a different pattern then or a few years earlier. I have worked extensively in both areas and have seen nothing beyond what I would label permanent and temporary habitations—nor have other researchers in recent years in Waimea. I would suggest that the archaeological interpretations of Clark and Rosendahl need reevaluation as to whether they truly reflect seasonal shifting settlement or some form of temporary housing (with the users likely living elsewhere in permanent habitations).

3. It is assumed here that King's and Ellis' counts per house are equivalent to counts per household. For Ellis, this is quite likely, as the *kapu* system had ended and multiple different-function houses within a household now became one. For King, one could argue that he might not have equated his "house" with households due to the multiple different-function houses that occurred with a house lot (Bushnell 1993, 120–121). The journal, however, in adding inland population to the Kealakekua Bay estimate, notes that there were "fifty families, or three hundred persons," or six per family (Cook and King 1784, 128). Men's houses (which were much larger), cookhouses, storage sheds, and family shrines (probably unroofed in most cases) would have been distinguishable and likely not confused.

4. While some twentieth-century social anthropologists have recorded higher average household sizes within Polynesia, it seems that one should be cautious about these, reflecting the impacts of modern medicine. There are average household counts from other Pacific ethnographic and historic records near contact and estimates from physical anthropology that suggest five to six persons per household is often a reasonable estimate

(Meggitt 1962, 160; Anderson 1970, 7; Houghton 1980). Also, Clark (1988) argues that use of average household estimates may not reflect changing composition of households over space and time. Estimates used here are contact estimates, so issues of possibly different average household sizes in earlier times are not relevant. Also, with no other averages than five to six, one must assume that these are reflective of different areas within the islands at contact until better data are available.

I find no basis for accepting Stannard's suggestion that the average household size was larger. He notes Loomis' identification of eleven people in a house in Kealakekua (Stannard 1989, 15), but this appears to be an example of a large household, representing one end of the range of household sizes, the other end being one person. He also cites the *Missionary Herald*'s 1823 publication of eight per house. This reference is for the port town of Honolulu (an immigrant hub with many nontraditional elements), and the count per house allows for "persons who are present from other districts and other islands" (*Missionary Herald* 1823, 315).

5. Even these areas have house-count problems. Hālawa includes coastal sand dunes that held houses where archaeological remnants are confusing mixes of postholes. Identifying the number of houses from postholes is extremely difficult, much less determining if they were permanent vs. temporary (Kirch and Kelly 1975).

6. Kaumuali'i, the ruler of the Kingdom of Kaua'i, stated before the *oku'u* in 1804 that his kingdom's population was 30,000 (Lisiansky 1814, 113), closely approximating Schmitt's (1971) estimate of 25,000, Dixon's of 27,000, and Cook's of 30,000 but below King's of 54,000 (Dixon 1789, 267). This bears some thought.

7. There is some debate whether Nānākuli and Lualualei were part of Wai'anae *ahupua'a*. Mahele land records identify Nānākuli as an *ahupua'a*. Lualualei's records are unclear. Here these lands are treated as if they were each *ahupua'a*.

8. One narrow strip of land (Wai'anae Uka) extended over the Wai'anae Range, across the central plateau of O'ahu, and up to the crest of the Ko'olau Range, the main eastern range (Cordy 2002a). Its archaeological record is limited and historical census information has problems. It is not covered in this chapter.

9. This situation is now changing. Over the last two years, beach parks have been improved, with archaeological work in some cases, and modern houses are being built, preceded by bulldozing.

10. These estimates differ slightly from those published elsewhere (Cordy 2002a) because an additional house was found in the survey area, three additional houses from the forest reserve, and 100 percent occupation of houses is assumed here.

11. These figures are different from those presented in Cordy (2002), where five people per household were used.

12. Green (1980, 12), using Monsarrat's 1878 and 1906 map data, estimated 226 ha of irrigated *kalo* land in Wai'anae. It is now clear that this estimate needs to be revised up with our new finds in the upper valley and the Kawiwi Swamp area. The 120+ ha intensive dryland fields also need to be included.

13. Extensive archaeology has been done only on the arid 'Ewa Plains, where very few permanent habitations were present (Tuggle and Tomonari-Tuggle 1997). The only other large projects have been around the Honouliuli floodplain (Wolforth et al. 1998) and in upper Hālawa Valley (Spear 1992; Bishop Museum, forthcoming).

8

BRENDA K. HAMILTON AND JENNIFER G. KAHN

Pre-Contact Population in the 'Opunohu Valley, Mo'orea

An Integrated Archaeological and Ethnohistorical Approach

> In the bottom of every valley, even to the recesses in the mountains, on the sides of the inferior hills, and on the brows of almost every promontory, in each of the islands, monuments of former generations are still met with in great abundance. . . . All these relics [belong to] a more populous era. — William Ellis

 Ellis' (1831) observation of the Society Islands, only forty-some years after contact, supports the mounting evidence that pre-Contact Pacific Island populations were much larger — and the impact of Western contact more disastrous — than what has traditionally been thought (e.g., Sand 1995, 213–254, 281–309; Spriggs 1997, 253–254; Stannard 1989). Clearly, a detailed assessment of pre-Contact population size in the Society Islands is in order.

The 'Opunohu Valley on the island of Mo'orea has one of the only pre-Contact Society Island settlement patterns that still remains intact, and thus it serves as an ideal locale for investigating pre-Contact population size from archaeological data. Here, a relatively long history of settlement survey work and more recent excavations is complemented by the rich ethnohistoric record from early European voyages to Tahiti and Mo'orea. This chapter integrates both lines of evidence, in addition to ethnographic, ethnobotanical, and soils data, in an effort to provide a more holistic, multiscalar perspective on demographic patterns at the time of contact.

Our investigation of Contact-period populations is based on reconstructions of Ma'ohi settlement and land use patterns. For 'Opunohu Valley and Mo'orea, estimates of population size at contact are drawn from archaeological and ethnohistoric data pertaining to Ma'ohi habitations. These numbers will be compared to carrying capacity estimates based on the potential productivity of the reconstructed pre-Contact Ma'ohi agricultural system and then discussed in light of overall population trends.

Population Estimates at European Contact

Early explorers' estimates of the population of Tahiti and Mo'orea convey the impression that the islands were densely populated (Table 8.1). Ma'ohi settlements appear to have been situated mainly along the coast and in lowland valleys in a dispersed pattern, but they also extended onto hillsides of the island interior; houses were typically interspersed among fruit trees and plantations (Bligh 1937, 2:423; Bougainville [1772] 1967, 228, 244; Forster 1778, 214; Hawkesworth 1789, 1:221, 3:11; Hooker 1896, 127, 133; Joppien and Smith 1988a, 3:46; Parkinson 1784, 23; Salmond 2003, 43–44).

In 1767, Robertson, shipmaster of the *Dolphin*, described Tahiti as "the most populous country I ever saw" and ventured an estimate of 100,000 on the basis of crowds that had gathered along the shore to view the ship (1948, 140, 234). A few years later, Cook similarly concluded that Tahiti was the most populous of the South Sea islands (Beaglehole 1967, 1:618; see also Sparrman 1944, 72). Islandwide population estimates proposed by Cook and J. R. Forster for Tahiti range from 120,000 to 204,000, based on the number of Tahitian war canoes participating in naval exercises in 1774 (Beaglehole 1955, 2:408–409; Forster 1778, 218). The Spanish explorers' estimates of 10,000 to 15,000-plus in the 1770s contradict a Spanish description of Tahiti as "thickly peopled"; for this and other reasons, Rallu views them as inaccurate (Corney 1913, 329; De Amat in Corney 1913, 16–17; Rallu 1991, 172; see Rallu, chapter 2 this volume).

The only early observer assessing Mo'orea's population in the Contact era is J. R. Forster, who proposed a population size one-fourth that of Tahiti's large peninsula, or roughly equivalent to 20,000 (1778, 218). Parkinson's comment that Mo'orea looked "like one continued village" suggests that Ma'ohi settlements were spread across much of the island (1784, 23). Adams later retrodicted an estimate of 40,000 for Mo'orea at contact, adding that 'Opunohu Valley once "swarmed with thousands of inhabitants" (Adams [1901] 1976, 4–6, 165).

Some later researchers have questioned the early estimates, after reconsidering the data from the historic naval exercises and/or warrior quotas given by Tupia, a Ma'ohi informant of Cook's (Hawkesworth 1789, 3:11, 57; Hooker 1896, 177). Revised estimates range from the 35,000 of McArthur (1967, 260) and Oliver (1974, 34) to 70,000 by Rallu (1990, 218; 1991, 172). The Tahiti estimates of the British explorers and later researchers imply a population of roughly 4,400 (based on McArthur and Oliver) to 26,000 (based on Cook in Beaglehole 1955, I2:408–409) for Mo'orea, if its population density was similar to that of Tahiti — a reasonable

Table 8.1. Survey of the available and most relevant ethnohistoric sources for Ma'ohi population.

Type of source	Date range	Strengths	Weaknesses
Early voyager accounts	1767–1789	Most valid for reconstructing Ma'ohi life at contact. Prior to significant European interference in Ma'ohi politics or economic affairs. Both written and pictorial representations.	Short stays, mainly in Matavai Bay, Tahiti. Many observations only from the sea, few inland observations. Local impacts. Tahiti-centric. Elite views. Some romanticized views of "noble savages." Start of depopulation cycle.
Later voyager accounts	1789 onward	Provide data on adoption of European goods and customs, effects of disease, depopulation.	Already significant post-Contact change. Protracted depopulation greatly affected social structure.
Missionary accounts	1797: arrival of *Duff* with LMS missionaries 1811: Mo'orea mission established at Papetoai	Long duration of stays (many missionaries lived on Mo'orea). Missionaries were interested in recording Tahitian culture and had some fluency in Tahitian. Best for documenting post-Contact transformations.	Biased by religious views and moral agenda. After widespread depopulation had occurred. Post-Contact changes in Ma'ohi settlement patterns and production systems evident.
Oral traditions	Early/mid-1800s (Henry) 1891–1893 (Adams)	Provide a Ma'ohi perspective. Legends sometimes have information about Tahitian culture difficult to find in other documents.	Collected well after contact, Henry is a second-hand account (Denning 1986). Dominated by male, elite focus? Dominated by accounts from Tahiti. Little information about daily lives.

assumption since similar physiographic characteristics and close proximity likely facilitated frequent interisland mobility and extensive social ties between kin networks (Hawkesworth 1789, 2:236; Hooker 1896, 95; Rallu pers. comm. 12/12/02; Rallu 1991, 175). Due to these similarities, Rallu posited a contact population of 9,300 for Mo'orea based on his estimate for Tahiti (1991, 172–175).

Missionary accounts provide estimates of Ma'ohi populations already in severe decline, due primarily to the impact of diseases and epidemics introduced as early as 1769 and secondarily to warfare among Ma'ohi chiefs (Adams [1901] 1976, 108, 149; Beaglehole 1955, 1:76, 98; Ellis 1831, 1:105–106, 2:65, 76; Forster 1778, 488; McArthur 1967, 244–247; Mortimer 1791, 64, 66; Rallu 1989, 131; 1990, 224; Wilson 1799, 403, 405). On Mo'orea, the sight of abandoned and burned-down houses became increasingly common as disease and warfare took their toll, almost completely depopulating some districts (Elder and Youl 1805 in McArthur 1967, 252; Ellis 1831, 2, 215; Mortimer 1791, 64–66; Thomas 2003, 63–64).

By 1815, Ma'ohi chiefs were lamenting the depopulation of their land and describing themselves as a "small remnant" of their former population (Ellis 1831, 1:104–105). Early-nineteenth-century missionary journals place Mo'orea's population at a mere 800 to 2,000 (Ellis 1831, 1:101–102; Gyles 1819 in Newbury 1961, 222–223; Jefferson to LMS, August 29, 1803, LMS Archives, in Oliver 1974, 35). The first censuses taken in Mo'orea in 1847 and 1848 put the island's population at 1,100 and 1,372, respectively (McArthur 1967, 255), suggesting a devastating 7-to-1 depopulation for Mo'orea (Rallu 1991, 172–175).

The discrepancies between early population estimates and their implications for the severity of the post-Contact Ma'ohi population collapse magnify the need to examine the archaeological evidence. Because the distribution and density of settlements are constrained by environmental factors, we will begin by considering the environmental setting of 'Opunohu Valley.

'Opunohu Valley: Background

Located in the Society Islands of French Polynesia, only 16 km from Tahiti, Mo'orea is a weathered high island of 133 km², with jagged peaks soaring up to 1,207 masl. The island is protected by fringing and barrier reefs (Jamet 2000, 8). Average rainfall ranges from roughly 2,250 mm near sea level to 2,750 mm at 100 masl, increasing significantly at higher elevations (5, 8, 13).

Extending from the coast 5 km inland, 'Opunohu is the largest valley on Mo'orea. Its numerous small upper-valley streams converge into a permanent stream that meanders through the lower valley. The upper valley contains tree- and fern-covered ridges, while the wide, mostly flat valley floor is covered by rich alluvium that is subject to inundation in places (Green 1961, 169).

In 1960, Roger Green and associates undertook a settlement survey and subsequent excavations in the valley in order to reconstruct inland settlement patterns and document the relationship between structure types in the prehistory of Tahiti (Green 1961, 1996; Green and Green 1967; Green and Descantes 1989). Excavation-based investigations were subsequently carried out by Lepofsky (1994, 1995; Lepofsky et al. 1996), Oakes (1994), Kahn (2003), and Kahn and Kirch (2001, 2003, 2004).

Though modern development has greatly modified the coastal zone and various factors inhibit the identification of surface remains in the coastal flat around 'Opunohu Bay (Green 1961, 169–170; Lepofsky 1994, 211, 281–288; Lepofsky et al. 1992, 305–306; Kirch 1986, 30), former settlement here is indicated by subsurface middens and local knowledge. In the lower valley about 1.5 to 3 km inland, extensive remains of settlement have been located. The steepest slopes of the innermost parts of the valley show no signs of settlement.

A Critical Assessment of the Ethnohistoric Sources

We examined available ethnohistoric sources to assess their potential usefulness for reconstructing aspects of Ma'ohi culture and estimating 'Opunohu Valley population size. While also consulting critical ethnohistoric reviews and historic works (e.g., Denning 1986; Lepofsky 1994, 1999; Newbury 1980; Oliver 1974; Salmond 2003), we reviewed three types of ethnohistoric literature: voyager accounts, missionary writings, and oral traditions and legends (see Table 8.1).

Critical analysis is needed to contextualize the explorer accounts in terms of the places visited, kinds of encounters, and length of anchorages (Lepofsky 1999; Lightfoot and Simmons 1998; Mills 2002; Rallu 1991; Stannard 1989). The early explorer accounts (1767–1789) to Tahiti and Mo'orea describe the islands in a state less affected by post-Contact transformations; thus we privileged them in our analysis (see Newbury 1980, 9). The early accounts are also more likely to be accurate due to their scientific orientation and more easily cross-checked because multiple crew members' journals are often available per voyage (Lepofsky 1999). To alleviate the bias of observations that were often made from the sea and filtered through a romanticized view of the "noble savage" (Denning 1986; Lepofsky 1999; Smith 1975), we focused on accounts from the most lengthy of the explorer visits and sought out references to inland visits (e.g., Banks in Beaglehole 1962, 1:252; Beaglehole 1962; Lamb et al. 2000, 60–62). Mo'orea was rarely visited during the forty years after contact; thus we use early accounts derived largely *from Tahiti* to reconstruct aspects of Contact-period Ma'ohi culture. Landscape renderings from several of the voyages often lack much detail (see Joppien and Smith 1985, 1:24, 2, 51), but in some cases specific cultivars can be seen (e.g., Webber's landscapes; see Joppien and Smith 1988b, 3:64, 65). From these sources, we gleaned information about Ma'ohi settlement patterns, settlement density, land use, and production systems.

Missionary accounts within the Society Islands become frequent after 1797, when the *Duff* landed with the first envoys of the London Missionary Society. While many missionary texts are filtered through moral agendas and ideological perspectives (see Smith in Lamb et al. 2000, 207), they offer a level of ethnographic detail rarely found in the voyager texts (see Edmond 1999; Newbury 1961). Mo'orea was a heavily missionized island, and several missionaries produced texts after 1811 while living for long periods at the Papetoai mission adjacent to 'Opunohu Bay (Newbury 1980, 37). We use these texts to supplement the voyager accounts with information specific to Mo'orea.

Tahitian oral histories, including chants, legends, myths, and genealogies, were recorded by Henry, Adams, and Emory from Tahitian informants. These collections of traditional Ma'ohi history were sometimes collected well after European contact (Gunson 1993). However, they offer occasional insight about family size and population, cultivars, warfare, and social production from an emic perspective not found in the other ethnohistoric documents.

Long-Term Population Trends in 'Opunohu Valley

By examining the available suite of radiocarbon dates for 'Opunohu Valley, we can infer long-term population trends while also tackling the important problem of site contemporaneity. Figure 8.1 shows the suite of ^{14}C dates from 'Opunohu Valley.[1] The series in the lower portion of the figure includes site-based dates and an off-site hearth; the other series is derived from off-site stream profiles (Green 1967, 130–182; Kahn and Kirch 2003, 33, fig. 5; Lepofsky 1995, 925–929; Lepofsky et al. 1996, 263; Oakes 1994, 77, table 4.2). Taking these dates as a rough proxy for population levels (see Dye and Komori 1992b), the overall pattern suggests that the valley began to be used as early as the seventh century AD. Population began to increase in the thirteenth century, with the most significant growth occurring in the later centuries prior to European contact (see Lepofsky 1994, 138, 298, 304).

Figure 8.2 plots the calibrated radiocarbon dates by 200-year time periods. Date spans for samples that overlap multiple time periods are counted in each period, breaking the nineteen site occupations into a total of twenty-nine potential date span segments. This figure shows that as many as fifteen, or 79 percent, of the 19 occupations could have taken place during the final interval prior to contact, from 1600 to 1767. Alternatively, the same period encompasses 52 percent

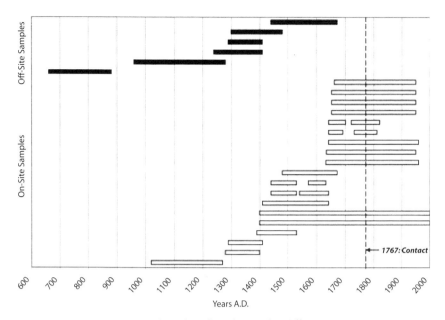

Figure 8.1. Calibrated radiocarbon dates from ʻOpunohu Valley.

of the twenty-nine potential date span segments for site-based dates. Overall, the pattern indicates that population may still have been increasing at the time of contact.

Habitation-Related Approaches to Estimating Population

We begin with a method commonly used by archaeologists: the *house-count approach*, wherein the total quantity of dwellings in an area is multiplied by a putative household size based on historical, ethnographic, or modern data (Cook 1972, 13; Hassan 1981). Several factors can affect the estimation of population from habitation remains. Those addressed in this chapter are family size; activity patterning and extent to which dwellings are used for specialized purposes; length of occupation and extent of reoccupation; and contemporaneity (Brown 1987, 16; Casselberry 1974; Cook 1972; Hassan 1981, 64, 73; LeBlanc 1971; Schacht 1981, 125, 131).

Implementing the House-Count Approach in ʻOpunohu Valley

Our calculation of pre-Contact population via the house count begins by summing the two types of Maʻohi houses in the valley—*fare haupape* (rectangular houses) and *fare poteʻe* (round-ended houses)—usually visible as curbstone out-

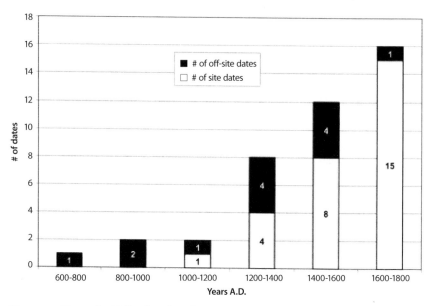

Figure 8.2. 'Opunohu Valley date distribution.

lines situated on naturally occurring flats or constructed terraces. The *fare pote'e* are thought to have served as houses for chiefs and lesser elites, receptions, and meetings, whereas the relatively smaller and architecturally simpler *fare haupape* may have functioned as commoner residences or craft activity areas (Davidson 1967; Ellis 1829; Green and Green 1967; Handy 1932; Kahn 2003; Oliver 1974; Orliac 2000). Archaeological survey and excavation records provide data for eighty-seven pre-Contact houses in the valley, up to eighty-five of which could have been occupied contemporaneously (Green 1967; Green and Descantes 1989; Kahn field diaries 1999–2003; Kahn 2003; Kahn and Kirch 2003, 2004; Oakes 1994).

Of fundamental importance to the house-count approach is the selection of an appropriate household size (Cook 1972). Ethnohistoric descriptions of Ma'ohi houses typically pertain to the residences of elites such as chiefs and their retinue, not to the average Tahitian family (Banks in Hooker 1896, 177; Ellis 1829, 2:66–68; Mortimer 1791, 46; Wilson 1799, 329). Such houses were crowded, occasionally sheltering up to sixty inhabitants who slept side by side on the floor (Mortimer 1791, 61–62; Smith 1813, 67; Wilson 1799, 358). For example,

> [T]he floor is the common bed of the whole household, and is not divided by any partition. The master of the house and his wife sleep in the middle, next to them the married people, next to them the unmarried women, and next to them at a little distance, the unmarried men; the servants, or Toutous, as they

are called, sleep in the open air, except it rains, and in that case they come just within the shed. (Banks in Hooker 1896, 134)

Though household social status was unspecified, Wilson noted an average Tahitian family size of six (1799, 184), whereas Oliver (1988, 43) later described household clusters (*utuafare*) of five to twenty persons interrelated by family ties. J. R. Forster mentioned that the largest Tahitian houses contain several families (1778, 214). Coconut and breadfruit origin legends recorded by Henry refer to family sizes of five and six, respectively (1928, 422–426).

Considering this wide range of numbers, we decided to examine the distribution of house sizes in the valley (Figure 8.3).[2] This facilitated the delineation of three size categories: (a) less than or equal to 45 m², with a mode of 10–15 m²; (b) 45 to 80 m², with a mode of 50–55 m²; and (c) 120 to 170 m². Interestingly, the average rectangular house size of 24 m² reported by early observers (Banks in Hooker 1896, 134; Hawkesworth 1789, 3:18) is close to that for ʻOpunohu Valley (mean = 26.77 m² for rectangular; 54.94 m² for round-ended houses). We assigned a household size of five to the smaller houses, twenty to the largest houses where chiefs may have lived, and twelve to the middle-sized houses, which might have been used by upper-class households or extended families within the same lineage or "House Group" (Kahn 2003). The following calculations give a resulting total of 575 persons in eighty-five houses:

- 65 houses measuring ≤ 45 m² in area x 5 p/household = 325 people
- 14 houses measuring >45 and <80 m² in area x 12 p/household = 168 people
- 3 houses[3] measuring >120 m² x 20 p/household = 60 people
- For the additional 3 houses not shown in the figure that lack dimensional data (2 rectangular and 1 round-ended), average sizes are assumed, corresponding to 2 5-person households plus 1 12-person household size of 12 = 22 people.

In light of the perishable nature of Maʻohi house construction, it is also important to estimate the number of houses not represented by surface structural remains in ʻOpunohu Valley. Many houses were built without (or later robbed of) curbstones, and excavations in terraces lacking surficial house remains have sometimes indicated residential functions for those terraces (Forster 1777, 1:348; Kahn and Kirch 2003; Lepofsky 1994, 207; Sparrman 1944).

Adjusting the Model for Underrepresented Houses. The ʻOpunohu Valley site records include data for 132 house terraces and living flats that lack definitive surface remains of house structures, as well as eighty-eight isolated pavements (Green 1961; Green and Descantes 1989; Kahn and Kirch 2003; Lepofsky 1994).

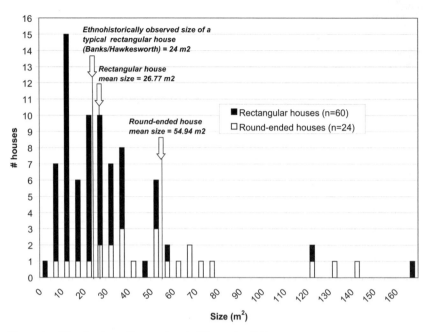

Figure 8.3. Distribution of house sizes in 'Opunohu Valley.

Isolated pavements may have been associated with destroyed shrines, former houses, and/or the remains of less permanent residences or activity areas (Descantes 1990, 43, 79; Green 1961, 171–172). Assuming that two-thirds of the eighty-eight pavements were associated with either a shrine or a temporary dwelling or activity area, we are left with twenty-nine pavements that may have been associated with a permanent residence.

If we assign one house to each of the 132 terraces and living flats and twenty-nine pavements, the number of houses in the valley then increases by 161. The corresponding household sizes are taken to be proportional to the ratio for the eighty-four existing houses shown in Figure 8.3: 77.4 percent, households of five; 16.7 percent, households of twelve; 6 percent, households of twenty. The calculations are

$$(.774)(161)(5 \text{ pp}) + (.167)(161)(12 \text{ pp}) + (.060)(161)(20 \text{ pp}) =$$
$$1{,}139 \text{ additional persons,}$$

thus increasing our population from 575 to 1,714.

A Reconsideration of Terraces. Recent excavations by Lepofsky (1994, 159–204) have found that not all terraces originally coded as agricultural ultimately showed evidence of agricultural activity. Some appear instead to have had domestic functions. In addition, there are at least 193 functionally undifferentiated terraces in the valley, some of which may have functioned as house terraces (Green and Descantes 1989; Kahn field notes 1999–2003; Lepofsky 1994).

Assuming that the terrace excavations are representative, we will reassess the function of 26 percent, or 120, of the valley's estimated 463 agricultural terraces that were surveyed, reflecting the proportion of test excavation units that did not yield diagnostic evidence of agricultural activity (Descantes 1990, 85; Green and Descantes 1989; Kahn field notes 1999–2003; Lepofsky 1994).

In general, terraces in 'Opunohu Valley were either residential or agricultural or are associated with religious structures or other features. The valley's relative distribution of structural remains among these three overarching functional categories is roughly 20 percent, 40 percent, and 40 percent, respectively, based on our review of structural evidence presented by Descantes (1990, 85). It follows that a residential function may be postulated for 20 percent (or 24) of the 120 terraces previously coded as agricultural, as well as 20 percent (or 39) of the 193 functionally undifferentiated terraces, thereby increasing the house count by 63 (assuming one house per terrace). If we again assume a household size ratio that mirrors the existing houses, we then have

$$(.774)(63)(5 \text{ pp}) + (.167)(63)(12 \text{ pp}) + (.060)(63)(20 \text{ pp}) =$$
$$445 \text{ additional persons,}$$

increasing the population from 1,714 to 2,159.

Specialized Activity Areas. Cook (1972, 13) defines the house dwelling as "the locus of the simplest but most important vital functions, eating, sleeping, reproduction, and care of the young . . . the space to which every human being must have access if he is to survive." Yet this definition does not neatly correspond to examples of traditional Ma'ohi dwellings. Ethnohistoric accounts suggest that each Tahitian family typically had one or more houses for sleeping and one or more cook houses or sheds; upper-class families tended to have additional residential structures such as a shelter for craft activities, a canoe house, and a steam house (Oliver 1974, 44, 162; Orliac 2000, 49). Reports that some houses served multiple functions further complicate the picture (Hooker 1896, 134). Because classification of Ma'ohi house structures is limited to *fare haupape* or *fare pote'e,* a closer examination is warranted (after LeBlanc 1971).

Excavations of twelve house sites in 'Opunohu Valley indicate that both *fare haupape* and *fare pote'e* could have served specialized functions such as tool working or wood sculpting or residential functions. Table 8.2 shows that 50 percent of the twelve houses were used for sleeping, and sleeping area represents 37 percent of the overall area. Granted, the sample is small and biased toward larger

Table 8.2. Function of space in 'Opunohu Valley excavated houses.

Site no.	Area (m^2)	Functional interpretation
Rectangular houses (*fare haupape*)		
Sleeping houses:		
ScMo-158 (period III)	15	sleep house (*fare ta'oto*)
ScMo-171A	29.25	50% primary sleeping house for craft specialist; 50% specialized function (adze production) (reinterpreted from Oakes 1994 by Kahn and Kirch 2003)
ScMo-171B	35	sleep house (*fare ta'oto*)
ScMo-171C	24.75	sleep house (*fare ta'oto*)
Special-purpose houses:		
ScMo-4B	12.96	specialized function: house for spectators of the dance or dance dressing hut
ScMo-103C (period III)	27	likely specialized function
ScMo-123A	13.5	specialized function
Round-ended houses (*fare pote'e*)		
Sleeping houses:		
ScMo-4A	81.27	sleep house (*fare ta'oto*) of lesser elite
ScMo-170	72	sleep house (*fare ta'oto*) of lesser elite
Special-purpose houses:		
ScMo-103C (period III)	154.44	specialized function: god house (*fare ia manaha*)
ScMo-120B	50	specialized function: wood-sculpting locale, possible *fare ia manaha*
ScMo-158D (period IIIb)	136.08	specialized function: *fare arioi* or meeting house
Total area:	651.25	
Total sleeping area:	242.65	→ 37% of total area was used for sleeping
Total special-activity area:	408.61	→ 63% of total area was used for special activities
# sleeping houses	6	→ 50% of houses were used for sleeping
# special-activity houses	7	→ 58% of houses were used for special-purpose activities*

*Sum of sleeping house and special-activity house counts exceeds 100% because one house has dual uses)

Sources: Green 1996, 221–222; Green and Green 1967, 175; Green et al. 1967, 139–140; Kahn 2003; Kahn and Kirch 2003; Kahn and Kirch 2001, 10; Oakes 1994, 109, 113; Orliac 1982, 237, 283; 1984, 237

houses, which we believe are more likely to be specialized. Yet until more data are available, it seems reasonable to reduce the population estimate by 50 percent to 1,080 to compensate for the specialized use of houses.

Contemporaneity. A comment made by J. R. Forster in 1778 while visiting Tahiti suggests that house occupancy was high: "All the houses are filled with people. . . . Wherever we walked we found the roads lined with natives, and not one of the houses was empty" (1778, 214). Nine of the twelve excavated house sites in 'Opunohu Valley show evidence of multiple occupations or episodes of refurbishment, such as double posthole patterns or curbstone border modifications, which may reflect a relatively long occupation and house use-life (Davidson 1967, 121–127, 134; Green and Green 1967, 166–169; Kahn 2003; Kahn and Kirch 2001, 2003; Oakes 1994, 78).

Site contemporaneity may be roughly approximated through an examination of the temporal data. The twenty-five radiocarbon dates obtained from valley sites (habitations, agricultural sites, and an off-site hearth) together represent a total of nineteen discrete occupations. Figure 8.1 shows that the dates for eleven of the nineteen site occupations (58 percent) cover much of the century prior to 1767 (first European contact) and may potentially be roughly contemporaneous. Assuming a 58 percent contemporaneity of houses at contact, we must then reduce our population estimate from 1,080 to 626. The resulting density across the estimated 2.85 km² of survey area is 220 p/km².

Implementing the Dwelling-Area Approach in 'Opunohu Valley

Although the house-count approach produces a culturally relevant and historically grounded approximation of the valley's population, for the sake of comparison we will also apply an alternative method. The *dwelling-area approach* typically divides the amount of per-person dwelling area derived from ethnographic studies into the total area covered by dwellings (Hassan 1981, 72–73). A commonly used measure is Naroll's 10 m² of dwelling area per person, based on his analysis of ethnographic data from eighteen traditional societies worldwide (Naroll 1962, 588; Schacht 1981, 128). Brown (1987), in his own Naroll-inspired reanalysis of floor area and population size, examined data from thirty-eight traditional societies, but unlike Naroll he explicitly considered intercultural differences and specialization of dwelling space. His result, which we apply here, is a revised measure of 6.1 m²/person (32). The calculations are as follows:

A. *Extant Houses.* Total area of 85 extant, potentially contemporaneous houses = 2,775.49 m².

B. *Adjustment for Nonextant Houses.* Of the 161 hypothetical additional houses, 115 may have been rectangular and 46 round-ended (if we assume the same 71.3 percent : 28.7 percent rectangular-to-round-ended ratio as for extant houses).

    1. 115 houses x [average area of a rectangular house] = 115 x 26.77 m^2
    = 3,078.55 m^2

    2. 46 houses x [average area of a round-ended house] = 46 x 54.94 m^2
    = 2,527.24 m^2

    3. Total additional habitation area = [1] + [2] = 5,605.79 m^2

C. *Adjustment for Functionally Reassigned Terraces.* We assume that the 63 additional house terraces reassigned in this step held 45 rectangular and 18 round-ended houses (again following the 71.3 percent : 28.7 percent ratio for existing structures).

    1. 45 x [average area of a rectangular house] = 45 x 26.77 m^2 = 1204.65 m^2

    2. 18 x [average area of a round-ended house] = 18 x 54.94 m^2 = 988.92 m^2

    3. Total additional habitation area = [1] + [2] = 2,193.57 m^2

By dividing the sum of (A), (B), and (C) by Brown's measure of 6.1 m^2/person, we obtain a population size of 1,734 people. After accounting for specialized activity space and contemporaneity, our estimated population decreases to 372 — approximately 40 percent lower than the house-count estimate of 626, yet resulting in a fairly high density: 131 p/km^2 (see Table 8.3).

Despite the divergence in estimates, we contend that the actual population would have been at least as high as the house count of 626. First, the strength of the house-count figure lies in the fact that it is contextually grounded, using both ethnohistoric and archaeological data. Second, our assumptions are very conservative. Other than hypothesizing houses for some documented terraces and pavements that lacked residential remains, we did not attempt to quantify the large number of additional houses thought to formerly exist. Low visibility and difficult access hindered the survey in parts of the valley, and many houses may have had no visible curbing or terracing (Green 1996, 221; Green and Descantes 1989, 7; Lepofsky 1994, 213).

On the 'Opunohu coastal plain, modern development and postdepositional disturbance have destroyed most evidence of ancient settlement (Green 1961, 169). Yet an "extensive but thin coastal midden" runs along both sides of 'Opunohu Bay, dating from European contact back to the thirteenth century; local knowledge suggests former coastal settlements; and four pavements were found on the inland edge of the coastal flat (Descantes 1990 14; Green 1961, 169; Rappaport and Rappaport 1967). The ethnohistoric literature similarly documents extensive

Table 8.3. Comparison of habitation-based estimates of valley population at contact.

Procedural steps	Population Estimates	
	House count, variable-sized households	Habitation area, Brown's 6.1 m²/pp
A. Existing houses	575 pp in 85 houses	455 pp using 2,776 m² dwelling space
B. Nonextant houses putatively assoc. with "houseless" house terraces, living flats, isolated pavements	+ 1,139 pp (161 add'l houses)	+ 919 pp (5,606 m² add'l dwelling space)
C. Nonextant houses on function-ally reassigned terraces	+445 pp (63 add'l houses)	+360 pp (2,194 m² add'l dwelling space)
Totals, prior to adjustment:	2,159 pp	1,734 pp
D. Adjustment for specialized ac-tivity areas (50% of *houses* used for sleeping; 37% of total house *area* used for sleeping)	2,159 × 50% = 1,080 pp	1,734 × 37% = 642 pp
E. Adjustment for contemporaneity (58%)	1,080 × 58% = 626 pp	642 × 58% = 372 pp
F. Resulting density in surveyed area	220 pp/km²	131 pp/km²

settlement along Tahiti's coast (Beaglehole 1955, 1:120; Forster 1778, 214; Hooker 1896, 127; Tobin in Oliver 1988, 96).

From this evidence, we surmise that the 'Opunohu Valley coastal areas likely held *at least* as many habitations as the interior valley (see also Lepofsky 1999, 19). At a minimum, then, our house-count estimate would need to be doubled to 626 x 2 = 1,252 inhabitants.

The Maximum Carrying Capacity Approach to Estimating Population

The analysis of carrying capacity provides an alternative line of evidence for es-timating maximum population size. Here we use Hassan's definition of carrying capacity (K) as the theoretical upper limit to which population might grow (1981, 164). Our assessment of carrying capacity resembles the approach used by many archaeologists in the Pacific (e.g., Bellwood 1972; Green 1973; Groube 1970; Shawcross 1970) in that it assesses the potential productivity of the environment within which settlements are situated. Our method estimates the amount of staple starch that could be produced and the population that could theoretically be supported if all available land was used for subsistence production.

The following reconstructed productivity model is intended to represent the variety of Maʻohi subsistence cultivation modes and land use patterns. It is grounded in diverse lines of evidence, including archaeological research (e.g., Lepofsky 1994), ethnohistoric data (e.g., Bligh 1937; Forster 1778; Hawkesworth 1789), ethnographic analogs (Kirch 1994, 1991; Kirch and Yen 1982), ethnobotanical observations (e.g., Wilder 1928), and soils data (Jamet 2000).

Zones of Cultivation

The Maʻohi production system spanned three physiographically distinct cultivation zones (see Lepofsky 1994, 63–66): the flat *coastal zone* (4 percent of ʻOpunohu Valley), which includes the coastal strand and plain; the *intermediate zone* (56 percent of the valley), which is mostly dominated by gentle to moderate slopes of 5–50 percent and extends from the inland valleys partway up the valley walls; and the *mountainous interior* region/upper valley walls (40 percent of the valley), characterized by medium to steep slopes of 50 percent or higher (Jamet 2000). Each of these zones offers a unique agricultural and agronomic potential.

It is primarily in the intermediate zone that ʻOpunohu Valley's ancient cultivation system is still visible today, in the form of terrace complexes and barrage pondfields (Lepofsky 1994, 152). Green classified the agricultural terraces as either *dry*, with moisture deriving only from rainwater, or *wet*, designed to hold water diverted from a stream or runoff (1961, 171). The wet terraces and barrages were probably used to cultivate taro or other aroids, whereas a combination of crops could have been grown on the dry terraces (Lepofsky 1994, 152). Repeated fire clearance associated with pre-Contact shifting, or swidden, cultivation appears to have been responsible for the large tracts of *Dicranopteris (Gleichenia) linearis* fern land now present on the slopes of the valley (Fosberg 1991, 19; Jamet 2000, 13; Lepofsky 1994, 114). Valley-floor trench excavations suggest that agriculture was established throughout the valley by the eleventh to thirteenth centuries AD, with landscape clearing continuing until European contact (Lepofsky 1994; Lepofsky et al. 1996). Other evidence such as breadfruit fermentation pits, coconut shell graters, identified traces of coconut, and breadfruit in excavations and sediment cores and observations of naturalized subsistence cultivars at many sites further guide our zone-based reconstruction (Green 1961, 169; Green and Descantes 1989; Kahn site records 1999–2002; Lepofsky 1994, 114, 193, 277, 289–290; MacDaniels 1947, 44; Parkes 1997, 192; Wilder 1928, 18).

Perspectives on the Maʻohi Subsistence Production System

Whether around houses or in plantations, the practice of tree cropping typified Maʻohi subsistence agriculture in the coastal zone, with taro cultivation likely prevailing in the marshy areas (Beaglehole 1955, 1:120; Cook in Hawkesworth 1789, 3:18; Ellis 1829, 358; 1831, 1:16–17, 43; Forster 1778, 162–163; Gore 1767 in Lamb et al. 2000, 60; Lepofsky 1994, 63–64). Viewing the eastern end of Moʻorea in 1767, Wallis described "the coast just within the beach [as] covered with cocoa-nut, bread-fruit, apple, and plantain trees" (in Hawkesworth 1789, 1:234). Of Tahiti's coastal zone, Forster noted,

> The whole ground is covered with coconut and breadfruit trees, which yield the chief subsistence for its inhabitants; all is interspersed with plantations of bananas, young mulberry trees for the manufacture of their cloth, and other useful plants, such as yams, eddoes [taro], sugar canes, and many others too tedious to enumerate. Under the shade of these agreeable groves, we every where behold numerous houses. (Forster 1778, 214)

In their 1805 description of the inland intermediate zone on Moʻorea, the missionaries Bicknell and Henry observed tree crops interspersed with houses at the back of the valley (in Green 1967, 221–222; see also Banks in Hooker 1896, 74; Parkinson 1784, 23). Two paintings of ʻOpunohu Valley in 1777 by Webber depict coconut and other trees along the coastal strand and, on inland slopes, dense stands of broad-leaved trees interspersed with putative fields of swidden cultivation and abandoned fern land (Joppien and Smith 1988b, 3:64–65). Inland on Tahiti, early visitors saw indications of swidden cultivation involving yams, sweet potato, taro, and bananas (Bligh 1937, 1:397, 2:40) and evidence of clearance by fire (Bligh 1937, 424–425; Forster in Sparrman 1944, 72–73; Hawkesworth 1789, 3:2). Plantings of aroids were irrigated along streams using barrage systems and water diversion channels (Forster 1777, 1:341–342; Forster 1778, 52; Lepofsky 1994, 62; Wallis in Hawkesworth 1789, 1:219).

Descriptions of the interior mountainous zone tend to describe steep, tree- and fern-covered ridges (e.g., Ellis 1831, 1:18, Hawkesworth 1789, 3:11). *Feʻi* bananas growing on precipitous cliffs were apparently gathered by climbing ropes of bark (Banks in Hooker 1896, 106–107; Parkinson 1784, 35). Sugarcane and bamboo may have also grown here (Lepofsky 1994, 66).

Subsistence Cultivars and Cultivation Modes

As seen in Table 8.4, the range of subsistence crops grown by the Ma'ohi was diverse. Taro (especially *C. esculenta*) was one of the most important starch-producing cultivars; under irrigation, it could produce the highest yields per hectare of any other traditional Ma'ohi cropping system (Kirch 1994, 183; Lepofsky 1994, 73–74; Oliver 1974, 249–250). Breadfruit was noted as being the "staff of life" for Tahitians (Ellis 1831, 1:40). Its seasonality influenced the naming of months (Oliver 1974, 245), and it played a central role in oral traditions (Henry 1928, 422) and communal feasts such as mass breadfruit bakings or *opio* (Davies and Darling 1851, 169; Ellis 1831, 1:40, 42; Oliver 1974, 226–228). Bananas, both *Australimusa* and *Eumusa*, also held a prominent position in the Ma'ohi diet. The roster of starchy crops was supplemented by yams *(D. alata* and *D. bulbifera);* giant taro *(Alocasia);* and sweet potato. (See Table 8.4 for additional references.) The availability of productivity data for these major crops, grown under traditional cultivation modes, allows us to incorporate them into our model.

The major starchy subsistence cultivars were typically grown in one of four different cultivation modes. The multistoried *arboriculture* mode was vital to the Ma'ohi production system. Here, breadfruit and coconut figured prominently in the upper canopy, bananas in the middle story, and yams, sweet potato, and taro were often grown in the lower story. Less important subsistence cultivars in tree-cropped areas could include *vi* apple, mountain apple, pandanus, sugarcane, arrowroot, *nono,* ti, and edible hibiscus (Fosberg 1991, 20; Kirch 1991, 122; Kirch 1994, 181–182; Kirch and Yen 1982, 39; Lepofsky 1994, 51–52, 54–57). Our model, detailed in Table 8.5, takes the average of two levels of arboriculture yields that were observed by Kirch (1994) on Futuna: 12.46 t/ha/yr.[4]

The second major cultivation mode was *dryland swidden cultivation* plots, likely involving yams, aroids, and bananas. For productivity data, we will again use Futuna as an analogy (Kirch 1994). Here, with a three-year successive cultivation cycle of yams, dryland taro, and *Eumusa* bananas followed by an approximate ten-year fallow period, roughly three-quarters of arable swidden land is under fallow at any given time, resulting in an average annual yield of staple starch of 5.41 t/ha/yr (Kirch 1991, 119–120; Kirch 1994, 113–123, 156, 187, 342; Lepofsky 1994, 57–59).

Often interspersed with tree crops where conditions permitted, the *wetfield cultivation of aroids* (mainly *Colocasia esculenta*) involved true irrigation or swampland drainage to control moisture, using terraces, raised beds, and/or barrages (Lepofsky 1994, 59–63; Spriggs 1984). Irrigated taro cropping could be carried out on valley slopes that facilitate water flow, whereas swampland taro cropping was likely used and is still seen today in the naturally inundated soils of floodplains

Table 8.4. Some subsistence cultivars in the Maʻohi production system.

	Cultivar[1]	Cultivation mode[5]	Coast	Inter-med.	Mtn.
				Cultivation zone[6]	
Cultivars of Primary Importance[2]	Breadfruit (ʻuru; Artocarpus altilis)	Arboriculture; Multi-cropped on edges of wet-field taro beds	C	C	—
	Banana (meiʻa; Eumusa banana/Musa paradisiaca)	Arboriculture; Dry swid-den cultivation	C	L	—
	Coconut (niu; Cocos nucifera)	Arboriculture; Multi-cropped in and around dry swidden plots	C	C	C
	Mountain plantain (feʻi; Australimusa banana/Musa troglodytarum)	Semicultivated or natu-ralized in mountainous interior; Arboriculture systems elsewhere	L	C	C
	Taro (Colocasia esculenta)	Wet cultivation in raised beds and irrigated fields; Dry swidden cultivation; Multicropped in arboricul-ture plots	C	C	—
Supplemental Cultivars[3]	Arrowroot (pia; Tacca leontopetaloides)	Arboriculture	C	C	—
	Greater yam (uhi, ufi; Dioscorea alata)	Arboriculture; Dry swid-den cultivation	C	C	—
	Mountain apple (ahia; Syzigium malaccense)	Arboriculture	L	C	—
	Screw pine (fara; Pandanus tectorius)	Arboriculture	C	L	L
	Sugarcane (to; Saccharum officinarum)	Arboriculture	C	C	—
	Sweet potato (umara; Ipomoea batatas)	Arboriculture	C	L	—
	Tahitian chestnut (mape; Inocarpus fagiferus)	Arboriculture; Multicropped on edges of wetfield taro beds	C	C	—
	Ti (Cordyline fruticosa)	Arboriculture	C	L	?
	Vi apple (vi; Spondias dulcis)	Arboriculture	C	C	—

Table 8.4. *(Continued)*

	Cultivar[1]	Cultivation mode[5]	Cultivation zone[6]		
			Coast	Inter-med.	Mtn.
Famine Foods[4]	Giant taro (*'ape; Alocasia macrorrhiza*)	Arboriculture; Dry swidden cultivation	C	C	—
	Lesser yam (*patara; Dioscorea bulbifera*)	Arboriculture?	—	C	—
	Nono (*Morinda citrifolia*)	Arboriculture	C	?	—

Symbols used: C = most common, L = less common

Sources: 1 = Lepofsky 1994; Petard 1986. 2 = Barrau 1961, 19, 40, 49; Beaglehole 1955, 1:120; Bligh 1937, 2:8–9; Bougainville 1967, 245; Cook in Hawkesworth 1789, 3:20; Ellis 1831, 1:43, 62; Forster 1778, 214, 441, 504–505; Henry 1928, 422; Lepofsky 1994, 93; MacDaniels 1947, 6; Morrison 1935, 152; Oliver 1974, 248; Parkinson 1784, 14, 19; Sparrmann 1944, 70; Varela in Corney 1913, vol. 2; Whistler 1991, 46; Wilder 1928; Wilson 1805, 132–133. 3 = Barrau 1961, 45, 60, 63; Beaglehole 1955, 1:120, 1967, 1:206–207; Bligh 1937, 1:392; Ellis 1831, 1:45–46, 48, 63; Forster 1778, 441, 443; Fosberg 1991, 18; Lepofsky 1994, 68; Oliver 1974, 245; Petard 1986, 106; Whistler 1991, 58; Wilson 1805, 154. 4 = Beaglehole 1955, 1:120; Ellis 1831, 1:44, 47; Forster 1778, 214, 443; Kirch 1994, 80; Whistler 1991, 56, 58, 59; Wilson 1805, 135. 5 = Bligh 1937, 1:424–425, 2:40; Bougainville 1967, 229; Ellis 1831, 1:25, 39, 44–45, 47, 60; Fosberg 1991, 20; Gore 1767 in Lamb et al. 2000, 60; illustrations by Hall (1773), Parkinson (1769), and Sporing (1769) in Joppien and Smith 1985, 1:29, 42; Kirch 1991, 116, 122; Kirch 1994, 86, 111, 119, 181–182; Kirch and Yen 1982, 39; Lepofsky 1994, 52, 59–63, 66, 69–73, 79, 81–82; MacDaniels 1947, 47–48; Papy 1954 in Lepofsky 1994, 81–82; Parkinson 1784, 38–50; Sparrmann 1944, 72; Whistler 1991, 55–56; Williams 1837 in Campbell 2003, 14. 6 = Banks in Hooker 1896, 95, 97, 105–107; Barrau 1961; Beaglehole 1955, 1:131, 2:769, 1962, 1:306; Bligh 1937, 1:369, 423–425; Cook in Hawkesworth 1789, 2:260, 3:2; Corney 1913; Ellis 1831, 1:25, 44–45, 48, 60, 63; Fosberg 1991, 18, 19; Henry 1928, 422; historic paintings and drawings by Ellis, Webber, Hodges, Parkinson, Sporing, and Hall in Joppien and Smith 1985, vols. 1, 2; 1988, vols. 3a, 3b; Jamet 2000, 11, 13; Joppien and Smith 1985, 1:42; Kahn site records 2000, 2001, 2002; Kirch and Yen 1982, 34; Lepofsky 1994, 69, 70–74, 76, 86; MacDaniels 1947, 10; Oliver 1974, 245, 248; Parkinson 1784, 38–50; Petard 1986, 116, 119, 280; Pickersgill Journal in Beaglehole 1955; Wallis in Hawkesworth 1789, 1:222; Whistler 1991, 56.

and valley bottoms (Lepofsky 1994, 59–63; see also Anderson et al. 2003; Campbell 2003). We will adopt a figure of 25 t/ha/yr for raw corms as a conservative mean minimum estimate of irrigated taro productivity, with 20 percent of the system in fallow at any given time (Kirch 1994, 155–156, 175, following Spriggs 1981, 1984). For simplicity we will assume the same productivity and fallow period for swampland taro cultivation. Swampland taro tends to have slightly lower yields

Table 8.5. Staple starch productivity of arboriculture systems.

	Planting density and production, per ha
Breadfruit	45 trees/ha; 5,310 kg/yr
Eumusa and *Australimusa* banana	450 trees/ha; 4,500 kg/yr[1]
Alocasia aroids	180 plants/ha; 450 kg/yr[2]
Colocasia taro	180 plants/ha; 450 kg/yr[3]
D. alata yam	135 plants/ha; 306.7 kg/yr[4]
Sweet potato	135 plants/ha; 306.7 kg/yr[4]
D. bulbifera yam (intermediate zone only)	(see note 4 below)
Total staple starch:	11,323.4 kg/yr (or 12.46 t/ha/yr)

Adapted from Kirch 1994, 182, with figures adapted from Massal and Barrau 1956, Murai et al. 1958, and Simmonds 1962.

1. Although Kirch (1994) found *Eumusa* bananas to be the most common banana in Futuna arboriculture plots, the popularity of the *Australimusa* banana among Tahitians (MacDaniels 1947) necessitates that it replace some of the *Eumusa* bananas in the Maʻohi arboriculture system. The production data remains the same as presented in Kirch 1994 (from Simmonds 1962).

2. Assumes, following Kirch 1994, a maturation cycle of 18–24 months and average yield of 5 kg per plant. The quantity of plants observed by Kirch has been reduced to accommodate some cultivation of *Colocasia* taro, with 1.6 *Colocasia* plants replacing each *Alocasia* plant due to differences in space requirements.

3. Assumes a 7–12 month maturation cycle (Massal and Barrau 1956, 8) and average yield of 2.5 kg per plant.

4. Replaces the *Xanthosoma* in Kirch's (1994) model, as *Xanthosoma* is a later introduction (Massal and Barrau 1965, 8; Pollack 1992, 18). Assumes a per-plant yield of 2.27 kg/yam plant (Massal and Barrau 1965, 13), which might also be reasonable for sweet potato. Assumes also that yams and sweet potatoes have similar spacing requirements as *Xanthosoma*.

than irrigated taro, but the difference is partially offset because the former does not require a fallow period (Spriggs 1984, 131).

A fourth cultivation mode, *short-fallow semicultivation of feʻi bananas*, was likely carried out on the steep upper-valley walls in the mountainous interior, where soil and access permitted (Lepofsky 1994, 80–81). Productivity of scattered bananas under short-fallow cultivation has been listed at 1.25 t/ha/yr by Massal and Barrau (1956, 17), and we will assume that 75 percent of land cultivated in *feʻi* would have been under fallow at any given time.

Table 8.6. Potential productivity of surveyed terraces.

	Est. total area of agri-cultural terraces*	Less area in fallow	x Productivity	= Yields
Wet terraces	5.6053 ha	1.121 ha	25 t/ha/yr (irrigated taro)	112.11 t/yr
Dry terraces	3.7980 ha	—	12.46 t/ha/yr (arboriculture)	47.32 t/yr
Total yields:				159.43 t/yr

* Includes those recorded in the original survey area, plus an additional .1605 ha of wet and 1.4445 ha of dry agricultural terraces documented at ScMo-285, outside of the original survey zone.For the small proportion (roughly 17%) of agricultural terraces that lacked dimensional data in the survey datasets (Green and Descantes 1989; Lepofsky 1994), we estimated measurements by reviewing site maps and descriptions or, in some cases, assigning a mean terrace dimension.

Implementing the Maximum Carrying Capacity Approach in 'Opunohu Valley

Our carrying capacity estimations start by assessing the potential productivity of the extant agricultural terraces that were surveyed, assuming for the sake of simplicity that all dry terraces were used for arboriculture and all wet terraces for taro cultivation. As shown in Table 8.6, the total amount of staple starch potentially produced from the archaeologically documented agricultural terraces in 'Opunohu Valley is 159.43 t/yr. Following Kirch (1994, 187, 342), if we assume a daily average intake of 3,000 calories in carbohydrates—roughly equal to 2.44 kg of staple starch based on average figures for bananas, aroids, yams, and breadfruit—annual per-person starch consumption would then come to 890.6 kg, or 0.98 t. The yield from the existing agricultural terraces could then support a population of 163, significantly less than our population estimates of 626 for the inner valley and 1,252 valleywide. The discrepancy suggests that there are many more agricultural terraces in the valley than those presently documented through survey (Green 1996, 214; Lepofsky 1994, 143, 148, 211). It may also suggest that nonterraced areas of the valley were being cultivated to supplement production from the terraces.

We now address the potential productivity of the valley. The valley and the island as a whole contain multiple soil types ranging from very fertile to strongly leached, as well as a diversity of slope gradients (Jamet 2000). Areas for each soil/slope category are shown in Table 8.7. The area of land theoretically available for

Table 8.7. Available land for cultivation by soil/slope category.

	Coastal zone (in ha)	Intermediate zone (in ha)				Upper valley/mountainous interior (in ha)		Totals
	A: Flat coastal plain	B: Lower valley alluvium/colluvium on 0–20% slopes	C: Leached soils on caldera's 5–20% slopes	D: Leached soils on 5–20% slopes in other catchments	E: Variably fertile soils on 20–50% slopes	F: Rocky, weakly developed soils on 50–100% slopes	G: Ridgecrests and eroded summits	
'Opunohu Valley								
Total areas	95.11 ha (4% of valley)	88.26 ha (3.7%)	333.34 (14%)	—	923.66 (38.8%)	716.65 (30.1%)	225.33 (9.5%)	2,382.35 ha (100%)
Less: wet agricultural terraces[1]	—	-.3053	-2.9876	—	-2.3124	—	—	-5.6053 ha
Less: nonagricultural structures[1]	-6.9445	-.34	-3.7629	—	-2.8416	—	—	-13.889 ha
Remaining available land[1,3]	88.1655	87.6147	326.5895	—	918.506	214.995[4]	—	1,635.8707 ha
Island Wide								
Total areas[2]	1,180 ha (8.9% of island)	335 (2.5%)	433 (3.3%)	540 (4%)	4,635 (34.8%)	5,287 (39.7%)	895 (6.7%)	13,305 ha (100%)
Potential available land[3]	1,173.1	334.4	426.2	540	4,629.8	1,586.1[4]	—	8,689.6 ha

Soil/slope categories

1. A comparison of maps revealed that structural remains generally tend to be situated on soil/slope types B, C, and E, which allowed us to estimate the amount of land of each soil/slope type that was consequently available for cultivation. In summing the total area of structures, for any structures whose area was unavailable we assigned a mean area for the relevant structural category, based on our computations and figures presented by Descantes (1990, 120). For the coastal zone, a settlement size equal to that of the inner valley is assumed (6.94 ha for nonagricultural structures).

2. Areas adapted from Jamet (2000), with adjustments made to categories C and F to account for our GIS and planimeter readings.

3. Excludes total area of nonagricultural structures surveyed for the valley and hypothesized for the coastal zone, as noted above. Also excludes the total area of the valley's wet agricultural terraces because these terraces were likely used to grow wetfield taro and thus their productivity is calculated separately (see Table 8.9). In contrast, the total area of dry agricultural terraces in the valley is *included* in this figure because they may have been used to grow a variety of crops in swidden or arboriculture.

4. Assumes 30% of this area has sufficient soil and access for cultivation.

Table 8.8. Reconstruction of subsistence cultivation system for 'Opunohu Valley and Mo'orea.

Cultivation zone	Soil/slope types (see Table 7 for details)	Subsistence cultivation modes in place on available land[1]
Coastal zone[2] (*95.1 ha of valley; 1,180 ha of island*)	A	A multicropped system composed of: 50%–arboriculture 50%–wetfield taro (swampland) cultivation on the coastal plain, using raised beds
Intermediate zone[3] (*1,345.26 ha of valley; 5,943 ha of island*)	B	Wetfield taro in documented terraces along streambeds in the valley. Of the remaining available land: 50%–arboriculture 50%–wetfield taro cultivation in raised swampland beds and irrigated fields
	C	Wetfield taro in documented terraces along streambeds in the valley; remaining area–dryland swidden
	D	Dryland swidden
	E	Wetfield taro in existing terraces. Of the remaining land: 50%–arboriculture 50%–dryland swidden
Mountainous interior[4] (*941.98 ha of valley; 6,182 ha of island*)	F	Short-fallow semicultivation of *fe'i* bananas in scattered patches, where soil and access are sufficient (30% of this area)
	G	No cultivation possible

Sources: 1 = Kirch 1991; Kirch 1994, 181–182; Lepofsky 1994, 63–66. 2 = Banks in Hooker 1896, 74, 127; Bougainville 1967, 215; Ellis 1831, 1:16, 250–251, 2:195, 215, 332; Jamet 2000; Wallis in Hawkesworth 1789, 1:234; artistic renderings of the coast of 'Opunohu Valley and Tahiti by Ellis (1777), Webber (1777), Hodges (1773, 1775–1776) and Parkinson (1769) in Joppien and Smith 1985, 1:29, 2:53, 62; 1988, 3a:354, 3b:63, 64. 3 = Bligh 1937, 2:40; Ellis 1831, 1:18; Gore 1767 in Lamb et al. 2000, 60; Jamet 2000; Robertson 1948; Wallis in Hawkesworth 1789, 1:221; artistic renderings of the intermediate zone of 'Opunohu Valley and Tahiti by Webber (1777) in Joppien and Smith 1988, 3a:375, 3b:46, 64–65. 4 = Cook in Hawkesworth 1789, 3:11; Ellis 1831, 1:18; Henry 1928, 422; Jamet 2000.

cultivation in ʻOpunohu Valley at contact was calculated using ArcGIS in conjunction with a soil map, while also accounting for the areas and locations of agricultural and all other archaeological structures documented through surveys.

According to Jamet (2000), the soils with the greatest agricultural potential are the immature, alluvio-colluvial soils that dominate the flat coastal plain (category A on Table 8.7) as well as the flat to gently sloping lower valley (category B). (Note that although the coastal plain also includes smaller areas of hydromorphic and calcareous soils, our model aggregates all of the coastal plain soils into category A for the sake of simplicity.) Cultivation of the leached, ferralitic patches of soil on the weak slopes of the caldera (C) and other catchments (D) is possible but would be enhanced if the soil was amended. Valley and islandwide, soil/slope categories E and F are the most prevalent. With varying fertility on steeper 20–50 percent slopes, category E soils are best cultivated using erosion control measures such as terracing and/or crops that do not require extensive tilling of the ground (e.g., perennial tree crops). Cultivation of the thin patches of weakly developed soil on the steeper rocky mountain slopes (F) may have been feasible, though difficult. Agricultural prospects were likely the worst on the steepest slopes of the ridge crests and summits (G) (Jamet 2000). Table 8.8 depicts the cultivation modes reconstructed for each zone based on our interpretion of the evidence discussed above.

Operationalizing the Model

After multiplying the areas of land assigned to each cultivation mode in our model by the hypothetical yields, the total amount of staple starch produced in the valley comes to 9,552 t (see Table 8.9). This figure assumes that all available land in the valley was under cultivation (as described above) and consistently productive and excludes from production the areas covered by nonagricultural structures (extant and hypothetical) as well as degraded fern land. The population size that could theoretically have been supported in the valley, if all staple starch was used for subsistence and per-capita annual starch consumption was 0.98 t, is 9,750 persons — about eight times our habitation-based estimate of 1,252. Islandwide, if we make similar assumptions about cultivation, productivity levels, and consumption, the available land on Moʻorea had the potential to yield a total of 57,246 t of staple starch, supporting a maximum carrying capacity population of 58,435.

Discussion

With an estimated minimum population of 1,252 based on the house-count method, ʻOpunohu Valley as a whole (approximately 23.8 km²) would have mini-

Table 8.9. Potential productivity of 'Opunohu Valley and Mo'orea.

Type of available land and cropping mode	Est. total area of available land (in ha) (see also Table 7)		Area (in ha) after subtracting area in fallow, if applicable		x Annual productivity	= Annual yields (in t)	
	Valley	Island	Valley	Island		Valley	Island
Surveyed wet terraces: *wetfield taro*	5.6053	5.6053	4.4842	4.4842	25 t/ha	112.11	112.11
Soil/slope A: *arboriculture*	44.0823	586.55	44.0823	586.55	12.46 t/ha	549.27	7,308.41
Soil/slope A: *wetfield taro*	44.0823	586.55	35.2658	469.24	25 t/ha	881.65	11,731
Soil/slope B: *arboriculture*	43.8074	167.2	43.8074	167.2	12.46 t/ha	545.84	2,083.31
Soil/slope B *wetfield taro*	43.8074	167.2	35.0459	133.76	25 t/ha	876.15	3,344
Soil/slope C: *dryland swidden*	326.5895 → 244.9421*	426.2 → 319.65*	61.2355	79.9125	5.41 t/ha	331.28	432.33
Soil/slope D: *dryland swidden*	—	540.0 → 405*	—	101.25	5.41 t/ha	—	547.76
Soil/slope E: *arboriculture*	459.253	2314.9	459.253	2314.9	12.46 t/ha	5,722.29	28,843.65
Soil/slope E: *dryland swidden*	459.253 → 344.440*	2314.9 → 1736.175*	86.11	434.0438	5.41 t/ha	465.86	2,348.18
Soil/slope F: *semi-cultivation of fe'i*	214.995	1586.1	53.7488	396.525	1.25 t/ha	67.19	495.66
Soil/slope G: *no cultivation*	—	—	—	—	—	—	—
Total yields in tons:						9,551.64	57,246.41

*To account for degraded, nonproductive fern land visible at contact in Webber's paintings (Joppien and Smith 1988, 3b:64–65), 25% of swidden land is removed from available land in soil/slope types C, D, and E.

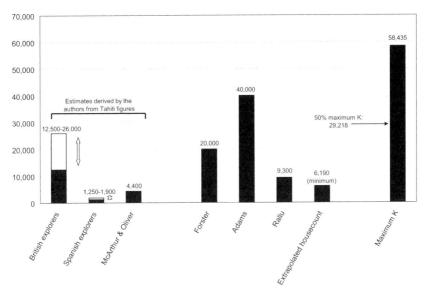

Figure 8.4. Island-wide estimates of population for Mo'orea at contact.

mally had a population density of 52–53 p/km². However, as shown archaeologically and ethnohistorically, the coastal and intermediate zones (14.4 km² in the valley, 71.2 km² islandwide) were the primary locus of Ma'ohi settlement and land use. The consequent population density in these zones of the valley would have been at least 87 p/km², giving an islandwide population (assuming a consistent density across these zones) of roughly 6,190 — a reasonable minimum estimation of the island's population at contact.

Figure 8.4 shows that our estimate falls between Rallu's 9,300 figure and McArthur and Oliver's (Tahiti-derived) figure of 4,400. Our estimate may have a closer affinity to Rallu's, however, because it represents a *minimum* estimate based on conservative measures, thus a somewhat larger population is within reason. One could also argue that the extremely low estimates of the Spanish explorers are questionable, as is Adams' high estimate. The British explorers' estimates, including Forster's, may appear overly high, yet they cannot be completely discounted since none of them exceed even 50 percent of the maximum carrying capacity.

Population Size vis-à-vis Carrying Capacity Estimates

Clearly, there is a large discrepancy between our house count or house area and our carrying capacity population estimates. Our islandwide habitation-based estimate of 6,190 at contact represents only 11 percent of the island's estimated carrying capacity. In his own analyses of carrying capacity for valleys in the Marquesas and the Cook Islands, Bellwood (1971, 1972) suggests that the maximum carrying capacity likely represents a productivity that is twice as high as the amount of food that a valley actually produced. The lower level might, then, be seen as the *optimum carrying capacity,* defined by Hassan (1981, 166–167) as the level that allows for resource shortages, population growth, or — as we will argue — other demands on production, such as social production for feasts and rituals.

There are many indications that population size in the windward Society Islands had not reached carrying capacity. To the voyagers, the Maʻohi appeared well nourished from a seeming abundance of food (Cook in Hawkesworth 1789, 3:12; Forster 1778, 346; Robertson 1948, 234). Though food shortages were occasionally experienced (Parkinson 1784, 34), semicultivated and wild plants and preserved foods such as *mahie* sustained the Maʻohi during less bountiful times of the year (Beaglehole 1955, 1:114, 122; Forster 1778, 504–505). Certainly not all of the food produced by the Tahitians was used for subsistence; numerous early accounts indicate that food, much of it staple starches, was often available in large quantities to trade for European-made nonsubsistence items (Banks in Hooker 1896, 90, 93; Wales Journal in Beaglehole 1955, 2:801; Wallis in Hawkesworth 1789, 1:192; see also Thomas 2003, 337).

Bayliss-Smith (1978) has distinguished between standard and maximum carrying capacity, arguing that "standard" population sizes do not usually reach 70 percent of the maximum carrying capacity. Reasons for this include the perceived need for surplus production (per Brookfield 1972) and varying levels of labor input that are linked to nonagricultural needs and perceptions of the quality of life. The Society Islands have long been recognized as one of the most highly stratified Polynesian chiefdoms (Goldman 1970; Kirch 2000; Oliver 1974; Sahlins 1958). It is reasonable, then, to invoke the chiefly system of tribute and its great demands on surplus food and labor (Adams [1901] 1976, 357; Banks in Hooker 1896, 176; Henry 1928, 177, 260; Kirch 1984, 166–167; Oliver 1974, 926; Sparrman 1944, 70; Wilson 1799, 375) as one of the most significant factors contributing to the discrepancy between our population estimations. Surplus food production was converted into social production, which supported the chiefly political economy. Foodstuffs were used as gifts, ritual offerings, and exchange items and were presented to the chiefs and the gods at large feasts to celebrate the ritual calendar and rites of passage (Ellis 1831, 2:203; Henry 1928, 198; Morrison 1935, 347). Foodstuffs were also fed to pigs and dogs, which were in turn eaten on elite feasting occasions and presented, often in great numbers, as ritual offerings at *marae,* along with seemingly copious quantities of other foodstuffs left to rot on the offering platforms *(fata)* (Banks and Solander 1770; Beaglehole 1955, 1:103, 113; 1962, 229–231; Bligh 1937, 402; Forster 1778, 189; Hooker 1896, 101, 170–175; Sparrman 1944, 70, 90–91; Tobin in Oliver 1988, 97, pl. 16).

Ethnohistoric accounts indicate that social production could impose severe demands on commoner production (Adams [1901] 1976, 27–29; Oliver 1974, 311). While there is no specific archaeologically based measure of social production for the Society Islands, conceivably 50 percent of surplus food production in ʻOpunohu could have been diverted into social and/or ritual production, if we follow Spriggs' and Kirch's findings from Anahulu Valley in a highly stratified Hawaiian chiefdom (1992). A high amount of social production, such as postulated for ʻOpunohu Valley, would be consistent with the divergence between population estimates and carrying capacity that our model has produced.

Perception of Population Pressure

From the radiocarbon sequence and environmental indicators, we infer that population growth was evident in ʻOpunohu Valley in the eleventh to thirteenth centuries, continuing until historic times. When considered in light of the large margin between population size and carrying capacity, this trend suggests that the population of the valley—and probably the island—was growing. At the same time, the valley's settlement pattern suggests that the Maʻohi inhabitants were perceiving population pressure, even though the environmental limits had not yet begun to seriously constrain population growth. Their population had reached an overall density of roughly 87 p/km² in the primary zones of settlement and land use. Yet within these zones, smaller pockets of concentrated settlement had reached a density of 220 p/km², not far below the high density of 242 p/km² observed on Tikopia (Kirch and Yen 1982, 56). Outside of the concentrated pockets, settlements were more lightly dispersed, even in areas that appear equally suitable for habitation (Lepofsky 1994, 259).

This nucleated, uneven concentration of settlement might be attributed to Maʻohi land tenure practices or sociopolitical boundaries that imposed restrictions on settlement (Descantes 1990; Green and Descantes 1989; Green et al. 1967; Lepofsky 1994, 260), which likely contributed to a perception of population pressure. As Kirch (2000, 309) explains, population pressure can be perceived socially and culturally—for example, in the claiming of territory—long before carrying capacity is reached.

Conclusions

The evidence suggests that the population of ʻOpunohu Valley—and likewise of Moʻorea—had not reached its maximum carrying capacity. Yet population pressure was manifested by certain Maʻohi practices—warfare, human sacrifice, and infanticide (Cook in Hawkesworth 1789, 3:29; Ellis 1831, 1:317; Williams 1837, 558, 562, 565; Wilson 1799, 218)—which can represent cultural controls on population growth (Kirch 2000, 309). The chiefly tribute system and restrictions imposed by chiefs on subsistence goods *(rahui),* characteristic of highly stratified Polynesian chiefdoms, can also be invoked as social responses to population pressure because they restrict access to food and land (Kirch 1984, 166–167). Social production likely also suppressed population growth by diverting a significant portion of production away from daily subsistence. We argue that population growth on Mo'orea at the time of contact was limited less by environmental factors than by the social practices that had been institutionalized in this stratified chiefdom.

It is possible that the valley's population would have continued to grow had it not been decimated by the devastating effects of diseases introduced by European contact (Rallu 1990, 1991). A comparison of the earliest censuses for Mo'orea, which counted 1,100 and 1,372 inhabitants (McArthur 1967), with our minimum estimate of 6,190 at contact suggests a 75–80 percent or greater decline in population, close to the 7-to-1 decline suggested by Rallu (1991, 74–75).

Our habitation-based estimate for Mo'orea assumes that the size and density of coastal settlements mirrored inland settlements, and that settlements did not extend significantly onto slopes exceeding a 50 percent gradient. Additional archaeological data, particularly from coastal contexts on Mo'orea or another windward locale, would allow us to test these assumptions.

In addition, the availability of additional radiocarbon dates would facilitate a closer look at population trends. Access to fine-grained information linking the location of agricultural terraces to specific soils/slopes would strengthen the assumptions we have made about the types of production systems practiced in the different zones, allowing for a more accurate estimate of potential productivity for the valley and island.

Our study supports the conclusion that there was a significant demographic collapse in the Society Islands following Western contact (Rallu 1991) and provides archaeological data for this pattern, which has heretofore been established on ethnohistoric grounds alone. We argue that archaeological reconstructions of prehistoric demographic patterns such as presented here can lead to a better understanding of the complex relationship between population, social and economic processes, agricultural intensification, and environmental change.

This study also underscores the value of using the ethnohistoric record and the importance of taking a comprehensive yet critical approach to the analysis of archival data. Equally significant, our investigation emphasizes the lessons that can be learned from reanalyzing settlement data, even decades after it was originally collected. The findings drawn from this study would not have been possible without the pioneering efforts of Roger Green, whose original settlement data — still the most comprehensive sample for a windward Society Islands context — continues to give us fresh insight.

Notes

We thank Patrick Kirch and Jean-Louis Rallu for inviting us to participate in the "Long-Term Demographic Evolution in the Pacific Islands Conference" on Moʻorea. Brenda Hamilton would like to thank Kirch and Gene Hammel for guidance and insight during the original drafting of this paper. This material is based upon work supported under a National Science Foundation Graduate Research Fellowship. Any opinions, findings, conclusions, or recommendations expressed in this publication are those of the authors and do not necessarily reflect the views of the National Science Foundation. Funding for Jennifer Kahn's field research in the ʻOpunohu Valley was provided by the U.C. Berkeley Gump Research Station and the Roger Green Foundation for Archaeological Research. Brian Chen is thanked for his work in producing the GIS database, Kathy Kawelu for production of the Freehand version of the soils map, and Christophe Descantes for sharing the digital database from the original ʻOpunohu survey. We especially thank Emeritus Professor Roger Green for his enthusiasm in sharing his original field data with us and for the many conversations we shared concerning the details of ʻOpunohu Valley archaeology and Society Island ethnohistory.

1. The percentage shown on each bar is the probability that the actual date lies within the given range. For consistency, all dates were recalibrated using Oxcal 3.8. The samples lacking a probability determination are those that yielded a questionable "modern" date. Therefore, as was recommended to Lepofsky, they have been assigned to the period from 1650 to 1950 (1994, 136). Forty years were subtracted from each date to compensate for the northern-to-southern hemisphere effect. In both figures, the site dates include an off-site hearth date. Three additional dates are not shown: CAMS-6253, which dates a recent coconut root; CAMS-6250, which also had a modern age determination; and GaK-367, whose modern determination conflicted with surficial evidence (Davidson 1967, 139; Lepofsky 1995, 923). In cases where the dates obtained from the same locus were not statistically different, they were combined using Oxcal 3.8 and counted once (following Glassow 1999, 49). Such dates are depicted as a single bar, or occupation, on the chart.

2. The houses shown in Figure 8.3 (n = 84) include seventy-eight whose length and width were provided in the dataset and six for which only the length was available but whose width we estimated using a linear regression–based "forecast" tool in Microsoft Excel (deemed appropriate because house length and width were somewhat associated: $r^2 = .63$ for rectangular houses and $r^2 = .55$ for round-ended houses). The figure excludes three additional houses for which neither length nor width was available. To account for rounded corners, the following formula was used to calculate the area of each round-ended house, thereby shaving off 10 percent from their area:

$$\text{Round-ended house area} = [\text{length} * \text{width}] - [\text{width}^2 - \pi\,(\text{width}^2\,/4)]$$

3. Although Figure 8.3 shows five houses in this size class, we removed two of them from our calculations because they were later superseded by rectangular houses and thus date to an earlier time period.

4. A high incidence of arboriculture suggests that Futuna is a good analogy for the Society Islands.

9

Estimating the Population of Hokatu Valley, Ua Huka Island (Marquesas, French Polynesia) According to the Archaeological Remains

 An assessment of Marquesan population at different moments in its history (before and after contact with Europeans) is of great interest for understanding the organization of the pre-Contact society and for estimating the drastic impact of post-Contact epidemics on the demography of the archipelago. Several sources, including narrative accounts of European navigators and first censuses by the missionaries and administrators, constitute important historic documents (Rallu 1990). In addition, archaeological remains in the valleys of the Marquesas document their spatial occupation and allow a synchronic approach that may complement the historic data. It is necessary to use specific case studies based on exhaustive archaeological surveys, as well as reliable methods.

Here we present a case study of Hokatu Valley on the island of Ua Huka, located in the northern group of the Marquesas (Figure 9.1). Our goal is to attempt to derive a potential demographic estimate based on archaeological data and available historic information. Demographic studies based on this approach have been attempted twice before in the Marquesas, and we refer to the work of Bellwood (1972) in Hanatekua Valley on Hiva Oa Island and that of Kellum-Ottino (1971) on Ua Huka in the valley of Hane, close to our own study location of Hokatu. We will specifically compare our own results with those of Kellum-Ottino for Hane.

Hokatu Valley

Hokatu is one of the three currently inhabited, principal valleys of Ua Huka (Figure 9.2), and like Vaipaee and Hane, it is located on the south coast. Its length is about 1.8 km. The well-protected bay favored human settlement, and the valley maintained its population even after the abandonment of most other valleys. At

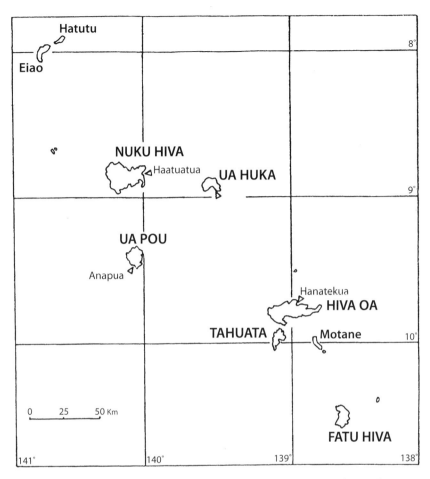

Figure 9.1. The Marquesas Islands, showing the location of the island of Ua Huka.

the time of European arrival, Hokatu was the territory of the Maku-oho tribe, which was, according to Handy (1923, 30), traditionally at war against the tribes of Vaipaee and Hane.

The current village is located in the lower valley, an area not usually densely inhabited in the pre-Contact period. Nevertheless, a stone platform is still located near the shore, and other structures are probably also present. Due to modern land use alterations in this lower part of the valley, our archaeological survey concentrated on the inland area (Figure 9.3). The fieldwork was carried out during several field seasons in 1999 by Eric Conte and Nathalie Tartinville (Conte et al. 2001).

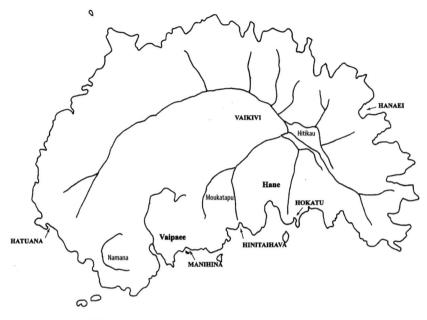

Figure 9.2. Map of the island of Ua Huka showing the location of Hokatu Valley.

Monumental Structures Recorded in Hokatu Valley

Eighty-seven stone structures were recorded; they constitute the basis of this attempt at demographic reconstruction (Figure 9.4). However, some structures such as walls were sometimes recorded and mapped without receiving an inventory number.

The structures recorded correspond to structures typically encountered in Marquesan valleys. We recorded thirty-four house sites, two of which were probably chiefs' houses based on their size (sites 33 and 39). The function of three structures could not be determined, but they may be houses and are recorded as "possible houses." Four other complex structures may be houses or *me'ae* (religious structures); one (site 48) is certainly a *me'ae*, as the present population still identifies it as such. We also recorded three *tohua* (ceremonial feasting platforms), three enclosures (one of which is a circular enclosure), and thirty-nine horticultural terraces.

We defined as "houses" the classical type of structure (Figure 9.5): a stone platform *(paepae)* with a paved zone in the front forming a veranda *(paehava vaho)* and, in the rear, a perishable superstructure *(ha'e* or *fa'e)* where the inhabitants slept. The floor of the house was divided into two parts over its whole length: in the front, a paved zone *(paehava oto)*, and in the rear, the sleeping area *(oki)*, covered with several layers of vegetable material and mats. The inhabitants slept side

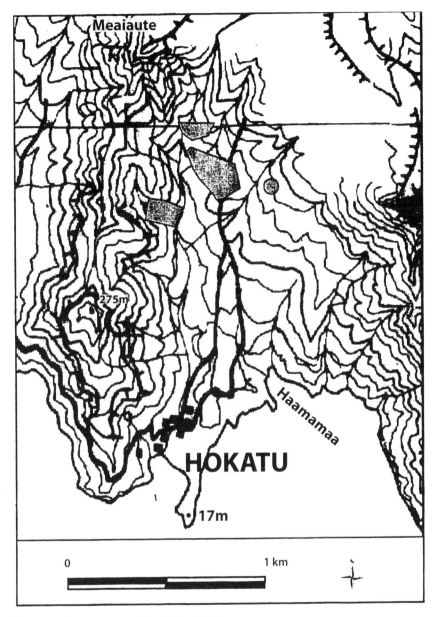

Figure 9.3. Survey areas within Hokatu Valley.

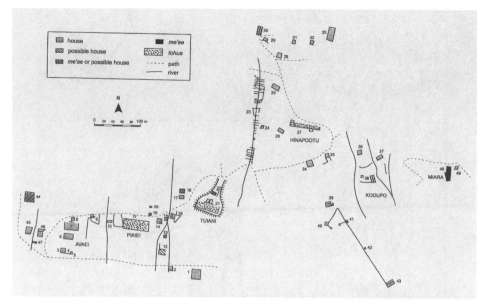

Figure 9.4. Map of stone structures in Hokatu Valley (see Table 9.1 for list of structures).

by side in the *oki,* with their heads positioned toward the rear of the house. Two posts crossed the length of the *oki,* one for resting the feet of the sleepers and the other one located at the rear of the house for laying their heads (Figure 9.6). This ethnographic information concerning Marquesan sleeping habits is critical for our attempt to calculate the number of inhabitants in Hokatu Valley.

Methods of Population Estimation

Possible Methods

To estimate a given population, we can rely on two principal types of data. The first — ecological data (such as the area of arable land or quantity of available resources) — are imprecise because they are influenced by too many parameters that are not well controlled (reconstruction of the natural environment in the pre-Contact period, estimation of cultivated and exploited surfaces, techniques of resources exploitation and yield, estimation of necessary quantity of food for each inhabitant, etc.). In our view, archaeological data are a priori more reliable because they have a material reality more readily accessed. However, most methods, such as those of Naroll (1962), Cook (1972), Casselberry (1974), and Soudsky (1962), use the surface area of the dwellings (of which it is necessary to define the space actually used) and, based on ethnographic data on traditional societies, make an evalua-

Figure 9.5. The classic form of Marquesan dwelling house (engraving by L. Lebreton 1838, "Cases de naturels à Nouku-Hiva," from the voyage of Dumont d'Urville).

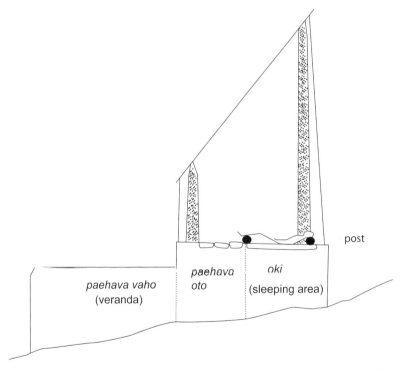

Figure 9.6. Cross section of a typical Marquesan house platform, showing the elevated sleeping area.

tion of the average surface per inhabitant. But according to Djindjian (1991), these methods yield variations of 1 to 5 according to the criteria chosen (type of family organization, type of settlement pattern, etc.), and this is not very satisfying. Moreover, one can question the use in Pacific studies of estimating the number of square meters required per person (e.g., Naroll 1962) based on ethnographic observations made outside of the Pacific area, typically of American Indians, who lived in ecological contexts and had organizational modes quite different from those of insular Pacific societies. Still, estimating the useful surface per inhabitant is often the only reliable method that can be used to estimate the population by its settlements. Therefore it would be valuable to have an ethno-archaeological study directed toward collecting of this type of data in different Pacific Island communities that have conserved a traditional lifestyle and are more representative of cultural areas in the region. Then it would be possible to refine estimates assuming better adapted criteria.

In the Marquesas, for Hane Valley, Kellum-Ottino (1971) proposed to calculate the population on the basis of five to seven people per house (while supposing that 75 percent of the houses were occupied simultaneously). Bellwood (1972) made an evaluation of the population of Hanatekua Valley according to several methods. He calculated the population according to Naroll's method (also used by Marimari Kellum-Ottino) using surface area per inhabitant. He also tried a complex estimation of carrying capacity of the valley—in our sense, not useful. But he also mentions a simple method of population assessment according to an indication given by Herman Melville, which describes that in a house of 10 to 12 m long, ten people could have slept side by side. On this basis, Bellwood proposed to estimate the population of a valley by dividing the total length of the sleeping areas of its house sites by 100 or 150 cm, in order to derive the number of inhabitants. It is this method that we chose to adopt here. We will compare it with the results derived from Kellum-Ottino's method.

The Adopted Method

As we are working with monumental structures in the absence of excavation results, our objectives are to estimate the population of the valley only from these surface remains, without trying to take into account ecological factors, for the reasons given above. We believe that the calculations based on the habitations' gross surface area were too imprecise because of the problem of defining usable zones or activity areas and because it is quite difficult and somewhat arbitrary to assign a per-person average surface area. It seems more appropriate to us, given the ethnographic accounts of Marquesan houses and sleeping habits, to base our estimations on the length of the sleeping area for several reasons. First, sleeping is an activity that concerns all inhabitants of the valley; second, the spatially defined sleeping areas are readily identifiable in the houses (even though some problems arise). Third, we possess precise ethnographic information on the manner in which people slept in the Marquesas. Therefore, our estimate is based on the length of the sleeping area in the houses. The sum of individual house lengths gives the total width of sleeping area available in the valley, and this can be divided by the space presumed to be necessary for each person to derive an estimate of population.

Some Methodological Problems

Problem of Survey Coverage. Although the other zones of the valley have been well recorded, the lower valley has not been studied. Therefore it is necessary to estimate the number of houses that could have been there in the past. According to historic information, confirmed by the available archaeological data, it seems that the Marquesan lower valleys were not densely occupied, notably because of the risk of seismic waves. Thus, Kellum-Ottino (1971, 163) mentions the missionary Crook (who never visited Ua Huka), who says that the inhabitants lived mainly in the bottom of the valleys, quite far from the sea. We decided to estimate the number of houses in the lower valley that were not recorded in the archaeological record. To do this, we calculated the percentage of houses found in the lower valleys in the Marquesas by other surveys (only those that provide this information) in relation to the total number of houses. In Hanatekua the proportion is about 20 percent (Bellwood 1972); in Haka'ohoka it is about 25 percent of the houses (Ottino and de Berg 1990). Based on these data, we decided to choose a maximal estimation of 25 percent and a minimal one of 15 percent. It is also important to estimate the average width of sleeping areas in these houses. This average is made on the basis of the average length of the houses in the rest of the valley.

Recorded Zones. Another sampling issue is whether we have in fact recorded all structures in the surveyed zones. Some sites might have escaped discovery, or some could have existed in the pre-European period but have subsequently been destroyed. On the first point, we stress that our inventory was undertaken in the course of several long field trips, and it seems unlikely to us that there are *paepae* still not recorded. Indeed, some features such as low walls and alignments have not been mapped on the general plan because they have not been precisely defined. But they are features less visible than the house platforms. Destruction of structures is certainly possible, but we note that out of the lower valley, there has been little recent disturbance, as evidenced by the number and the state of conservation of the recorded monuments. We did not notice any obvious traces of destruction, such as piles of stones or recent terracing. We can assign a common percentage to estimate houses that were not recorded; this percentage will be integrated into the final calculation. We propose a high evaluation of 10 percent of nonrecorded houses and a low value of 5 percent. The length of these houses will be calculated as indicated previously.

Possible Houses without Stone Construction. The inventory of stone monuments raises the question of the possible existence of houses that may have been built without any associated stone foundation or pavement and that would therefore not be detectable through standard surface survey. Most authors working in the Marquesas have given little attention to this problem and implicitly assume that all houses would have a stone foundation conserved. Without being so categorical, if it is true that if the function of the stone platforms (to elevate the inhabitants from the damp and the mud) is so important, it is difficult to understand why people would have chosen to dispense of this comfort, especially since stones are commonly available in the valleys so that transport distance is not a major factor. We do not want to reject the possibility of houses without stone foundations out of hand, but we think that if they existed, they were few in number. We have dealt with the possibility with two options: first, that there were no houses of this type, and second, by adding an estimate of 10 percent to account for the possible existence of such houses built entirely of perishable materials.

Identifying the Houses. Among the recorded monuments in Hokatu, 34 are undoubtedly houses, for they present the classic plan of the dwelling *paepae*, and their definition does not pose a problem (Table 9.1). We call these structures "houses." In some cases, they present a more complex plan (e.g., one dwelling *paepae* with another platform), and one has to determine if the habitation includes one or several sleeping places. In this case, we give a high evaluation (two sleeping areas) and a low one (only one sleeping area). In general, the monuments are in a good state of preservation, but sometimes the platform is damaged; in this case, we give one high and one low evaluation of the length of sleeping areas. Three structures may be houses, but we are not certain; they are named "possible houses." The function of four other structures is ambiguous, as they might be houses or religious structures *(me'ae);* we label these "house or *me'ae.*" Excavations in these structures and analysis of artifacts might resolve these functional uncertainties. Nevertheless, for estimating the ancient population, we must propose options that include counting these structures as houses or not as houses.

Contemporaneity of Houses. This question is problematic and concerns all surface surveys. If we had one date for each group of structures, this question would be less problematic. Even in that case, it would give an idea of a global evolution in the use of the group of structures as a whole, rather than a possible differential

Table 9.1. Stone structures identified in the Hokatu Valley survey.

Number	Type of site	Length or mean length (m)	Maximum length (m)	Minimum length (m)
1	house	7.5		
2	house	7		
3	house	7.5	10	5
4	enclosure			
5	house	6		
6	2 houses	18		
7	3 houses	24	29	19
8	house	6.5		
9	house	12		
10	house	9		
11	*tohua*			
12	possible house	16		
13	possible house	6		
14	house	7.5	10	5
15	house	6.5		
16	house	4.5		
17	house	7		
18	house / *me'ae* ?	15		
19	house	5		
20	house	2		
21	*tohua*			
22	house /*me'ae* ?	10		
23	agricultural terraces			
24	house	5.5		
25	house	8		
26	house	10		
27	*tohua*			
28	house	4.5		
29	house	8		
30	house /*me'ae* ?	6		
31	enclosure			
32	house	9		
33	chief's house	9.5	14	5
34	house	11		
35	house	7		
36	house	8		
37	house	4		
38	house	14.5		
39	chief's house	8		
40	house	7		

Table 9.1. (Continued)

Number	Type of site	Length or mean length (m)	Maximum length (m)	Minimum length (m)
41	house	4		
42	circular structure			
43	house	8		
44	chief's house /me'ae ?	12		
45	house	3		
46	house	7	9	5
47	possible house	8		
48	mea'e			
49	house	7		

use for each structure. However, we have only one radiocarbon date for the valley, which is not helpful in this discussion. Since the monuments do not present notably different states of preservation, we can assume that they date primarily to the last period of the prehistory of the valley or even to the early post-European period. In short, we believe that the settlement dates to approximately between the seventeenth and eighteenth centuries. Considering that 90 percent of the houses were occupied contemporaneously is our high estimation. For a lower estimation, we chose the same option as Kellum-Ottino (1972) for Hane, estimating that 75 percent of the houses were used at the same time.

Dwelling House Occupation Rate. The calculations of high and low estimates concern the sleeping areas' potential capacity, assuming they were all maximally occupied. However, a house might be constructed to shelter an extended family and, as children became adults, they might settle in a new house, while the parents' house was as a consequence less fully occupied. Therefore it seems appropriate to make calculations that take into account variable rates of occupation. We propose two rates of occupation: one maximal (100 percent) and another lesser value of 60 percent.

How Much Space to Assign to Each Person. Finally, to calculate the number of individuals by sleeping area, we have to define an individual's necessary sleeping space. We believe that a width of 100 cm per person probably corresponds to the reality of Marquesan sleeping habits. But it is necessary to consider, as Bellwood did, a possible value of 150 cm; these values will produce population estimates more or less high.

Table 9.2. Low estimation of population.

No. of houses	34
Length of sleeping area	256.5 m
Average length	8 m
Lower valley (15%)	5.1 houses: 40.8 m
Exhaustiveness of the inventory (5%)	1.7 houses: 13.6 m
Houses without lithic support (0%)	0
Subtotal of sleeping area	310.9 m
Contemporaneous habitation (75%)	233 m
Occupation rate (60%)	140 m
No. of inhabitants (100 cm)	140
No. of inhabitants (150 cm)	93

Estimating the Population of Hokatu Valley

Applying the various parameters defined above and depending on the high or low values, we can derive a number of population estimates. We will not review all of the possible variations in detail, for this would be irrelevant to our purpose. Rather we will present only the estimates of potential lowest and highest populations.

The lowest estimate of the valley's population takes into account thirty-four structures identified with certainty as houses. Of the two possibilities for mean sleeping area, we take the shortest. The total length of the thirty-four houses is 256.5 m, and the average length of these houses is 8 m; these will serve as the base for our calculations. Table 9.2 gives the details of our calculation, which — taking all the lowest options — permits us to obtain two low estimates according to the area per person: 140 inhabitants (using 100 cm per person) or 93 inhabitants (using 150 cm per person). The high estimate takes into account all possible houses in the valley (forty-one structures). Of the two possible values for length of the sleeping area, we have chosen the longest one, giving a total length of 362.5 m. The average length of these 41 possible houses is 8.85 m; this will be the basis of our calculations.

Table 9.3 gives the details of the calculation and, choosing at each time the highest option, yields two high estimates of the population: 315 inhabitants (with 150 cm per person) and 473 inhabitants (with 100 cm per person). Thus, according to the sleeping area allowed to each individual, we obtain the following range: (1) at 100 cm per person, between 140 and 473 inhabitants; (2) at 150 cm per person, between 93 and 315 inhabitants. We can now compare these estimates with the calculation of population according to Kellum-Ottino's method, who estimated

Table 9.3. High estimation of population.

No. of houses	41
Length of sleeping area	362.5 m
Average length	8.85 m
Lower valley (25%)	10.25 houses: 90.7 m
Exhaustiveness of the inventory (10%)	4.1 houses: 36.2 m
Houses without lithic support (10%)	4.1: 36.2
Subtotal	525.6
Contemporaneous (90%)	473 m
Occupation rate (100%)	473 m
No. of inhabitants (100 cm)	473
No. of inhabitants (150 cm)	315

Table 9.4. Low estimation of population according to the method of M. Kellum-Ottino (five inhabitants per house).

No. of houses	34
Lower valley (20%)	5.1 houses
Exhaustiveness of the inventory (5%)	1.7 houses
Houses without lithic support (0%)	0
Subtotal	40.8 houses
Contemporaneous (75%)	30.6 houses
No. of inhabitants (5 inhab/house)	153

five to seven inhabitants per house. With forty-one houses as maximal number and seven persons per house, we obtain a high estimate of 287 inhabitants. With thirty-four houses as minimal number and five people per house, the lowest estimate would be 170 inhabitants. If we use Kellum-Ottino's method with the criteria used in our method (Tables 9.4 and 9.5), we obtain a low evaluation of 153 inhabitants and a high one of 375 inhabitants.

Several remarks can be made. First, with regard to the results obtained with our method, it is obvious that the difference between the minimal and the maximal estimates is significant (a ratio of 1:3). On the whole, however, these estimates all indicate a population on the order of several hundred and certainly less than 500 inhabitants for the entire valley. Comparing methods, we note that the derived estimates are relatively close between our method using 100 cm per person and that of Kellum-Ottino (140 and 153 inhabitants minimum estimate and 473 and 375 maximum estimate). This lends a certain confidence to the accuracy of

Table 9.5. High estimation of population according to the method of
M. Kellum-Ottino (seven inhabitants per house).

No. of houses	41
Lower valley (25%)	10.25 houses
Exhaustiveness of the inventory (10%)	4.1 houses
Houses without lithic support (10%)	4.1
Subtotal	59.5 houses
Contemporaneous (90%)	53.5 houses
No. of inhabitants (7 inhab/house)	375

the proposed estimates. However, because the houses of Hokatu present variable sizes, we judge that the length of sleeping areas allows a better precision.

Are these estimations of population in accord with historical information available on Ua Huka and, particularly, on Hokatu Valley? The first known contact between inhabitants of Ua Huka and Europeans dates from 1791 (American Captain Joseph Ingraham). The first estimate of population (considered by most authors as completely erroneous) was in 1838 by Du Petit-Thouars, who estimated 2,000 to 3,000 inhabitants for Ua Huka. Vincendon-Dumoulin gave the same numbers in 1842. In 1856, Jouan counted 300 inhabitants for the whole island (Bailleul 2001, 83), indicating that this low number was a consequence of the depopulation following diseases in 1855–1856.

In 1867, the resident Lawson made a detailed enumeration of population by tribe. At this date, 287 people lived on the island, of which 264 were indigenous and 23 were foreigners. Lawson also says that 73 Marquesans were from the Maku Oho tribe in Hokatu (Bailleul 1995, 84). Bailleul (2001, 103) indicates that in 1875, Eggiman, the French resident in the Marquesas, counted 254 inhabitants in Ua Huka. According to Rallu (1990, 50), when the first reliable civil census was taken in 1886, the inhabitants of Ua Huka numbered no more than 130, a decrease of half the population in about twenty years. Rallu estimates that a decrease of the same extent could have occurred in the 1830s and 1840s because of the numerous wars and famines on the island. This leads him to estimate the population in the 1840s (at the time of French annexation of the Marquesas) at 600 to 800 persons instead of the 2,000–3,000 persons attributed by Vincendon-Dumoulin and Du Petit-Thouars.

Note that in 1867, the seventy-three Marquesans from Hokatu Valley represented 38 percent of the entire population of the island. If we apply this percentage to the low estimate of Rallu for the entire island (600 inhabitants), we can estimate the population of Hokatu in 1840 to have been about 230 inhabitants. If we use the high evaluation, we obtain about 300 people for Hokatu. We notice that the low and high estimates obtained by our regressive demographical calculation, although indeed rough, yield results of the same order as those obtained by the different census methods. One indication allows us to consider that we are not far from the reality: Kellum-Ottino (1971, 165) evokes a surprise attack conducted by about a hundred Maku Oho warriors against Europeans in 1841. This supposes a total population of about 300 people if we take into account the extrapolations made elsewhere for the total population from the number of warriors (Rallu 1990, 48). The limited documentary information does not allow us to say much about the period prior to 1840, but given the known conditions leading to population decrease in the archipelago (documented famines in Marquesas in 1797–1798, 1804, and 1820), we can suggest a population more numerous for the period that can be linked to the archaeological house sites between the seventeenth and the beginning of the nineteenth centuries.

Population Density

In addition to estimating total population, density per unit area of land is another way to apprehend the demographic situation, and we attempt the exercise for Hokatu Valley. The valley's surface area from the crest to the beach is about 1.4 km². This would give an approximate density of between 66 and 225 inhabitants p/km² for our lowest estimations (using 150 cm sleeping space per person) and between 100 and 337 inhabitants p/km² for the highest estimations (using 100 cm sleeping space per person). One can note that even the density corresponding to the lowest estimation is high when compared to those commonly given by anthropologists working on Pacific societies.

We believe, however, that the density of a Marquesan valley cannot be compared directly with valleys on other Eastern Polynesian islands or with the density of coastal plains. Besides, it would seem to us erroneous to compare such a density to the density of entire islands. So it would be unreasonable to apply such an average density value to the island of Ua Huka in totality. Moreover, it seems just as hazardous to apply it to other valleys of this island.

On the first point, the Marquesas valleys were the principal place of settlement, as coastal plains do not exist. In contrast, valleys in the Society Islands are interdependent with extensive coastal plains, over which settlements were more or less intensively distributed. In the Marquesan valleys, where the great majority of the population was concentrated, settlement densities cannot be compared either to valleys or to coastal plains from other archipelagoes. Similarly, Marquesan valleys can be considered as population agglomerations, as surface surveys have shown that many areas were not settled permanently; thus the density of valleys cannot be compared to evaluations for entire islands. In short, one cannot apply the densities estimated for Hokatu to the entire island. We possess some historical information on tribes that, at the time of contact with first Europeans, had settled some valleys of Ua Huka that are today deserted. At least for this recent period, a calculation is possible and would permit a rough population estimate. But this would be only an approximation, because the dynamics of each valley may have led to substantial differences in their populations. This is to say that population density does not have any value in itself. It has to be considered in relation to the ecological and cultural context, and all comparison can be done only in relation to comparable situations. Thus for Hokatu, the material possibility of lodging about 200–300 persons in this valley is a false question; 135 persons are living today in the lower valley alone. Similarly, when considering the resource base for this population, one must include secondary resource zones such as the valley's sides, little adjacent valleys, and perhaps the neighboring mountains, which constitute a very important source of vegetal and terrestrial animal products. We have noticed one horticultural system of irrigated terraces in the valley, probably for taro culture. In addition, breadfruit trees were planted near the settlements and helped to sustain people, but they are impossible to count today. Finally, sea products (fish, shellfish, crustaceans, and seaweeds) have to be added to the resources used by the inhabitants of Hokatu. Considering all these factors, it seems entirely possible that 200–300 people once lived in this valley.

Conclusions

The valley of Hokatu is perhaps not an ideal space in which to attempt an assessment of pre-European population based on archaeological remains, partly because the whole lower valley has been disturbed. Yet it illustrates the difficulties met in most valleys of Ua Huka that are still inhabited (the same situation applies in Hane and in Vaipaee) and in the Marquesas in general. Thus, the solutions proposed to compensate for lack of information on the lower valleys could be applied in other areas and contribute to a more systematic survey of the pre-European demography. Unfortunately, there is a significant gap between the high and low estimates, which presents a consistent margin of uncertainty. In addition to the destruction of monuments, this uncertainty is due to the variables taken into account and especially to their imprecise quantification. The method of estimating the population on the basis of sleeping areas could be improved through excavations that would help to specify the function of specific monuments and by dating that would permit an assessment of contemporaneity.

Beyond the Marquesan situation, where this simple and relatively accurate method can be applied, it is obvious that an estimation of population alone at a given time, without its long-term evolution, poses knotty problems. Notably, the contemporaneity of dwelling structures can be resolved only by multiple dating, requiring a budget not available for most research projects. We have also shown that the method of evaluation of the population based on surface area necessary per inhabitant results in variable estimations according to different authors and, indeed, according to the ethnographic references chosen. To limit this problem — and because in Oceania we have the opportunity to study prehistoric populations whose descendants still perpetuate (in some places and to a certain extent) ancient lifestyles — it seems more appropriate to use or collect ethnographic data on Pacific societies rather than using criteria from populations out of the Pacific zone. Finally, one can question the utility of calculations of the carrying capacity of a territory in order to estimate the population size. Indeed, such calculations, no matter how sophisticated, can give only an idea of a virtual (or possible) population. They cannot answer the only interesting question: What was the real number of people living in this place?

To conclude, estimating ancient population — while it poses numerous theoretical and practical problems — cannot remain our sole preoccupation if we want to understand prehistoric demography. As with present populations, we need to evaluate birth, mortality, growth rates, life expectancy, and so on; that is to say, we need to use other sources (such as from mortuary archaeology) and to confront other difficulties. As we strive to gain better understanding of past populations, such data will be of primary importance to assess the bases of demographic dynamism, which depends both on historical trajectories and sociopolitical transformations — major research themes in Oceanic prehistory.

DAVID V. BURLEY

10

Archaeological Demography and Population Growth in the Kingdom of Tonga

950 BC to the Historic Era

Considerations of pre-European population size, other aspects of demography, and the methods by which these are measured have long been of concern to Oceanic historians, anthropologists, and archaeologists. As Kirch (2000, 307–313) further asserts, research concerns with potential interest and importance on a global scale are based on an understanding of long-term demographic patterns and principles on islands of the Pacific. In this chapter, I examine the issues and data bearing upon these types of questions in the principal islands of the Tongan archipelago of Western Polynesia. Beginning with the pioneering studies of Gifford (1929) in the 1920s, there has been ample focus on Tongan demographic patterns (Rogers 1969; Walsh 1970; Green 1973; Maude 1965, 1973), and aspects of Tongan data have been drawn into more general debates on models of demographic growth and their applicability (Kirch 1984; Sutton and Molloy 1989). A secondary objective, therefore, is to explore the implications of the Tongan data for theoretical or methodological problems in demographic archaeology as a whole.

In its broadest sense, demography involves the study of human populations, including their size, growth, density, and distribution. To the social demographer, it further includes analysis and study of underlying causal factors, including statistics on fertility, birth, gender, marriage, disease, and mortality. Unless one is dealing with exceptional and representative burial assemblages, the latter variables are all but invisible in the archaeological record. Archaeologists alternatively use proxy data for insight into population change both over time and in space (see Hassan 1981; Chapman 1999). Proxy data can be diverse and can vary considerably in their ability to reflect upon population and its transformation. As a result, archaeological demography is a considerably different and less exact field from that practiced in sociology, anthropology, geography, or history. Yet archaeological data have the unique ability to provide insight into the *longue durée* of human existence, and archaeological demographers are able to broadly ascertain demographic patterns that have taken place. This insight can be acquired in no other way.

Here I examine long-term patterns of demographic change in Tonga by first reviewing those factors that have been critical to or impacted upon settlement and population growth within the kingdom as a whole. I also review historic population trends and population distributions in different parts of the archipelago, and I assess previous attempts to estimate population size on the eve of sustained European contact in the eighteenth century. Given the almost three millennia of occupation in these islands, this latter population must represent a theoretical maximum for carrying capacity threshold, and its correlates should be recognizable in an archaeological context. Second, using earthenware ceramics and archaeological sites as demographic proxy data in prehistory, I next examine Tongan population trends and dispersal during the colonizing Lapita phase (ca. 950 to 700 BC) and through the sequent Polynesian Plainware phase (700 BC to AD 400). These data clearly illustrate transformational patterns in settlement and economy, although population growth rates and distribution vary substantially in time and in different areas within the archipelago. Finally, archaeological correlates for population and its transformations in the dynastic chiefdom of later Tongan prehistory are discussed. With full population levels not attained until later in prehistory, the emergence of this chiefdom and its expansion into adjacent islands in Western Polynesia are argued as a consequence of population growth and as a density-dependent control over its rate.

Historic Population Trends and an Estimated Population Threshold

Tonga is an archipelago of over 160 islands stretching along a 750-km-long southwest to northeast linear axis on the western flank of the Polynesian Triangle (Figure 10.1). The archipelago incorporates two parallel and geologically distinct chains of islands, each having important implications for human colonization. To the west is the Tofua volcanic arc, a series of islands typically ranging from steep-sided volcanic cones to violently erupted caldera remnants to occasionally active seamounts. With the exception of Niuatoputapu in the far north, the shorelines of these islands lack extensive coral reefs, reducing their potential for human exploitation and making them difficult to access. At the same time, these islands are a valuable source for andesitic basalts needed for adze production, oven stones, and other uses, and by at least later prehistory most of the larger volcanic islands had been settled in some fashion (Burley et al. 2003). The eastern

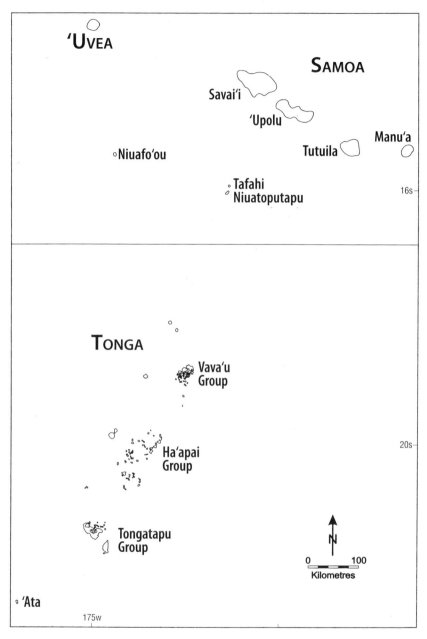

Figure 10.1. Kingdom of Tonga and other islands in Western Polynesia.

chain incorporates a series of coral limestone islands and sand cays situated atop the forearc platform of the submerged Tonga Ridge. These islands vary in size and elevation, but all are incorporated within a complex system of reefs supporting a rich and diverse range of fish, as well as molluscan and crustacean faunas. The coral limestone islands also have well-developed agricultural soils whose parent materials are an andesitic tephra blanket originating from eruptive events along the volcanic arc. The coral limestone islands were a focus for first settlement in the archipelago, and the vast majority of the Tongan population in prehistory and at present is concentrated here.

Islands within Tonga are referred to as occurring in three geographic groups: the Tongatapu Group (south), the Ha'apai Group (central), and the Vava'u Group (north), with a fourth cluster, the Niuatoputapu Group, sometimes called the Niuas (Niuatoputapu, Tafahi, and Niuafo'o), also occurring to the extreme north. Archaeological research into the discovery and initial settlement of these groups by Lapita peoples has been extensive (see Poulsen 1987; Kirch 1988; Burley et al. 2001). Reasonably it can be estimated that the earliest landfall occurred on Tongatapu by 950 BC (Burley and Dickinson 2001), with population expansion northward during the ensuing century. Tongatapu is the largest island in the archipelago (260 km²), supported the largest population through prehistory, and by AD 950 was the political center for the dynastic Tongan chiefdom (Kirch 1984; Burley 1998). Population densities on some of the inhabited islands of Ha'apai similarly were high through the eighteenth and nineteenth centuries, though in this case it was limited land, not overall population size, creating this density. Typically, the coral limestone islands of Ha'apai are small, with the largest being no more than 13 km² in area and the majority under 2 km² (Crane 1992). The islands of Vava'u are the highest in the archipelago composed of coral limestone, and on many the majority of the shoreline is cliffed or steeply sloped, making access for a maritime-adapted people difficult. The principal island, Vava'u, has an area over 89 km², and, given a subsistence economy centered on agriculture, it could be expected to support a large population in prehistory. That this may not have been entirely the case is an exception to be examined later.

Demographers working with Tongan data emphasize the difficulties of gaining accurate insights into pre-twentieth-century population sizes and distributions (see Maude 1965; McArthur 1967; Green 1973). There is little doubt that the densest concentrations of people were in western and central Tongatapu as well as on the principal coral limestone islands of Ha'apai (Maude 1970, 58). Beyond this, however, we are left only with the impressionistic estimates of explorers and missionaries for population size. These led early scholars such as Gifford (1929, 4) and Wood (1943, 90) to suggest an eighteenth-century population of 25,000 for the whole of the archipelago. More recent estimates for the same period of

Table 10.1. Census data for different island groups in Tonga based on numbers given in Maude (1965), Wood (1943), Walsh (1970), and Thayman (1978).

	1891	1911	1921	1931	1956
'Eua	—	362	387	348	1,933
Tongatapu	7,308	8,550	9,740	12,357	31,204
Ha'apai	5,631	5,803	5,976	6,410	9,947
Vava'u	5,292	5,161	5,787	7,643	12,504
Niuatoputapu	—	705	761	790	—
Other	1,737	1,130	1,108	1,291	56,838
Total	19,968	21,712	23,759	28,839	56,838

time by Maude (1965, 27) and Kirch (1984, 98) respectively range between 29,700 and 40,000 individuals. The first official census carried out in the kingdom in 1891 documented a total population of 19,968 individuals (Table 10.1), suggesting a nineteenth-century population decline of between 33 and 50 percent if we accept the Maude or Kirch estimates. Even the most conservative of demographers support some decline (e.g., McArthur 1968, 71–75). Internecine chiefly wars, European introduced epidemics, and other maladies are well recorded from the late eighteenth through mid-nineteenth centuries.

After 1891, census data for Tonga were regularly collected and population distributions and transformations between the different island groups can be explored. Table 10.1 provides these data for a select number of years up to 1956. What these numbers immediately illustrate are quite variable rates of population growth through the first half of the twentieth century. For example, between 1891 and 1911, the Tongan population rose only at a rate of 0.44 percent per annum; between 1911 and 1931, this increased to 1.64 percent per annum, while the interval between 1931 and 1956 had a dramatic increase of 3.88 percent per annum. Maude (1965), Rogers (1969, 220), and others (Walsh 1970, 32; Thaman 1978, 90) suggest that the post-1931 growth was not so much fueled by increased fertility as by decreased mortality, this being a consequence of modern medical practices and developing immunities to European disease. Further apparent in the census data is the fact that population distributions and growth in different island groups also are variable, with Tongatapu and Vava'u increasing their populations between 1891 and 1931 at respective rates of 3.2 and 5 times that occurring within Ha'apai.

Population growth and densities within sedentary agricultural societies such as Tonga are almost always linked to the potential for agricultural production as an operational measure for carrying capacity. In this, and speaking specifically for Polynesia, Kirch (1984, 98) emphasizes the association between population and arable land, concluding that "agricultural resources were a significant limiting factor to population increase." Traditional Tongan agricultural practice is centered on mixed-crop dryland farming, supplemented with poultry and pig husbandry. While the islands of Tonga are almost entirely without freshwater streams, annual rainfall patterns are capable of supporting productive yields of yam *(Dioscorea alata)*, giant taro *(Alocasia macrorrhiza)*, taro *(Colocasia esculenta* and *Xanthosoma saggitarius)*, and sweet potato *(Ipomoea batatas)*, as well as the more recently introduced cassava *(Manihot esculenta)*. This agricultural system is based on a shifting cultivation pattern, one no doubt originating in swidden garden practices of the initial Lapita settlers (Kirch and Green 2001, 128). Fallow cycles vary to meet local conditions and requirements, with cropping periods of from two to five years over an eight-to-ten-year cycle (Green 1973, 65–66). Tree crops, including coconut *(Cocos nucifera)*, plantain *(Musa* sp.), bananas *(Australimusa sp.)*, and breadfruit *(Artocarpus altilis)* are further integrated into field systems and residential complexes. The apparent productivity of agricultural practices on Tongatapu so impressed Cook in 1773 that he favorably compared Tongan gardens to the most fertile plains of Europe (Beaglehole 1969, 252).

Soils for each of the island groups in Tonga have been classified and mapped in a series of reports by the New Zealand Soil Survey Branch (Gibbs 1976; Wilson and Beecroft 1983; Orbell et al. 1985). The structure, characteristics, and productivity of these soils for different crops provide some insight into population distributions in at least later prehistory and the historic era. The most widespread soils are friable loams *(Kelefatu* and *Haʻapai)* formed from recent ash falls (ca. 5,000 BP), a silty clay *(Keleʻumea)* formed from deep, older ash (ca. 20,000 BP), and a sandy loam *(Touʻone)* found along coastal strips and on sand cays. Drainage patterns and structure of the silty clay and sandy loam substantially reduce their capabilities for the production of deep-rooted crops central to the traditional Tongan economy (Crane 1992, 107–108). High population densities reported for central and western Tongatapu as well as Haʻapai correlate well with the agricultural capacity provided by the loams. Eastern Tongatapu and ʻEua, often categorized as "arable" land by demographers (Maude 1965, 167), are in fact dominated by silty clay with significantly lowered capacity for root crop production (Figure 10.2). Population densities in eastern Tongatapu remained low into the nineteenth century, with ʻEuaʻs population continuing to be diminutive until well into the twentieth (see Table 10.1). And, in the case of ʻEua, its more recent population expansion was fully a consequence of government-planned resettlement, first by 200 residents evacuated from the southern outlier of ʻAta in the 1860s and then by a full-scale transplantation of 1,300 individuals in 1946 after the volcanic eruption of Niuafoʻo (Crane 1992, 82, 95).

That factors other than agricultural potential and soil type influenced past

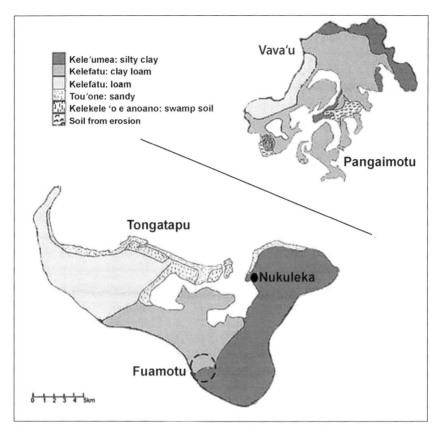

Figure 10.2. Principal soil types on Tongatapu and Vava'u adapted from Crane (1992, 108–109).

population distributions and emically perceived limits of carrying capacity seems indicated in the case of Vava'u. Like Tongatapu, considerable variation in population distribution occurs, with islands to the southeast having comparatively high densities of people and those to the west being more limited. In this case the correlation of soil type and population does not hold, for the productive loams are widespread throughout both areas. Population distribution in Vava'u, rather, is a reflection of shoreline variation and island topography, where "low biogenic productivity" and cliffed or steep-sided slopes on the western islands have substantially reduced supplementary subsistence resources of the reef and limited settlement access by a maritime people (Roy 1997, 192). Returning to the case of Tongatapu and Ha'apai, Walsh additionally notes that, while the population densities here do correlate with high agricultural capacity, the same areas also have exceptionally high productivity in reef and maritime resources. To Walsh, thus, population "densities are generally determined by a *balance* of both land and sea resources" (1970, 31, emphasis in the original).

Maude (1965, 1970) carried out extensive research in Tonga on agricultural production, landholding sizes, and the per capita amount of land required to support basic subsistence needs. This work is especially relevant, for it provides an operational measure for carrying capacity constraints and, arguably, helps to establish an upper limit for population size in each of the island groups within the archipelago. Focusing only on villages where cash cropping was limited, Maude reported that an average of 0.32 acres per person per annum was put in crop (1965, 142–143). Over a cultivation cycle of two years production and five years in fallow, this requires a minimum of 1.12 acres of arable land per individual. Green (1973, 66–67) believes Maude's estimates to be on the low side, for he has not taken into account land needed for tree crops nor variations in the production/fallow cycle. Adding an additional 0.28 acres for the former and calculating ranges for the latter, Green provides a revised estimate of 1.8 ± 0.2 acres per individual. These numbers, if accurate, allow a maximum population density of between 124 and 221 individuals p/km² for areas with productive agricultural soils, provided all land is used for cropping.

Ha'apai census data from 1891 to 1931 implicitly support the preceding estimates for agricultural land required for subsistence economy. Tongatapu and Vava'u populations, as earlier noted, were undergoing substantial growth over this forty-year period, respectively averaging 1.73 percent and 1.11 percent per annum. The annual average growth rate in Ha'apai, however, was only 0.35 percent. I believe this slower rate of growth is a direct consequence of agricultural production limits on a highly restricted land base rather than being caused by social conditions. That is, the 1891 population of Ha'apai appears not to have been significantly below the upper threshold of carrying capacity, thereby forcing population growth to remain in check over subsequent decades. The amount of arable land available per person in Ha'apai ranges from 2.19 acres per person in 1891 to 1.92 acres per person in 1931 (Table 10.2). This provides a population density range between 112.8 and 128.7 p/km² over the forty-year period. Given that some land was required for settlement and uses other than cropping (roads, grave sites, etc.), even minor adjustments to these numbers allow them to comfortably fall within the range predicted by Green. By 1931, wage employment, cash cropping, imported foods, fertilizers, and modern agricultural technologies allowed for an upward spiral in population in Ha'apai and throughout Tonga — one that continued into the later decades of the twentieth century.

Finally, I return to the pre-Contact population estimates of 40,000 by Kirch and 29,700 by Maude to assess the veracity of these numbers relative to agricultural subsistence capacities given above. To do this, I first calculated the hypothetical

Table 10.2. Acres of arable land per person for each of the main island groups in Tonga.

	1891	1911	1921	1931	1956
Tongatapu	5.05	4.32	3.79	2.99	1.18
Ha'apai	2.19	2.12	2.06	1.92	1.24
Vava'u	4.72	4.84	4.32	3.27	2.00

Total acres of arable land as given by Maude (1965, 167) are 55,400 for Tongatapu, 16,746 for Ha'apai, and 24,978 for Vava'u. In the calculations, the Tongatapu number was reduced by a third to 36,930 to account for poor agricultural soils in the east, and the estimate for Ha'apai was reduced to 12,320 to exclude the volcanic islands as given by Green (1973, 68).

population that could be sustained given acres of arable land on the principal island groups of Tongatapu, Ha'apai, and Vava'u using a carrying capacity threshold of 2 acres of productive agricultural soil per individual as is suggested above (Table 10.3). For Tongatapu, I also adjusted Maude's (1965, 167) arable land values downward by one-third to account for reduced productivity of the silty clay in the eastern part of the island. Resulting calculations of 18,195 for Tongatapu and 6,160 for Ha'apai seem highly acceptable, these also being approximations predicted by Green and generally supported by the few available eighteenth-century accounts (Green 1973: 63-64, 68, 73).

The same calculations for Vava'u give an estimated population of 12,489, which is clearly out of line. Unless Vava'u was subject to severe depopulation in the eighteenth century that has gone unrecorded — and this seems improbable — then the 1891 to 1931 census data indicate a population slightly below or equal to that of Ha'apai (see Table 10.1). The Ha'apai number of 6,160, thus, is taken here as an adjusted population size for Vava'u.

Lastly, one must add in a population total for the remaining islands throughout the archipelago ('Ata, Tofua, Late, Niuatoputapu, Tafahi, and Niuafo'o), a number Maude estimates as 10.4 percent of the overall population (1965, 27). If correct, these other islands can be calculated as having 3,542 individuals. The total potential population for Tonga based upon a theoretical carrying capacity threshold for agricultural production, then, is 34,057 — an estimate virtually midway between those of Kirch and Maude. The 40,000 of Kirch and the 29,700 of Maude provide a comfortable range for maximum and minimum limits of population size on the eve of European contact.

All Pacific Island demographers, anthropologists, and archaeologists recognize the fact that founding populations throughout Remote Oceania had the

Table 10.3. Projected Late Prehistoric population estimate based on 2 acres of arable land per person, with downward adjustments for Vava'u. The adjusted estimate for the other islands is taken as 10.4 percent of the total as calculated by Maude (1965:27).

	Arable land	Population estimate	Adjusted estimate
Tongatapu	36,930	18,467	18,467
Ha'apai	12,320	6,160	6,160
Vava'u	24,978	12,489	6,160
Other	—	—	3,436
Total	—	—	34,223

potential to rise quickly to significant population sizes if left unchecked, even with extremely slow rates of growth. Applying Carneiro's formula for length of time to full land utilization by shifting cultivators, Kirch (1984, 222) illustrates the implications of unrestrained population growth for the island of Tongatapu. Even incorporating the less than productive silty clays of eastern Tongatapu as arable land and a growth rate of 0.005, he calculates a total of 1,091 years for a founding group of 100 to arrive at full land capacity. Looked at another way, and given exponential growth as the expected norm, the same founding population with the same rate of growth literally doubles in size every 139 years. Tongatapu's population alone thus could theoretically have risen to over 200,000 individuals in its first 1,500 years of prehistory. This could not and did not happen, insofar as the maximum population threshold is estimated at between 30,000 and 40,000 individuals for the archipelago as a whole. Determining how and when the Tongan population rose to its maximum size, what its correlates in the archaeological record are, and what these can tell us about population transformations in the past are questions of considerable importance to Tongan prehistory, with implications for archaeological demography as a whole. It is to the Tongan archaeological record that I now turn.

First Lapita Settlement: Economy and Population Distribution (950–700 BC)

Systematic examination for and excavation of Lapita period sites throughout Tonga have been extensive over the past half century (Burley 1998, 342–349). With the results of recent surveys on twenty-two islands in the Vava'u Group now in hand (Burley and Barton 2004), few if any other archipelagoes in Oceania have a comparable database by which to infer chronology, settlement expansion, distri-

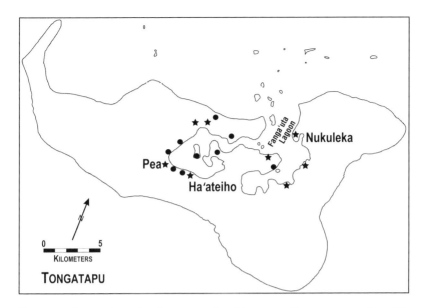

Figure 10.3. Lapita phase sites (950–700 BC) on Tongatapu. Stars represent sites with substantial cultural deposits. Dots represent either surface finds of decorated Lapita ceramics or sites with evidence for a limited Lapita phase occupation.

bution, economy, and other characteristics for this initial phase of colonization. For Tonga, the earliest of these sites is Nukuleka, a settlement strategically positioned at the northeast entrance to Fanga 'Uta Lagoon on the island of Tongatapu (Figure 10.3). Radiocarbon dates place first landfall here in the interval 850–950 BC (Burley et al. 2001, 95), while select ceramic motifs and ceramic temper analysis support a western Lapita origin for the founding group (Burley and Dickinson 2001). Over the next half century, Lapita settlements were established in other locales around the lagoon, as well as to the north on the principal coral limestone islands of Ha'apai, in a small number of locales in the southeastern islands of Vava'u, in a single settlement on the far northern outlier of Niuatoputapu, and, ultimately, into Samoa (Figures 10.4 and 10.5).

A suite of ceramic decorative types, most including simplified geometric or curvilinear motifs, literally demarcates this settlement episode (Burley et al. 2002). Overall variation of these eastern Lapita ceramic assemblages is low throughout the archipelago, thereby implying an integrated and related community of potters. And equally important, contemporaneous assemblages from most locales in Fiji outside of the southeastern Lau Group are distinctively different, most appearing to have closer relationships with western Lapita style ceramics of central Island Melanesia (Nunn et al. 2003). These observations lead to three important conclusions for demographic consideration in early Tongan prehistory. First, the

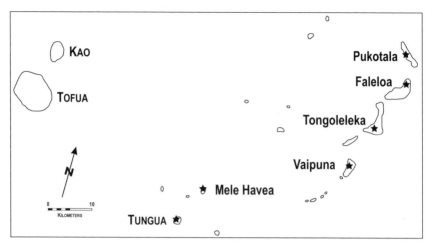

Figure 10.4. Lapita phase (950–700 BC) occupation sites where excavations have been conducted in the principal northern islands of the Ha'apai Group.

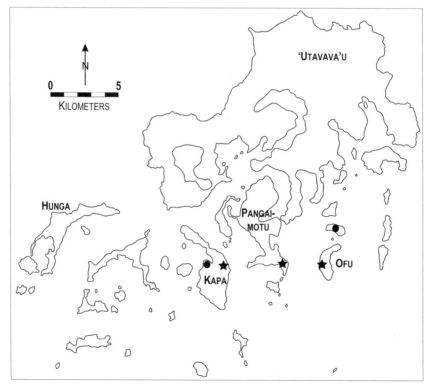

Figure 10.5. Lapita phase sites (950–700 BC) on the islands of the Vava'u Group. Stars represent sites with substantial cultural deposits. Dots represent sites with evidence for a limited Lapita phase occupation.

eastern Lapita ceramic series as expressed in Tongan sites — and the people who made this pottery — derive largely from the ancestral population of Nukuleka. Second, stylistic homogeneity over time and between sites implies limited if any in-migration from central or western Fiji after initial colonization. And third, this same homogeneity suggests regular interisland voyaging and persistent communication, despite the 400 km north/south distance of the archipelago's axis. If these interpretations hold true, the initial settlement at Nukuleka becomes the nucleus to which all of Tonga can trace its ancestry (Burley and Dickinson 2001).

All Lapita sites in Tonga occur on former back-beach sand flats or ridges having access to open water but within proximity to a reef where shellfish and other marine resources could have readily been gathered. Excavated faunal assemblages illustrate an economy centered on reef and maritime exploitation, with considerable numbers of indigenous birds, iguana, and turtle also being taken. I cannot deny linguistic and other arguments for the spread of an Oceanic agricultural complex associated with Lapita colonization, as inferred by Kirch and Green (2001, 121). It is equally impossible, however, to ignore the substantial and substantive evidence for a Lapita foraging economy that occurs in sites throughout Tonga. Whether defined as foragers with supplementary swidden gardens or as horticulturalists with supplementary foraging activities matters little, for northward exploration and settlement through the archipelago was almost certainly fueled by the exploitation of new and pristine resource locales (see also Anderson 2001, 2003). In fact, the limitations of these resources for a Lapita subsistence economy may have defined an upper threshold for population expansion itself. In Fanga ʻUta Lagoon, where extremely dense populations of the bivalves *Anadara* and *Gafrarium* were present (Spennemann 1987; Burley et al. 2001), multiple settlements occur at dispersed locations around the shore (see Figure 10.3). To the north in Haʻapai, Vavaʻu, and Niuatoputapu, cumulative foraging potential was more restricted. This consequently led to a settlement distribution where single sites were established in optimal locales on individual islands (Burley 1999) (see Figures 10.4 and 10.5).

Estimating the size and rate of growth of the Lapita population in Tonga are not simple tasks. Despite the extensive survey coverage that has taken place, one can question what percentage of the actual site population has been documented. There also is no way to determine if recorded Lapita settlements — or even different areas within individual sites — were contemporaneously occupied given the limits of radiocarbon dating. And since most Lapita sites are deeply buried, gaining the most basic understanding of site boundaries and size has been difficult. My overall impression, nevertheless, is that the majority of these settlements are now known and that only a small number of additional sites remain to be

Table 10.4. Lapita site size by island group in Tonga.

	Number	Range	Mean
Tongatapu	7	750–7,500 m^2	3,100 m^2
Ha'apai	5	1,000–1,750 m^2	1,180 m^2
Vava'u	3	1,000–1,500 m^2	1,165 m^2 ?
Niuatoputapu	1		3,000 m^2

For Tongatapu and Ha'apai, only those sites are included where a reasonable estimate of site boundaries exists. The size estimates for Vava'u are impressionistic, based on surface area. The Niuatoputapu site size is from Kirch (1988).

discovered. It also is my impression that most of these sites are extremely small hamlets, ranging between 750 and 1,500 m^2 in area (Table 10.4). Such a settlement would accommodate between two and three residential (household) units, with probable populations not exceeding twenty to twenty-five individuals at most. If we put caution to the wind and speculate the full number of contemporaneously occupied Lapita sites in Tonga to be twenty-five, and if we further acknowledge that a few of the larger settlements had populations exceeding twenty-five individuals, then a Lapita population for Tonga is suggested to fall between 600 and 700 persons by ca. 700 BC. Approximately half of this population would have been situated around the shores of Fanga 'Uta Lagoon.

An estimate of 600 to 700 individuals for the Lapita phase seems high given the estimated 250-year period over which it developed. For example, if we accept a founding population of 100 and a growth rate of 0.005 as Kirch (1984) proposed, then the population theoretically should have grown to no more than 300 to 400 individuals during the Lapita phase. If one accepts Hassan's (1981, 140) assertions that a rate of 0.0052 is "the probable maximum" for prehistoric groups, then we must either conclude that the founding population exceeded 100 or that it was supplemented by continued in-migration after first landfall — or a combination of both. The archaeological record is not well enough known to assess securely the appropriateness of either situation, nor can it be used to evaluate Hassan's claims for a maximum population growth rate for prehistory. Yet as Kirch (1984, 108) observes, colonizing propagules are not subject to density-dependent controls, and population growth rates might well have been higher than would be the case in later prehistory. Brewis et al. (1990, 352), for example, estimate a rate of 0.00875 for New Zealand prehistoric populations based on skeletal data, a number roughly equivalent to that proposed by Rallu (2003) in his demographic growth model for pre-Contact Polynesia. Notably, a rate of 0.008 would fully account for the projected Lapita population in Tonga with a founding population size of 100 or slightly fewer.

The end of the Lapita period in Tongan prehistory, as elsewhere in Remote Oceania, is demarcated by the loss of decorated ceramics and, in a few cases, loss of the vessel forms to which the decoration had been applied (Kirch 1997). The sequent phase — referred to as Polynesian Plainware after its associated ceramic style — spans the period from 700 BC to AD 400. Encompassing over a millennium, it is a critical period for transformation and development of an ancestral Polynesian society within Tonga and Samoa (see Kirch and Green 2001). Indeed, it is near the end of this phase that exploration and settlement of Eastern Polynesia commenced, an event one might read as a potential correlate for population pressure within the ancestral Polynesian homeland.

Agricultural Intensification and Population Dispersal in the Plainware Phase (700 BC to AD 400)

Dedicated archaeological research into the Polynesian Plainware phase in Tonga has been limited, and our understanding of ceramic types, unfortunately, does not yet facilitate fine-grained chronological control. Plainware assemblages are dominated by large, thin-walled, subglobular jars with restricted orifices (Burley 1998, 361–362). These jars have a relatively large holding capacity (Groube 1971, 299) and most likely were used for storage. Smaller bowls and cups also occur but diminish in frequency with time (Dye 1996). We presently have an inadequate understanding of how, at what rate, and why pottery disappears at the end of this period. While impressionistic, ceramics seem to not only decrease in volume as the period progressed, but ultimately become thicker and more crudely manufactured. Green (1974) proposed this pattern for Plainware ceramic transition in Samoa as well.

Interpretation of Plainware sites relative to their potential for archaeological demography, as was the case with Lapita, is prone to problems. Many of the recorded sites represent no more than scatters of surface sherds in ploughed fields or other exposures, and their correlation with or comparability to distinct settlement locales remains dubious. This is particularly the case on Tongatapu, where Spennemann's (1986, 1989) mid-1980s surveys documented abundant ceramic scatters throughout all areas of the island (Figure 10.6). In other cases, such as Kirch (1988, 38–40) found on Niuatoputapu, Plainware ceramics can be associated with an optimal landform and occur over several kilometers in an almost continual distribution. Defining site boundaries for comparison of spatial extent to settlements of the Lapita period or between islands during the Plainware phase

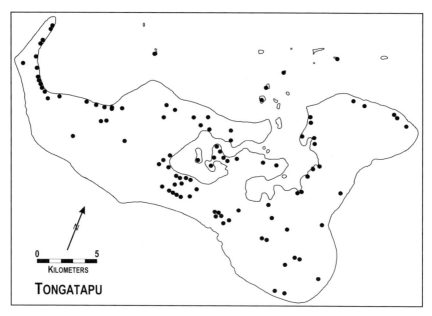

Figure 10.6. Plainware phase (700 BC–AD 400) ceramic sites on Tongatapu adapted from Spennemann (1986). With the exception of several sites on Fanga ʻUta Lagoon and a small number in western Tongatapu, most of these sites are limited scatters of surface ceramics in agricultural fields.

becomes impossible. Finally, the absence of even coarse chronological control means that Plainware site distributions on the landscape are a cumulative record of 1,100 years or more, without possibilities for tracking population shifts or settlement expansion. Yet at the same time — and as tentative as the Plainware ceramic data may seem — they do reflect upon significant demographic and economic changes taking place throughout the archipelago during the period 700 BC–AD 400.

Perhaps most important in the Plainware dataset is a clear indication of an extensive distribution of ceramics — and presumably people — during this period. On Tongatapu, for example, Plainware ceramics occur in all areas of the island, suggesting an expansive if not full use of the landscape by the end of the phase. In Haʻapai, all islands with agricultural soils have a thinly dispersed veneer of ceramics that — should systematic and intensive survey of inland fields be undertaken — would give a comparable site distribution to Tongatapu if plotted as equivalent dots on a map. And Plainware ceramics indicate not only a movement over the principal islands of the archipelago, they illustrate a use or settlement of the smaller and more marginal offshore islands as well as islands in the Tofua volcanic arc (Dye 1988, 285–286; Burley et al. 2003). Only Vavaʻu appears as a partial exception to this pattern. Here Plainware ceramic sites are largely concentrated on the southeastern group of islands, following a pattern established in Lapita times. The few scattered sherds found in contemporary villages on the principal island of Vavaʻu by Davidson (1971) and in more recent survey (Burley and Barton 2004) imply a probable expansion of population into the hinterlands of this island, but one beginning only at the very end of the ceramic era, ca. AD 400.

All recorded Lapita sites in Tonga had a continuous and expanded occupation through at least the early part of the Plainware phase. In some cases the spatial extent of the Plainware archaeological component indicates a substantial transformation of the former hamlet into a village-sized complex. On the Haʻapai island of ʻUiha, the early Lapita site of Vaipuna was confidently estimated to be no more than 25 x 40 m in extent; the subsequent Plainware settlement spread out for over 1 km in length, with the village facing the leeward coast (Burley 1996). Equivalent types of expansion can be noted for Lapita/Plainware sites elsewhere in Haʻapai and also on Fanga ʻUta Lagoon on Tongatapu. Increasing population densities in these original settlement locales gave way first to settlement expansion in other locales along the leeward coast and then into inland or windward areas or to other less favorable islands. On Lifuka, also in Haʻapai, settlement expansion during the Plainware era at the early Lapita site of Tongoleka again was considerable. Five additional settlement nodes were situated subsequently along the leeward shore over a distance of almost 5 km; a few others were then scattered inland or founded along the windward coast on the more extensive southern end of the island (Figure 10. 7) (Burley 1994, 390–393).

Dispersal of settlement in the Plainware phase on Tongatapu and the islands of Haʻapai appears to be correlated with a fundamental transformation in economy, where intensive dryland farming practices had been developed and where agricultural production had become a central concern. In fact, the widespread distribution of ceramic scatters on Tongatapu as recorded by Spennemann is explainable only by the use of field systems extending over the island's interior. Foraging of reef resources continued, but the critical role foraging seems to have played in Lapita settlement pattern is no longer supported by the faunal data. This economic transition is indirectly documented in the archaeological record in two ways. First, comparative analysis of faunal assemblages between Lapita and Plainware components suggest Lapita foraging activities had significant impacts on indigenous birds, iguana, shellfish, and perhaps turtle, leading to extinctions, localized extirpations, or population reductions (Dye and Steadman 1990; Steadman et al. 2002b). As a corollary, Plainware faunal assemblages other than fish have far fewer indigenous species, with greater representation of domestic animals (Steadman et al. 2002a). Second, sediment accumulation in many Plainware sites is often substantial, resulting in deposits of 1 m or more. Episodic volcanism

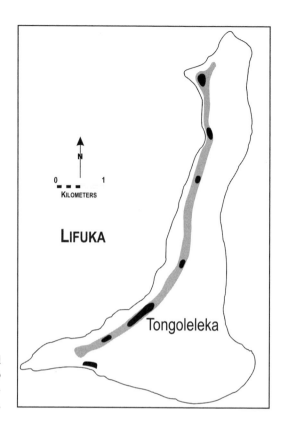

Figure 10.7. Midden ridge and Plainware phase (700 BC–AD 400) settlement sites on the island of Lifuka, Haʻapai Group.

LIFUKA

Tongoleleka

(Taylor 2003) or other geological processes (colluvial, aeolian, etc.) may explain these sediments in part but not fully. Rarely are the deposits uniform in thickness within a site or between sites, nor are they evenly distributed between the site and other areas of the landscape. I suggest that these deposits resulted largely from a long-term accumulation stemming from significant inputs of sediment transported from adjacent gardens by adhering to root crops, people, pigs, and in other ways.

An economic transition to intensive dryland agriculture expanded the carrying capacity threshold appreciably in Tonga, potentially allowing for populations to rise to the maximum predicted by Kirch and Maude. A population of 600 at the end of the Lapita period given an exponential growth rate of 0.008, as previously suggested for Lapita, would have reached the projected maximum around 200 BC. Even if the rate of growth had slowed to 0.005, full land capacity would have been accomplished by AD 200, two centuries prior to the end of the Plainware phase. Plainware ceramic distributions and site characteristics illustrate a widespread use of the landscape, a more dispersed population than was the case

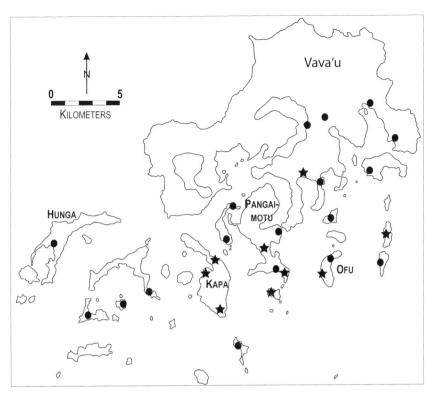

Figure 10.8. Plainware phase (700 BC–AD 400) ceramic sites on the islands of the Vava'u Group. Stars represent sites with substantial cultural deposits. Dots represent surface finds of Plainware ceramics.

earlier, and dense concentrations of people along leeward coastlines. Close examination of the Plainware archaeological data, however, does not support the kinds of population density predicted for later prehistory in all three island groups. Vava'u is the most notable exception in this respect, with significant parts of the group remaining largely unoccupied despite the presence of viable agricultural soils (Figure 10.8). And sites on Tongatapu — other than those on the lagoon or in some locales on the western leeward shore — are ephemeral deposits at best, representing limited occupations if not a single event. Only in the small islands of Ha'apai do Plainware sites give the impression of population size reaching full land use capacity. The origins for each of the contemporary villages in Ha'apai are documented in the Plainware period, and a range of other no longer occupied but substantial Plainware sites supports this interpretation.

If the Tongan population did not reach its maximum threshold based on agricultural production potential during the Plainware phase, then the growth rate of

0.008 predicted for the Lapita era must have been reduced substantially. In fact, a rate of 0.003 or slightly less accounts for a population size of about half of the predicted maximum by AD 400, a number in keeping with my general impression of the archaeological record. The factors contributing to this reduction are unknown, nor are archaeological correlates for population pressure or controls yet recorded — with one possible exception. That exception, as noted earlier, is the renewed evidence for long-distance voyaging during the late Plainware period as witnessed in the settlement of Eastern Polynesia, as well as limited evidence for the emergence of a long-distance exchange network (Burley and Clark 2003, 242–243). Whether a population reaching carrying capacity stimulated either of these is debatable.

A population growth rate of 0.003 over the Polynesian Plainware phase is attractive for more than its rough correlation of population size with what I perceive to be site distributions and ceramic densities in the archaeological record. Importantly, it would delay the attainment of a full population capacity for Tonga until well into the first millennium AD. And not insignificantly, it is only then that the archaeological record and traditional history begin to document large-scale changes taking place that can confidently be correlated with substantial population increases. These changes relate to the emergence, consolidation, and hegemonic expansion of a Tongan maritime chiefdom.

Considerations of Later Prehistory and the Tongan Maritime Chiefdom

The disappearance of ceramics from the Tongan archaeological record creates a problem for archaeologists first in our ability to succinctly identify settlement locales and second in the related loss of a proxy for tracking population distributions. These problems are further compounded by the absence of monumental architecture, burial tumuli, or other features until nearly the end of the first millennium AD. While this intervening period has been labeled an "archaeological dark age" (Davidson 1979, 95), it is assumed that the slow rate of population growth suggested for the Plainware phase continued, with increased population size increasingly absorbed into vacant or underutilized land, especially in areas such as Vavaʻu, the windward coast of Tongatapu, smaller and less desirable islands throughout the archipelago, and on to the volcanic outliers. The political emergence of a dynastic Tongan chiefdom under the control of the paramount Tuʻi Tonga ultimately began to appear by AD 950 on the island of Tongatapu (Gifford 1929, 50). Oral traditions interestingly enough suggest that the origins of this dynasty did not come from the densely populated shoreline areas of Fanga ʻUta Lagoon or in western Tongatapu. Rather it was in the Fuamotu area of southeastern Tongatapu (Gifford 1929, 52; see also Spennemann 1989, 439), a locale overlapping the margins of the agriculturally productive loams and the more marginal silty clay (see Figure 10.2). This type of borderline locale with a lower carrying capacity threshold parallels circumstances elsewhere in Polynesia where population pressure in marginal environments gave rise to complex chiefly polities (Kirch 1984, 204, 1994).

Kirch (1984, 223) specifically has correlated increasing population pressure on agricultural productivity and competition for land with the emergence of a complex centralized chiefdom in Tonga. As he models it, a full land situation near the end of the first millennium AD on Tongatapu would result in a series of constantly competing regional chiefdoms with ever-increasing assimilation of smaller groups by larger ones. These regional chiefdoms, accordingly, are marked lexically by the appearance of the Tongan title Tu'i, literally translated as "Lord of the Place" (Kirch 1984). Continued competition for land between regional chiefs led to political consolidation by a single paramount line—the Tu'i Tonga. Traditional Tongan history, even with its metaphorical elements and mythologized vagaries (Gunson 1993), lends support to Kirch's interpretation. By no later than AD 1200, the Tu'i Tonga had gained full control of Tongatapu and moved his capital and ceremonial center first to Heketa on the leeward shore and then to Lapaha on Fanga 'Uta Lagoon (Kirch 1984, 227–232; Burley 1998, 373–374). The location of the latter is telling, for it provided an accessible harbor for an expanded and expanding maritime polity. By AD 1450, a widespread campaign of consolidation and control by the twenty-fourth Tu'i Tonga was waged throughout Ha'apai, Vava'u, and Niuatoputapu and into other areas of Western Polynesia (Kirch 1988; Burley 1995; Sand 1999a; etc.). This campaign was the inspiration for Guiart's (1963, 661) characterization of the later Tongan chiefdom as *"un empire insulair."*

The purpose of this chapter is not to document in detail archaeological or other evidence for the dynastic Tongan chiefdom. Rather, what is important from a demographic perspective is the emergence of this integrated polity as a theoretical response to and probable correlate of population pressure as carrying capacity limits were being reached (after Carneiro 1970). What is also important is that this maritime chiefdom, with its well-reported hegemonic expansion throughout Western Polynesia, created a series of density-dependent control mechanisms allowing the population within Tonga to stabilize at or below its maximum threshold. The principal mechanism was a straightforward out-migration of younger males. This first occurred as part of the conquest and subjugation process associated with Tongan expansion. Later it involved Tongans as mercenaries in overseas wars and as participants in long-distance voyages for the purposes of trade or acquisition of exotic goods (Davidson 1977; Burley 1998; Kaeppler 1978; Aswani and Graves 1998). Not insignificantly for demographic considerations in Tonga today, this pattern of out-migration established in prehistory continues to persist (Cowling 1990). Now, however, it has reduced competitive demands on land to the point where some islands in Haʻapai are all but abandoned (Evans 2001, 169).

Other than emigration, the dynastic chiefdom brought with it a variety of social and political responsibilities and protocols related to marriage regulation, chiefly servitude *(fatongia)*, warfare, and in other areas, with substantial repercussions for fertility, mortality, and population growth. Some, such as the wholesale slaughter of captured enemies and their families, are direct (see Gifford 1929, 204–227). Others, particularly those related to marriage regulation, can be subtler. Although related to land shortages and population pressure in the mid-twentieth century rather than in the dynastic chiefdom period, Rogers (1969, 218) provides an excellent illustration of how this latter type of check on population might work. Between 1956 and 1966, census data indicate a significant population rise throughout Tonga (36 percent) and a rapidly growing number of landless males. What the data concomitantly illustrate is a time-transgressive delay in the age of marriage for both sexes, a pattern with obvious implications for longer-term fertility rates. In part, as Rogers suggests, this was due to out-migration of landless males, much as we anticipate in the dynastic Tongan chiefdom. Yet this pattern of delayed marriage also was in part due to increasing costs associated with traditional Tongan marriage rites. And in the latter, we have a no less significant cultural response to create a density-dependent control.

Further associated with the Tongan chiefdom was yet another fundamental transition in the nature of settlement pattern throughout the archipelago, one most likely rooted in continued competition for land. Whereas Lapita and Plainware phase settlements were aggregated hamlets and village-based residential units, the later population became dispersed across the landscape on traditional estates of chiefly lineages. Central to this pattern was the residential and ceremonial complex of the chief, a site clearly marked by monumental architecture, including an ancestral burial mound complex and freshwater bathing well (Kirch 1988; Burley 1994, 1998). Tongans describe this system of land use as creating *fanongonongo tokoto*, where news literally could be shouted from one household to the next as it traveled from one end of an island to the other (Bott 1982, 16). Dispersed settlement by the extended lineage and followers of a chief provided security of chiefly land tenure. It also maximized usage of the productive land base insofar as land-using groups were widely scattered, and in this latter capacity it may well have raised the carrying capacity threshold.

Our only direct insight into Tongan prehistoric demography comes from the excavation of two dynastic chiefdom burial mounds by Davidson (1969a) at ʻAtele on Fanga ʻUta Lagoon. Pietrusewsky (1969) analyzed the ninety-nine individuals that were recovered, being able to place sixty-one of these into age-specific classes.

These data subsequently allowed Kirch (1984, 112) to construct a life table profile for comparison to other Polynesian datasets. The 'Atele burial sample is particularly notable for its high levels of infant and child mortality, as well as having the lowest expectation for survivorship in all of the populations examined by Kirch. It is believed that the 'Atele mounds were constructed and used after the Tongan population had reached its maximum threshold. To Kirch, this low expectation of survivorship was a direct response to "density-dependent effects," the latter serving to stabilize the population at or below the island's carrying capacity limit (116). Kirch does not clearly define what density-dependent effects he is referring to, but his reference to "nutritional status" suggests food stress as a most likely explanation.

Conflict and warfare are inherent in many demographic models where populations are able to rise to their maximum capacity (see Carneiro 1970). In Polynesia this is well recorded for Easter Island, Tahiti, Hawai'i, the Marquesas, New Zealand, and elsewhere (Kirch 1984, 195–216). For the dynastic Tongan chiefdom, this conflict was first directed outward, expanding territorial conquest throughout the archipelago and into other island groups in Western Polynesia by the mid-fifteenth century AD. Hegemonic expansion, as I have argued, became one of several density-dependent control mechanisms, helping to regulate population growth in islands at the chiefdom's core. By the late eighteenth century, this no longer was the case. Incongruities in the appointment to chiefly title, regional rivalries, dense population throughout the archipelago, and competition for land led the chiefdom to literally implode, and for the next half century Tonga became engaged in intense and destructive warfare. This event, combined with European disease, quickly led to the severe population decline that was evident in the 1891 census.

Conclusion

My intent has been to explore demographic patterns and processes in the historical and archaeological data of the Tongan archipelago with two objectives. The first relates to Tongan prehistory and what a demographic approach can tell of population dispersal, expansion, rates of growth, and transformation from first Lapita settlement of 950 BC up to the late dynastic Tongan chiefdom of the nineteenth century AD. Because written records and direct observation are lacking for much of this time, proxy data including different ceramic types, site distributions, and site sizes are necessarily applied. The second objective was to examine the implications of these data and consequential patterns for theoretical or methodological problems in demographic archaeology as a whole. In this, and as Kirch asserts (2000, 307–313), a concern for archaeological demography within

Oceania takes on a measure of importance far beyond the archipelago to which it specifically relates.

In examining the *longue durée* of the Tongan past, I necessarily have urged caution with respect to the veracity of the data at hand and its reliability as a demographic proxy. Equating ceramic dispersal with population distribution and site size with population density can be legitimately criticized, for they lead only to hypothetical scenarios and speculative inferences. And using these results as a basis upon which to calculate or infer population growth rates, as has been done here, can be no more than conjecture. When all of the other unexamined variables that affect population growth are taken into account, one can only conclude that the data at hand are insufficient to say more than the obvious: Populations did in fact grow over time (see Clark 1988, 29 for a similar assessment for Hawai'i). Yet I would argue that patterning in the data reflects generally upon demographic trends in Tonga, and in this the data relate to the broader debate on the nature and form of demographic change in Oceania as a whole. One of the most important of these issues, as highlighted by Kirch (1984, 2000; see also Rallu 2003), is on the type and shape of the population growth curve itself, whether of exponential, logistic, or some other type.

Kirch asserts (1984, 103), and others are in agreement (see Clark 1988, 26), that some type of logistic process or sigmoid-shaped curve characterizes population growth on most Polynesian islands in prehistory. This includes a period of initial unrestrained exponential growth that ultimately is leveled off by density-dependent controls as a population nears its carrying capacity threshold. Data from both the early and later periods in the Tongan archaeological sequence well support this model. Population growth during the initial colonization episode does seem unrestrained and at a pace far higher than what appears the case in later prehistory. Thus, based on what we know of Lapita archaeological data, an estimated founding population of 100 grew to between 600 and 700 individuals dispersed throughout the archipelago during the first 250 years of the Tongan past. This increase requires a growth rate of ca. 0.008, a number in keeping with other areas in Polynesia as has been noted. We can also be reasonably certain that by the end of the first millennium AD, the Tongan landscape had reached or was close to reaching its maximum population threshold, one estimated at between 30,000 and 40,000 individuals. Thereafter, and as is characteristic of the logistic model, density-dependent controls served to check and stabilize population levels within carrying capacity limits. Discussions of these controls importantly relates them to the origins of the Tongan maritime chiefdom and eventually its expansion to other areas in Fiji and Western Polynesia.

As a conclusion based on the above, it is easy to concur with Kirch on the logistic nature of demographic processes taking place through Tongan prehistory. Yet it must also be acknowledged that the nature of population growth in the critical and lengthy interval between 700 BC and AD 1000 remains unclear. If exponential growth were continuous, as a logistic curve would assume, then a significantly reduced rate of less than 0.003 is required to account for lag time to maximum population size. Since this would be correlated with a transformation to and intensification in agricultural production in subsistence economy, it cannot easily be explained. This reduction, in fact, is the complete opposite of what we should expect, for agricultural populations are well documented as having significantly higher fertility rates than foragers or mixed horiticulturalists (Kelly 1995, 244). Anticipating such problems, Kirch notes that the logistic model's "underlying assumptions may not accurately reflect a 'real world' situation" (1984, 103). And because of this, he alternatively presents a number of modified logistic variations to potentially be taken into account. I suggest that one of these, the "stepped" model, provides an equally applicable if not more attractive hypothesis to consider in the Tongan case.

Stepped growth models incorporate alternating periods of exponential growth that — as carrying capacity limits are approached — become held in check by density-dependent controls. In the density-dependent interval(s), improvements in agricultural production systems or other technologies lead to an upward shift in carrying capacity limits, facilitating renewed exponential growth (Kirch 1984, 103). The growth curve thus appears stepped rather than continuous, and the consequential effect is a delay or reduction in the overall rate of growth through prehistory, as appears to be the situation in Tonga. The Plainware archaeological data in Tonga are not fine grained enough to identify population plateaus and periods of accelerated growth. These also, no doubt, varied significantly in the different island groups that constitute the archipelago. It nevertheless is assumed that the significant exploitation impacts on terrestrial and reef resources recorded in the Lapita phase led to an archipelago-wide lowering of carrying capacity in early Plainware times. A correlative reduction in the population growth rate, if not an actual density-dependent plateau, can be expected. By the middle to late Plainware period, it can further be hypothesized that the carrying capacity threshold was pushed upwards again, no doubt the result of refinements and intensification in dryland agricultural production. The consequence of these improvements was widespread population expansion and the permanent establishment of inland and windward settlement nodes. A stepped model of population growth might even be characteristic of population shifts in the late chiefdom phase in Tongan prehistory. The significant transformation in settlement pattern from aggregated hamlets to widespread dispersal arguably served to raise carrying capacity and the corresponding thresholds for population maxima.

The Tongan archaeological record may never provide the secure and detailed data that demographers consider instrumental for analysis of population distributions in the past. Its basic structure with changing rates of population growth, differential expansion and densities in different island groups, the economic integration of agricultural production with reef and marine resources, and the nature of density-dependent controls within the Tongan maritime chiefdom are nevertheless illustrative of the complex and difficult issues we face in gaining an understanding of population and its transformation in the *longue durée* of Oceanic prehistory. Future and directed research in these areas, particularly in the period 700 BC to AD 1000, will be essential.

Notes

The majority of fieldwork on which this chapter is based has been supported by grants from the Social Sciences and Humanities Research Council of Canada between 1990 and the present. I am also extremely grateful to the government of Tonga for assistance and support over this period of time, especially that given by the Prime Minister's Office and the Tongan Traditions Committee. I thank all of the participants in the Moʻorea Long-Term Demographic Evolution workshop for their feedback and the collegiality offered to a newcomer to this field. I am also grateful to Dr. Margaret Purser, Sonoma State University, for her insight and input. Finally, I thank Andrew Barton and Jessi Witt of Simon Fraser University for their skill in preparation of the figures included herein.

11

ROGER C. GREEN

Protohistoric Samoan Population

Editors' note: The first portion of this chapter is the text of a
manuscript drafted by Roger C. Green in 1972 — and until now
unpublished — addressing the question of protohistoric Samoan
population. At the editors' request, this manuscript was distributed
to the participants of the 2003 Mo'orea conference. Professor Green
has kindly agreed to the inclusion of this important document in
the present volume and has added an addendum (see "Concluding
Commentary: September 2004") based on his reflections some three
decades after the original analysis was penned. (Note that usage of
"Western Samoa" has been retained throughout the original essay.
The name has now been officially shortened to "Samoa.")

Drawing upon reconnaissance surveys of prehistoric and early
historic sites throughout Western Samoa and on settlement
pattern surveys in selected project areas, archaeologists have
demonstrated the territorial extent of former settlement (with
fairly continuous occupation) inland from the coastal zone, as
well as its antiquity. These patterns furnish an obvious contrast to modern settlement, where the distribution was overwhelmingly coastal. This modern distribution, which we know from historical studies, dates back to the AD 1840 period,
although not necessarily earlier. Villages *(nu'u)* in the traditional nucleated Samoan pattern that are known to be from this early historical period (from 1840
onward) occur rarely — or not at all — in the archaeological record, particularly
in zones inland from the coast. Was the change from the prehistoric situation as
defined archaeologically to that of the 1840s pattern and after simply one of population *redistribution,* or did it also reflect population *change?* The archaeological
data from Samoa, I conclude, are sufficient to make further examination of this
question worthwhile. Figure 11.1a locates the islands of Samoa within the central
Pacific and provides the names of its main islands, while Figure 11.1b locates them
within the wider Pacific region.

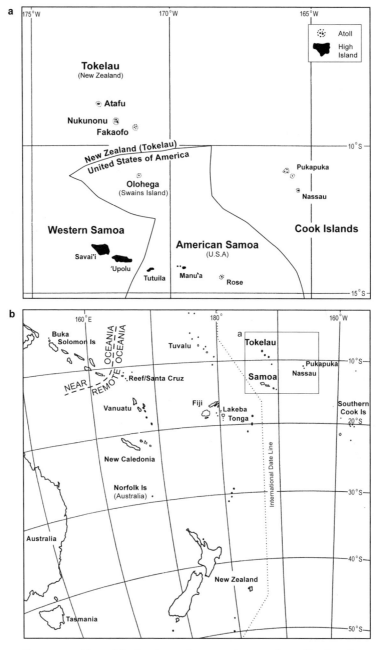

Figure 11.1a. Map of the South Pacific region showing the atolls of Atafu, Nukunonu, and Fakaofo and Olohega (Swains Island) and the islands of Samoa and American Samoa, with negotiated international maritime boundaries. (Amended from *Atlas of New Zealand Boundaries* [Kelly and Marshall 1996, fig 1.2], by courtesy of the authors.)

b. Map of the South Pacific region showing New Zealand and Samoa, with the atolls of Tuvalu, Tokelau, and Pukapuka.

Three aspects of the problem require discussion:

1. The earliest reliable estimates of Samoan population size and distribution, which involves a review of the relevant historical sources;
2. Estimates of the amount of occupied and cultivated land probably required by a population of this size, which involves an analysis of former Samoan cultivation practices; and
3. The extent of occupation and cultivation in prehistory based on the archaeological record, which involves an analysis of land usage that relates the archaeological record to population size.

Each topic will be examined separately in support of the claim for a greater population in the past than obtained in the mid-nineteenth century. The implications for Samoan prehistory will then be taken up in the conclusion.

The Historical Record

The question of Samoan population size as inferred from historical records has already been extensively discussed by Watters (1958, 3), Freeman (1964, 565, fn 3), Pirie (1963, 1968), McArthur (1967, 98–115), and Davidson (1969). McArthur's position (1967, 115) is that the historical documents do not warrant inferring a population for all Samoa of greater than 37,000 or 38,000 for the period after the late 1830s, when the missionary efforts at census began to be reasonably effective. More importantly, no reasonable evidence for a population greater than 40,000 in the early 1800s or before was forthcoming (104), despite some general estimates in the literature to the contrary. A second position is that "it is possible with graph, map and high frustration tolerance to reconstruct the distribution of the population of Samoa in the 1840's, and to trace its growth trend through until the first official censuses after partition, all within an acceptable margin for error" (Pirie 1963, 43–44, 63–64, and fig 4). This leads us to believe that the population was more than 40,000 in AD 1844–1845 and even higher in the 1830s and before.

All investigators seem agreed that the historical records are sufficient to claim approximately 33,900 as a reasonable estimate of population size for Samoa in 1853, after which it continued to fluctuate up to 1921 approximately as shown in Figure 11.2. Then, with an improvement in health services and reduction in infant mortality, it began a steady and unabated rise to well over 130,000 in the last decade (referring to the early 1970s, when this essay was originally written).

The controversial issue is the hypothesis of a marked population decline in the 1820s to 1840s, which was only partially recorded in the historical records. Pirie (1968) was initially led to this conclusion by inferences from the historical records and demographic considerations, and he has been further encouraged in

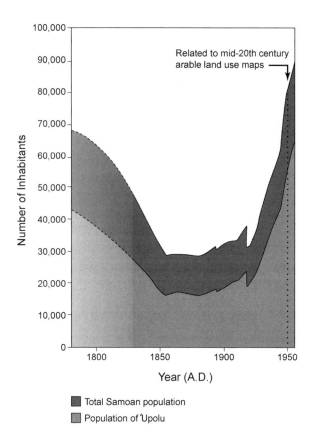

Figure 11.2. An enhanced representation of Samoan population history from AD 1790 to 1950 (after a figure in Pirie 1963).

In the figure:
- Y-axis: Number of Inhabitants (0 to 100,000)
- X-axis: Year (A.D.) (1800 to 1950)
- Annotation: Related to mid-20th century arable land use maps
- Legend: Total Samoan population; Population of 'Upolu

this view by the archaeological evidence that has subsequently been accumulating from Western Samoa. Davidson (1969b) has assembled archaeological evidence that shows that the distribution of population between 1820 and 1840 has certainly changed, from one more widespread both on the coast and inland to one of more tightly nucleated villages almost solely on the coast. She examines the hypothesis of correlating this change with reduction of population size and concludes that the hypothesis of a larger population requires serious consideration given the archaeological evidence of far greater settlement inland in the past than obtained in AD 1840. I contend that the hypothesis is one that deserves serious consideration, as it cannot be disproved on the basis of the historical record alone, and it receives some support from the archaeological record.

Scholars who have examined the Samoan records generally agree that estimates for the nineteenth century must be based on missionary sources because only they had the contacts and organization necessary to produce satisfactory results (Pirie 1968, 44). There is nothing in the accounts of the early explorers or local residents to suggest they had more than an impressionistic basis for their figures, and they will not be discussed here. However, the estimates provided by Wilkes in 1839, by Home in 1844, by Maxwell in 1848, and by Erskine in 1849, because they derive from the missionaries, deserve a careful assessment.

Close study of the population estimates given in the records between 1832 and 1845 indicate that missionary endeavors slowly changed from rough approximations in round numbers based on general impressions to fairly good approximations based on repeated head counts. Thus the 1845 census, which Stair (1897) describes as the first successful one, becomes an important control for population size in the 1840s when placed in its historical context. Its assessment requires a brief review of the mission estimates that preceded it.

General estimates of the Samoan population begin with Williams (1832) of the London Missionary Society (LMS), who in 1832 suggested a population of 40,000 to 50,000 for the Leeward Group (Western Samoa). Turner (1835), the Wesleyan missionary, began his Samoan work in 1835 with an impression that there were about 25,000 people, of which the Wesleyans had 2,000 as adherents. By 1836 he revised this to 30,000 and claimed 7,000 adherents (1836). He cited no further figures for total population, but by 1837 he was able to claim an establishment in Western Samoa, with its stronghold in Savai'i, of 13,000 adherents, eighty chapels in villages, and 1,000 Samoan employees (Gilson 1970). That his claim is not unreasonable is indicated by Heath's citation of it in December of 1837 and the fact that the London Missionary Society at this time was willing to credit him with 10,000 converts (Gilson 1970, 85, fn 56).

Buzacott (1836–1837), another LMS visitor in 1836, continued the tradition of general impressions when he placed 20,000 on each of the larger islands, giving as his opinion "That it may be more, but could not think it less." The LMS claims in 1837, first to 14,000 adherents on 'Upolu and Manono (Mills 1838), and then 18,000 adherents for all Western Samoa, are more open to dispute than Turner's. While it is difficult to tell whether the people enumerated were nominal adherents of the LMS, Wesleyans also counted as LMS, or "heathens," it is apparent that at this time and thereafter the missionaries were counting heads and revising their estimates accordingly. Moreover, their comments reveal that they were now aware of the problem of shifting population, though this factor continued to plague census efforts in Samoa for a long time thereafter. Mills and Heath, for example, initially counted houses and arrived at 14,000 adherents on 'Upolu and Manono based on an average number of occupants per house. The figure was reduced to 13,000 after Heath (1838a) counted heads (5,800) in his district, in the course of which he found that some 600 or 700 adherents were previously counted in Mills' district. Mills, he noted, had not yet counted heads, though his district was the most populous. By this he meant some 7,200 people — the value arrived at if one subtracts his 5,800 adherents and the 5,000 he said they had counted on Savaiʻi from his estimate of 18,000 adherents for the whole Leeward (Western Samoa) Group.

In 1839, Turner and the Wesleyan missionaries were forced by a decision of the parent societies in England to abandon the mission in Western Samoa, leaving the field clear for the LMS (Gilson 1970). In the same year, the LMS missionaries reported to Wilkes that 12,500 in Western Samoa had "actually embraced Christianity"—that is, they were able to read and had passed through the initial stage of Christian "inquiry" to baptism (95–96). On the other hand, about two-thirds of the whole population was reported to belong to the Christian party (Wilkes 1845, 2:130). Two-thirds of the 46,000 total for Western Samoa cited by Wilkes yields 30,667 who were nominal Christians, and among this number presumably there were 13,000 Wesleyans, 12,500 LMS church members, and some 5,000 others who were Christian adherents. What is important is that the LMS was now able to number its church members and pupils fairly closely. Thus there is little reason to doubt the figures given to Wilkes in those two columns of Table 11.1, although the same does not apply to the column for total population.

The Wilkes estimates of total population can be shown to be inaccurate for a number of its island categories. For instance, a fairly accurate census taken in 1840 for American Samoa counted 4,300 people on Tutuila and 1,174 on Manuʻa (Murray 1840; Heath 1840a). Clearly the estimate of 10,000 given to Wilkes in 1839 as the total population for American Samoa is in error, although the figures for church members and pupils appear quite reasonable. In the same way, the figure of 500 for the total population on Apolima is high; it should probably be 75, in line with the 100 church members and 120 pupils reported and the observation of 75 people in twenty houses by Wilkes (1845, 2:108). The Manono figure is, on the other hand, probably fairly accurate. In 1832, Williams noted in a brief visit some 2,000 people on Manono and 100 on Apolima. Turner in 1835 reduced his Manono figures to between 1,000 and 1,500, and Heath in 1838 says 1,000.

By 1840 only the earlier figures of 25,000 for ʻUpolu and 20,000 for Savaiʻi remained unverified and still in need of revision. By the 1845 census, both of these figures as well as the others had been reduced to acceptable levels. In 1844, Home was given an estimate by Mills, the LMS missionary stationed at Apia, which shows that all the Western Samoan figures had been revised except the long-repeated estimate of 25,000 for ʻUpolu (Table 11.2). This remained unchanged. By now the situation of Methodist and LMS adherents had been clarified and the Savaiʻi figures revised accordingly, as were those for Manono and Apolima. The estimated number of heathens in Western Samoa, moreover, had dropped significantly from the figure of ca. 15,000 given to Wilkes to 5,600.

In the next year, the LMS took its first recorded census of the population for

Table 11.1. Population of Samoa in 1839.

	Population	Professed Christians	Pupils
Eastern Group (Manu'a)	2,000	150	150
Tutuila	8,000	2,200	1,900
'Upolu	25,000	8,000	6,200
Savai'i	20,000	4,000	3,700
Manono	1,100	400	230
Apolima	500	100	120
Total	56,600	14,850	12,300

Source: Wilkes (1845, 2:130)

Table 11.2. Population of Western Samoa in 1844 according to the LMS missionary Mills.

	Population	Comments
'Upolu	25,000	(with 5,000 "heathens")
Savai'i	16,000	(with 600 "heathens")
Manono	1,400	(with all Christians; presumably including Apolima, for which no separate figure is given)

Source: Home (1844) as cited in Pirie (1964, 43)

the entire group. At this point, only the standing estimate for 'Upolu still required radical revision. Stair says: "Of the population in 1845 it is possible to speak with some accuracy since a successful census was made at that time. But even then, through native prejudices, it was difficult to obtain correct return from some of the districts. It was considered that the population at that time was about 40,000; an underestimate probably, but it certainly did not exceed 45,000" (1897).

Confirmation of the 1845 census results as being a better estimate than that given by Wilkes is contained in Pritchard (1845): "It has been stated that the whole group contains 60,000 but from a census lately taken by the missionaries it is evident that they do not exceed 40,000." As Pirie notes, it was Stair rather than Pritchard "who was likely to have been best informed about the methods used in taking this census" (1963, 43). As he probably had some hand in its organization, it is significant that Stair thought it was an undercount.

Although no details of the census seem to have survived, it is not difficult to derive population figures for Western Samoa from it. Pirie adopts a conservative position by taking 5,250 persons as an approximation for the eastern group and subtracting this from 40,000 to arrive at 34,750 for Western Samoa. In light of Stair's appraisal of the 40,000 figure as an underestimation of the total population, I have simplified Pirie's figures to 5,000+ for American Samoa and 35,000+ for Western Samoa. If these values are placed in the context of the other population figures available from 1840 to 1853, the result is a very consistent pattern from which several trends can be extracted (Table 11.3). First, reasonably well-supported figures for American Samoa indicate a population decrease of some 14.8 percent between 1840 and 1853. A decline of a similar order for Western Samoa, 16.5 percent, is also in evidence. Moreover, figures for the intervening years provided by Maxwell for 1848 and Erskine for 1849 are in line with those postulated for American and Western Samoa in 1845, given the respective positions of each within a general framework of population loss. Finally, an attempt to set out population sizes by individual islands from 1840–1844 to 1853 yields equally acceptable values for 1845 consistent with those discussed above and a total population of 40,000+ (Table 11.4). Only the 'Upolu figure given to Home in 1844 requires a massive downward revision on the order of 6,400. As noted above, this was to be expected because it was the one much earlier estimate whose unreliable origin had not been revised subsequent to 1845 as a result of increasingly better head counts.

It is worth noting that in Table 11.4 the total population figures for Samoa throughout the 1840s are reasonably well supported by independent historical sources and in correct yearly order. The same applies to eight of the fourteen estimates for individual islands during this period. Among the six remaining figures, five belong to 1845, for which no returns by island are available. These results perhaps adequately demonstrate that by the 1840s it is possible to reconstruct estimates for the distribution of the population within the Samoan group to an acceptable margin of error. From the historical evidence, we can conclude that in the early 1840s the Samoan population was of the order of 42,000 ± 1,000, and in some thirteen years or less it had decreased by around 18 percent to about 33,900. The early 1840 population may be divided with some assurance into approximately 5,500 people in American Samoa and 36,500 in Western Samoa and with somewhat less assurance into the population sizes by island as set out in Table 11.4.

Before 1840, population estimates recorded in the Samoan literature, whether by missionaries or casual visitors, are too impressionistic to serve as reliable guides and may not be used to assess former population size or its distribution. It is also unlikely that the documented decline from the 1840s to 1853 constitutes the total extent of that loss as commonly recorded in the early stages of regular European contact in the Pacific — in the Samoan case, providentially caught by the portion of the historical record judged to be reliable. The continuous historical record by

Table 11.3. Census estimates and population decline in Samoa, 1840–1853.

	1840–1844	1845	1848	1849	1853	% decline
Western Samoa	42,000[1]	35,000	33,000	32,000	29,237	16.5% (1845 to 1853)
American Samoa	5,474[2]	5,000+	—	5,000	4,664	14.8% (1845 to 1853)
Total	47,474	40,000+	—	37,000	33,901	15.2% (1845 to 1853)

[1] In 1844, based on a census in which the estimate for 'Upolu was still too great by about 6,400 people.

[2] In 1840, based on a fairly accurate census.

Sources: 1840 (Murray 1840; Heath 1840a); 1844 (Home 1844); 1845 (Stair 1897); 1848 (Maxwell 1848); 1849 (Erskine 1853); 1853 (Samoan Reporter, No. 15, 1854).

the missionaries, reviewed above, begins ten years earlier, and general observations on the subject go back to La Pérouse in 1787. Regular contact with Europeans, including a small number of resident beachcombers (Maude 1968), begins in the mid-1820s, before which recorded contacts were few, brief, and irregular. Still, there is an interval of regular European contact whose length is more than equal that of the period of recorded population loss. During this interval, introduced diseases or local wars could have taken their toll, and the numbers involved have gone unrecorded, just as they did in nearby Tonga (Green 1973). Unfortunately, few good accounts of the introduction of such diseases or of the epidemics that usually follow are recorded in the early documents or traditions before 1840 (Pirie 1963, 21–28). The only two with reasonable documentation are influenza epidemics in 1830 and 1839 (59). This unusual circumstance leads Pirie (23) to suggest that perhaps the initial introductions of some of the more common European diseases were prior to the 1830s and a result of known contacts in the 1800–1830 period with Tongan visitors from a population that had suffered serious population loss in this period from such diseases. On the other hand, traditional accounts of wars in the 1800–1830 period are well documented (Kramer 1902). The last of these, in 1830, which featured the political rise of Malietoa Vaninupo, seemingly had devastating though probably exaggerated historical consequences, at least for the population of A'ana (Heath 1838b). Thus, given large but historically unrecorded population loss in nearby Tonga between 1800 and 1850 as a result of disease and war, a similar decline in Samoa should be viewed as a reasonable hypothesis for examination by other methods.

The problem is how to demonstrate such a decline using other than historical

Table 11.4. Estimates of Samoan population size by island, 1840–1853.

	1840–1844	Internal estimate for 1845	1848–1849	1853	1840–1844 to 1853 % change
'Upolu	18,600[1]	18,200	18,000[4]	15,587	16.2% decline
Manono	1,400[2]	1,300		1,015	14.0% decline
Apolima				191	
Savai'i	16,000[2]	15,500	15,000[4]	12,444	22.3% decline
Western Samoa	36,000	35,000+	33,000	29,237	18.8% decline
Tutuila	4,300[3]	3,800	3,600–3,700[5]	3,389	21.3% decline
Manu'a	1,174[3]	1,200	1,300–1,400[5]	1,275	8.0% increase
Samoan Group	41,474	40,000+	38,000	33,901	18.3% decline

Sources:

[1] The 25,000 estimate given by Home (1844) has been corrected here to 18,600 to bring it into line with all other figures.

[2] The figures, also from Home (1844), appear to be in line with the later estimates.

[3] These figures for 1840 are from Murray (1840) and Heath (1840a). A figure of 4,000 for 1843 is given by Erskine (1853, 60); see fn 5 below.

[4] These figures are from Maxwell (1848), whose total of 33,000 is only 1,000 greater than the 32,000 of Erskine (1853, 103) in 1849. However, Erskine's apportionment of the 32,000, placing 20,000 on 'Upolu, including Monono, and 12,000 on Savai'i, appears to be in error. An internal adjustment of 2,500 is required to bring Erskine's figures into line with the others before and after.

[5] These figures for 1849 are from Erskine (1853, 60), who remarks: "It is feared that the population is decreasing though not rapidly, as is now estimated by the missionaries, who have the means of knowing with tolerable exactness, at from 3,600 to 3,700 souls, having been called 4,000 ten years before." Elsewhere (1853, 104) he places 5,000 on Tutuila and Manu'a, yielding the quite reasonable result of 1,300–1,400 for Manu'a.

evidence. Here a technique employed in Tonga would appear appropriate, particularly as the results can be related to archaeological and historical observations on land use prior to the period for which we have adequate census figures (Green 1972). Moreover, the procedure may be tested on the 1840 American Samoa population figures before being utilized in population estimates for Western Samoa prior to 1840.

Land Use in American Samoa in 1840

The approximate amount of cultivated land required by a population of 42,000 in Samoa can be calculated with a fair degree of accuracy. In addition, a total for the amount of land occupied by such a population can be estimated within reasonable limits and the results related to historical studies of the extent of settlement ca. AD 1840. The question can then be asked whether such a population would equally well account for the extent of prehistoric settlement recorded in the archaeological records or whether a greater population at some point in the past is required.

In these calculations, there are several reasons for beginning with American Samoa as an initial test of the procedures. First, of the early figures on population size reviewed above, those for American Samoa in 1840 are among the most reliable. Next, an analysis along the lines employed here has already been carried out for American Samoa by Lay (1959) as part of a method he developed for estimating prehistoric population sizes on Polynesian islands. While I do not agree with his general method, I nonetheless find the data for American Samoa helpful. Finally, the American Samoan results go some way toward providing a check on the application of the method independent of its application in Western Samoa, where the results become crucial to arguments over population sizes in the period before 1840.

Lay's initial analysis involves estimating the amount of cultivable land that would have been required by a contact population in American Samoa. Using extensive agricultural data collected in the late 1920s for a population of 8,987 and previously analyzed by Coulter (1941), he attempted to determine how much land was required for each of the traditional subsistence crops and arrived at acceptable values for taro, bananas, yam, arrowroot, and miscellaneous root crops, as well as for breadfruit. Only the coconut, also involved as a cash crop, presented difficulties requiring certain corrections. The figures obtained were then modified slightly to approximate more closely the prehistoric situation, with a population of 5,500 — the population of 1840 — using 2,750 acres in any one year. The result is that root crops were found to require about 0.24 acre per person and tree crops (breadfruit and coconuts) about 0.26 acre. The figure of 0.5 acre/person/year of cultivated land for American Samoa at which Lay arrived was judged to have uniform application throughout Polynesia as a means of estimating prehistoric population size. I would disagree with this, arguing that while it applies to American Samoa, it requires adjustment on other islands with different crops and soils (Bellwood 1971, 1972; Green 1973).

For American Samoa, Lay notes that the arable or potentially cultivable land is about one-third of the total, or about 14,144 acres, with Tutuila accounting for 9,408 acres. By his methods, if 50 percent of the cultivable land on Tutuila was in use, a population of 9,400 would result; if 33 percent, a population of 6,200; and if 25 percent, a population of 4,700. On this basis, the 1840 Tutuila population of 4,300 would have used some 23 percent of the arable land in any one year. His calculations, however, avoid the distinction between root crops that are planted in cultivation cycles and include intervals of fallow and tree crops that are not and use the same ground through several cycles. They also do not contain information on the amount of land required over the course of a complete cultivation cycle; that is, no allowance is made for the amount of land that is left in fallow when the rest is in cultivation.

To overcome this defect, a table employing typical Samoan crop-fallow cultivation cycles (Coulter 1941, 26; Farrell and Ward 1962, 199–200, 201–210) has been constructed using Lay's figures of 0.24 acre for root crops and 0.26 acre for tree crops. In addition, figures of 0.30 and 0.34 acre for root crops have been added on grounds justified below in connection with Western Samoa. These Samoan figures, it is worth noting, lie between the values of 0.35 and 0.40 acre that appear to have characterized prehistoric and early historic requirements in Tonga, where the dominant crop was yam, and the modern values of 0.11 and 0.15 acre recorded in relatively isolated Atiu (Crocombe 1964, 138; Barrau 1961, 25), where wet taro formed the dominant crop.

Estimates of total land areas and the percentage cultivable in American Samoa vary slightly in the literature. Coulter (1941, 28) gives a third, while more recent sources suggest 28 percent (*Annual Report* 1967) and 30 percent (*Pacific Islands Yearbook* 1972). Employing the commonly cited figures of 52 mi^2 for Tutuila and 19 mi^2 for the Manu'a Group, this yields totals in the 13,000 to 16,000 arable acres range. Holmes (1974, 102) notes that in all American Samoa, 14,830 acres were under cultivation in 1950, decreasing to 11,321 acres in 1960. Arable land in American Samoa can therefore be placed at ca. 15,000 acres with some degree of confidence. Of this, about 10,000 is on Tutuila and 4,000 in the Manu'a Group, with the rest on Swains Island. These figures for arable land differ only to a minor degree from those employed by Lay.

Using 1.3 ± 0.2 acres from Table 11.5a, land use requirements can be generated for various sizes of population as in Table 11.5b. In Table 11.5a the requirements of an 1840 population of 5,500 are calculated, which in contrast to Lay indicate that some 43 to 59 percent of the arable land was actually in use. The overall results are similar to those for eighteenth-century Tonga and imply conditions where a population is approaching substantial use of its arable land — but not a point at which it is putting an undue pressure on this resource. At 4,300, the population of Tutuila would be only slightly under values where the extent of land use in relation to carrying capacity might be expected to raise the threat of an impending land shortage and where reduction mechanisms bringing the population toward a fluctuating though steady state could be expected to begin. The requirements of 1,200 people on Manu'a, on the other hand, were well below these values (Table 11.5a).

Could higher populations have obtained in the past? Table 11.5b goes some dis-

Table 11.5. Cultivated land requirements in American Samoa, 1840.

Part a

	No. of cultivated acres			% of arable land in use		
	Total	Tutuila	Manua	Total	Tutuila	Manua
Population:	(5,500)[1]	(4,300)[1]	(1,200)[1]	(14,000)[2]	(10,000)[2]	(4,000)[2]
Acreage per person						
1.1	6,050	4,730	1,320	43	47	33
1.3	7,150	5,590	1,560	51	56	39
1.5	8,250	6,450	1,800	59	65	45

Part b

				6,500[1]	7,000[1]	7,500[1]
Population:	6,500[1]	7,000[1]	7,500[1]	(14,000)[2]	(14,000)[2]	(14,000)[2]
Acreage per person						
1.1	7,150	7,700	8,250	51.1	55	58.9
1.3	8,450	9,100	9,750	60.4	65	69.4
1.5	9,750	10,500	11,250	69.6	75	80.3

[1]People
[2]Acres

tance toward answering this question. While population may have been more, it could not have been of the order of the 10,000 recorded by Wilkes, as without an unrecorded degree of agricultural intensification, a population of this size would have involved up to 100 percent use of the arable land. Nor does it support Lay's maximum value for annual land use of 50 percent, which implies a population of 9,400 on Tutuila, for example, as this too is impossible without some kind of intensification of the agricultural system. Such intensification did not occur in American Samoa. It is absent from the archaeological record for the prehistoric period and is not recorded ethnohistorically during the 1840s (Watters 1958). In short, there is little evidence of wet or dry terracing, permanent field boundaries, pondfields, or other features that are the typical archaeological indications of intensification (Kikuchi 1963). In fact, Lay's average value for annual land use of 33 percent, implying a Tutuila population of 6,200, in reality would have required use of between 68 and 93 percent of the arable land when the necessary allowances for fallow are made. A more likely total for the prehistoric population of American Samoa is 6,500, which would have involved use of some 51 to 70 percent of the arable land. With up to 6,500 people, a population could be maintained at a steady state, as it is below the 7,000 to 7,500 people and 60 to 80 percent land use values that might be expected either to trigger off population reduction mechanisms or induce intensification within some aspects of the agricultural system.

There are three important points here. First, before AD 1840, subsistence agriculture in American Samoa not only could have supported 6,500 people, but a population of this size could easily have been achieved in the more than 2,800 years it had been occupied, even at minimal rates of population growth. That it had a larger population than the 5,500 of 1840 is suggested, though not yet satisfactorily demonstrated, by the initial archaeological survey of Tutuila. This revealed extensive prehistoric settlement of areas inland that are only now being returned to cultivation (Kikuchi 1963). Second, in the fifteen years before 1840, an unrecorded decline of 15 percent from a population of 6,500 is quite in line with the approximately equal decline from 5,500 to 4,650 people recorded between 1840 and 1853. The hypothesis of an overall population decline of 28 percent in American Samoa resulting from contact with Europeans in the 1830s and 1840s thus seems warranted and deserving of closer examination. In this respect, it is interesting that it is the more isolated population of Manu'a, where utilization of the arable land was less than 50 percent, that little or no decline was recorded in the 1840 to 1853 period. Third, the method employed here confirms independently that Wilkes' figure of 10,000 for 1839 is not acceptable and also that Lay's maximum and average values are unreasonable because they do not allow for sufficient fallow. On the other hand, the basic figures given by Lay for prehistoric root and tree crop requirements, when combined with typical cultivation cycles, do produce satisfactory results.

With this background and assessment of the method, it is possible to turn to the more controversial case of Western Samoa with greater assurance. Here, some modification is required of Lay's basic figures to cope with the slightly different landforms and soils of 'Upolu and Savai'i. A study of modern villages on 'Upolu and Savai'i revealed that the average area of occupied land in Savai'i is 27 percent greater than on 'Upolu, the main difference being the cultivated land requirements as a result of the poorer, more rocky soils of Savai'i. It is for this reason that slightly higher figures of 1.5 ± 0.2 acres per person for 'Upolu and 1.7 ± 0.2 acres per person for Savai'i have been proposed as realistic (Table 11.6; summary at bottom of table).

Concluding Commentary: September 2004

At this point, typed and pen-corrected draft of my 1972 manuscript ended. What was published elsewhere derives from a text, still in my usual handwritten form, intended to be the next publication. Having consolidated these thoughts into a

Table 11.6. Individual cultivated land requirements in prehistoric Samoa.

Root crop acreages per person:	Root crop land per capita in acres			Root and tree crop land per capita in acres		
	.24	.30	.34	.24	.30	.34
Crop/Fallow cycles						
2/8	1.20	1.50	1.70	1.46	1.76	1.96
3/10	1.04	1.30	1.43	1.30	1.56	1.69
2.5 or 4/10	.84	1.05	1.19	1.10	1.31	1.45

(plus .26 acre for tree crops)

Range: 1.10–1.96 acres in cultivated land per person.

Land required by typical cultivation cycles in:

American Samoa: 1.3 ± .2 acres based on .24 of an acre and covering all except upper values of .30 acres; 'Upolu, W. Samoa: 1.5 ± .2 acres based on .30 of an acre and covering all except the lower values of .24 acres; Savai'i, W. Samoa: 1.7 ± .2 acres based on .34 of an acre and covering all except the lower values of .30 acres.

short data-packed abridgement, drawing together what was to form a discussion and conclusion, a two-author polished version was published as the penultimate paragraph to Section 9, the "Conclusions" of *Archaeology in Western Samoa*, volume 2 (Green and Davidson 1974, 278–282). At that time, it formed a sort of final reprise by Green and Davidson after editing some 560 pages in two volumes on the archaeology of [Western] Samoa. Given our newly obtained archaeological knowledge, the inclusion of this paragraph (outlining the case for a greater former population size than 37,000–40,000) was a means of briefly addressing the vexed issue of how much larger a Samoan population might be proposed for the period before AD 1830. In 1974 the data seemed to favor a number up to 70,000 in AD 1790, if not more, as suggested by Pirie from historical extrapolation.

In fact, Davidson (1969) had already examined the issue of the size and distribution of a pre-Contact Samoan population, drawing on Pirie (1963) and our initial archaeological results. That theme was repeated with respect to several island cases during my presentation to the twelfth Pacific Science Congress in 1971 (Green 1972). Unsurprisingly, that effort led to a savage critique from Derek Freeman in his own congress contribution, which he focused on the Samoan example rather than topics on which he was scheduled to speak. Later, McArthur (1974) also strenuously objected to any upward revision (Green 1973) of her estimates for Tonga, and by inference Samoa, based on the common methodology both employed. Nevertheless, over time the views of many on these matters of contact population size, its distribution, and its history, generally and for Tonga and Samoa in particular, have dramatically changed, as witnessed by contributions to the present volume. For this reason, the published Samoan "abridgement" is reprinted here, together with three figures extracted from Pirie (1963), an unpublished Ph.D. thesis. Each figure has been redrawn and enhanced (see below) to better indicate the arable land under cultivation by 1950 that is alluded to in this paragraph. Moreover, the summation is now preceded by the intended text that covers the background and analytical methods employed and needed for its interpretation. Of parallel importance, the ideas can now be embedded within various paragraphs of additional commentary based on expanded archaeological knowledge of 'Upolu and Savai'i and on participation in the 2003 Mo'orea conference.

With respect to the 18.3 percent calculated average annual population decline from 1840 to 1853 (the exception being an 8 percent increase in the Manu'a Group), one should now add consideration of the early effects of gonorrhea on Samoan women's fertility. Not present earlier (Houghton 1996, 212–215), this STD is identified as a significant contributing factor in this decline (in addition to other communicable diseases of European origin; cf. Pirie 1971), although the effects probably began with the arrival of beachcombers and deserters from ship's crews during the period 1790–1830. Over the next decade, outside trade increased markedly with the establishment of ports at Apia and Pago Pago, and this increased opportunities for interpersonal contacts. Despite mission efforts to control the new diseases, the economic aspects of the changes were accompanied by a further decline in Samoa's population into the 1850s, as illustrated in Figure 11.2. Yet it is also evident now that an active interaction sphere, with long-standing exchanges of goods and movements of people, encompassed Tonga and Samoa. Identifiable in the early ethnohistorical accounts and oral traditions from Samoa, this exchange sphere also constituted a source for the persisting transmission of those European diseases known to have had devastating effects in Tonga and Lakeba in the 1790–1840 period. Initially, this was a tentative inference by Pirie (1963, 27–24, 58–59) as a probable cause of initial nineteenth-century population decline because the increasingly sustained contact from 1830 onward seemed to show a relatively less than expected impact. I would now give that cause and source more prominence.

In Figures 11.3 and 11.4, illustrating land use in 'Upolu and Savai'i ca. 1954–1957, the numerous crops grown on the arable land (each indicated on the original maps by a different symbol) have been reduced to one category: "arable land under cultivation." In addition, the area of the Apia "urban" region has been restored to the arable category, while obvious strips through the tropical forest (representing clearances on either side of roads) have been reinstated as forest.

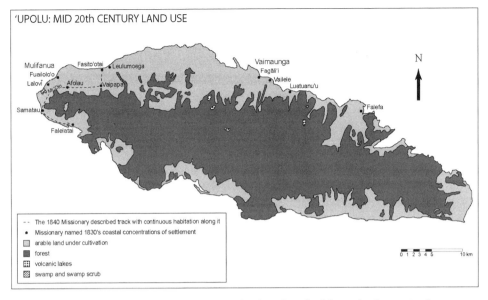

Figure 11.3. 'Upolu: Mid-twentieth-century land use based solely on the distinction between forest and arable land in cultivation/habitation. A famous major inland trail of ca. 1840 and earlier, at the western end of the island, is also indicated (after a base map in Pirie 1963, without the representation of finer crop categories that it includes).

The areas of land use on 'Upolu (Figure 11.3) may be directly associated with Figure 11.2; population size may then be related to (a) arable land use in the 1950s and (b) that to be expected in the period 1790 to 1830. Figure 11.4 leaves little doubt that the population of Savai'i in 1790 and thereafter was significantly smaller than that of 'Upolu. Indeed, from 1790 to the 1950s, the population of 'Upolu has consistently been twice that of all the rest of Samoa. As I note elsewhere (Green 2002, 138, 148), the concentration of settlements on the northwest and west-central coast of 'Upolu is a situation that appears to have a 2,000-year antiquity as revealed by archaeology and as still reflected in present circumstances.

When evaluating a very early and suspect 1830 population estimate for Savai'i by John Williams, more recent archaeological investigations make it easier to understand how he erred in making a general inference from it:

Our natives who went inland informed us the houses were very numerous there also [as well as along the coastal pathway in both directions] so that we thought the inhabitants in the immediate vicinity of the teachers [then just starting their stay in the Sapapa(a)li'i Nu'u or district] would amount to several thousands. And if the Inhabitants are numerous in proportion all round Savai there can not be less than 20 or 30,000 inhabitants. (Moyle 1984, 77)

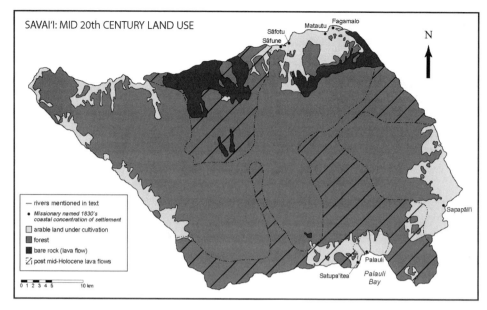

Figure 11.4. Savaiʻi: Mid-twentieth-century land use based solely on the distinction between forest and arable land in cultivation/habitation, although separating from these the raw lava of late-eighteenth/early-nineteenth-century volcanism. The base map is enhanced by a symbol indicating the extensive area of post–mid-Holocene volcanism, with at least some of its Puapua volcanic series perhaps coinciding with the period of human settlement. (After a map figure in Pirie 1963, with volcanic enhancement from Green (2002, fig 3); representations of the original finer crop distinctions are again suppressed.)

Again, on his 1832 visit by boat to the coastal portion of the Satupaʻitea Nuʻu (one of two substantial settlements noted in Palauli Bay), he says, "Having obtained all we could I went through the settlement. It is rather large contains many houses and perhaps near a 1000 people" (Moyle 1984, 166). By March 1836, Platt confirms that, through mission efforts, Sapapa(a)liʻi had the biggest congregation on Savaiʻi, with Satupaʻitea the next largest, thus providing yet further support to the 1832 population observations (1835–1836a).

The other large *nuʻu* in Palauli Bay (Figure 11.5), documented by records of some historic coastal remains as old Vailoa village, has been identified in the archaeological surveys of Savaiʻi (Scott 1969, 85). It corresponds to a coastal settlement that lay just behind the beach around the mouths of the Seugagogo and Vailoa Rivers that was reported during the mission era. In 1837 it was referred to as Palauli by the Rev. Peter Turner, who at that time was living in nearby Satupaʻitea, preaching there as well as in Palauli and complaining about the incessant "worldly" demands — to Turner (1837, 43–44) — of the seemingly ungrateful chief of Palauli. The rival chief in Satupaʻitea was, of course, the far more powerful local para-

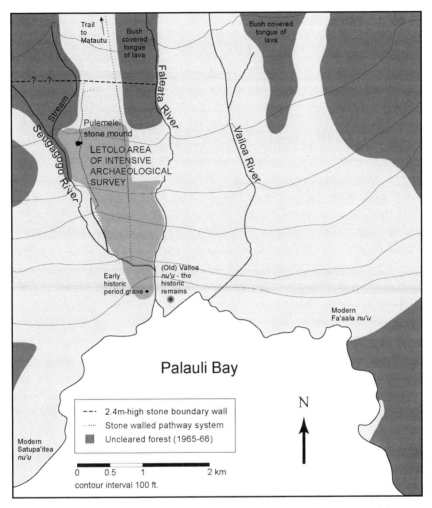

Figure 11.5. Palauli Bay showing the two principal named coastal settlements of the 1830s; the trail that connected them to the major east coast settlements of Savaiʻi; the trails, boundary walls, and zone of archaeological site survey within the Letolo Plantation. (Map is a composite of figs 32 and 38 in Buist 1969 and in Scott 1969 and detail from fig 2, Jennings et al. 1982.)

mount Tuinaula, holding one of the three principal ancient titles of Savaiʻi — that of Lilomaiava. Having converted to Methodism in Tonga in 1829, he was directly responsible for Turner's presence in Palauli Bay as one the first of the non–LMS missionaries in Samoa. His "acquisition" stemmed in part from his petition for a missionary that was finally acted on by the Wesleyan (Methodist) Mission in Tonga (Moyle 1994, 74 and fn 124, 257–258). Palauli Bay not only provided both a safe canoe landing place for two very populous *nuʻu* in the 1830s but appropriate locations for "large" concentrations of coastal habitation with "many" dwellings, all accessed from the main pathway passing through the settlement, as described by Williams (166–167). This same path eventually led east, inland across the narrow part of the peninsula on the southwest corner of Savai'i to its east coast, where it formed the main coastal pathway through a number of *nu'u* such as Sapapa(a)li'i (Platt 1835–1836b). This main around-the-island pathway was used, for example, by a visiting LMS missionary party that walked it to Satupa'itea and back in 1832 (Moyle 1994, 126). Like Williams' account after his visit by boat a short time later (above), they too reported the Satupa'itea settlement under the authority of Lilomaiava to be "very large containing near one thousand people."

We now need to add to such historical records our archaeological knowledge about the large tract of excellent arable land, later a commercial plantation, behind old Palauli (Vailoa) village, for we have a detailed habitation map with trails documenting 1,059 raised platforms within 300+ walled household units. Access to them was by a branching system of wall-lined paths (the main one situated centrally), leading far inland. Although the detailed map is only for a part of the Letolo Plantation portion, it indicates that between the two river boundaries forming the noncoastal part of district there were once literally hundreds of the contiguous stone wall–bounded household units, each with an average size of 0.6460 ha.

These bounded household units extended far inland, well beyond the mapped 2 km point where the huge stone mound of Pulemelei is situated. All this suggests that a rather large number of people once lived there. This *nu'u*, starting at the coast, extends to a high stone boundary wall, with an east-west alignment, located some 4 km inland. A sociopolitically related inland *nu'u* with still further mounds lies beyond the *pa tonga* wall (Scott 1969, 77–79; Jennings et al. 1992, 88–89). The main pathway that passes through this *nu'u* went on to cross the "mountainous" interior of Savai'i from north to south and, although "very rough" through the center of the island, this "old road" (as one missionary called it) followed a wide and well-defined walled pathway for many kilometers at either end, as we know from the mission reports and from archaeology (Davidson 1974a, 240). It was traversed over five days by Platt and his party coming from Matautu in May 1842. Some later observers tend to aver that no such prehistoric trails accessing the Savai'i interior ever existed, and only a few inland ones were known on 'Upolu. Yet archaeology has revealed that those described for inland A'ana, including the Vanimonimo and Mt. 'Olo sectors, once had extensive zones of adjoining wall-bounded household units (Davidson 1974b, 199; Jennings et al. 1982), just as recorded in Stair's most telling description from a time within the period 1838–1845. This reports adjoining households along a 9-to-10-mile inland trail, from southwest coast Falelatai to east coast Fasito'otai, along which he suggested "a child could wander safely the entire distance and never be out of earshot of a habitation" (Davidson 1969, 54).

Sometimes a raised causeway, sometimes a sunken one, and at other times following the surface with low walled alignments on either side (Davidson 1974a, 239–240), in my view various portions of that major trail and boundary marker separate the zone of the *'aiga 'i uta* of each *nu'u* from that of the *'aiga 'i tai*. (Davidson (1974b, 199). Parts of the trail have been described and mapped by different archaeologists at various times (i.e., Green 1969b, 268; Davidson 1974b, 202, fig 81) for the portion from Samatau on the coast to Faia'ai on the inland southern edge of the Mulifanua project zone (Green 1969a, fig 1). This trail continues to Mt. 'Olo, where it is shown as raised, walled, and trenched in its various portions as it extends for some 2.6 km along the seaward boundary of the inland Mt. 'Olo zone of household units and wards, as mapped by Jennings and Holmer (1980, figs 3a to 3c).

There is also a much smaller but similar map for one modern plantation zone lying 0.5 km inland of Sapapa(a)li'i. It too exhibits the same kind of density, with habitation platforms and walled household units (Jackmond and Holmer 1980), confirming the reports cited above that were brought back to Williams by the Cook Island native teachers. Williams, who stayed at the coastal residence of Maleitoa Vaiinupo(o) in 1830, also obtained other local reports (Moyle 1994, 76). Again, archaeology has demonstrated that these inland household units were serviced by a wide central pathway from the coast that proceeded yet farther inland to a high, north-south cross-cutting stone boundary wall. The path passes through the wall and leads into a separate though probably sociopolitically related dense zone of settlement — one said to possess a different name and belong to a different chief (Buist 1959, 51). In these matters, Williams' observations of size and density in the early 1830s now stand as quite firmly supported by archaeology.

However, in William's first-impression estimate for the population of Savai'i in 1830, major troubles reside in his assumption that what he observed closely on its southeast coast, or in Palauli Bay in 1832, prevailed "in proportion at that time" all around Savai'i. It did not. The one other main cluster of really dense settlement, evidenced by the usual abundant archaeological remains for pre-Contact habitation well inland, is in the Fagamalo, Matautu, Sa(a)fotu, Sa(a)fune part of northern Savai'i (Buist 1969, 45–50, figs 34, 35). One of the controlling factors on Savai'i is the distribution of the various fairly recent and exceedingly stony post–mid-Holocene Puapua volcanic soils possessing extremely poor fertility. Thus they are not easily gardened productively under a Samoan horticultural regime such as that reconstructed in the analysis presented in the text and summarized in Tables 11.5 and 11.6. Therefore, they were not cleared of their tropical forest bush cover until recently, if then (see Figure 11.4). Savai'i was certainly far larger in total area than 'Upolu, but just as our calculations for different amounts of arable land required for cultivation on the two islands suggest, its population never grew as large as that of 'Upolu in prehistory. As a result, nothing like the same amount of land on Savai'i was ever under cultivation in the past, and for comparative purposes, the density of population by island size is almost meaningless.

A certain amount of confusion has obtained in relation to Samoan settlement patterns, which Davidson (1969, 55–57) attempted to clarify; it is that usage that is followed here. *Nu'u* are conceived as clusters of title names and holders for various points in time who form a landholding administrative "parish," with regional geographic boundaries well known to its residents. Within these boundaries are numerous actual residential areas that may exhibit considerable variation in their distribution and that change markedly over time. The *nu'u* titleholders act as a localized sociopolitical entity and exercise authority — *pule* — over a bounded territory within the landscape that is demarcated by streams and other natural features, together with built features such as earthen or stone walls or pathways (raised, sunken, or level) with stone alignments along them. *Pitonu'u* are spatially distinct portions within *nu'u* (Jennings et al. (1982) called them "wards" when found inland; in his 1840 reconstruction, Watters (1958) called them settlements, a part of a village or a village section). "Section" is a common English designation for them when they are found in modern coastal concentrations of habitation referred to either as a village or a named *nu'u*, although the portion of village garden land inland of the habitation zone is, in fact, also involved.

In addition, archaeologists have found it convenient to talk of household units, centered around remains from raised residential foundations for dwellings — *fale* — along with various outbuildings and ovens, usually set off and demarcated by low stone walls, sunken ways or pathways, and raised causeways. The measurement along a path — *fua-ila* — is one Samoan term for indicating these residential units of *'aiga*.

Larger territorial divisions — districts and subdistricts — joining adjacent *nu'u* formed recognized regional groupings that usually also possessed a locality name. Their formation had a more political basis, and their constitution changed frequently with altered circumstances and fortunes. Commonly, the reach of certain titles in powerful *nu'u* extended well beyond the *nu'u* in which the current titleholder resided. Other even more powerful titles related to major islandwide divisions such as A'ana, Tuamasaga, and Atua on 'Upolu, and investiture into one or more of them could lead to one being considered a *tupu*, or paramount chief. On the basis of other high titles, it was also possible to be termed the *tupu* of Savai'i (Heath 1840b), or even the *tupu* and/or the *tafa'ifa(a)* or holder of the four high titles of the major island divisions of 'Upolu—thus a linguistically dubious use of "the king" in European parlance.

In his essay, Watters (1958) presented maps indicating the major known and named coastal "settlements" of over 400 inhabitants in AD 1840. Also shown were socially and politically allied adjoining village sections of 100 to 400 inhabitants, along with a few isolated "settlements" (mostly inland and with known coastal alliances) that he placed in the category of under 100 inhabitants. These "settlements" and "sections" served as the basis for an attenuated physical conception of the Samoan *nu'u* of that period in that it lacked full recognition and portrayal of the associated gardening lands. Some 96 percent of the population—ca. 52,000 inhabitants in 1840—were deemed to have lived near the coast and certainly not more than 1.6 km (a mile) from the sea. Most settlements were on the *faga* of calcareous sandy alluvium inland but adjacent to the beach, where the habitation zone focused around dwellings and their outbuildings. Each familial social entity usually possessed one or more *fale* surrounded by low boundary walls of volcanic stone or sapling fences. These helped to keep out the pigs and defined what the archaeologists would call household units. Well-trodden trails led off from settlements in multiple directions through coconut groves to the main taro garden clearings of the *vaifanua* on the slopes behind. These plots were cultivated in rotation as part of a fallow and cultivation cycle. Watters (1958, 9) even drew an imagined plan for the typical major kind of "settlement" of the 1840 period, complete with its large central grassed *malae* and guesthouse or *faletele* (Figure 11.6a). The core of the inhabited strip focused on a reef channel maintained by a permanent stream from inland that often bisected the main village section.

It is the establishment of this pattern, ethnohistorically well attested in the accounts of 1839–1840 (Watters 1958, fn 1), that provided a foundational format for the nineteen coastal village sections, with their inland strips of mixed crop garden zones, mapped in intricate detail in the mid-1950s by the Fox and Cumberland (1962) team. Those maps also provide nineteen sets of substantive figures on various cropping cycles and the amounts of land in various kinds of cultivation in 1956. Compiled into a summary table of land statistics for particular village sections (Farrell and Ward 1962, table 13), they are accompanied by detailed maps and textual discussion for many of the individual cases in order to display the variation that results. Four complete coastal village maps are also presented (figs 27 to 30) to show the major variations among them. Moreover, the map for the modern coastal portion of the *nu'u* of Asaga on Savai'i (Figure 11.6b) fairly closely approximates the main portion of the typical coastal settlement as imagined by Watters for 1840 (see Figure 11.6a). Apart from their similarity, the notable feature of these two examples separated by 110 years is the almost complete con-

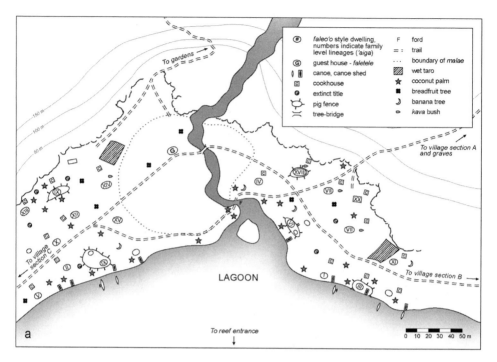

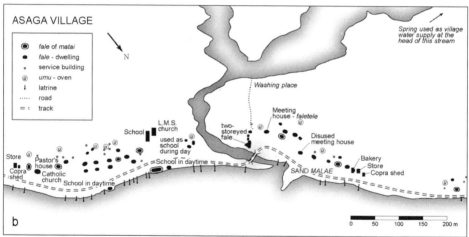

Figure 11.6a. An illustrated perception of a typical structural pattern created by settlement buildings and related features, compiled from multiple text descriptions of the AD 1839–1840 period. It relates to the central section, within a coastal settlement of three sections, of the ca. 1840 period (after Watters 1958, fig 5).

b. The actual internal patterning found in Asaga Village *(nu'u)*, Savai'i, in 1956 (after fig 29, Farrell and Ward 1962).

trast with information of a similar kind obtained from the various large-scale archaeological project map exercises and from more general surveys undertaken by archaeologists and applying to an earlier period. These revealed a quite different distribution of former dwelling platforms and household units (largely assigned to the centuries before 1830), sometimes possessing time depths of up to five or more centuries. It is this period for which archaeological settlement pattern information is greatest (Green 2002).

Davidson (1969) was the first to compile in detail the archaeological case for a different distribution of a much greater Samoan population in the seventeenth and eighteenth centuries AD. She drew heavily on firsthand archaeological observations in the field and a settlement pattern–oriented interpretation of them, bolstered by close examination of the earliest ethnohistoric accounts from the 1830s. In light of the ever-increasing body of archaeological information then forthcoming, she forwarded two propositions. One was that the former size of the population before 1840 was very much greater than the majority of researchers writing on Samoa in the 1960s (other than Pirie) would allow. The other was that the former distribution of households was vastly different from the prevailing conceptions known from the last 100 years of the historic period, the basis of inferences by these authorities, Pirie included, in extensions several hundred years into the past (Davidson 1969, 50). Moreover, it was Davidson's supposition that the observations of the early 1830s only just caught the tail end of this major transformation in landscape use on 'Upolu and Savai'i. By 1974, with the publication of volume 2 of *Archaeology in Western Samoa*, we were reasonably convinced this was the case. Only shortly thereafter, a series of intensive household survey projects of long-abandoned archaeological remains simply tended to further confirm the propositions we had developed (Jennings et al. 1982).

In short, we strenuously disputed the inference that Samoan settlement pattern and use of the landscape had remained the same over the centuries leading up to 1840. Theoretically, we postulated that a variety of forms of settlement could exist on *nu'u* district lands without altering fundamentally the social and political system operating within these "parishlike" territorial *nu'u* zones that had formerly stretched from the coast to well inland (Davidson 1969, 55–56; 1974c, 159–161). Our argument was first for a marked decline in population size from 1790 to 1850, along the lines set out in this essay. The second claim was that, during this reduction in population size, a significant parallel shift had taken place in the former dispersal of household units over the landscape, especially with respect to those once located 1.6 km to 4 km or more inland and now long abandoned. We also recognized that special circumstances prevailed in the broad, deep Falefa Valley — and perhaps elsewhere — that were exceptions to this general pattern. A third proposition was that inland in the Falefa (and more generally from the coast to some distance inland at number of localities investigated on both ʻUpolu and Savaiʻi), it was possible to document a marked change in the form and physical layout of the household units and the platform bases that served for dwellings. However, change did not occur to the same degree in *fale* dwellings themselves until well into the twentieth century. Thus the ubiquitous stone boundary walls (around what were often adjoining household units served by well-delineated pathways of all types — raised, sunken, and level) that obtained in the past gave way to more compact or tightly nucleated habitations without any obvious surrounding walls or other markers delineating their boundaries. Inland in Samoa, this change was concretely attested to in the wall-less nucleated dwellings of the 1840 hamlet-sized community of Sasoaʻa (and in those of modern Falevao village), where their associated agricultural fields lay at some distance from the zone for residential units (Davidson 1974c, 157, 160). On the coast, new maps of the densely packed former household units inland within the Letolo Plantation of Palauli Bay (Jennings et al. 1982, fig 2) contrasted with a map for the wholly coastal modern village of Faʻaala and its closely packed dwellings that were entirely lacking in boundary walls (Jennings et al. 1982, fig 5), where the village gardens were inland. This illustrated better than anything previously the profound difference in household layout and house platforms in two adjacent situations. In fact, it was similar to what Davidson (1974b) had already tentatively outlined as applying in the intermediately situated commercial zones of the Mulifanua Plantation region in relation to its current wholly coastal modern villages. Jennings et al. (1980) then solidly reinforced Davidson's claims through a fully inland Mt. ʻOlo survey that revealed a densely packed strip of household units in which a major boundary-marking trail followed along its seaward edge (see above).

However, only since the transformation of settlement pattern archaeology theory (under which these projects were carried out and interpreted) into the social symbolic concerns of landscape archaeology may one advance the interpretation for Samoa further toward a more familiar and widespread model of Polynesian land tenure. Sahlins (1958, 251–252, 263–266), for example, was misled by an 1840s model of resource distribution and use related to land tenure in Samoa. He contrasted this Samoan descent line system — nucleated or village settlements and rich resource zones clustered into small areas supporting a limited range of crops exploited by a single household — with a quite opposite arrangement observed in Eastern Polynesia. That, he thought, explained the differences in social organization and stratification between Eastern and Western Polynesia. His interpretation, however, was soon shown to be defective in significant empirical facts.

Consequently, the current framework thought to have applied within most high volcanic islands of the central Pacific is that land tenure arrangements for the territory of each of its communities in the past, at contact, and at times well into the historic period cut across a sequence of ecological niches. In their idealized form, those progressed from the reef and lagoon across the beach and the sandy area often backed by a swamp to a zone of the most fertile soils rising through ever-steeper inland slopes, until they reached the steep central forested ridges and mountainous interior. Frequent descriptors for these tenure patterns are wedge-shaped portions of land, from the coast to inland summits, containing the island's major resources. Ward (in Denoon 1997, 90–91), whose summation this is, points to examples from Lakeba and Moala in Fiji, the *nu'u* of Samoa, the *tapere* of Rarotonga, and even those on the raised coral island of Atiu in the southern Cook group. He also notes the uncertainly termed valley and ridgetop territorial markers of the windward Society Islands (Oliver 1989, 906, 913, 1,189 fn 12) and the well-understood *ahupua'a* systems of Hawai'i (Kirch, this volume).

The last example proves especially instructive in demonstrating that where suitable natural features were lacking, cultural constructions (such as trails, pathways, and stone stacks, along with dry stacked stone or even earthen walling) were erected to mark these important sociocultural boundaries. In Samoa, analytical studies now underway are attempting to more precisely identify archaeologically some of these *nu'u*-based landholding social units, not only for the best documented pre-Contact Paluali/Letolo case, but also at Sapapa(a)li'i on the east coast of Savai'i and Sa(a)fune and Sa(a)fotu on the north coast. Similarly, on 'Upolu a restudy of the archaeological survey evidence allows further endeavors along these lines, including an in-depth reinterpretation of existing evidence from Mulifanua, Vailele, Luatuanu'u, and Falefa Valley.

Following is the data-packed paragraph embedded in the "Conclusions" to volume 2 of *Archaeology in Western Samoa* (Green and Davidson 1974, 281–282), which will still serve as a fairly concise summation for the previous text that led to this construction and conclusion:

The question of Samoan population size at the end of the eighteenth and beginning of the nineteenth century is a source of conflict. Some writers, such as McArthur (1968: 104, 115) and Freeman (1964: 565, fn. 3; pers. comm.) believe that the population of Western Samoa was never more than the 37,000 to 38,000 people indicated by the missionary censuses of the late 1840s and early 1850s. Others, such as Pirie (1963: 43–44, 63–64; 1968; 1972: 196–202), believe that population in the early nineteenth century was declining, and that before this period population was perhaps twice the generally accepted estimate of about 38,000 for the mid-1840s. The issue has been examined from an archaeological perspective by Davidson (1969: 72–77). That study and the more detailed evidence presented in these two volumes certainly show that the distribution of population between AD 1820 and 1840 changed from one less nucleated and

more widespread, both on the coast and inland, to one in more tightly nucleated villages almost entirely on the coast, as documented by Watters (1958).
Davidson therefore examines the hypothesis of correlating this change with a
reduction in population size and concludes that the prospect of a larger population requires serious consideration, given the extent of archaeological evidence
implying much greater use of the inland parts of Samoa than obtained either
in the 1840s or for a number of decades thereafter. Green, having made a study
of probable population size on Tongatapu (1973) on the basis of former agricultural land use requirements, has followed up the arguments on population size
and land use in Samoa presented by Pirie (1972: 199), by applying the methods
used for Tonga to the Samoan situation. It appears very unlikely, either on the
basis of modern village figures of 1.5 acres (0.61 ha) of cropland per person in
'Upolu and 1.8 (0.73 ha) in Savai'i (Farrell and Ward 1962: 186) or reconstructed
figures of 1.5 ± 0.2 acres (0.71 ± 0.08 ha) for 'Upolu and 1.7 ± 0.2 acres (0.69 ±
0.08 ha) for the time of contact (Green MS, this volume), that 38,000 Samoans would ever have required the use of more than 80,000 acres (32,375 ha)
of arable land to supply completely their requirements under a low-intensity
subsistence system of swidden agriculture, and no more than 100,000 acres
(40,469 ha) of occupied land in total. In an island group with 699,200 acres
(282,956 ha) of land, of which more than 200,000 acres (80,937 ha) are able to
be cultivated, only 155,960 acres (62,151 ha) were occupied by a population of
97,237 in the mid-1950s (Farrell and Ward 1962: 186; Cumberland 1962: 318-321).
It is evident, therefore, that Western Samoans in the 1840s needed to use, and
were occupying, only the coastal part of their islands in much the way that the
historical records attest. Thus Watters (1958: 7) concluded from those records
that only 4 percent of the population (and 14 percent of the settlements) were
located inland; the remaining 96 percent was on or within 1 mile (1.6 km) of the
coast. Whether Samoans lived in dispersed settlements, as in the past, or were
concentrated in coastal villages, as in the 1840s, the one obvious explanation
for the extent to which the landscape in Western Samoa has in fact been occupied, much of it continuously, for agriculture and residence over a long period
of time, is a much larger population. It seems that only a population twice the
size of that in the 1840s, or one with a radically different subsistence-settlement
pattern basis, would require the amount of arable land which archaeology indicates was once in use. The possibility of such a population size thus continues
to deserve close examination and further investigation, however unacceptable
it may seem to those concerned with traditional Samoan social organisation.

Notes

Author's note: It is a pleasure to recognize assistance from Dorothy Brown in locating the complete bibliography for the original paper among the 1972 files. Of similar importance, in 1971 and again this year, was Janet Davidson's provision of references and certain topical extracts from the vast corpus of unpublished missionary accounts necessary for this enterprise. Richard Moyle provided additional similar help, especially with regard to the journals of Peter Turner. Valerie Green helped to edit the new addition to the original manuscript and to update the references.

Patrick V. Kirch knows that a publishable paper would never have eventuated if it had not been for his bursts of persuasion. First, it was necessary to convince me to retrieve the draft and notes from yellowing files dated 1972; he knew of their existence from photocopies he has conserved for decades. That effort achieved the presentation of a desktop version presented to conference members in December 2003. Subsequently, after further revision in mid-2004, the essay is in a form more suited for inclusion in this volume. *Faafetai lava.*

12

VALERIE J. GREEN AND ROGER C. GREEN

An Accent on Atolls in Approaches to Population Histories of Remote Oceania

 Atolls, which did not emerge as stable landforms suitable for human habitation until the late Holocene (after sea-level stabilization), represent more recently occupied landforms dispersed across Remote Oceania. High Pacific isles were well populated by communicating groups of settlers before tropical atolls were sought out and transformed into habitable environs for the voyagers whose kin became atoll people. Nonetheless, last need not be least in their contributions to our understanding of population trajectories in Remote Oceania during the decades preceding and encompassing the early European contacts. The primary purpose of this chapter is to accent atoll populations, using the case of Tokelau, which has particular cogency as perhaps "the closest real case equivalent of a Polynesian founding population" (Molloy and Huntsman 1996, 56). Several discernible responses of the atoll populations to demographic challenges and crises during the decades around European contact have wider relevance for investigations of the migration, settlement, reproduction, and endurance of populations in Remote Oceania, from Lapita voyaging to the post-Contact era.

No account recovers the past (Lowenthal 1985, 215), and all representations of the past are contestable. Informative population studies include conceptual acknowledgement of culture and of history, of events and trajectories, of continuities and contingencies. The people are active participants in the times and spaces investigated in such studies (Sahlins 1985, vii–xix). Although this chapter introduces only text sources in its representations of the past, the sources of those texts are diverse: Oral narratives and ethnographies, historical and ethnohistorical documents, mission and bureaucratic reports and correspondence, archaeology and demography research papers, and international legislation are referenced. Each presents a distinctive manner of interpretation and communication for intended or imagined audiences. They are interrelated but seldom interchangeable contributions. Within the constraints of this essay it is not possible to explore the associated implications, but the selected texts are used to increase understanding of the settlement, reproduction, expansion, migration, constraint, loss, and recovery of population on the atolls of Tokelau.

For the groups of islands in Remote Oceania, population histories relating to the period of occupation before sustained European contact have featured two research strategies. One is the census approach of historical demographers, whose recent efforts have separated estimates of Contact-period maximal population size from reassessments of enumerated island populations. Records of the latter type, whether compiled by a mission or colonial administration, usually start somewhere around the mid-nineteenth century AD. The second strategy encompasses a range of proxy methods employed by archaeologists and human geographers in attempts to link their representations of a deeper past with the more secure enumeration records dating from around AD 1840; examples relevant to Samoa are Pirie (1963) and Green (chapter 11, this volume).

An ethnohistoric approach usually starts with first conjectures of population size, however imprecise, and proceeds using chronological census records of missions and European administrations. Reported estimates are critically assessed and the most trustworthy selected. The strategy then employs demographic reconstructions and projects these back through time as far as convincing propositions allow — typically less than a century. In relation to Remote Oceania, McArthur (1967) is a standard reference for the use of this strategy, although Schmitt (1968, 1973) provides a widely cited foundation for the Hawaiian islands, while Pool (1977, 1991) fulfills the same purpose for New Zealand. Rallu (1989, 1990) offers a contemporary reassessment for Oceanic populations (excluding New Zealand) during the nineteenth and twentieth centuries (see chapter 1, this volume).

Whether examining the careful estimates of ethnohistorians or those in proxy studies, it is evident that contemporary revisions of contact population size are invariably upward (e.g., Green 1972 for Tonga; chapter 11, this volume for Samoa). Indeed, the amplification of contact population numbers for Hawai'i (Kirch 2000, 311–313) and La Grande Terre of New Caledonia (Sand 1995, 287–309; Sand et al., chapter 15, this volume) lead these two researchers to conclude that new approaches are now needed. Among their critiques are the following:

1. Sand argues, citing the multiple difficulties, that there are just too many uncontrolled variables to make further continuation along these well-traversed lines of investigation either productive or more accurate.
2. Sand also points out that since each researcher chooses to accord singular importance to one or another historical text or a particular proxy method, careful researchers reach totally different conclusions that cannot easily be faulted by others.

3. Kirch avers that historical demography for the periods before the mid-nineteenth century AD — especially when based on reassessments of historical estimates, early "census" reports, and the initial proxy propositions of some archaeologists — belongs to a line of debate that is not likely to get us very far. New practices are needed.

Real case studies have been marginalized among strategies for investigating population histories in Remote Oceania. Yet, peculiar to a context (such as atolls) and configured with caveats as they may be, such studies stand as valuable complementary resources in the preparation of models and the interpretations of other approaches. Real case studies nurture thinking about the behavior of real people responding to the complexities and contingencies of survival, reproduction, and migration in Pacific communities and environments.

Writing from the perspective of biological anthropology, Brewis and Allen (1994, 8) surmise, "One characteristic of Pacific populations *which may set them apart from other populations,* is a long-term tendency towards growth, coupled with habitual periodic population collapses, most particularly under atolline conditions" (emphasis ours). When required, very high fertility rates are a known strategy of island populations, and Molloy and Huntsman (1996, 41) reiterate Brewis' (1993) argument for a model presuming flux rather than stasis, since island life is beset with periodic disasters.

Atoll population cases from Tokelau raise questions about the use of Pitcairn as the common reference population for historical demography in Remote Oceania. As Rallu (this volume) acknowledges, the Pitcairn case presents significant problems; using Tokelau data overcomes several of these difficulties. Atolls present quite different landscapes and resources from those in other Pacific environments, but the separate histories of these atoll populations reveal purposeful social practices that should inform demographic research within this region. Molloy and Huntsman (1996, 41) support Brewis' proposition that the pre/post-Contact period may be perceived as a continuum along which many demographic challenges among island populations remained similar. In this chapter, the term *"pericontact"* refers to this period.

The Atolls of Tokelau

Tokelau is the contemporary inclusive reference for three Pacific atolls — Atafu, Nukunonu, and Fakaofo — that lie in relatively close proximity but do not provide intervisible landfalls. Within the equatorial zone, 8 to 10 degrees south, the atolls are located along a 150 km northwest-southeast axis between longitudes 171 and 173 degrees west (see Figure 11.1). They were not available for human occupation until around 1,000 BP (Dickinson 2003). Linguistic research suggests that Tokelau and Tuvalu were centrally located in the arc of atolls that formed the homeland for expansionary migrations of an Ellicean language subgroup (Marck 1999, 119; 2000, 129). Despite hints of discovery by canoe voyagers (Matagi Tokelau 1991, 1), it is autochthonous ancestors rather than mythical isles of origin that feature in the Tokelau *tala anamua* ("traditional tales of happenings in times long ago") (Wessen et al. 1992, 31; Huntsman and Hooper 1996, 127–139; Matagi Tokelau 1991, 11–18). The only archaeological investigation indicates that "thriving communities"—evidently in communication with other regional populations—existed on at least two of these atolls by the tenth century AD (Best 1988, 117). Later, an atoll realm was established by conquest and sustained until the pericontact period. This polity was disestablished mid-nineteenth century after a sequence of climate, obeisance, and depopulation crises sundered the hegemony of Fakaofo. As a negotiated outcome of the British appropriation in 1877, three of the equatorial atolls, now known as Tokelau, are politically located "within the boundaries of New Zealand," according to the Tokelau Act of 1948 (Angelo et al. 1989, 30–35).

Individually and in association, the reef-bound coral islets of Tokelau have been identified, misidentified, and documented under an assortment of names since 1765, when Byron (Gallagher 1964), aboard HMS *Dolphin*, first mapped the position of northernmost Atafu. United States Exploring Expedition (USEE) accounts show that Hudson ([1846] 1981, 58), recognizing linguistic and other population links, recorded the three atolls as "The Union Group." An unintended consequence was the exclusion of Olohega (Olosenga or today's Swains Island), ca. 200 km south of Fakaofo, which the people traditionally included among *na motu e fa o Tokelau* ("the four islands of Tokelau") (see also Matagi Tokelau 1991, 37–43; Macgregor 1937, 22–23). The loss of Olohega to U.S. jurisdiction (as part of American Samoa) was belatedly legislated in the Treaty of Tokehega 1983, but Tokelauans consistently reiterate their earlier claim that "it rightfully belongs to us" (e.g., Tokelau Fono Agenda, 8.6.1976; see also Hooper 1975).

Tokelau lies beyond the range of the direct effects of regional volcanism, but other episodic natural disasters such as droughts and cyclones are among the greatest threats to atoll residents. Olohega and Atafu once served as subsistence resource reserves when storms devastated other settlements and islets. Following some six years of climate-induced food shortages, missionaries coerced a migration of hundreds from Fakaofo to ʻUvea in 1852. It is also apparent that risk was always aboard voyaging canoes, and it increased during interatoll journeys. Attempts to manage risk, including convoy travel, may have reduced but did not prevent the loss of unknowable numbers of voyagers.[1]

The remoteness and benign environments of Tokelau atolls and their lack of deep water access for ports meant that the effects of endemic and introduced diseases were comparatively minimal.[2] Early Europeans observed only a few cases of elephantiasis and skin infections: Hale ([1846] 1981, 41, 43) reported Tokelau populations "healthy and well conditioned," the men possessing "fine forms and manly looks."[3] Tinielu (1972, 9) implies that dysentery, infective hepatitis, tuberculosis, and skin diseases became common after European contact and several outbreaks of some of these diseases claimed some lives. A singular "catastrophic denudation" of Tokelau population occurred in 1863 when 47 percent of the atoll residents — including almost all able-bodied males (Maude 1981, 73) — were transported on *vaka kaihohoa tagata* ("people-stealing boats") by European agents for labor enslavement in Peru.

Some relevant landscape characteristics of the three atolls officially designated Tokelau for which sound information has been published are summarized in Table 12.1. It has been compiled from the extensive corpus of literature now available and referenced throughout this chapter.

Nukunonu

Insofar as the concern here is primarily the population trajectories of the pericontact period, recounted states of flux during earlier times are merely indicated. Many generations before Europeans appeared, Nukunonu[4] was subjugated by the elites of more populous Fakaofo, who established the polity of Tokelau through conquest, exercised hegemony, extracted burdensome annual tributes, took women of Nukunonu as wives, and relocated kin groups there after natural disasters depleted their own land resources (details in Hooper and Huntsman 1973; Huntsman and Hooper 1985, 133–149; Hooper 1994, 307–320; Huntsman 1994, 321–338; Huntsman and Hooper 1996, 136–139). Thus, the people occupying the largest Tokelau atoll were accustomed to population influx and decline within comprehensible parameters.

Nukunonu was first documented in 1791 by Edwards ([1790–1791] 1915, 47), who found the village deserted after he observed several voyaging canoes crossing the lagoon. This episode exemplifies the Nukunonu response to early European visitors: Never were they welcomed in ways that permitted population estimates. Even when adult men greeted arriving ships and their crews, they first ensured the "protection" of atoll women (and children) by placing them on canoes in the lagoon or concealing their presence on densely wooded islets — a strategy Europeans observed on each atoll. During the 1820s and 1830s, sporadic and brief encounters with a few Nukunonu men preceded the arrival of the USEE in 1841.[5] However, since Hudson was unable to land anyone on this atoll, there are no substantive estimates of population until a mission visit in January 1863.

Table 12.1. Tokelau: Vital landscape characteristics.

	Fakaofo	Nukunonu	Atafu
A. Total land area c. 12 km²	4 km²	4.7 km²	3.5 km²
B. Lagoon area	59 km²	109 km²	19 km²
C. Land area suited to arbori-culture (largely coconut, with cultivated pandanus)	2.49 km² (612 acres)	2.65 km² (650 acres)	2.03 km² (502 acres)
D. Marginal land area, with "forest" pandanus and strand vegetation	1 km²	1.35 km²	0.5 km²
E. *Pulaka (Cyrtosperma chamissonis)* production in artificial pits	Numerous pits, eastern islets	None	A few pits, eastern islets
F. Fresh water source/s	One village well; permanent supply, easily accessed, valued and care-fully maintained	No village well; one small un-reliable well, on southeast islet, not maintained for permanent use	Two known but unreliable wells distant from vil-lage, not main-tained for perma-nent use

Note: During the pericontact period, groundwater supplies were supplemented by rain-water catchment in pools and in *tugu* carved low on trunks near the base of coconut trees.

Sources of data: Richardson (1925); Hooper and Huntsman (1973); Yaldwyn and Wod-zicki (1979); Wessen et al. (1992); Huntsman and Hooper (1996); with additional and corroborative information from other texts in the listed references.

Population depletion and recovery is central to the narrative of Nukunonu published by Molloy and Huntsman (1996). It is an ethnohistoric case study cov-ering the six decades from 1860 to 1920 that offers an atoll population reconstruc-tion based on genealogy, mission, and other historical records. The interpretation and use of these records is informed by general and specific ethnographic under-standings that are an outcome of Huntsman's three decades of Tokelau research.[6] There are inherent difficulties in the approach, but the authors clearly outline these and their methodology.

The Nukunonu case study has an informative value because the reproductive population that reassembled after evading the Peruvian labor recruitment raids of February 1863 is so small.[7] This remnant group is perceived to be around the size of a successful founding population during the migrations of people across

Remote Oceania. The derived number is well supported (Maude 1981, 68–69, 73), and a large majority of individuals and their progeny have been identified in documented genealogies and church baptismal records. Maude offers an estimate of 140 residents from the records of a brief mission visit to Tokelau in January 1863; he calculates that seventy-six people were transported on the recruitment vessels termed "slave ships" in his regional investigation. Of the three Tokelau atolls raided, Nukunonu lost the highest proportion of population (54.3 percent) and retained the smallest number of people. In effect, Molloy and Huntsman define the reassembled population of potentially reproducing residents as less than forty, although the cultural knowledge, subsistence labor, and child care of other survivors would have contributed to the recovery and endurance of the group. In addition, contact with neighboring atolls provided some spouses and settlers who had kin affiliations. Of the sixty-four atoll residents in the remnant population, Molloy and Huntsman (1996, 44) state that there were: (1) Five people (four male, one female) of an age to be grandparents (born 1820s or earlier); (2) Thirteen people (six male, seven female) of an age to be parents (born 1830s and 1840s);[8] and (3) Twenty people (eleven male, nine female) of ages regarded as children (born since 1850). Twenty-six individuals are not able to be assigned to these cohorts; either they did not survive to adulthood or they did not contribute to Nukunonu population regeneration.

Immediately after the "slave ships" departed, the discernible remnant population declined further when a group left to seek assistance in Samoa.[9] The baptized survivors returned aboard a sailing vessel within a few months. During their absence two atoll-born men arrived back from 'Uvea; subsequently, other people with Nukunonu ancestry or kin affiliations (thus readily reincorporated into local patterns of subsistence living) came from Atafu, Fakaofo, Olohega, and Samoa (Huntsman and Hooper 1973, 378; Maude 1981, 68; Molloy and Huntsman 1996, 45). Obviously, the integrity and functioning of *kaiga* (extended family groups with shared property rights) was destroyed by the removal of most able-bodied members; the crisis management response on Nukunonu included the temporary institution of *toga* (cooperating groups of remnant *kaiga*) to facilitate the activities of subsistence (Huntsman and Hooper 1996, 223–224, 336 fn 3). When population increase allowed it, near the end of the nineteenth century, Nukunonu reverted to more traditional cognatic descent groups with a contemporary reallocation of resources.

By AD 1872, the number of residents has reportedly risen from sixty-four to eighty. At the end of another decade, the figure of ninety-six is strongly supported by the genealogical analyses. This is not incompatible with two separate enumerations, of ninety and ninety-nine, by the priests who visited in 1882; discrepancies may reflect classifications of "Tokelauan," "resident," or even "baptized" individuals (e.g., Portuguese and Samoan spouses were resident before that date). Molloy and Huntsman (1996, 45) summarize the identified members of this genealogically attested community as

9 people of age to be grandparents (4 male, 1 female)

36 people of age to be parents (17 male, 19 female)

51 people of ages regarded as children (27 male, 24 female).

After the immediate crisis response (a repatriation of people with Nukunonu ancestry or affiliation), there was a continuous steady population growth. Maude (1981, 173) calculated that Nukunonu achieved a 4.4 percent average rate of increase during the two decades after the "slave ships" (significantly lower than Atafu and Fakaofo; see below), a trend that reflects social strategies being implemented. On one hand, little emigration is discernible (Molloy and Huntsman 1996, 49), and later incidents of overt discouragement are on record.[10] On the other hand, newcomers with kinship links are welcomed, but a riskier strategy of soliciting or even encouraging other immigrants is not evident. While the numbers and the rate of increase are central to the Nukunonu case, the social processes and strategies revealed in this population regeneration carry other implications for regional demographic studies.

Molloy and Huntsman (1996, 50–51) are explicit that "monogamous lifetime unions" remain the principal pattern of marriage on Nukunonu. A high fertility rate is detectable during the crisis-response period, averaged out as a family size of eight children in the initial 1860–1879 cohort. As population recovery proceeds, average family size lowers to 5.6 children by the turn of the century. While this trend is demonstrable, there is little variation around the central tendency of 6.2 children (53, table 2). Such data may be used as indicative of, although not determinative of, population associated with each dwelling (see below). A reasonably constant juvenile mortality is shown, averaging 36 percent over the sixty years under study. For this period of regeneration, the authors characterize Nukunonu as a high fertility/high mortality population.

The data assembled by Molloy and Huntsman (1996, 53, 56) reveals that "high fertility did not mean uncontrolled fertility," but the social controls do not feature the commonly cited triplet of abortions, infanticides, and banishment by boat. Rather, the process of repopulation was managed and a number of strategies are evident. Birth intervals and age of cessation of reproduction are probably influenced by various ethnographically attested practices. These include breastfeeding infants for six months or longer; customary uxorilocal residence that facilitates maternal supervision of daughters and infants (as well as "protection" of new mothers for a period of postpartum abstinence), and a cultural preference that women cease reproduction before their daughters commence. It is also apparent that ex-nuptial births and polygamy are rare. Indeed, women without children are more numerous in the later cohorts: After a destructive cyclone in 1914, there were fewer male residents for a couple of years or more while a group worked on Ocean Island.[11] In contrast to Atafu and Fakaofo, population increase on Nukunonu owed little to begetters of other ethnicities. However, the pool from which potential spouses were drawn did include Catholic youth from Fakaofo *kaiga*.[12] For the sixty years following the "slave ships" depopulation, the calculated average growth rate is 4 percent. This confirms the rate offered by Maude (1981, 173) and indicates that although Nukunonu was viewed as "lagging" behind the very high rates on Atafu and Fakaofo during the initial phase of the crisis response period, this atoll population exercised social controls to manage population recovery with consistent growth over a longer period. Unlike the case of Pitcairn, where Kirch (1994, 96) also calculates a 4 percent rate (r =.04), the Nukunonu data possesses real coherence and ethnic integrity.

Certainly it is with some justification that Molloy and Huntsman (1996, 56) claim Nukunonu as possibly "the closest real case equivalent of a Polynesian *founding* population" (our emphasis). It is an atoll case study that has critical relevance for demographic reconstruction of colonization events, social processes, and population trajectories in the wider sphere of Remote Oceania.

Atafu

The very useful advancement of Nukunonu as such a real case equivalent has obscured another pertinent atoll population case. Moreover, it is one for which there are Tokelau *tala* of a founding settlement and a genealogically ascribed "founding population." Evidence concerning the first-time settlement of Atafu remains equivocal and can now only be unraveled by archaeology. Best (1988), sampling on the present village islet, indicates that occupation there began by ca. AD 1100, although evidence of the first residents has yet to be located. Oral traditions claim that barbarian occupants, who had "utterly overwhelmed" both Fakaofo and Nukunonu earlier, were tricked into abandoning Atafu by Fakaofo voyagers (Huntsman and Hooper 1985, 137–139; Matagi Tokelau 1991, 33–36). Thereafter, people resided on the atoll intermittently, using it as the northern outlier resource reserve and sole source of *kanava (Cordia subcordata)* wood for Tokelau canoes and houses. Eventually, whether by inclination or edict, a pioneer group of kin left Fakaofo under the leadership of a junior lineage *aliki* (chief) and established a colony on Atafu that became an enduring settlement.

As to when this resettlement of the atoll occurred, a date independent of genealogical analyses cannot yet be promulgated. Byron searched the atoll in 1765 without finding evidence of occupation, but Edwards readily located established dwellings, canoes, fishing gear, and a place with ritual artifacts near the present village in 1791, yet he did not see people, despite "a most minute and repeated search."[13] Such historic reports, associated with genealogies, prompted Raspe (1973, 10) to conclude, "a late 18th century date for the [Fakaofo] colonization of Atafu seems most appropriate"; overpopulation of the source community was the suggested probable reason. Raspe based her analyses on detailed Atafu genealogies compiled by Huntsman in 1971 and used in the Tokelau Islands Migrant Study (TIMS).[14] Computer punch cards were employed for data entry and various statistical analyses, and an assumption was made that resettlement took place 180–190 years before the genealogies were collated. Citing other studies from Polynesia (including Macgregor 1937, 35) as warrants, Raspe proposed a "generation" of eighteen years and investigated Atafu as "a breeding isolate" through "a manageable span of nine generations" of the demographic structure, ca. 1791 to ca. 1971.[15] There are problems with this less sophisticated methodology and the definition of Atafu as a breeding isolate across the generations investigated (see also Huntsman and Hooper 1976, 268). However, the interest in this limited analysis resides with its broader affirmations of other parallel and supporting information.

Our compilation of some relevant data is found in Table 12.2. Acknowledging the existence of certain irresolvable conundrums, a collation of available material is used in order to view trends over time rather than to determine precise numbers at particular dates. Thus, on Atafu, an apparent trend is a steady increase in numbers of people and dwellings, yet the average number of people associated with a dwelling seems to remain fairly constant.

Tokelau narratives name Tonuia, from a junior line of Fakaofo elites, as the *aliki* (chief) of the founding migrants. His wife Lagimaina (formerly of Nukunonu), their six children (four male, two female), and the youngest son of Tonuia, child of a second wife, accompanied him. An Atafu concept of "social order" is marked by the seven *puikaiga* founded by the progeny of Tonuia and collectively termed Falefitu ("Seven Houses") of Atafu. Among the other members of the founding group were the spouses of these progeny and two brothers of one son's wife. In addition, there were "two companions of Tonuia" (i.e., the same generation); one "had no issue," while the second was with three of his children, two male and one female (Macgregor 1937, 54–57; Raspe 1973, 9). Thus, there is "a small founding population whose relationships with one another were largely unequivocal" (Huntsman et al. 1986, 20). The cross-referenced genealogies are internally consistent with the frequently recounted *tala,* none of which are considered privileged esoteric knowledge.

The first Atafu-born children are not named, but Macgregor (1937, 55) includes information provided by an elder concerning the original houses and their known locations; the names of Tonuia, his progeny, and his companion's children

Table 12.2. Atafu: "Generations" and sibships.

Generation	No. of sibships	No. of Males	No. of Females	Additions to population each 18-year generation
1	0	2	1	3
2	3	10	8	18
3	13	43	34	77
4	45	74	88	162
5	71	145	141	286
6	124	223	229	452
7	143	216	215	431
8	65	113	123	236
9	14	14	18	32
Total		840	857	1,697

Source of data: Raspe 1973, Tables 1 and 2.

are each associated with one dwelling as the named responsible occupant (refer also to Matagi Tokelau 1991, 44–45). An estimated sixty to seventy residents occupy the first ten houses. Subsequently, additional settlers arrived from Fakaofo (five named men and their "families") and constructed another five ordinary dwellings, increasing the population in this new village by approximately thirty people (Macgregor 1937, 54–56;[16] Matagi Tokelau 1991, 43–45; Huntsman and Hooper 1996, 138, 171–173). Dwellings and "living space" under roof in relation to number of associated people serve as a another kind of corroborative proxy that is explored further below.

In this pre-mission era, there are clear indications of polygyny (Raspe 1973, 43). The founding *aliki* Tonuia had two named wives, and four members of his children's generation were twice married, but the frequency of such marriages in this small population is not determined. For the people of Tokelau, this is a time preceding "enlightenment" *(te malamalama),* and the practice of polygyny reputedly ended after two resident LMS teachers guided the Atafu conversion to Christianity between 1861 and 1863.

In Table 12.2, derived from data in Raspe (1973, tables 1 and 2), Generations 1 and 2 represent the incoming founding adult migrants in the group led by Tonuia. Consequently, Generation 1 has no sibships, and only three sibships are nominated in Generation 2 (i.e., the migrant children of Tonuia's two wives and the children of his "companion"). As a crude measure of population increase over time, the steady increase in number of sibships for some generations "is characteristic of the rapid growth of a population finding itself in a previously unexploited environment" (37). This coherent and well-supported assessment is fundamental to forwarding the case of Atafu as another Polynesian founding population equivalent to and an exemplar for a Diuternal Settlement Model (see below).

Thus, an estimated population of around ninety (Tonuia's founding group plus the five identified settler "families") apparently increased steadily despite the perils common to atoll populations, only some of which are revealed in the genealogies and interpretations augmented by narratives and historical records. The USEE accounts of the Atafu visit include a low estimate of 100 persons, a high of 160, and the preferred report by Wilkes ([1845] 1981, 7–8) of 120 people. In 1841, these residents occupy around twenty dwellings (Hooper and Huntsman 1973, 369–378; Hale [1846] 1981, [151–152] 40; Wessen et al. 1992, 38).

Raspe is not equating "generation" with chronological time intervals, nor is she concerned with population figures on a given date; the "additions" in her study are genealogically attested atoll births. (Thus, these include individuals who later died, emigrated as spouses or kindred, or became temporary residents on the other atolls, including Olohega.) Certainly some Atafu people were elsewhere during the USEE visit in 1841 — for example, on 'Uvea as driftaways yet to return to their atoll or in Samoa. Yet the dwelling spaces of the contemporary settlement support other indications that there were not large numbers of absentees. The extent of migration that is genealogically evident before the "slave ships" arrival affirms that spouses were sought from other atolls; as the size of the population increased, spouse selection more closely approached "the preferred mating types according to Tokelauan kinship ideology" (Raspe 1973, 82).[17]

An LMS mission record places ca. 140 residents on Atafu in January 1863, shortly before the arrival of the "slave ships" (Maude 1981, 63; Hooper and Huntsman 1973, 376). Since the thirty-seven able-bodied men removed were still of reproductive age, this depopulation directly and subsequently seriously affected Generations 4, 5, and 6 as defined by Raspe. It is in Generation 4 that the first consanguineous (nonincestuous) first cousin marriages are discernible. Despite the regeneration crisis in the atolls, Atafu is characterized as showing low inbreeding for the structure of its population.

How did Atafu respond to the 1863 depopulation? The atoll responded effectively and with alacrity. Maude (1981, 173) estimates that, despite a remnant male population of just six ("left through age and infirmity"), Atafu achieved a remarkable rate of increase averaging 13 percent over the first five years. Indeed, during the latter part of the nineteenth century, Atafu had more residents than any other Tokelau atoll (Huntsman and Hooper 1996, 336), and before 1900 the population was more than double the 1863 mission figures.[18] Even without precise numbers of residents, the Raspe study indicates an intensified population recovery effort affecting the genealogical "additions" in Generations 5, 6, and 7 (see Table 12.2).[19]

How did Atafu achieve such a rate of recovery? In the view of Molloy and Huntsman (1996, 56–57), Atafu was able to increase rapidly because its women were spared by the recruitment agents, and this atoll experienced the smallest loss in numbers of people (thirty-seven, all men). In part, this is attributable to an alert teacher's warning and his efforts to deceive recruiters (Maude 1981, 71). Atafu was also spared the virulent dysentery that caused fatalities on Fakaofo (see below). And missionaries repatriated five Atafu male driftaways aboard a canoe that landed on Tutuila. In addition, immigrant males of varied ethnicity were accepted as spouses; irrevocable bequests in the gene pool include those of European and other Polynesian begetters. In managing this regeneration crisis, one Atafu elective was exogamous marriages while there was a paucity of Tokelauan males of reproductive age.

This brief review of Atafu indicates that a small founding population can quite quickly raise reproductive rates, expand or recover, and sustain an overall growth trajectory. Swinbourne (1925), in his final report before the transfer of administrative responsibility to New Zealand, lists the population of Atafu at 380. So in this case, over a period of 130 years (ca. 1795–1925), the calculated average growth rate is about 2.5 percent (Table 12.3).

Olohega

The are no analyses of the population history of Olohega; it is the contested international status of this atoll that attracts interest (Hooper 1975; Skaggs 1994, 213–214; Huntsman and Hooper 1996, 306, 338). Nevertheless, numerous historical records as well as *tala* affirm that, under the hegemony of Fakaofo, Tokelauan people occupied this atoll. It was an outlier resource reserve, particularly valued and used after cyclones or during other periods of food shortage, an integral part of the realm although seldom inhabited by more than a few households (representing *kaiga*) at any one time. The USEE, unable to land, reported no signs of habitation from their shipboard view of the densely wooded island, but people moved on and off Olohega and were certainly there during Fakaofo famine years from 1846 onward.

It is an implausible proposition that Olohega was "not occupied" when claimed by an American trader, since people from the other atolls were in residence (e.g., see Macgregor 1937, 23; Hooper 1975; Skaggs 1994, 213, app. 227; Huntsman and Hooper 1996, 335 fn 15). After the sequestration of Olohega, traders continued to offer employment to Tokelauans as processors of coconut oil and copra. With regard to the "slave ships," Maude (1981, 206, fn 9) concluded that "[t]here is no reason to suppose a single recruit was taken from Olosenga, where the only islanders were Jennings' own family and his plantation workers with their families." The

Table 12.3. Atafu: Dwellings and population per dwelling.

	Est. no. dwellings	Est. population	Est. average associated population per dwelling
1. Population end of eighteenth century (before European contact) Tonuia's Settlement "Founding Population" ca. 1785–1795	10	[60]	[6]
With additional settlers ca. 1795–1800	15	[90]	[6]
2. Population 1841 Wilkes and USEE observers			
Low estimate: Reynolds	15	100	6.7
Reported by Wilkes	20	120	6.0
High estimate: Hudson	28	160	5.7
3. Population 1863 Mission census before "slave ships"	[23]	140	[6.0]
Recorded after "slave ships"		103	
4. Population 1900–1925 "Contract labor" period (increased male emigration)			
1900 Hunter Ms (Hooper and Huntsman 1973)		375	
192 — July, Swinbourne (NZNA correspondence)		380	

Interpolated values (in brackets) for missing data (a) are consistent with other values in this table; (b) take cognizance that women on Nukunonu produced an average of 6.2 children but only 1.2 reproducing daughters (in the period AD 1860–1920, see Molloy and Huntsman 1996) in estimates of population associated with dwellings.

Abbreviations: USEE: United States Exploring Expedition, 1841; NZNA: New Zealand National Archives.

teacher on Atafu identified Jennings aboard the first "slave ship" and recounted his enticement of men who trusted him as a trader known in Tokelau since 1856.

In discussions of Tokelau atoll populations through time, Olohega was part of the polity, although its landlocked lagoon became a brackish lake and it lacked permanent underground potable water in quantities to support a large settlement. In the absence of population estimates for the pericontact period, the significance of Olohega is that the temporary residence of men and household groups has an indeterminable yet acknowledged effect on reproduction trends, population estimates, and official enumerations of source villages (e.g., people who evaded "slave ship" raids and twenty from Atafu on Olohega in 1902). Since some people subsequently used Olohega birth or residence as a route to American Samoa, Hawai'i, and U.S. citizenship, it cannot be assumed that Tokelau people counted there at a particular time would return to their villages of origin (even if such affiliations were recorded).

Fakaofo

Finally, we offer a brief consideration of Fakaofo, the suzerain of Tokelau after the "three unrelated warring populations" (Huntsman and Hooper 1985, 144) were subjugated into one polity. Undoubtedly, for centuries before the pericontact era, the largest population (with lineages of elites who controlled a ritual and political hegemony of Tokelau) occupied the small islet on Fakaofo that provided a permanent underground water supply. After the conquest of Nukunonu, Fakaofo appropriated women and other resources from that atoll.

What is known of the Fakaofo situation during the pericontact period reveals complex population issues. Perusing only the nineteenth-century context, impediments to formal analyses include the significant population displacements and depletions associated with cyclones, drought, famine, voyaging losses, emigration, immigration, and disease. And then, the "slave ships" transported 53 percent of the survivors who were resident in February 1863. The USEE reports (e.g., Hale [1846] 1981, 48; Hooper and Huntsman 1973, 372) estimate 500–600 people in 1841. After a cyclone in 1846 there were apparently some six years of drought conditions leading to famine.[20] A fleet of twenty canoes left for the other atolls; only two are reported to have reached land, on larger islands (Wessen et al. 1992, 40). In 1852, missionaries coerced a migration of about 500 residents to 'Uvea, leaving 90–100 residents — elders who refused to abandon their atoll and forty younger kin left to assist them (cf. Monfat [1890] 1981, [304–310] 92–93).

How many migrants returned, and when, has not yet been determined. Maude (1981, 65) states that sixteen of these people, converts to Catholicism, returned from 'Uvea in 1861. Clearly, most migrants were not repatriated; one decade later missionaries recorded only 261 residents in January 1863. Some driftaways returned on that mission voyage; several hosted dysentery contracted in Samoa and a few died aboard. Subsequently, there were sixty-four deaths during the outbreak on Fakaofo before the "slave ships" appeared.[21] Infected individuals transferred dysentery when taken aboard, and most passengers died before the vessels reached Callao. Only one Fakaofo survivor is known, a male who was later left on Rapa; his son visited once but did not remain in Tokelau (Maude 1981, 184).

A total of 140 people were transported from Fakaofo in February 1863 (sixty-four men, seventy-six women and children) — over 53 percent of the population (Maude 1981, 194). This atoll was left with sixty residents, but not as a founding population with selected reproductive potential. There were thirty women and twenty-one children; only six men remained (four Tokelauans, two Samoan teachers, and one U.S. trader), although three men soon returned from Tutuila after one "slave ship" left them ashore.

This remnant population was increased by the driftaways who landed on Savai'i (four men, three women, eight children), one Fakaofo woman from the Atafu canoe that beached on Tutuila, and four couples with an unknown number of children who returned from Olohega. Maude (1981, 68, 173) suggests that regeneration began with at least eighty-four (seventeen men, thirty-eight women, and twenty-nine children) and calculates that Fakaofo achieved an average rate of 12 percent increase over the first seven years to 1870. Molloy and Huntsman (1996, 57) attribute this recovery rate to a return migration of reproductive-age individuals (from Olohega, Samoa, and elsewhere). Hooper and Huntsman (1973, 372), citing manuscripts by Newell and Cusack-Smith, report 278 people on Fakaofo in 1896; that is still less than the population at that time on the smallest atoll of Atafu. For the period of population recovery (1870–1925), our calculated average growth rate for Fakaofo is 2.1 percent. Attempts to calculate a rate from the baseline of 1841 population estimates (at this time, Hale [1846] 1981 ponders the maintenance of a resource/population balance when he writes of the "very well peopled" Fale islet) indicate an overall decline exceeding 2 percent when the endpoint is 1925.

Stated succinctly, the Fakaofo population loss from the 1841 USEE estimate (500–600 residents) — through the six-year famine of 1846–1852 (perhaps ca. 300 deaths), the disappearance of eighteen voyaging canoes, the coerced migration in 1852 (ca. 500 people), the dysentery outbreak (sixty-four victims), and "slave ship" recruitment (137 villagers) in 1863 — represents a sequence of depopulation episodes over two decades that leads to dissolution of the traditional atoll polity and the annihilation of the Tokelau religion. Yet, despite the successive displacements under duress, never did the population of Fakaofo abandon the atoll.

An Atoll Population Proxy: Archaeological and Demographic Aspects of the Ethnographic Tokelau Dwelling

Dwelling space has been used as a proxy for calculating population numbers in prehistory. The original ethno-archaeological study of floor area and settlement population by Naroll (1962) indicates only the potential of this approach. In this study, four Pacific examples (Tonga, Vanua Levu, Ifalik Atoll [Yap], and Tikopia) are incorporated with data from two communities in Papua New Guinea. However, a careful review of source data shows only that for Tikopia is apt: An ethnohistoric figure provided for this island, at 6.8 m² per person (m²/p) of floor area, can be usefully employed in analyses for Remote Oceania. Brown (1987) employs more appropriate data in a restudy involving thirty-eight societies in different world regions; this yields a comparable figure for "outdoor" (as opposed to "indoor") societies of 6.1 m²/p — close to that for Tikopia derived earlier — with a reported sample range from 4.7 to 7.5 m²/p.

An archaeologist's ethnological study of this relationship in several Samoan villages (LeBlanc 1971) yields figures for traditional style dwellings of modern construction: 8.7 and 11 m²/p (i.e., greater than the high end in the Brown study). Employing extensive habitation data from archaeological investigations in former Western Samoa, with additional ethnographic information, Davidson (1974, 235–236) carefully assesses this relationship for pericontact dwellings. She concludes that "the average floor space requirements per individual" appear closer to 8 m²/p than to the Naroll (1962) world standard of 10 m²/p available at the time.

As yet, there are neither archaeological nor early historic observations on dwelling size for any of the Tokelau atolls. The only archaeological survey of Tokelau (Best 1988) has not yet attracted Pacific researchers to offer the atoll people an acceptable program of archaeological and complementary investigations. So, is there an ethnographic situation in Tokelau, comparable to that of Samoa, that offers a relevant proxy for consideration in the archaeology and paleodemography of Remote Oceania?

Village maps of Atafu (1970) prepared by Huntsman and of Fakaofo (1968) by Hooper, have been published (Matagi Tokelau 1991, 157; Huntsman and Hooper 1996, 28–35).[22] For each village, there is a photograph of one *fale* (dwelling structure, house) identified as characteristic, and for general consideration such material can be associated with population figures for the years 1951, 1961, 1966, and 1971, the period leading up to and around the time the fieldwork maps were prepared (AJHR 1951, 1966, 1971).

An extrapolated average population figure for association with each village map has been calculated for the 1951–1971 period. During these years there was a rise followed by a fall in the number of people on each atoll; reasons for the recorded population changes are known.[23] A population estimate for each map could be derived from either an interpolation between the 1966 and 1971 data for the 1968 or 1970 year or from an average of the four figures, as is done here. The result is 477 people for Nukunonu, 738 people for Fakaofo, and 561 people for Atafu.

Table 12.4. Tokelau: Calculations of modern ethnographic dwelling size and associated population numbers.

Atoll village	Avg. pop. 1951–1971	No. of dwellings	No. of people per dwelling	Avg. size in m² of platform dwelling[1]	Area per person under roof in m²
Fakaofo	708	83	8.5	64.1[2]	60.0[2]	7.76
Atafu	561	68	8.25	64.5	70.9[3] 57.9	7.0
Nukunonu	477	68	7.0	68	52.2	7.4

1. The estimated floor area of a dwelling under roof.

2. For thirty-six more traditional examples in which illustrated sizes of dwelling and platform sizes are nearly congruent.

3. For forty-seven examples for which only illustrated dwelling size was measured in relation to various kinds of much larger platform bases, or a household's area around a dwelling was demarcated by stacked stone walling, often without an obvious pavement or platform base.

The methods employed in assembling the data summarized in Table 12.4 are fairly straightforward. On greatly enlarged versions of each map, church and public buildings (described by Huntsman and Hooper 1996, 32–35), cookhouses, and other ancillary buildings have been removed from consideration. Huntsman and Hooper report that in Tokelau, "low platforms upon which most houses are set extend more than a meter beyond the interior space," and there are particular features of *fale* on each atoll. "Fakaofo houses characteristically have low walls and sometimes are perched directly on their stone foundations rather than having platforms around them." To give mathematical effect to this statement, using only the thirty-six "characteristic" Fakaofo dwelling platforms, an average ca. 64.5 m² size as a basis for calculating living floor area is reduced to an average of ca. 60 m².[24]

For Nukunonu, "houses are set on foundations retained by courses of coral slabs and always have low or full side walls." In contrast to the stone-built foundations of Fakaofo and Nukunonu, the foundation platforms of Atafu are reportedly often filled with coral rubble and "retained by sections of *kanava* timber embedded in the ground." Dwellings are more open (i.e., with minimal fixed walls or no walls), and a demarcation between living space under roof and that beyond is not as clearly indicated.

A numbered habitation platform database was compiled, and approximate measurements for habitation structures were calculated. The tabled summary of detailed calculations here is in a form deemed most useful to archaeologists wishing to consider such data in proxies of population figures from house size and numbers. In this atoll case, there is also a different relationship where exceptionally large platforms in the formerly dominant village support habitation structures with an average size much greater than the "characteristic" traditional dwellings on all three atolls.

The results shown in Table 12.4 allow the inference that a Samoan figure of 8 m²/p in current use might well be further reduced to 7–7.5 m²/p when working with pericontact period dwelling data. As with other data developed for Tokelau atolls, this may have wider relevance for research in Remote Oceania. For "outdoor" societies throughout that region, a figure toward the high end of the Brown (1987) "world" sample of ca. 7 m²/p is forwarded as a productive guideline when estimating numbers of people from archaeological data related to "living space" under roof (when it can be restricted to a *fale* or a similar and common type of habitation unit). However, with respect to averaging the number of associated people per dwelling (a proxy "house-count approach" in archaeology), the early ethnohistorical figures of five to six cited (and widely applied) are still supported by the nineteenth-century Tokelau data, rather than the seven or eight indicated by modern ethnographic data (such as that assembled for Tokelau ca. 1970, or the eight and eleven assessed for Samoa at that time).

Concluding Review

In considering Pacific population issues, there is an underestimated value in examining real cases to understand more about how island population groups establish, reproduce, conserve, recover, and constrain the numbers necessary for the endurance of their communities. The case of Atafu and that of Nukunonu, supplemented by the less structured data compiled for Fakaofo, are pertinent atoll contributions to ongoing debates about population processes on many islands in Remote Oceania.

Brewis (1994, 53) writes of a "Pacific Islands Model" (based on Firth's [1957] description of Tikopia and other historic cases) used in attempts to provide a foundation for modern theories of preindustrial fertility control. One concern is to elucidate how island populations could — and more importantly did — internally regulate population size through examining "real case" examples. Some social mechanisms commonly cited in the control of reproduction — abortion, celibacy, infanticide, and emigration (from solitary departures to substantial movements of "breeding propagules") — are noted above in reference to Tokelau. Real case studies and supplementary data from these atolls contribute the following new insights to these issues:

1. They establish that founding populations in Polynesia may not have been of the kind postulated for preindustrial societies (in which fertility was deemed to be high and mortality low), with active population regulation only in cases of environment stress. Rather, the atoll cases based in real locations reveal that social practices are more flexible than thought.

2. They also demonstrate that such Polynesian founding populations possessed a very high degree of potential fertility and — significantly — they reveal a high mortality. Moreover, under most conditions pertaining to the pericontact period (eighteenth and nineteenth centuries), some sociocultural regulation of fertility was practiced, rather than reactively instituted in response to periods of population and/or environmental stress.

3. They expand the range of reproductive controls cited in the literature. One addition is the relatively long birth intervals suggested by Nukunonu data. Others in evidence include a relatively short average reproduction span (that includes maternal and paternal mortality); a cultural preference that women cease reproduction by the time their daughters commence; and maternal oversight of daughters and their newborns associated with (a) breastfeeding for a desirable period of six months or longer and (b) prolonged postpartum abstinence (facilitated by customary uxorilocal residence).

4. They affirm that founding populations in the order of sixty to ninety can successfully establish, reproduce, and sustain migrant settlements that endure to become cultural communities even within the constrained ecology of atolls that experience periodic calamitous events.

5. They reveal that strategies of maintaining contact with communities of origin and association for a period after the founding of migrant settlements have pragmatic and evident effects in ensuring access to spouses of acceptable kin relationship distance within culturally affiliated populations.

6. They exemplify the strategy of occupying and incorporating neighboring isles as outlier reserves of resources (common and scarce) to be accessed periodically by authorized atoll representatives but not necessarily inhabited on a permanent basis.

Turning now to some aspects of the atoll economies, it is apparent that Tokelau cases reflect the basic food resource minimums with which founding populations could establish and survive. Modes of occupation, survival, reproduction, and expansion are clear without recourse to notions of "strandlooping" or to notions of highly mobile populations in "skimming" mode, depleting resources on one island and then moving to the next, "in a form of non-agricultural colonization" (Anderson 1995, 2003, 7). The latter stance is an important element of the "dispersal" model that entertains an effective foraging economy throughout the initial movements into the region of Remote Oceania. The "dispersal" model also proposes that migrants departed from an agricultural base (if that existed among the early Lapita populations of Near Oceania). In this construction, tuber gardening and arboriculture, in a nonsystematic and piecemeal fashion only, appear much later and toward the eastern end of Lapita distribution (usually at the end of the 300-year phase of dentate-decorated Lapita traditions of southern Vanuatu, New Caledonia, Fiji, Tonga, and Samoa [Anderson 2003, 8]).

The Tokelau data suggest that, even under the environmental constraints imposed by an atolline island, immigrant founding populations of ca. sixty (two double-hulled or outrigger oceangoing canoe loads) can establish settlements that endure 100, 200, and even more years. This is accomplished by using (a) the marine resources of fish, shellfish, and turtles, combined with (b) land birds, young coconut crabs, and the wild varieties of coconut and pandanus trees that preceded all human habitation in these islands and, subsequently, (c) higher yielding cultivar varieties introduced after arrival, as well as imported root cuttings of breadfruit trees (*Artocarpus altilis*) where feasible.

In seventy years (e.g., with 300 residents on the .05 km² Fale village islet), the atoll people can greatly enhance their diet, just as on Fakaofo. If there is a deep lens of underground freshwater, *pulaka (Cyrtosperma chamissonis)* pits can also be constructed. On the minimal Fakaofo evidence available, the result sustains a substantial population of 300–350 (even up to 500; see Table 11.4). Such an atoll population could exhibit significant fluctuations during periods of environmental and social stress, yet easily endure for up to 1,000 years. Even if such a limited enhancement of the subsistence system is not feasible, a population of 140 and more enduring over several centuries seems a reasonable proposition. This would be easily achievable after the prevalence of wild coconuts is largely displaced by cultivated types in managed plantations and a similar strategy undertaken with introduced, cultivated forms of fruiting pandanus.

Predation soon after settlement limits the contribution made by wild land and seabirds, and large overmature shellfish soon disappear. However, a supply of shellfish is always obtainable. Turtles become scarce and a food reserved for elites. But neither "strandloopers" nor "foragers" appropriately describes the foregoing as the economic behavior of pioneer settlers on the atolls. As for founding populations on many of the larger raised atolls, smaller volcanic islands, or larger islands west of the Andesite Line, within a century or so they would be growing at a steady pace and relocating kin-affiliated groups of people every few generations to occupy new niches as they cleared more arable land.

This chapter represents a more complex and comprehensive phase in the development of a flexible Polynesian founding population growth model. A longer-term objective of the underpinning study is to refine the contribution of atoll populations to the Diuturnal Settlement Model (Green and Green 2002) for the migration and settlement of people in Remote Oceania, from Lapita migrants to their numerous descendant populations. To distinguish the principal characteristic from the commonly used concept of "established," its designation emphasizes the *enduring* character of the pioneering migrant settlements. Over generations, they are transformed into cultural communities that — in geographically separated locations requiring transoceanic journeys to sustain social contacts — differentiate as language groups through time.

A Diuturnal Settlement Model offers a useful framework for discussing the characteristics of migrations and founding settlements throughout Remote Oceania. It is relevant to settlements on offshore atolls, raised coral islands (e.g., the main Reef Islands), and similar islands (as in Vanuatu, the Loyalties, and the Isle of Pines) that served as stepping-stones for migrations during the Lapita expansion eastward. During a later time interval, ca. 1,000 BP, this model is also applicable to atolls across the longitudes from Tokelau/Tuvalu west and north to Nukuoro, Kapingamarangi, Ontong Java, and Takuu (i.e., the Samoan-Ellicean-Outlier expansion, Kirch 2000; Marck 2000), as well as eastward to the Northern Cook Islands and from Pukapuka to the Tuamotu Archipelago. Finally, ca. 800 BP it engages with the settlement of the Tuamotus from the Society Islands. The model incorporates only minimal initial conditions of subsistence resources (any more becomes a plus) for the pioneering migrants, a founding population in the range of sixty to ninety with effective social processes to control fertility, along with transport resources and skills to maintain contacts with the source and associated communities (Kirch 1988; Irwin 1992). The atolls of Tokelau offered the minimal subsistence resources. What they lacked was arable land and the means for further horticultural intensification over time. These populations demonstrated a repertoire of strategies for successful transport and settlement of a founding population, as well as voyaging skills that enabled migrants to sustain regional social networks. The atoll populations used flexible social processes for the control of fertility and rates of reproduction; they actively managed recovery from the demographic challenges of contingency events and ensured their continuity as atoll populations occupying enduring settlements.

Notes

Authors' note: The authors wish to thank the participants who debated the issues associated with atoll settlement and population reproduction during the conference on Mo'orea and Jeffrey Lang, who worked on the habitation database.

1. Wessen et al. (1992, 40) indicate potential voyaging losses: Of twenty canoes on an interatoll journey, only two are known to have made landfall — on Savai'i and 'Uvea.

2. Kirch (2000, 308) observes that human populations found themselves occupying healthier environments once they were beyond the malaria vector regions of Near Oceania. Houghton (1996) surveys the spectrum of indigenous diseases.

3. Hooper and Huntsman (1973, 402) cite Pirie: Only filariasis *(Wuchereria bancrofti)* and a skin infection were present in Tokelau before 1863. In the 1960s, "filiarial fever [is still the] principal cause of ill health" (Wessen et al. 1992, 251; McCarthy and Carter 1967).

4. Traditionally, an atoll name may also be used as a reference for its population.

5. Huntsman and Hooper (1996, 140) list documented European visits between 1765 and 1841.

6. Genealogies clearly associate the present with the past in culturally patterned and selective reporting of ancestral and generational linkages that reflect (and often legitimate) significant social relationships. In this chapter, they are considered and used as representations of the past that have validity, but their representations differ from those of other cultural idioms or historical texts (see also Huntsman et al. 1986).

7. Hooper and Huntsman (1973), Molloy and Huntsman (1996), and Huntsman and Hooper (1996) offer detailed data; Maude (1981) offers a meticulous narrative of the Peruvian labor recruitment raids and their effects on Pacific Island populations.

8. Of these, four couples are regarded as the founders of four maximal kin groups termed *puikaiga* (Molloy and Huntsman 1996, 44), the *Falafa* ("Four Houses") of Nukunonu.

9. Maude (1981, 68, 172) reports fifteen voyagers; some died in Samoa. His number may represent survivors: Huntsman and Hooper (1996, 336 fn 22) write that nineteen voyagers left for Samoa — the eighteen baptized there (including women and children) and the chief's son, Takua.

10. Nukunonu elders, parents, and some women reportedly objected to plans for men to undertake labor contracts in the Phoenix Islands (Matagi Tokelau 1991, 121–122).

11. Tokelau *tala* recount at least two devastating cyclones before Europeans arrived, but the 1914 event was the worst recorded from people who remembered the experience. Some atoll residents drowned, nearly all dwellings were destroyed, and copra production ceased. Matagi Tokelau (1991, 58–59 plates) includes photographs of Nukunonu; no *fale* remained. After another severe storm the following year, a group of men was sent in 1916 to obtain money for *kaiga* needs by working eighteen-month labor contracts.

12. Molloy and Huntsman (1996, 51) identified twenty-seven of ninety-seven parents as not from Nukunonu. Of these, twenty-two were from other Tokelau atolls (Fakaofo sixteen; Atafu six); apart from one Portuguese male, all others were from previously contacted Pacific islands.

13. Edwards ([1790–1791] 1915, 45). Since Tokelau canoes are laboriously crafted from lashed sections of valued *kanava* wood found only on Atafu, abandonment of the described settlement is less likely than absence for a return voyage to Fakaofo. Tokelau *tala* indicate that a small group completed a return voyage immediately before Tonuia's founding settlers emigrated (Matagi Tokelau 1991, 43), a strategy modeled as characteristic of Polynesian voyaging expansion.

14. The Tokelau Islands Migrant Study (TIMS) was a long-term (1966–1984), compre-

hensive, multidisciplinary study of the effects of migration and social change on the people of Tokelau (Huntsman 1975, 183–192; Prior et al. 1977; Wessen et al. 1992). The Raspe (1973) analysis was "a preliminary demonstration" that ethnographic genealogies could be linked and coded to produce biological information. The genealogies from each atoll were subsequently used to construct a "synthetic" genealogy used by other TIMS researchers (Huntsman et al. 1986).

15. Later analysis of Nukunonu data (Molloy and Huntsman 1996, 51) supports the Raspe rejection of 25 years for a generation. For Raspe (1973, 19), "generation" is concerned with a unit of transmission of genetic data rather than a discrete period in time; her "population" comprises individuals born or permanently resident on Atafu. The Atafu genealogies represented ancestral histories of 46 *kaiga*. They provided a "clear, highly consistent" record. "The entire population of Tokelau may be represented in 230 terminating four-generation pedigrees" (Huntsman, Hooper, and Ward 1986, 18, 24).

16. During Atafu fieldwork in 1932, Macgregor (1937, 3) obtained most "information of the history" from an elder who was a child when "missionaries first came . . . in 1859."

17. The reported culturally desirable separation is fourth degree of relationship; Huntsman (1976, 271–272) indicates that second cousin marriage transgresses custom and first cousin marriage is culturally unacceptable.

18. Hooper and Huntsman (1973, 372) cite manuscript sources of Atafu population figures: Newell and Cusack-Smith (1896, 350); Cusack-Smith (1897, 351); Hunter (1900, 37). Richardson (1925, 8) recorded 363 residents (thirty more women than men, but thirty men were on Olohega) on October 1, 1925.

19. There were other impediments to Atafu population growth in the early twentieth century. Severe droughts foreshadowed certain mobility patterns (e.g., twenty people on Olohega in 1902; sixty-four in the Phoenix Islands in 1904). A 1914 dysentery outbreak resulted in thirty-four deaths (Huntsman and Hooper 1996, 306).

20. Wessen et al. (1992, 35) refer to a Padel report of trenches in Fakaofo village containing 300 bodies (deaths during five months). In the village, there were no coconuts, and inflorescence of felled palms was being eaten (indicative that the food shortage was extremely serious).

21. The driftaways were survivors from six of eight canoes missing from an interatoll voyage in December 1862; eventually, six landed on 'Upolu, one on Savai'i, and one on Tutuila. People in the 'Upolu group contracted dysentery before boarding the mission ship that returned them to Fakaofo; they infected atoll residents (leading to sixty-four recorded deaths), and the dysentery was then transferred to passengers on at least three "slave ships" (see Maude 1981, ch 9).

22. Of the periods used for preparation of these maps (1968–1970), Huntsman (1971, 318) writes that "the islands still maintain a subsistence economy based on fish and coconuts." Even in 1971, "[t]he subsistence economy prevailed. Houses were all made of local wood and thatch, and transport was by sailing canoes" (Huntsman and Hooper 1996, 39), and Hooper (1981, 16) states that "[t]he principles of the neo-traditional [i.e., post-1863] social order held."

23. During these years, New Zealand removed emigration permit requirements. In the late 1950s there were about 500 members of the Tokelau Association who purchased land near Apia (Goldsmith 1974, 1975). When Western Samoa attained independence (January

1962), Tokelauans became aliens. With information about impending changes, many returned to the atolls earlier, increasing the density of village populations (on Fakaofo, the 783 residents in 1961 represent the highest number ever recorded). The reactive repatriation increased the Tokelau population to over 1,900 in 1966, with a marked gender imbalance. Some individuals initiated kin-sponsored migration to New Zealand. Subsequently, government schemes sponsored around 350 migrants, but most Tokelauans remained on the atolls.

24. Of the house platforms on Fale (Fakaofo village islet), it is not possible to distinguish platform versus boundary differentiation of forty-seven very large habitation structures shown on the map. For the other thirty-six dwellings, the "characteristics" described by Huntsman and Hooper (1996, 33) apply. Averaging floor area at ca. 60 m² means that some of the "characteristic" thirty-six *fale* retain a size of ca. 64.5 m² and others are reduced to ca. 58 m² yet still possess the traditional small ledge around the outside of the dwelling under roof.

13

Prehistoric Population Growth on Kosrae, Eastern Caroline Islands

Understanding prehistoric population dynamics, including size and growth rates and their changes over time, without question should be one of the major goals of archaeology. Few archaeologists would dismiss the subject of population dynamics as a major system state variable driving adaptation and the evolution of human cultural systems. Recognition of the fundamental significance of population characteristics (e.g., size and density) to the behavior and ecology of nonhuman biological organisms has been a major theme in ecological literature for a long time (e.g., Kingsland 1985; Turchin 2003). There is no reason to believe that population attributes would be any less significant for understanding human evolution and adaptation (e.g., M. Cohen 1977). However, when it comes to looking at particular archaeological cases and regional archaeological sequences, the specific data relating to human population dynamics quickly become slippery, ambiguous, and difficult to interpret (e.g., the case for Hawai'i as presented by Stannard [1989]; see chapter 4, this volume). Consequently, archaeologists more often than not avoid the issue altogether, which is unfortunate because so little effort is being made to overcome the problems inherent in prehistoric population studies.

It is often said that islands are natural laboratories for studying the ecology and evolution of both natural organisms and humans (Williamson 1981; Kirch 1997). Islands are relatively small and manageable isolates that are comparatively free from significant outside influences or "disturbances" — thus the term "natural laboratories" is well conceived (though obviously key variables cannot be experimentally controlled the way they could in a real laboratory). To develop approaches for understanding prehistoric human population growth, therefore, archaeologists working in Oceania almost certainly have a special advantage over scientists working in continental areas. Having this advantage, it is imperative that archaeologists working on the Pacific Islands do more to understand prehistoric population dynamics.

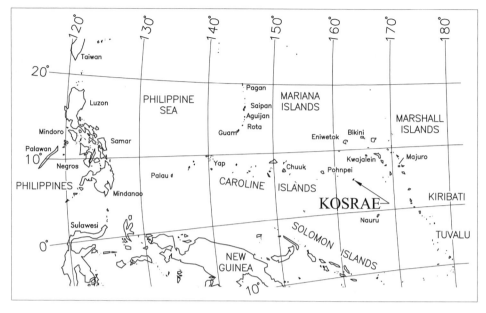

Figure 13.1. Map of the western Pacific Ocean showing the location of Kosrae in the eastern Caroline Islands of Micronesia.

For this discussion, advantage will be taken of one particular natural laboratory in the western Pacific where archaeological and historical data are particularly good. This is the small high island of Kosrae, located in the eastern Caroline Islands of Micronesia (Figure 13.1). The quality of the Kosrae data makes it possible to highlight and elucidate a number of important issues related to the study of prehistoric population dynamics.

Although determination of the size of an island population at contact — essentially evaluating the accuracy of historic population estimates — is a major goal of prehistoric population studies for the Pacific Islands, it is far from the only goal. Such questions as the size of the initial founding or colonizing populations and growth rates and possible changes through time constitute extremely important domains of inquiry. There is also the question of whether density-dependent pressures, following initial high growth rates, led to a later reduction of growth rates.

Another important population issue — to this writer's knowledge one not addressed in the literature — concerns size and density parameters for the onset of the formation of prehistoric stratified chiefdom societies. Population size and density estimates for chiefdoms, such as have been published (e.g., Drennan 1987), derive only from Contact-period information (always of questionable accuracy) long after the formation of social stratification. However, it appears that there never has been an attempt to determine size and density of such societies at their *inception*. Yet this issue is critical for understanding human evolution and adaptation. Pacific Island cases of prehistoric social complexity offer a unique opportunity to discover if there are patterns or regularities in population characteristics for the formation of social stratification. While it would be premature to draw general conclusions at the present time, the Kosrae case provides a starting point for such an inquiry.

The approach advocated here for Kosrae uses the available data to establish a number of parameters or constraints regarding prehistoric population growth on Kosrae. The parameters to be developed include (1) historical information about population size from the time of earliest Western contact; (2) archaeological data of various types impinging on the issue of population size; (3) information on the carrying capacity of the environment; and (4) what we know about general population growth models. This information is then used to construct a number of alternative population growth models for Kosrae — some realistic, given the parameters, and others wholly unrealistic, given the parameters. By this means, several important characteristics of prehistoric population growth on Kosrae can be approximately determined, presumably with a fair degree of confidence within the limits of the parameters. Whether these findings have a broader applicability to other islands will have to await additional studies. However, the approach — essentially a multidimensional constraints approach — should be useful for the study of other prehistoric island populations.[1]

Kosrae: Geographical Baseline

Kosrae is a small, tropical, lushly vegetated, high volcanic island in the eastern Caroline Islands of Micronesia. It is situated about 550 km east-southeast of Pohnpei, the closest neighboring high island, and 5° latitude north of the equator. The small coralline atolls of Pingelap and Mwoakilloa (Mokil) are situated between Kosrae and Pohnpei. East of Kosrae, the nearest atoll of the Marshall Islands, Namorik, is some 600 km distant.

Kosrae, with a land area of 109 km² (42 mi²), consists primarily of a rugged mountainous interior with only a narrow coastal plain (Figure 13.2). The mountains rise to a maximum elevation of 629 m (2,064 ft) above sea level. According to Whitesell et al. (1986), nearly 70 percent of the island has steep slopes. Only 15 percent of the land area is made up of foothills, alluvial fans, and bottomlands, with most of the remainder (14 percent) consisting of mangrove swamps. A fringing reef surrounds the island. There is no barrier reef.

The climate of Kosrae is tropical, with high rainfall (5,000 mm annually, with higher amounts in the island's interior) and high humidity year around. The island is situated at the edge of the trade wind belt to the east, which exerts only a slight effect on Kosrae's climate from about February through April. During this

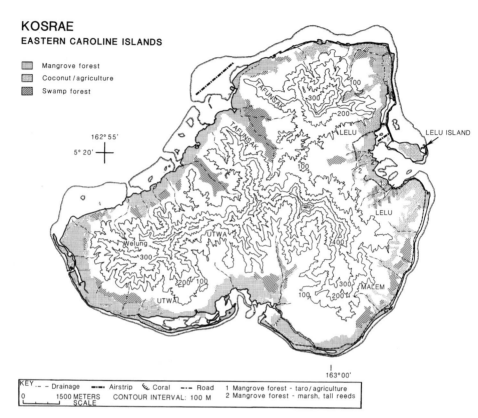

KOSRAE
EASTERN CAROLINE ISLANDS

░ Mangrove forest
▒ Coconut / agriculture
▨ Swamp forest

162° 55'
5° 20'

LELU ISLAND

TAFUNSAK

LELU

LELU

Welung

UTWA

UTWA

MALEM

163° 00'

KEY .– – Drainage ▬▪▬▪ Airstrip ☙ Coral –▪– Road 1 Mangrove forest - taro / agriculture
0   1500 METERS   CONTOUR INTERVAL: 100 M 2 Mangrove forest - marsh, tall reeds
         SCALE

Figure 13.2. Map of Kosrae. Note rugged interior topography and extensive coastal swamps and mangrove wetlands.

time, rainfall decreases somewhat and offshore winds become more noticeable. Kosrae rarely experiences typhoons, which tend to have their origins to the west off the coasts of Pohnpei and Chuuk and then move westward. At present, approximately 63 percent of the island is in forest, leaving 23 percent in agroforest (primarily breadfruit, coconut, and banana), 11 percent in secondary vegetation, and 3 percent nonforested (Whitesell et al. 1986). Geologically, Kosrae is a young island, having formed some 1–2 million years ago over a hot spot trace in the earth's crust (Keating et al. 1984; see Mattey [1982] for geological details).

Besides the main volcanic landmass, Kosrae also has a much smaller 70-ha volcanic island, Lelu, which is located adjacent to a natural deepwater harbor on its northeast side (see Figure 13.2). The east side of Lelu consists of a large and steeply sloping volcanic hill (Finol Poro) that rises to an elevation of 111 m. In contrast, the western half of Lelu, encompassing some 27 ha, is entirely man-made. This is the location of the impressive and well-known megalithic ruins of a late prehis-

Figure 13.3. Dwelling compound of a high chief at Lelu showing houses and people as depicted in sketch by Alexander Postels of the *Senyavin* (Lütke 1835, pl 18). Fyedor Lütke, captain of the *Senyavin,* is at the far left distributing gifts. Pandanus leaf mats cover the ground in front of the houses.

toric chiefdom center (Cordy 1985a, 1993; Morgan 1988, 86–115). The reef flat here was purposefully filled with lagoonal sediments to raise the surface above the high tide level for construction of residential, ritual, and mortuary compounds for the paramount and high chiefs, plus their families and retainers (Figure 13.3). Although filling of the reef flat began about AD 1200, megalithic construction did not start until about AD 1350 or 1400. Expansion of the Lelu compounds on the reef flat continued up to about AD 1800 (Cordy 1985a, 1993, 228–233; Athens 1995, 79–80).

Lelu Island was the prehistoric political center of Kosrae and continued to be the island's administrative center after first European contact in 1824 and on through the whaling, German, Japanese, and American periods (see Cordy 1993). Although the municipal government remains in Lelu, the state government is now centered in Tofol on the main island. Lelu nevertheless continues to be the most important population and commercial center on the island, having approximately 2,500 people. This compares to approximately 1,200 to 1,700 people it is estimated to have had during the late prehistoric period (Cordy 1985a, 256; 1993,

164–165). Kosrae's total population at the time of European contact in 1824 was probably not much more than double this number at best (Ritter 1981; further discussion of historic population estimates is presented below).

Traditional Kosraean Society and Agriculture

The earliest Western visitors to Kosrae — the French and Russian exploration ships *la Coquille* and the *Senyavin* in 1824 and 1827, respectively (see Ritter and Ritter 1981) — described the island as politically unified with a population of no more than 3,000 people, which was divided into four distinct social strata. At the top was the paramount chief, who was both the secular and sacred head of Kosraean society and who held ultimate title to all land. Under the paramount there were about ten high chiefs, usually male relatives that were appointed by him. The high chiefs, who were obligated to live in Lelu with the paramount, controlled named land units called *facl* that ran from the high mountains to the reef. There were about fifty such *facl* in Kosrae. The paramount also had his own *facl*. Below the high chiefs were forty or fifty low chiefs who were land managers or overseers of the *facl* and who resided on the land for which they were responsible. Agricultural production was primarily the responsibility of the commoners, who occupied the lowest social strata. Low chiefs saw to it that needed food, labor, and tribute were provided to the paramount and high chiefs in Lelu.

Cordy (1985a, 256–257) describes Lelu as

consist[ing] of about 100 walled compounds (dwellings, two royal burial compounds, and 17 sacred compounds) connected by sea piers, an internal canal system, and a paved network of streets. The dwelling compounds of the four social strata differed greatly. The ruler's and high chiefs' dwelling compounds were clustered in central Leluh and had massive basalt walls as high as 6 m. Within were multiple houses, with a large feast-house near the main entrance. Here the ruler entertained his visitors and retinue. Earthen ovens were located near this feast-house, and numerous food-pounding and *seka (Piper methysticum)*-pounding stones were present within the house.

Figure 13.3 shows houses and people in the dwelling compound of a high chief as depicted in a sketch by Alexander Postels of the *Senyavin* (Lütke 1835, pl 18).

As for traditional Kosraean subsistence, René Lesson (in Ritter and Ritter 1981, 46), medical officer of the *Coquille,* observed that "the tree which furnishes the principal base of the existence of these islanders is the breadfruit tree *[Artocarpus altilis]*. It is so common that the fruit of this tree litter the ground."

A widespread zone of agroforest, of which breadfruit was the chief constituent, is suggested both by the early descriptions of Kosrae and the present distribution of these trees. Other cultigens identified in the early historic literature included the giant swamp taro (*Cyrtosperma chamissonis*), taro (*Colocasia esculenta*), bananas, yams (*Dioscorea* spp.), coconuts, and sugarcane (see Ritter and Ritter 1981; Hunter-Anderson 1991). Lesson also specifically mentions *Arum macrorrhizon* (*Alocasia macrorrhiza*), though it appears that he may not have recognized the distinction between it and *Cyrtosperma chamissonis*, presenting a description that appears to be an amalgam of the two (see Ritter and Ritter 1981, 46; Athens 1995, 11–12). Friedrich Kittlitz, a naturalist on the *Senyavin* expedition, however, does refer to "both of these giant aroids" (Ritter and Ritter 1981, 177), leaving little doubt about the presence of two large aroids on Kosrae at the time of contact.

Dogs and pigs were absent from Kosrae at contact, and birds were scarce except for pigeons and chickens. Fyedor Lütke, Captain of the *Senyavin*, noted that "fish and crayfish are the only animal food that they [Kosraeans] eat" (Ritter and Ritter 1981, 123).

Historic Population Estimates

A detailed examination of historical records indicates that Kosrae's population at the time of known European contact in 1824 must have been "between about 2,500 and 3,500 with 3,000 being a reasonable estimate" (Ritter 1981, 13). The important point for purposes of this presentation is that, unlike for many islands, these estimates can be regarded with more confidence than is usually the case with the earliest population estimates of newly discovered islands. This is because the first ships to visit Kosrae — the *Coquille*, captained by Louis Duperrey in 1824, and the *Senyavin*, captained by Fyedor Lütke in 1827/1828 — were specifically charged with exploration and making scientific observations. While there are gaps in the information — and historical population estimates, in general, are notoriously unreliable (McArthur 1970, 1,101) — the Kosrae case offers population figures based on observations at contact by men who sought to accurately record and document what they saw on a relatively small island. Lütke, in fact, provides a listing of all adults in each *facl* (though as Ritter [1981, 13] argues, his estimate is too low for several reasons). Considering the various estimates and factors that distorted the historic estimates, Ritter is able to ascertain that the size of Kosrae's population at contact must have been somewhere in the neighborhood of 3,000 people or perhaps 3,500 at most. Based on the historical observations, there is not much leeway in adjusting these figures up or down.

For heuristic purposes and to be absolutely certain population size is not underestimated, a population size double Ritter's high-end estimate — or 7,000 people — can be considered. However, it is very clear that there were *not* 10,000, 15,000, or even 20,000 people on the island at contact. Such high figures are well beyond reason, given the quality of the earliest observations. Thus, we have an important constraint for a population model for Kosrae.

Carrying Capacity

An island's carrying capacity represents the upper limit of sustainable population size based on the availability of resources. For societies dependent on agriculture, of course, carrying capacity will be primarily based on agricultural productivity. Any calculation of carrying capacity, however, must be defined in terms of long-term resource availability in which populations can be sustained without degradation of the environment, and it should also factor in the lower limits of natural fluctuations in the availability of needed resources (as from storms or droughts), as well as seasonal variations in productivity (see discussion in Hassan 1981, 164–175 with references; also Dewar 1984).

Calculation of the carrying capacity of an island is useful because it provides a figure for the upper limit of population growth, which is obviously an important constraint for modeling prehistoric population growth and for evaluating historic estimates of population size at contact. A difficulty in calculating carrying capacity for human populations concerns the process of intensification, whereby productivity per unit land area can be increased through technological (e.g., domestication and improvement of cultivars, irrigation, storage) and cultural innovations (e.g., exchange, redistribution). Thus, any calculation of carrying capacity must take into consideration the possibility for intensification.

Unfortunately, there is no specific information on agricultural carrying capacity for Kosrae based on what is known about traditional subsistence (i.e., primary dependence on breadfruit, with bananas, coconut, and taro). Nevertheless, it is still possible to develop some useful "ballpark" figures based on land area available for agroforest and taro cultivation and productivity information concerning the main cultivars.

As indicated by Whitesell et al. (1986), 23 percent of Kosrae's land area is presently in agroforest and 11 percent is in secondary vegetation. Roughly, these figures — totaling 34 percent — provide an indication of how much land on Kosrae is potentially available for agriculture. This amounts to 37 km², or 3,700 ha. Based on Lesson's previously quoted observation, breadfruit would have been the main food crop, and presumably the other main components of agroforest production — coconut and bananas — would have contributed some smaller percentage to the total dietary intake. These cultigens do well in the foothills, alluvial fans, and bottomlands and generally require little management or labor input for their maintenance. In addition to agroforest production, the landward fringes of mangrove swamps and the freshwater swamps (see Figure 13.2) could also have been devoted to taro cultivation *(Cyrtosperma* and *Colocasia).* The percentage of wetlands devoted to taro is difficult to estimate, but it would have been relatively small and much less than the total. Although speculative, an estimate of the land devoted to taro might be somewhere around 5 percent of the total available for agriculture, amounting to 185 ha.

If the high-end historic contact population estimate is used — that is, 3,500 people — about 1.1 ha of agricultural land would have been available per person on Kosrae. If we assume that the contact population was double this size — almost certainly a substantial overestimate — there would have been 0.55 ha of agricultural land per person.

As for the amount of land needed to sustain a person, a rough estimate can be derived from breadfruit productivity figures. For the island of Pohnpei, which is geographically very similar to Kosrae, 1 ha of breadfruit trees produces on average 6,866 kg of fruit per year, with low-season monthly values of 8.2 and 16.8 kg (January and February) and high-season monthly values reaching 1,748.5 and 2,789.6 kg (June and July; see Raynor 1989, 95–96). Regarding seasonal variation in production, this can be somewhat mitigated if the cultivator is careful in selecting different varieties with offsetting fruiting seasons (during the few months of each year when breadfruit supplies are most limited, fermented breadfruit can also be stored, and taro, yams, and bananas can be substituted). As breadfruit supplies 103 kcal of energy per 100 grams of fruit (USDA National Nutrient Database for Standard Reference), productivity calculates as 7,071,980 kcal per ha. As adult humans require about 2,000 kcal per day or about 730,000 kcal per year, the produce from a single hectare of breadfruit trees obviously far exceeds (by a factor of almost ten) the caloric requirements needed to sustain a single individual. Although this productivity calculation does not take into consideration seasonal variation of breadfruit production or yearly fluctuations in productivity due to climate or other factors or other nutritional needs (beyond gross caloric intake), it does demonstrate that the caloric needs of an individual on Kosrae can be met by just slightly more than 0.1 ha of agroforest land. Obviously, people were eating other foods and presumably obtaining a certain percentage of their diet from marine resources. These other foods, however, would have only a minor impact on the carrying capacity calculations and need not be considered for purposes of this discussion (marine foods, for example, should slightly reduce the agroforest land area needed to supply a person's dietary requirements).

If, for the sake of argument, it is assumed that Kosrae's contact population was 3,500, there would have been about 1.1 ha of agricultural land available per person. Given that only about one-tenth of a hectare of agroforest land is needed per person, we are left with the obvious conclusion that the population of Kosrae at contact was likely very considerably below its carrying capacity (in other words, carrying capacity was about ten times higher than the actual historical population estimate). This supports historical observations. As Ritter (1981, 24) notes, "the early explorers felt that Kosrae could have supported many times the current population." Even if the population size were double — surely an overestimate — carrying capacity would have been almost five times what was actually needed.

The early exploration accounts also suggest that Kosraean fertility appeared to be relatively high and illnesses were few (Ritter 1981, 24). Obviously, however, it would be difficult for the early visitors to evaluate mortality from such causes as childbirth, infant infections, and so on. Thus, relatively high fertility *and* high mortality could account for Kosrae's low contact population relative to its carrying capacity. While there is some indication from historical records that the perceived low population size at contact might have been the result of a late precontact typhoon (24–25), it seems doubtful that such a storm would have been responsible for killing thousands of people on a high island (as might result from an ensuing famine).

The Archaeological Record

Initial Settlement

There are only a few points concerning archaeology that are germane to a consideration of prehistoric population growth on Kosrae (for details and a bibliography, see Cordy 1993; Athens 1995). One of the most important is the date of initial settlement. Fortunately, the information is rather strong that settlement occurred close to AD 1 (or about 2,000 years ago). We know this from both well-documented archaeological evidence and the independent paleoenvironmental record (see Athens 1990, 1995; Athens et al. 1996). This initial date of island settlement provides a critical foundation for modeling Kosrae's population growth.

Prehistoric Agriculture

Another important aspect of the archaeological record concerns evidence for a rather static agricultural production system for almost the entire period of human occupation. By about AD 500, an agroforest production system had been established on the lower slopes, foothills, alluvial mouths, and bottomlands throughout the island based on the cultivation of breadfruit, coconut, and most likely banana (banana has not been confirmed archaeologically, though it was present at contact; Athens et al. 1996). Agroforest production was supplemented by the cultivation of the aroids *Cyrtosperma* and *Colocasia* in the landward margins of mangrove swamps and other locations with freshwater hydromorphic soils (*Alo-*

casia was also present). There is no evidence for intensification to any significant extent at any point in time, and there is nothing to suggest that new cultigens were introduced during the prehistoric period. Rather, the production system seems to have remained virtually unchanged from the time that the agroforest was established at around AD 500.

Immigration/Outside Contact

As for the possibility of immigration to Kosrae during prehistoric times, there is no archaeological evidence to suggest a later wave of settlement after initial colonization. Likewise, there is no evidence in the archaeological record of trade or exchange with other islands. In this regard, it is notable that at contact Kosraeans did not have oceangoing canoes. Kosraean society clearly evolved isolated and virtually untouched by outside influences for almost 2,000 years, until the advent of the Western ships of exploration.

Radiocarbon Density Plot and Population Growth Rate Changes

Because a rather large amount of archaeology has been undertaken on Kosrae since the late 1970s, there is an exceptional body of data for the island. One of the results is a large number of radiocarbon dates from sites around the island. These dates — 109 of them — allow construction of a radiocarbon density time series plot (Figure 13.4).[2] This may be regarded as a proxy for population growth. The underlying assumption is that the amount of charcoal in the environment is related to the number of people living in the environment at any given point in time (see Dye and Komori [1992a, 1992b] for a full explanation). Obviously, there are uncertainties regarding the use of a radiocarbon density plot as a proxy for population growth. However, a density plot is only a model, and it can serve a valuable heuristic purpose. Granting this, there are three main points to note in the Figure 13.4 curve. These are (1) the date when there first begins to be a significant rise in the curve, which occurs around AD 500 or 600; (2) the date for the sudden spurt in radiocarbon densities and hence population, which occurs about AD 1200; and (3) the date when the curve begins to level off following a major growth phase, which is about AD 1425.

The late prehistoric leveling of the radiocarbon density curve is most interesting in the context of the present discussion because it suggests a significant decrease in the *rate* of population growth at this time. This in turn suggests that density-dependent population controls may very well be in evidence (see Dye and Komori 1992b, 124–125 for the case of Hawai'i). Such a density-dependent response is expected when populations begin to confront limitations in needed resources. The result is a logistic growth curve, as originally presented by Verhulst and developed further by Lotka and Volterra and later by others (see Harris

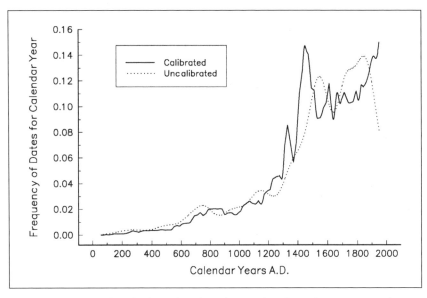

Figure 13.4. Density plot of radiocarbon dates from archaeological sites on Kosrae's main island (see Athens 1995, 21–27 for data and discussion).

2001, 20–23; Wilson and Bossert 1971, 92–143; Kingsland 1985). While there is much experimental research to suggest the validity of density-dependent control mechanisms for many organisms, acceptance of this mechanism as a regulator of human populations remains controversial and unproven. To be sure, a dampening of population growth starting around AD 1425 in Kosrae does not necessarily demonstrate the operation of density-dependent control mechanisms. Nevertheless, it is very interesting that the radiocarbon density plot suggests a significant decrease in the *rate* of population growth in late prehistoric times, for whatever reason.

Emergence of Social Stratification

The emergence of social stratification represents a significant change in prehistoric Kosraean society, and therefore it may bear on the question of changes in population growth rates. Theoretical constructs suggest that the formation of hierarchical societies is itself a density-dependent response (see Athens 1977, 1978, 1992). Megalithic construction at Lelu, including the attendant residential, ritual, and mortuary compounds for the paramount and high chiefs, was underway by about AD 1400 to 1450. This has been regarded as the time that Kosrae became unified under a single chief (Cordy 1985, 1993; Athens 1995, 358). The highly stratified Kosraean society at contact was well described by the earliest Western visitors (see Ritter and Ritter 1981). What is interesting is that the timing of political unification and evidence for significant social stratification occurs at the same time that the radiocarbon date density plot indicates a substantial decrease in the rate of population growth. While the significance of this correlation must be evaluated with further evidence, it does support the notion that density-dependent pressures may have begun to be operative at this time.

Human Burials

Skeletal remains are not preserved in Kosrae due to its moist tropical climate. Thus it is not possible to obtain direct information about prehistoric fertility and mortality (e.g., Johansson and Horowitz 1986; Jackes 1994; Brewis et al. 1990; Buikstra et al. 1986; and others).

Comparison of Selected Growth Rates

This section reviews the applicability of different population growth rate scenarios for Kosrae in light of what is known archaeologically and historically about the island. Some of the growth rates are historically documented for different parts of the world or have been used for Pacific Island populations and are therefore known to have validity in terms of their applicability to human populations. A few, however, are contrived just for purposes of this analysis. The data are presented in Tables 13.1 through 13.3. Population growth rates were calculated using the standard formula (e.g., Sarfati nd).

The models in Tables 13.1 and 13.2 are based on the assumption of twenty people colonizing Kosrae at AD 1. It is obviously impossible to determine the number of people that actually made landfall on Kosrae 2,000 years ago, but twenty seems reasonable for a single-hulled oceangoing canoe, considering both the probable large amount of time the boat would have been at sea and the possible uncertainties at the outset of the voyage about where and when landfall would be made (see Law 1977). It is possible, of course, that prior exploration had determined the location of Kosrae and that multiple initial colonizing voyages occurred, resulting in a starting population of perhaps 50, 100, or even more people. To take this possibility into account, the models in Tables 13.3a through e are built around the assumption that there were three boatloads of immigrants, with arrival of single boats at AD 1, AD 50, and AD 100.[3]

A constraint inherent to remote island colonization by small numbers of immigrants concerns the demographic viability of small populations. Primarily due to an imbalance of the sex ratio, small populations are inherently unstable. According to Bocquet-Appel (1985), small populations can avoid eventual extinction only by means of a high migratory flow. This was mathematically determined to be 11 percent for a group of 20 individuals, 7 percent for 50 individuals, and 3 percent

Table 13.1. Comparison of single population growth rates for selected time intervals, single colonizing voyage.

Rate %	200 years	500 years	1,000 years	1400 years	1824 years
0.042	22	25	30	36	43
0.25	33	70	243	659	1,901
0.30	36	89	400	1,325	4,730
0.35	40	114	658	2,654	11,797
0.45	49	189	1,782	10,738	72,065
0.90	120	1,764	155,666	5,606,124	250,332,486
1.50	393	34,201	58,488,737	22,567,795,854	1.24478E + 13
1.78	682	135,598	919,340,797	1.04904E + 12	1.89379E + 15
3.00	7,387	52,437,545	1.37485E + 14	1.87562E + 19	5.20149E + 24

Table 13.2. Comparison of multiple population growth rates for selected time intervals, single colonizing voyage.

Rate %	300 years	Rate %	500 years	Rate %	1,000 years	Rate %	1400 years	1824 years
0.52	95	same	267	0.35	1,532	0.042	1,806	2,159
0.52	95	same	267	0.35	1,537	0.25	4,183	12,058
0.75	188	same	839	0.35	4,830	0.15	8,810	16,634
0.90	294	same	1,764	0.52	23,713	0.30	64,378	186,038
1.5	1,741	0.35	3,514	0.25	12,277	0.15	22,394	42,279
1.5	1,741	0.90	10,542	0.35	60,692	0.20	135,235	315,502

for populations of 350 to 400 individuals. These figures are based on statistical probabilities, and they would be presumably applicable to Pacific Island populations. They suggest that in the early stages of settlement, there almost had to have been an influx of new people to Kosrae in the form of a second or possibly even a third canoe landing. Thus, successful colonization as a result of a single canoe landing may have been improbable.[4] At a minimum, therefore, there is a need to build at least several additional canoe landings into the modeling analysis.

Another problem with small colonizing populations concerns possible marriage rules, including monogamy, incest prohibitions, clan exogamy, and so on, that serve to restrict the pool of potential mates (see Black 1978, 1980). The result may be that an already vulnerable small population is made even more vulnerable by its failure to optimize reproduction because of culturally imposed marriage rules.

Table 13.3. Comparison of multiple population growth rates for selected time intervals, three colonizing voyages (20 people at AD 1, 20 people at AD 50, and 20 people at AD 100).

a

Rate %	50 years	100 years	300 years	Rate %	500 years	Rate %	1,000 years	1400 years	1824 years
0.042	40	61	67	same	73	same	89	106	126
0.90	51	101	605	0.90	3,629	0.90	320,136	—	—
0.90	51	101	605	0.52	1,700	0.15	3,583	6,526	12,321
0.90	51	101	601	0.30	1,093	0.042	2,309	2,732	3,263
0.90	51	101	601	0.30	1,093	0.15	2,312	4,210	7,949
1.50	62	152	2,979	0.15	3,967	0.15	8,394	15,288	28,865

b

Rate %	50 years	100 years	200 years	Rate %	500 years	1,000 years	1400 years	1824 years
1.50	62	152	672	0.15	1,040	2,200	4,007	7,566

c

Rate %	50 years	100 years	200 years	Rate %	500 years	1,000 years	1400 years	Rate %	1824 years
1.50	62	152	672	0.15	1,040	2,200	4,007	0.042	4,787

d

Rate %	50 years	100 years	200 years	500 years	Rate %	1,000 years	1400 years	1824 years
1.50	62	152	672	58,524	0.35	331,953	—	—

e

Rate %	50 years	100 years	200 years	500 years	1,000 years	Rate %	1400 years	1824 years
0.35	44	72	103	292	1,675	0.15	3,048	3,645

The time between the postulated multiple canoe landings on Kosrae, of course, is anyone's guess. They might have been separated by just days — or possibly hundreds of years. For purposes of the present investigation, a second canoe will be assumed to have landed at AD 50 and a third at AD 100. After that, colonization presumably ceased. As noted in the discussion of Kosrae's archaeological record, there is nothing to suggest interisland contacts during the long trajectory of Kosrae's prehistory. Even in the case of Pohnpei, where oral accounts are so much better preserved and richer in detail (e.g., Bernart 1977; Fischer et al. 1977), there is only a very limited indication of possible long-distance interisland contacts during prehistoric times. Contacts, of course, are but one side of the coin, as such contacts, if they ever occurred, may not have involved immigration.

In preparing the tables, the following may be noted about the annual rates of population increase that were used:

1. The 3 percent growth rate is documented for the United States between the 1670s to the 1850s (Harris 2001, 14).[5] A rate of 3 or 4 percent is also documented for Pitcairn Island (Brewis et al. 1990, 354). Although this range is probably not the highest intrinsic rate of increase possible for humans, it represents a reasonably well-documented high-end value for preindustrial populations. If there are no controls on fertility, the environment is relatively benign in terms of health risks (i.e., relatively low mortality), and the food supply from agriculture is plentiful and without serious production risks, a rate of growth of 3 percent or more should, in theory, be attainable by a Pacific Island colonizing population.

2. The 1.5 percent growth rate is a conservative rendering of the 1.78 percent growth rate implied by the "Pacific model," derived from Pacific Island mortality and fertility schedules (McArthur et al. 1976; also see Stannard 1989, 35).

3. The 0.9 and 0.5 percent growth rates are derived from the McArthur et al. (1976) simulation study (the simulations were run with two, five, and seven couples and with different mixes of age brackets and a "Pacific model" of mortality and fertility). As they report, more than 90 percent of the "successful" simulations (ones in which the population grew and became viable) had growth rates between 0.9 and 0.5 percent (see Stannard 1989, 35). This compares to a rate of 0.875 percent derived by Brewis et al. (1990, 352) in their model of prehistoric Maori population growth. At the low end of the McArthur et al. range, Hassan (1981, 140) advocates a rate of 0.52 percent, which he estimates "as the probable maximum growth rate for prehistoric groups, and a prolonged child-spacing period of 40 months."

As he notes, the population doubling time at this rate is 133 years, or about seven generations.

4. The lowest growth rate of 0.042 percent is from J. Cohen (1995, 78) and is the estimated world population growth rate between AD 1 and 1650.[6] This estimate is for a period characterized by preindustrial revolution agriculture. Interestingly, it falls within the estimated population growth rate ranges estimated from the time that people first became dependent on agriculture about 10,000 years ago (0.021 percent and 0.051 percent), suggesting a very stable and low rate of population growth for agricultural populations until the beginning of the industrial revolution (note that with the beginning of agriculture about 10,000 years ago, the population growth rate increased "by a factor of at least ten to several hundred" from what it had been [J. Cohen 1995, 78]). Thus, while Hassan (1981, 140) sees a *maximum* growth rate for prehistoric groups as 0.52 percent, the average is clearly far less.

Low growth rates of 0.15 percent, 0.25 percent, 0.30 percent, and 0.35 percent are also used for heuristic reasons, though they are not based on specific empirical data. Application of the model growth rates to Kosrae (Tables 13.1–13.3) yields a number of insights, and these are summarized below.

Results: Table 13.1

One of the most obvious conclusions to be drawn from Table 13.1 is that unchanging modest to high population growth rates throughout the 1,824 years of the prehistoric period do not seem to work and therefore could not have characterized the Kosrae situation. These results clearly call into question the McArthur et al. (1976) simulation results. Only the 0.25 percent and 0.30 percent rates produce end results that are reasonably close to the historic contact population estimates. While the 0.35 percent rate is not unreasonably high, the results of the other rates from 0.45 percent to 3.00 percent are completely untenable. There is also a concern with the lower rates of 0.25 percent and 0.30 percent, which is that the population sizes are so low during the first 500 years that the chances of the population remaining viable during such a long interval has to be very low. A higher colonizing rate, therefore, seems essential if the population is to have a chance at remaining viable. As for the lowest rate — 0.042 percent, the average global growth rate for preindustrial agricultural populations — Table 13.1 demonstrates that it is wholly unrealistic for a colonizing agricultural population.

There is also another problem with the low rates. The archaeological data indicate that by about AD 500 the entire island was mostly occupied and the lowland forest had been entirely (or perhaps mostly) transformed into an agroforest. It is impossible to see how this could happen with populations of just seventy and eighty-nine people at AD 500, as indicated by Table 13.1 for the 0.25 percent and 0.30 percent rates. It is probably safe to conclude that a model utilizing a single very low population growth rate and having a colonizing population of twenty people does not work for Kosrae.

Results: Table 13.2

In Table 13.2, an attempt was made to build a more complex population growth model using higher initial growth rates followed by a two- or three-step slowing of the growth rate (essentially a density-dependent logistic growth model). As with Table 13.1, a single twenty-person colonization event is assumed. Only one model, with a starting growth rate of 0.52 percent, produced a result that can be regarded as somewhat close to reasonable after 1,824 years. This is the one that ended with a population of 2,159 people. All of the other growth models reached their terminus having populations that were far too high to be considered reasonable in view of the historic population size constraint. With respect to the one potentially viable model, its only negative aspect has to do with the relatively small number of people generated by AD 500, which is 267. This is probably too low considering the agroforest data and the implication that the lowland landscape of the *entire* island should be occupied and in production.

The single potentially viable model indicates that by AD 1400 there would be 1,806 people on the island. In regard to pressures that would foster the development of hierarchical social and political organization at this time, the figure seems a little low considering the size of the island and its probable carrying capacity.

Overall, what is notable about the results of the Table 13.2 models is that the 0.52 percent rate for initial colonization seems reasonable. The higher rates are untenable and cannot be considered realistic. This fits with Hassan's (1981, 140) estimate for the probable maximum growth rate for prehistoric populations, though it clearly far exceeds the average calculated growth rate for preindustrial revolution agricultural populations of 0.042 percent as indicated by J. Cohen (1995, 78).

Results: Table 13.3

The models of Tables 13.3a through 13.3e assume three colonizing voyages of twenty people each over a 100-year period using different colonizing growth rates and various other growth rate combinations during later time periods. In most of the models, a relatively high growth rate was used for the initial period of colonization, followed by an assumption of a dampening of the high growth rate later on as a result of the onset of density-dependent conditions.

The results indicate five potentially viable models. Two of these are in Table 13.3a, and both start with an initial growth rate of 0.90 percent and end with populations of 3,263 and 7,949. These models both overcome the deficiency of the "viable" model in Table 13.2 in that they both generate a relatively high population size by AD 500 (1,093), which nicely conforms to the agroforest data mentioned above. They also achieve a significant population size compatible with the formation of a chiefdom by AD 1400.

The other three viable models are in Tables 13.3b, c, and e. The model in Table 13.3b assumes a relatively high colonizing population growth rate (1.50 percent), though it drops down to just 0.15 percent after 200 years, and remains at this rate through AD 1824. The model generates populations of 1,040 at AD 500 and 7,566 at AD 1824. The AD 500 population is reasonable in view of the agroforest data. However, the 7,566 figure for AD 1824 is a little high, as it is so much above the historical estimate. One way to fix this would be to add further density-dependent dampening to the growth model, assigning a value of 0.042 percent at AD 1400 when the paramount chiefdom formed. This result is presented in Table 13.3c, which shows a population end-point size of 4,787. While this estimate is still high compared to the historical figure, it is very reasonable and suggests that the Table 13.3c growth model could be viable.

The model in Table 13.3d is obviously not reasonable, demonstrating that if the colonizing rate starts as high as 1.50 percent, it can stay this high only for several hundred years at most (Tables 13.3b and 13.3c); otherwise the total population spirals to unreasonable levels as early as AD 500. The model in Table 13.3e, while ending with a very acceptable population size (3,645), suffers from the previously noted flaw of not generating enough people by AD 500 to be compatible with the agroforest data.

Conclusions

The study of prehistoric island populations is inherently extremely difficult. However, few would doubt its fundamental significance for understanding social and political processes of island societies. Although it will probably always be impossible to nail down specific numbers of people at any given point in time during the prehistoric past, the Kosrae case provides an example of how the problem can be approached using a combination of different types of data that provide constraints for population models. To do this, of course, high-quality archaeological data are extremely important. In the example of Kosrae we can be confident of the date of initial settlement, the date for the transformation of the lowland forest to an agroforest, the probable date for the development of hierarchical social organization, and the date for changes in the radiocarbon date density curve. In addition — and of immense importance — we have relatively good historical data on population size at the time of earliest Western contact. Also, the carrying capacity data seem to be based on reliable information concerning agricultural productivity. So what have we learned about Kosrae's prehistoric population that was not already known?

The most important implication of the Kosrae data is that population growth rates always must have been relatively modest, at least compared to twentieth-century growth rates and some other high-end estimates in the historical literature. This finding runs against conventional wisdom for prehistoric Pacific population studies. The highest reasonable rate for a colonizing population landing on Kosrae is 0.90 percent, though a rate as high as 1.50 percent could have been operative if it was limited to no more than several hundred years. Rates significantly lower than 0.90 percent have the problem of not being able to generate a high enough population by AD 500 to be compatible with the agroforest data. Also, populations with growth rates lower than about 0.52 percent, especially for the single voyaging canoe models, would have had a high risk of extinction (as a result of sex ratio imbalances and other factors), so such low estimates are doubly unrealistic.

Nevertheless, it is clear that Kosrae, an island particularly well endowed by nature, had a prehistoric population that never grew at rates anywhere approaching what could have been the case given the productivity of its agroforest, the quality of the natural environment, and the likely absence of significant mortality due to disease. While it is difficult to imagine that the people of an extremely small colonizing population would employ measures to significantly limit their numbers from what they could have been (see Tanner [1975] for discussion of population limitation measures in Polynesia), the viable growth models presented here certainly show that such measures had to have been adopted within 500 years of colonization. Also, the models show that these limitation measures must have been more vigorously employed thereafter as population size increased with the passage of time. It is impossible to see how it could have been otherwise. Such a model, which assumes a dampening of the growth rate with the passage of time, implicates the operation of density-dependent processes during the later part of Kosrae's prehistoric sequence. Empirical support for such an interpretation is suggested by the radiocarbon date density curve (see Figure 13.4).

The final conclusion of this study concerns population size on Kosrae at the time the paramount chieftaincy formed in the fifteenth century AD. An estimate in the range of 2,500 to 3,000 people seems likely for the AD 1400 time frame given the high-end Contact-period population estimate and allowing for the possibility of a somewhat higher population level.

Notes

1. This approach is not new by any means (e.g., Brewis et al. 1990 for the New Zealand Maori; Stannard 1989 for Hawai'i), though I believe the particular mix of data available for Kosrae makes it possible to carry the approach further.

2. The many radiocarbon dates obtained from the Lelu archaeological site are not included in this analysis because, being mostly late and from a single offshore site, it was believed they would bias the results. Radiocarbon dates obtained just from the main island should provide a better indication of settlement and land use intensity—and hence population.

3. Black (1978) provides an interesting discussion of founding population sizes on islands and the likely consequences this has for growth and survival. Black's simulation experiments used starting population sizes of forty and eight people.

4. If small populations are inherently unstable, and if remote island colonization is as difficult and dangerous as many believe, then we might expect to see archaeological evidence for colonization failures. This would be seen archaeologically in the form of a gap in the early occupation history of an island. As far as this author knows, archaeological evidence of this nature is generally lacking for the Pacific Islands. However, perhaps early occupation histories for many islands should be reexamined with this possibility in mind.

5. Immigration from England was a factor in this high rate, though birthrates were very high and mortality rates were likely declining (Ehrlich et al. 1977, 192).

6. Using different data, J. Cohen (1995, 79) cites estimates of a growth rate of 0.092 percent from AD 1 to 1750 and another of 0.039 percent for the same period. By way of comparison, Ehrlich et al. (1977, 190) cite a growth rate of 0.3 percent between AD 1650 and 1750, which presumably represents the first spurt of the growth rate with the beginning of the industrial revolution.

14

Population in a Vegetable Kingdom

Aneityum Island (Vanuatu) at European Contact in 1830

In giving the population of this or any other of these islands I must preface my remarks by saying that I put little or no confidence in the numbers stated. I consider that in an island of any size it is absurd to think you can even go near the population without a census or from constant and careful intercourse with the tribes, all over the island, obtain the number of each, and thus of the whole[.]

As to a census in any of these western groups having ever been taken, I won't believe it, and the other alternative I consider nearly equally impossible, owing to the fact that there are scarcely two islands where it would be safe to trust yourself amongst the natives in the way that is necessary to establish the number of the population. But there is a third plan, and I believe it to be the one most generally followed, that is for missionaries, or sandalwood traders to "chance" some round number of hundreds or even *thousands*! and put that down as the population whenever asked, perhaps believing themselves that they are strictly close to the mark. If asked are the natives numerous at such a place? The answer is probably, Oh Yes, they flocked down in hundreds to the sea — the beach was literally *covered* with them etc., etc. and so a number is fixed upon, and ever after adopted. The missionaries I believe take more pains about it, but I fear they are little nearer the truth, excepting in those islands where they have been long resident, and which if not altogether converted are so far civilized as to enable them to visit all parts, this is the case more to the Eastward[.]

The population here is said to be 2000. — P. D. Vigors, *A Private Journal . . .*

 Aneityum or Anatom (20°10' south latitude, 169°50' east longitude) is the southernmost inhabited island of Vanuatu (Figure 14.1) and is situated within TAFEA Province (an acronym referring to the five main islands of southern Vanuatu: Tanna, Aniwa, Futuna, Erromango, and Aneityum). It is a high island formed from two coalesced Pleistocene volcanoes. It is 160 km² in area, with the highest peak reaching 852 m. The geology is mainly basaltic volcanics with one small area of Pleistocene raised reef and extensive areas of recent alluvium that in part overlie reefal materials laid down just above present sea level in the mid-Holocene. The soils reflect this relatively simple geology, but climatic zona-

tion and human influence have complicated the picture. Some 88 percent of the soils are strongly leached ferrallitic soils (ferralsols and cambisols) of poor to moderate fertility. The other main soil type is that of the alluvial soils, which form about 9 percent of the area, and these are the most fertile soils on the island (Quantin 1979).

A description from a visiting missionary in 1860 gives a good idea of the appearance of the island during the early European contact period:

> As you coast along in a boat you observe three belts or zones, in many places pretty well defined, which we may name the alluvial or arable, the sterile, and the woody. The first lies along the shore, is flat, and consists of a dark rich soil. As it furnishes a great proportion of the food, most of the natives are found on it. Here flourish luxuriantly the Cocoa-nut and bread-fruit trees, with taro, bananas, sugarcane etc. The second or sterile is of larger extent, and can best be seen. In some places there is no vegetation, nothing but red earth. On the most of it, you find grass, ferns, and a few stunted trees. . . . The woody belt occupies the summit and centre of the island. (RPM: J. Copeland, October 1860, 346)[1]

Today the main difference is that the "sterile zone" is now largely a zone of plantation pine trees, put in by the government in the 1970s and 1980s to control erosion and provide a future source of income for the people of the island. When I first visited Aneityum in 1978, however, its appearance was exactly as Copeland had described it over a century before.

The island was sighted from some distance by Captain Cook in August 1774 (Beaglehole 1961, 508–509, 524), and Aneityumese people were among those his expedition met at Port Resolution on Tanna during his sojourn there. In July 1809, Golovnin, commanding the Russian sloop-of-war *Diana*, came in close to shore near Anelcauhat on the south coast of Aneityum and observed several outrigger canoes and "a considerable number" of people on the beach who were waving long spears. He didn't land but proceeded to Port Resolution on Tanna, where again there were Aneityumese people present (Barratt 1990, 39–41).

The first Europeans known to have landed on the island were Ward and Lawler of the brig *Alpha* in March 1830. They landed at and named Port Patrick on the north coast of the island, and their crew cut sandalwood (Bennett 1831). There were reports recorded by the first missionaries of sightings of other ships, or perhaps this same ship at other locations on the island at about this time (McArthur 1974, 2; Shineberg 1967, 22–23). In 1841 the London Missionary Society landed Samoan catechists, but before that date various sandalwood or whaling vessels presumably visited the island, as there is a short account of it in the *Colonial Magazine* for 1841 (Anon. 1841, 335–336) that describes canoes, houses, and the appearance of the inhabitants. In June–July 1842, when the mission vessel returned,

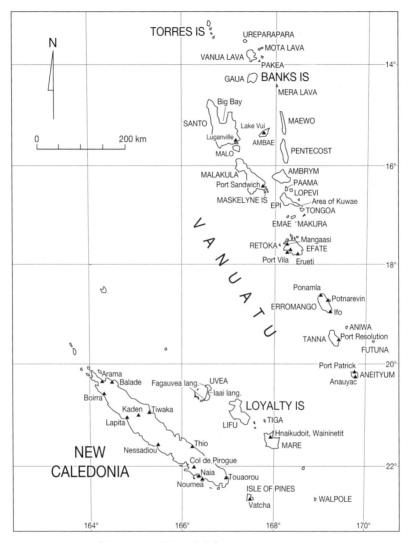

Figure 14.1. Map of Vanuatu and New Caledonia.

three sandalwood vessels were seen trading at the island, and in 1844 Captain Paddon opened a sandalwood station and trading depot on Inyeuc islet, just off Anelcauhat and now the site of the island's airstrip. From this date Aneityum became a frequent port of call for sandalwood and other vessels. In February 1848, after a devastating hurricane, Paddon moved his depot to Anelcauhat on the mainland, and it remained there until 1853 when it was removed to the Isle of Pines in New Caledonia (Shineberg 1967, 58–61, 100–106).

European missionaries arrived in 1848 (there had been London Missionary

Society catechists on the island continuously since 1841), the first to land in May being Catholic Marists who had fled from New Caledonia. They departed in 1850, largely because of sickness. In July 1848 the Reverend John Geddie of the Presbyterian Church of Nova Scotia arrived, and he remained until 1872. He was joined in 1852 by the Reverend John Inglis of the Reformed Presbyterian Church of Scotland, who remained until 1876. It is mainly from records left by these two men in the form of books, a diary, and published letters that we can glean what we know of the early Contact-period history and geography of Aneityum (see Spriggs 1981, 21–22 for sources).

This chapter attempts to reconstruct the population of Aneityum at effective European contact in 1830. It is based largely on chapter 4 of my Ph.D. thesis (Spriggs 1981), but I give no apology for essentially repeating it here as the thesis has never been published outside of a microfilm series, and the methodology used does not yet appear to have been taken up by anyone else working in Pacific archaeology. I subsequently used a similar approach in examining post-Contact population and production levels in Anahulu Valley on O'ahu in the Hawaiian Islands (Spriggs and Kirch 1992). I have discussed some aspects of the Aneityum example in two further papers (Spriggs 1986, 1993).

Aneityum in 1830

A range of written and oral historical sources allows us to gain an impression of the settlement pattern and social organization on Aneityum on the eve of European contact (see Spriggs 1986, 11–15). It must be recognized, however, that none of the substantive accounts of social organization are contemporary accounts; in fact, they begin with the arrival of European missionaries some eighteen years later. All of them thus represent memory culture to varying extents.

At contact, the island appears to have been divided into seven dominions or chiefdoms, each further divided into some fifty-odd districts (Figure 14.2). These dominions are called *nelcau* (canoe) in Aneityumese and had at their head a *natimarid* (high chief) with a number of *natimi alupas* (district chiefs) subservient to him. Chiefly power was based on ritual rather than physically coercive powers — power of sorcery against enemies, power over the elements to control success in agriculture and fishing, and so on. Chiefs were distinguished from commoners by various practices, not least by their polygamy, three wives being the maximum recorded by the missionaries. *Natimarid* were most clearly differentiated from others at their death. The usual method of disposal of the dead was burial at sea, but *natimarid* were buried in the floor of their houses with their heads exposed. Food offerings were placed before the corpse until the head could be separated from the body, and then the skull was placed on a pole as an object of worship.

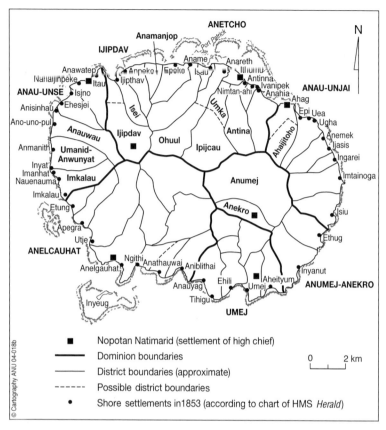

Figure 14.2. Dominion and district boundaries on Aneityum (Anatom) in the early Contact period. The boundary between Ijipdav and Anetcho is uncertain.

The basic settlement unit was the district under a *natimi alupas,* with households dispersed among the gardens. These districts usually consisted of a single catchment from the central chain of mountain ridges to the shore, forming wedge-shaped territories incorporating a range of environments from reef flat to cloud forest. These districts, fifty-one to fifty-five in number, are analogous to Hawaiian *ahupuaʻa* (Earle 1978; Hommon 1986).

The agricultural system consisted then — as it does in part today — of both dryland and irrigated gardens, with taro *(Colocasia esculenta)* as the main staple, grown in *inhenou, inmegaiwai,* and *inwete* (different types of taro swamps) and in *incauwai* (canal-fed, furrow-irrigated gardens). Several dryland swidden techniques were also practiced (see Spriggs 1981, chap 3).

The drudgery of women's lives is recorded in detail in oral and written sources (Spriggs 1993). Much of the garden work, the collecting of marine foods, and cooking were done by them. When missionaries Geddie and Inglis took the first census in 1854, they noted a marked imbalance in numbers between the sexes, which they attributed to preferential infanticide of female children and the strangling of women upon the death of their husband or sometimes other close relatives.

A rule of endogamy restricted marriage usually to within the dominion and perhaps ideally within the district or contiguous districts. Chiefly marriage links were wider, however. Sister exchange was the preferred form of marriage and there was no operation of bridewealth. The imbalance between the sexes meant, as noted by missionary Geddie in a letter of 1854, that "no less than 600 men are doomed to a life of hopeless celibacy" (MR: Geddie, August 1855, 124–126).[2]

Warfare was endemic, with continuously fluid and shifting alliances being the pattern of relations between dominions. Pressure on resources does not appear to have been the reason for warfare, territorial conquest was not its aim, and few men appear to have been killed in battles.

Population Estimates for Aneityum in 1830

The quotation from Vigors at the head of this chapter accurately represents the way in which population estimates were arrived at during early European contact with the Pacific Islands, and it sagely assesses the reliance that can be placed upon such figures. An independent check is needed to assess population estimates for the period, and one of these is discussed in this chapter.

A central theme of demographer Norma McArthur's thesis on Aneityum (1974) was a discussion of the population and population structure during the early period of missionization and the massive population decline brought about by epidemics of diseases introduced by visiting European ships from 1861 onward. This catastrophic population decline is charted here in Figure 14.3. Figures for population decline in other islands of Vanuatu after European contact are summarized in the 1967 census report (McArthur and Yaxley 1968) and discussed further by McArthur (1981).

During 1854, a census was conducted on Aneityum by Geddie and Inglis: "We have on our list about 3800 names, but Mr. Inglis and I are of the opinion that the population is about 4000" (MR: Geddie, August 1855, 125). By 1858, Inglis was of the opinion that the true population was "about 3500" (MR: Inglis, October 1859, 151), but whether the 300 to 500 people had disappeared because of more accurate counting or because of a real population decline in this period is not totally clear (cf. McArthur 1974, 60–69). Populations for some individual dominions and districts are also given by the missionaries. Anau-unjai Dominion contained 450 people attending seven schools in June 1856 (RPM: Inglis, April 1857, 103), while in December 1854 the population of Anau-unse was given as 300. Reported also at

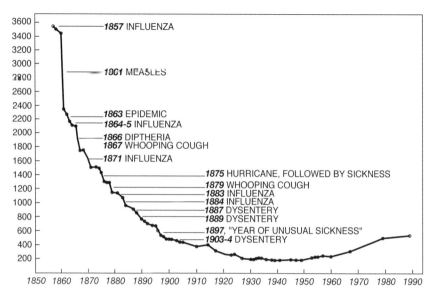

Figure 14.3. Population decline and recovery on Aneityum, 1850–1990 (from Spriggs 1997, 258).

that time were a "large inland settlement of Inwai-jipthav, containing 100 people, and three smaller settlements all heathen; besides two settlements on the shore, partly heathen containing more than another 100" (RPM: Inglis, April 1855, 173).

The two shore settlements are presumably those at the mouths of the Ijipdav and Isei Rivers. It is not clear whether Inglis knew of and included the inland population in the Isei Valley, perhaps one of the three smaller inland settlements referred to. The period referred to is prior to the change in the western boundary between Geddie and Inglis' parishes from the Anau-unse-Anelcauhat dominion boundary to a point within Anau-unse between Anauwau and Ehesjei Districts (see Spriggs 1981, appendix 7). Thus, the "several large settlements, mostly heathen" contiguous with and to the other side of Anau-unse, also mentioned in Inglis' account, must have been within Anelcauhat Dominion. There is no record of when the Umanid-Anwunyat District (with two settlement foci) was missionized, and this was evidently still heathen at the time. To the southeast was Imkalau District, still heathen in February 1854 (Miller 1975, 176) and having "recently abandoned heathenism" in January 1855 but which had at that time no teacher settled there (195). Iteg, the next district (Etung on Figure 14.2), was already missionized by December 1854, having had a teacher stationed there since February 1853 (153) and a school that was in a "hopeful state" when visited by Geddie in August 1854 (187).

Inglis' figure of "at least 700 heathens, being all in contiguous districts, and of these Anau-unse is in the centre" (RPM: May 1855, 173) would thus seem to refer to the population from Isei (Anpeke, the adjacent district, was already missionized by January 1853; see RPM: Inglis, November 1853, 355) to Imkalau District. Of these, over 500 people are from identified areas — say 520 if the "more than another hundred" reference to the Ijipdav and Isei shore settlements is taken as about 120. Thus Umanid-Anwunyat and Imkalau ("several large settlements") and the smaller settlements inland in the Ijipdav area would have had a population of about 180–200 between them. Inglis' June 1856 report (RPM: April 1857, 102–103) notes that 100 of his flock were transferred to Geddie's jurisdiction by the parish boundary change mentioned above. The 100 people referred to were the inhabitants of Anauwau. I suspect, however, that this figure comes from the fact that Inglis had lost one out of his three Anau-unse districts and so assumed it contained one-third of the Anau-unse population (hence 100 people). From the archaeological survey, however (Spriggs 1981, 51–55, appendix 10), it would seem that the Anauwau Valley was much more densely occupied than the other two districts, and so this population figure should be taken with a pinch of salt.

Inglis (1887, 75) gives the combined population of Epeke, Aname, and Isav Districts as 120, notes that Ipijcau had "about 70" inhabitants in November 1855 (RPM: December 1856, 408), and mentions in October 1854 that an "important inland district" in his parish had a population "upwards of eighty," some of whom had been recently converted to Christianity. Although the district is not mentioned by name, it is almost certain that it is Ohuul to which he is referring.[3]

Geddie's accounts are always short on statistics. Patterson (1882, 347), ostensibly quoting Geddie, gives the population of Anauyac as fifty in 1853, but as McArthur notes (1974, 63), no source for this figure has been found. Anumej had "nearly 300 souls" in 1854 (MR: Geddie, August 1855, 124) and is the only district population figure mentioned in Geddie's writings. It is for this reason that the discussion of Aneityum's 1830 population and the archaeological survey on which it was based concentrated on Inglis' parish rather than Geddie's.

Although population decline on the island because of introduced diseases from 1861 onward has been documented in detail (McArthur 1974, chap 3), McArthur noted but dismisses evidence for two previous epidemics on the island occurring sometime in the period between 1830 and 1848 (1974, 93–103; 1981, 18–20). Her dismissal was first on the grounds of inconsistencies in the written accounts and second that "there is also some reason to doubt that any exotic disease introduced before the mid-1850s could have had such a widespread incidence as measles had in 1861" (1974, 96); but this was, as she admitted, "largely because of the parallels with a legendary epidemic in the Hawaiian Islands in the early 19th century" (97). Apparently there is evidence to suggest that the Hawaiian epidemic never took place. Such a "parallel" demonstrates that we should show caution when examining missionary and other sources, but as evidence for the nonoccurrence of epidemics before the arrival of missionaries on Aneityum, it must be ruled out of court.

Since 1974 and McArthur's further study of 1981, additional evidence for the two epidemics has come to light. All the accounts can be traced back to the testimonies of two men: Williamu, an Aneityumese eyewitness to the second epidemic and reporter of the first, and Simeona, a Polynesian catechist also present on Aneityum during the second epidemic (sources given in Spriggs 1981, appendix 9).

The clearest evidence for the occurrence of two epidemics is the eyewitness account by Williamu in a letter written in 1860, quoted by Inglis in his 1890 book (322), and the occurrence of the second is closely dated by Hardie's 1851 account of the life of the Polynesian catechist "John Griffin" (Simeona) (MR: February 1852, 23). Simeona was at Malua Institution, Samoa, in 1851 and Hardie's account is clearly based on conversations with him at that time, less than ten years after the second epidemic had occurred. From Hardie's account, it is clear that it occurred soon after Simeona's settlement on Aneityum in 1842, as the house he was building at the time was unfinished when the epidemic started. An 1842–1843 date for the second epidemic is supported by the known occurrence at the same time of epidemics on the neighboring islands of Futuna, Tanna, and Erromango (McArthur and Yaxley 1968, 5, 8, 10). All accounts of this second epidemic place it as occurring between the settling of Polynesian teachers on the island (the first ones were landed in 1841) and the arrival of Geddie in 1848. The "inconsistencies" noted by McArthur rest on the confusion by Geddie and Gill between events that occurred in 1842–1843 and 1846; these are the 1842–1843 epidemic on Aneityum — and death of one of the teachers — and the flight of teachers from Tanna to Aneityum in 1846 after they were blamed for causing epidemics in that year on Tanna (MR: February 1850, 24; Gill 1856, 153–154). The accounts by Hardie, Inglis, Williamu, and Brenchley are consistent in their dating of the second epidemic (Spriggs 1981, appendix 9). Only in his 1890 account does Inglis give an inconsistent date of "probably 1844 or 45" (177–178), perhaps after reading Gill's 1856 account.

Williamu was described by Inglis (1890, 304) as "a lad of fourteen or so" in 1841 who "attached himself to the teachers." Williamu's 1860 account raises the question of when the first epidemic occurred, which he did not himself witness. If he was about 12–14 in 1841, he would have been born around 1827–1829. Either the epidemic occurred soon after he was born or it did not directly affect the area where he lived (Aname). Inglis' 1854 account does not mention the first epidemic, and apart from Williamu's letter there is no mention of it until 1867 (RPM: Inglis, December 1867, 448), when it is noted as occurring between 1830 and 1841.

Inglis stated that he could find no traditions of any epidemic disease occurring before that time. Brenchley's information obtained from Inglis during his 1865 visit (1873, 196) was that it occurred "about the year 1836" and was a disease "like cholera," noting the 1842 outbreak as similar. In 1890 Inglis was of the opinion that both epidemics were "of the nature of cholera," and he gives a date for the first of "about 1837 or 1838" (1890, 177–178). In 1854 he had identified the second epidemic as "dysentery," and the accounts of the 1842–1843 epidemic on neighboring islands also note it as an outbreak of "dysentery" (McArthur and Yaxley 1968, 5, 8).

The weight of evidence for the 1842–1843 outbreak appears conclusive, coming as it does from two eyewitness accounts. The evidence for the first epidemic is largely from Williamu and while the date for it cannot be accurately established, the fact that it is first mentioned by an Aneityumese rather than a European visiting many years later distances it from any legendary Hawaiian parallels.

Without any clear indication of disease type or mode of transmission, it is very difficult to estimate the kind of mortality involved. Talking of the second epidemic, Hardie states that "many died," and Inglis in 1854 wrote that "great numbers died. . . . The population seems to have been considerably reduced before the epidemic disappeared" (MR: February 1852, 23; RPM: August 1855, 274). Williamu wrote: "Around the whole island the people died; they fell like the leaves from off the trees" (Inglis 1890, 322). It should be noted that Simeona and Williamu would have only had direct experience of the effects of the epidemic in the Epeke/Aname area of the north coast. Inglis was the first to hazard a number for the pre-Contact population and the mortality from the two epidemics. In 1867 he wrote that the population "could not have been less than 12,000; some have thought that it might be 20,000" (RPM: December 1867, 448). Who the "some" might be is never stated. He gives mortality of "at least one third" for the first epidemic (i.e., 4,000), describing the second epidemic as "equally severe," leaving about 4,000 people when Geddie and Inglis conducted the census in the 1850s. The figure of one-third would seem to have come from analogy with the 1861 measles epidemic that is known to have killed about a third of the existing population.

Brenchley's account (1873, 196) would appear to be drawn directly from Inglis but, being phrased slightly differently, falls into a humorous statistical lapse that as McArthur noted (1974, 95) would in fact have left no people at all on the island after 1861! In his 1890 account, Inglis details how the 12,000 figure was arrived at, reporting how in the early years of the mission,

Both at the two principal stations, and at four other important stations, as we had with us the most intelligent and best informed men on the island, we took down the names of all the men who had died at these places respectively during both the first and second epidemics; and making allowances for a fair proportion of women and children, we calculated that fully 4000 people must have died during each of the epidemics. (1890, 177–178)

If Inglis is to be believed (and it is most strange that Geddie never mentions this process and that Inglis only mentions it long after he had left the island), his estimate is still little more reliable than a number picked out of the air. What is a "fair proportion of women and children"? According to Williamu, in the second epidemic "there were no little boys or infants died," so both epidemics may have had age- and sex-specific mortality patterns of which Inglis would not have been aware. We have only Inglis' rather suspect tabulation of deaths at Aname and Anelcauhat and "four other important stations" (presumably Umej, Anekro, Ahaij, and Itau?) that the effects of the epidemics were felt all over the island. Simeona and Williamu could only really vouch for the Aname/Epeke area.

One reason for McArthur's skepticism about these epidemics was that epidemics could not have spread as easily before missionization as they did afterward, when most of the population met for an hour each day in the district schoolhouses and many attended the two main churches every Sunday for services (McArthur 1974, 103, 137; 1978). Such conditions were obviously extremely favorable to the spread of various diseases and had no equivalent in the pre-mission period. As McArthur notes (1974, 137), there were traditional occasions such as the competitive feasts when different districts and dominions would be in contact, and the men of any one district met regularly at the *intiptag* (men's area) to plan communal activities. She concludes that although the chances of a communicable disease spreading throughout the island would have been less, "the effect on the district [dominion in my terminology] immediately concerned may have been no different under either the traditional cultural system or the early years of some form of Christianity." Given that various dominions would have been allied at any one time and that people related by marriage could pass through or into hostile chiefdoms (Spriggs 1981, 63), contact between them may not have been as restricted as the missionaries suggest. I would thus conclude that while it is unlikely, it is not impossible that mortality rates on the island as a result of communicable disease before missionization could have approached those that occurred later.

We are thus left with a series of population estimates for the pre-Contact period, none of which is very convincing. If we dismiss the evidence of the two pre-missionary epidemics, we are left with figures on the order of 3,500, 3,800, or 4,000 — in other words, the censal population. The evidence, on the other hand, that serious epidemics did occur between 1830 and 1848 is strong, particularly for the second one. We would thus expect that some population decline had occurred prior to the 1850s. The figure given by Inglis of 12,000 as the pre-Contact population is little (if at all) better than a "chance" figure, while in considering the opinion held by "some" nameless persons that there were 20,000, I can only follow Vigors as quoted at the beginning of this chapter: "I won't believe it"!

Archaeological Evidence for Population: A Bridge Too Far?

To obtain an idea of the magnitude of possible depopulation of the island prior to missionization, we must now turn to the field remains of settlement and agriculture on the island. In 1848 Mrs. Charlotte Geddie had noted that "there is sufficient land to raise food for three times the number of people" (Miller 1975, 39), a point echoed by John Geddie, who wrote in the following year: "The land if cultivated seems capable of sustaining a population many times greater than its present number" (MR: February 1851, 23–25). Once again, a similar point was made by Copeland in 1860: "A very small part of the island is cultivated; were all that is suitable for the raising of food turned to account, it would support four times the present population" (RPM: October 1860, 346).

The distribution of remains of agricultural systems on the island does not appear to tally with these descriptions, as considerable areas of the island have evidently been cultivated at one time. The archaeological evidence and the early mission accounts can only be reconciled if, as a result of previous epidemics, a proportion of cultivable land had become abandoned at this time. As stated by Inglis, at about 1830 "the island was populous, and most of the available land under cultivation" (RPM: October 1860, 346).

McArthur was one of the sterner critics of archaeological methodologies and assumptions concerning demography. In her thesis she attacked the assumption of demographic growth toward carrying capacity (the left-out clause of "population pressure" so used and abused by generations of archaeologists) and dismissed house size and number and settlement area as population indicators. She then made telling points against estimates based on the amount of land cultivated or needed to be cultivated to provide food, as the age and sex structure of both the general population and the workforce must be taken into account, and such considerations are rarely worked into usually simplistic archaeological models. She weighed in against the converse argument, and here I quote from her thesis: "The converse argument of some arbitrary acreage required to provide adequate sustenance per head of population, irrespective of the structure of the population, is also simplistic and becomes more so when the estimates of acreage or quantities required derive from contemporary land use and modern varieties of food crops, and take no account of what Lea (1969) described as the 'non-nutritive functions of food'" (McArthur 1974, 16). Her criticism of Green (1973) was based on these arguments, trenchantly summed up by the undeniable point that "The demonstration that an area might be capable of supporting some number of people is not proof that any such number was ever there, no matter how long the area might have been inhabited" (32).

Having dismissed site number, house size, house number, land area, and other potential sources of archaeological data as indicators of population number, the question is again posed: How can archaeologists give reliable or reasonable estimates of former populations for which there is little or no documentary evidence? McArthur in fact ended her thesis with some suggestions, starting with a survey to

> establish the topographical, geographical, geomorphological, botanical, etc., etc., factors that contributed to the selection of the various areas for settlement and assess the extent of the exploitation in each. Ideally the ground survey would indicate where people had lived, and hopefully suggest some alternatives for how. Part of the how must include hypotheses about the structure of the population, even if only in the simplest terms of the proportion of adults regardless of sex, because the size of the settlement and the average size of households will have been determined by this and not by the dimensions of dwellings, either singly or in their totality. (McArthur 1974, 147)

The outline given in her concluding chapter was not intended to be any more than "reflections," so where can we go from here?

As has been made all too clear, human populations rarely (if ever) live near their ecological carrying capacity. Instead of examining such hypothetical maximum population levels, it is better to look at the parameters that would be associated with populations at various levels below carrying capacity. Green (1973) attempted to do this for Tonga in the prehistoric period. Various writers have suggested estimates for the pre-European contact population of the Tongan Group varying from 8,000 to 20,000 (see chapter 10, this volume). Obviously, it will never be possible to compute an exact figure, but Green examined the claimed population range with regard to how much land would have been in cultivation at different population levels. He modified recent land use data to suit the pre-Contact economy and suggested that in Tonga the per capita requirements of arable land ranged from 0.64 to 0.8 ha. The lower figure implies a more intensive system with a shorter fallow period needing, as a result, greater labor input into clearing, weeding, and the like in order to maintain yields. He calculated the carrying capacities at these different intensity levels (i.e., when 100 percent of the arable land would have been in use) and then for various populations below this the percentage of total arable land necessary for their support. The range of population figures ("standard populations") that he considers the "best fit" for the pre-Contact situation are those that demand use of 50–70 percent of arable land, this range being hypothesized from the earliest European reports that describe large areas of Tongatapu being under cultivation. In her thesis, McArthur raised a host of objections to Green's approach, not least being the validity of his extrapolations from modern land use data for per capita arable requirements (1974, 32–33).

Our problem is similar to Green's: a range of population estimates for the pre-Contact period on Aneityum of 3,500 to 20,000. As in Tonga, we will never be able to give more than "best-fit" approximations of the immediately pre-European contact population, but I feel an approach is possible that answers McArthur's forcefully expressed objections. Green's assumptions have been criticized, but the idea of "standard populations" that he was certainly the first archaeologist in the Pacific to use does indeed point the way forward.

Bayliss-Smith's Model: The New Deal

My approach to the problem is based closely on the geographer Bayliss-Smith's model for a "welfare" approach to carrying capacity and related questions. His approach was detailed in two papers (Bayliss-Smith 1978, 1980), the latter specifically considering taro-based societies. His approach works variable levels of output and input into the carrying capacity models. He notes that in addition to subsistence production, there are important forms of social and trade production for which the motivation is not primarily subsistence (cf. "the non-nutritive functions of food" quoted by McArthur [1974, 16]). In addition, there can be variable labor inputs in different societies depending on what is perceived as a tolerable level of agricultural work input. Taking these into account, his model involves ten steps for establishing measures of "standard populations" for any given area, for different levels of leisure (or more properly, nonsubsistence activities), and different levels of surplus. The matrix produced can then be examined given hypothesized ranges of population for the "best fit" with other evidence. I will list each step and examine them in relation to sources of data from Aneityum to show that such a procedure is feasible there. The ten steps *(in italics)* are as presented by Bayliss-Smith (1978, 133–134), except that "manhour(s)" has been changed to "person-hour(s)".

Step 1. Definition of the territory available to the population and its classification in terms of the areas suitable for different land uses.

This step has been accomplished by establishing the boundaries of districts and dominions from oral and written sources and the dominant topography that divides the island into a series of catchments radiating from the central spine of mountains (Figure 14.2). The archaeological survey and reference to environmental information (Spriggs 1981, chap 2) allowed land use classification (Table 14.1). Although various districts on Aneityum were in direct contact with parts of Tanna, Aniwa, and Futuna, these links do not appear to have involved any significant exchange of food items. Thus for our purposes here, Aneityum represents a closed system.

Step 2. Definition of a feasible economy, in terms of the types of environmental exploitation (e.g. crops) and the proportion of the total energy (E) needs of the population that each product should provide.

On Aneityum we have a rare chance to investigate this, as the agricultural land available to the Late Prehistoric period population is delineated by stone walls, terraces, and the like. The layout of these distinctive archaeological remains allows us to examine the proportion of irrigated taro to dryland crops. This involves an assumption that all garden systems located in the archaeological survey could have been used in 1830. The exceptions are garden systems known to informants to have been built in the period after missionization, which are not included in the calculations. The assumption is that if the garden systems (or parts thereof) were not actually in use in 1830, they were in fallow within a given rotation. Swampland systems *(inhenou, inmegaiwai, inwete)* are assumed to be permanently in use without fallow. Three fallow regimes are considered for canal-fed *incauwai* and dryland gardens: five years fallow to one year's use, six years fallow to one year's use, and six years fallow to two years' use. Other rotations were found either not to allow sufficient fallow periods for soil fertility to recover or to be of longer duration than necessary, needing undue effort in clearing regrowth. Three years' use (or longer) was considered to be too long in general for yields to be maintained on Aneityumese soils (see Spriggs 1981, 38).

The perimeter of the area within each district used for gardens was plotted on the basis of the archaeological survey, and the area within this was calculated using a digitizer. The dryland component was calculated by deducting from this figure the areas of *inhenou, inmegaiwai, inwete,* and *incauwai* that were estimated in the field.

Various soil types on Aneityum appear to have been unsuitable for any kind of agriculture (Spriggs 1981, table 1). Clearly the soils of the perihumid or cloud forest zone usually found above about 400–500 m (soil type 6) could not have been used, and much of the area of these is in fact virtually inaccessible. Other areas of exceptionally steep land nearer the coast, the soils of which are eutric rhegosols (type 1), are equally unsuitable. The heavily eroded soils of the ridges near the coast (type 7) appear to have already been rendered useless for agriculture at some time prior to 1830 because of garden clearance without sufficient antierosion precautions (1981, chap 5). These three soil types, making up about 30 percent of the land area, were excluded from consideration as garden land.

The most productive land is found on the coastal flatlands and the Pleistocene and Recent alluvial terraces, as well as on some other minor soil types (types 2, 3,

Table 14.1. Northern Aneityum: Land area and land use in 1830.

Dominion and District names	Total area (ha)	Land below 300 m (ha)	Dryland gardens* (ha)	Incauwai (ha)	Other wetland gardens (ha)	Gardens as % of land <300 m**
Anelcauhat						
1. Imkalau	355.0	220.5	25.64	—	—	12
2. Umanid	439.6	249.2	22.12	—	0.1145	9
Anau-unse						
3. Anauwau	487.0	245.8	97.36	3.044	0.8222	41
4. Ehesjei	241.9	186.8	33.01	—	0.0475	18
5. Itau	322.7	247.1	54.48	0.040	0.6595	22
Anau-unse Total	1051.6	679.7	184.85	3.084	1.5292	28
Ijipdav and Anetcho						
6. Ijipdav (coastal)	91.0	91.0	17.27	0.850	1.058	21
7. Ijipdav (inland)	550.1	183.6	52.37	0.130	0.3154	29
8. Isei	204.7	110.4	27.04	0.100	0.0875	25
9. Anpeke	224.9	148.4	22.14	—	0.3120	15
10. Anamanjop	122.2	112.5	17.95	—	0.2990	16
11. Epeke	278.3	231.2	56.17	1.525	0.3921	25
12. Aname	483.1	299.5	52.67	6.095	0.1872	20
13. Isav	69.6	69.6	16.25	7.000	0.2860	34
14. Itad	85.1	85.1	52.67	8.500	1.3155	73
15. Anetcho-Idumu	62.3	62.3	46.00	4.750	0.0750	82
16. Umka	220.0	215.2	38.52	15.500	0.5795	25
17. Ohuul	451.2	154.2	23.52	9.450	0.3249	61
18. Ipijcau	624.2	247.8	37.67	7.800	—	18
19a. Antina (lower valley)	95.2	95.2	26.98	7.600	—	36
19b. Antina-Anejpou	359.4	199.5	25.9	1.075	0.3100	14
20. Anetcho Ecsina ***	77.8	77.8	7.61	21.000	0.658	38
21. Anaia	348.5	266.1	54.31	8.750	0.9678	24
Ijipdav and Anetcho Total	4347.6	2649.4	575.04	100.125	7.1679	26
Anau-unjai						
22a. Ahaij	213.0	191.2	16.35	12.000	1.8402	16
22b. Ahaijitoho	253.7	119.8	23.60	2.250	0.5620	22
23. Uea	303.9	240.7	53.79	14.425	2.0077	29
24. Ijassis	272.3	174.4	31.00	12.125	0.2407	25
25. Igarei	106.1	93.7	6.15	5.075	0.4531	12
26. Imtania	420.2	261.5	36.95	8.250	0.4284	17
27. Isia	329.2	245.6	39.47	3.135	0.2405	17
Anau-unjai Total	1898.4	1326.9	207.31	57.260	5.7726	20

Table 14.1. *(Continued)*

Dominion and District names	Total area (ha)	Land below 300 m (ha)	Dryland gardens* (ha)	Incauwai (ha)	Other wetland gardens (ha)	Gardens as % of land <300 m**
Anau-unse, Ijipdav, Anetcho, and Anau-unjai	7297.6	4656.0	967.2	160.469	14.4697	25
Imkalau to Isei Total Epeke, Aname, and	2691.9	1534.3	329.28	4.164	3.1046	22
Isav Total	831.0	600.3	125.09	14.62	0.8653	23

* 20% has been deducted for unusable land within the garden area.

** Some garden areas are found above 300 m and this slightly distorts some figures.

*** Consists of Anemtanahie and Ivanipek.

4, 8, 9, 10). Structural remains associated with both dryland and irrigated gardens are concentrated on these soils, which are included within the area of arable soils. They make up only about another 9 percent of the total land area, however, and the remaining 61 percent consists of "problem" soils of type 5. Their tendency to rapid erosion when cleared of their forest cover necessitates antierosion measures to allow sustained agricultural use (cf. Quantin 1979). A large percentage of the area of type 5 soil occurs on slopes probably too steep to be usable for gardens. It is thus assumed that only those areas of such soils showing structural remains associated with gardening, such as stone terracing and storm drains, could have been used for agriculture in 1830.

The area of gardened land could have been extended by further terracing of type 5 soils and intensified in some locations by the construction of irrigation systems in areas previously used only for dry gardens. The area measured as garden land in use in 1830 therefore does not represent the potentially usable land at that time, which was much greater. In no sense is any notion of ultimate carrying capacity being investigated here — only the productive capacity given the amount of land known to have been in use at that time. It is worth noting, however, that all of the best garden land (agricultural aptitude 1 and 2 in Spriggs 1981, table 1) seems to have been in use in 1830, and the main avenue for expansion would have been in extending hillside terracing on the "problem" soils higher up the valleys. Some districts even then had exceeded the limits of their own catchment water supplies and had some of their irrigated gardens fed via long canals from adjacent valleys. In these districts, the potential for further intensification of production was seriously limited.

The area of dryland gardens was adjusted down by 20 percent to allow for house sites, sacred areas brought into production only in the mission period (cf. Spriggs 1981, appendix 3: items 11, 14, 15, 23, 63b), and areas of unusable land (river and streambeds, rock outcrops, particularly steep slopes, etc.) within the perimeters of the gardened area. The 20 percent allowed is a subjective judgment made on the basis of the field survey.

The crop grown in *inhenou, inmegaiwai, inwete,* and *incauwai* was taro, and an assumption is made that the dryland garden crop was also taro or that other dryland crops (yams, bananas, etc.) gave equivalent yields and needed similar labor inputs. It is assumed for ease of comparability that all dryland gardens were burned off before planting and were not mulched. Energy requirements met from root crop sources have been taken to represent 80 percent of total energy requirements. The other 20 percent of energy requirements would have come from tree crops, fish, shellfish, gathered plant foods, and hunted and domestic animals, birds, and bats. In considering the precolonial economy of Batiki Island in Fiji, Bayliss-Smith (1980, 81) suggested that 29 percent of diet needs were from other than root crop sources: 9 percent from fish and shellfish and 20 percent from coconut. Midden sites on Aneityum are generally small and contain few fish bones. This may in part be related to differential preservation, but from oral historical and some documentary sources it appears that fish was not an important element in diet on the island, although both marine and freshwater shellfish evidently were (Spriggs 1981, appendix 3: items 20j, 20k, 21, 49a, 64; but see also 4, 5 for a contrary view on the importance of fish). Although coconut cream was used in traditional food preparation methods, it seems unreasonable to assume that 20 percent of energy would have been from that source. Inland, where much of the population lived, only one or two coconut trees are found in association with old settlement sites, and the dense stands of coconuts found along the shore today are an artifact of the island's later marginal involvement in capitalist production. In the 1850s, the missionaries encouraged coconut planting to start a copra industry and noted that the trees were "comparatively few" (MR: Geddie, March 1859, 36). While other early accounts mention a profusion of coconut trees, it must be remembered that our appreciation today of what constitutes large numbers of coconut trees is very different from anyone living in the 1840s and 1850s before copra plantations had gotten underway in much of the Pacific.

The importance of other tree crops such as breadfruit and *Inocarpus edulis* is difficult to assess. *Inocarpus* seems to have been important mainly in times of failure of other crops, but breadfruit was clearly important in some areas (particularly around Inglis' mission station) at certain seasons of the year (Spriggs 1981, appendix 3: items 15, 26, 36, 37, 46, 64b). It is difficult to assess the importance of breadfruit in the diet, but I have assumed that on a yearly basis it could be included within the 20 percent of energy from other sources. In several years it was reported that the breadfruit crop was damaged by storms and hurricanes, to which it was particularly prone — for instance, in 1853, 1857, 1858, 1861, and 1862 (items 17, 32, 36, 37, 50, 52, 54, 64b). It would thus appear to have been somewhat unreliable as a food source. Gathered plant foods ("wild" yams, etc.) were important in the diet only in periods of crop failure. The significance of both hunted and domestic animal food would appear to have been as protein and fat sources rather than for their caloric contribution. There is no evidence that large herds of pigs were maintained, and they would appear to have been consumed mainly at feasts and not as an everyday item on the menu.

Step 3. Specification of what is the minimum productivity level (E units per person-hour) which will be culturally acceptable. Empirically, 1750 kilocalories (7330 megajoules) per hour appears to be at or below the minimum actual yield of major economic activities in subsistence or part-subsistence communities.

Bayliss-Smith bases this figure on comparative data from many societies, and I have accepted 1,750 kcals as the lowest acceptable productivity limit. The study of current labor inputs on Aneityum (1981, chap 3) was adjusted to reflect a presteel economy (tables 4, 8; cf. appendix 4). The adjusted figures show that all observed gardening techniques have a minimum productivity level higher than 1,750 kcals, except tilled dryland gardens where only corms are harvested (1,288 kcals/hour). This is thus not included as a viable technique, and it is assumed that corms and cormels were harvested. Dryland tilled (higher yields), *incauwai* tilled (low yield), and *inhenou* (minimum yield) approach the lower acceptable limits of labor productivity.

Step 4. Specification of the energy yields for each major land use (E units per hectare) at various levels of labor intensity around the maximum intensity level defined in Step 3. Such data, showing yields per hectare in relation to different yields per person-hour, will often be unavailable, especially for subsistence crops. Sometimes such data can be determined by fieldwork, or through ethnographic comparisons.

The figures used (Table 14.2) were determined from yield trials on Aneityum (Spriggs 1981, appendix 5). I have made the calculations for the model using a set of fixed yields and fixed labor inputs rather than a range as used by Bayliss-Smith. From available comparative figures, he constructed a curve relating labor input and yield (fig 4), and while some of the techniques used on Aneityum would fit this curve, others deviate markedly from it. Bayliss-Smith (1980, 74) found exceptions where "abnormally high labor inputs were needed to sustain perennial cultivation . . . in an unfavorable environment," such as on Ontong Java Atoll (Solomon Islands) and where "high labor inputs reflect an unusual situation of recovery from hurricane damage to other food supplies," such as Nasaqalau on Lakeba (Fiji) and Uafato (Samoa). Considerable variation was also found in pro-

Table 14.2. Garden labor and productivity on Aneityum in 1830.

Garden type	Labor hours/ha	% male labor	% female labor	Energy expenditure/ha *(kcals)	Yield (million kcal/ha/yr)	Productivity (kcal/hour)
Inhenou (max. yield)	9,137	33	67	1,598,975	(a)43.407 (b)35.357	(a)4,751 (b)3,870
Inhenou (min. yield)	8,111	37	63	1,419,425	(a)25.043 (b)20.698	(a)3,088 (b)1,798
Incauwai (tilled)	10,628	37	63	1,796,900	(a)24.208 (b)19.597	(a)2,358 (b)1,909
Incauwai (untilled)	3,612	13	87	632,100	(a)21.704 (b)17.570	(a)6,008 (b)4,864
Dryland (tilled)**	9,635	40	60	1,686,125	(a)17.215 (b)12.408	(a)1,787 (b)1,288
Dryland (untilled)**	3,449	19	81	603,575	(a)17.215 (b)12.408	(a)4,991 (b)3,598
Dryland (av.)***	6,542	35	65	1,144,850	(a)17.215 (b)12.408	(a)3,389 (b)2,443

 * Following Bayliss-Smith (1980), average energy expenditure in garden tasks is taken to be 1,750 kcal/hour.

 ** The growth period is usually less than a year (ca. 9 months); adjustment has been made to give yearly totals.

*** This average (half tilled, half untilled) is of course a purely notional technique. It can be taken to represent a situation where in one district both tilled and untilled beds may be found depending on microenvironmental conditions.

(a) = yield from corms and cormels.
(b) = yield from corms only.

ductivity between individual farmers and in different environmental conditions within a small area.

Such deviations occur on Aneityum (and elsewhere) because of a factor Bayliss-Smith does not take into account: the presence in many areas where wetland taro is grown of a permanent infrastructure of canals, terraces, and ditched beds that can be brought back into commission at any time without high labor inputs. Canal-fed systems reactivated on Aneityum in 1980 had not been in production for over eighty years, but beneath tall secondary forest the terraces and canals remained in good condition as a permanent improvement of the land for agricultural purposes. This permanent infrastructure allows an enhanced return for labor over other forms of agriculture such as the building of yam mounds, which would have to be dug over anew each year and thus do not represent a permanent infrastructure.

Two models of yield and return for labor have been used. In Model 1 (minimum yields), it is considered that of all dryland gardens in any area, half have been tilled (high labor input) and half were untilled and that all *inhenou* were less densely planted (thus representing a slightly lower labor input). Two submodels allow that *incauwai* were untilled (1a) or tilled (1b). In Model 3 (maximum yields), *inhenou* are more densely planted, all *incauwai* are tilled, and the submodels consider that dryland gardens were either all tilled (3a) or half were tilled and half left untilled (3b).

Models 1 and 3 encompass the full range of yields and return for labor, and no extra information appeared to be gained by considering models intermediate between them, so these were dropped from the calculations. The submodels allow us to take account of a degree of environmental variation in our calculations. Tillage was used on some soils under a grassland cover to improve yield of both *incauwai* and dryland gardens, as well as in the narrow valleys where crop growth would be restricted by limited sunlight hours (Spriggs 1981, chap 3). On the leeward side of the island, tillage of dryland gardens may have been necessary to obtain worthwhile taro yields as a response to the frequent droughts encountered there (cf. Spriggs 1981, chap 2).

Step 5. Calculation of K, or the carrying capacity population. This is the population that will be sustained at subsistence level by the production of all available land, exploited to the maximum extent compatible with the constraint imposed by Step 3 above. For its calculation, the land areas specified in Steps 1 and 2 are combined with the maximum yields from the relevant land uses specified in Step 4. This generates a total energy output (E units per year). The maximum number of people that this output can support can be calculated by assuming that subsistence will not require, on average, over 800,000 kcal (3.35 million MJ) per person per year.

We have allowed for only 80 percent of energy needs to be met from garden production, and so subsistence is thus taken to require 640,000 kcal per person per year. Given the figures and models used in previous steps, a range of K levels was generated for the northern half of the island from 3,776 persons (6 to 1 fallow regime, minimum yields) to 9,003 (6 to 2 fallow regime, maximum yields). If we assume that the percentage of population on the north side of the island in the 1850s (52.6 percent) is a constant value over time, then the K levels for the whole island range from 7,200 to 17,100. The highest estimate for the population in 1830 (20,000) thus could not have been supported given the technology and land use patterns operative at the time, and so the figure must be dismissed as improbable. If the minimum range for K is accepted, then Inglis' 12,000 figure must also be rejected; but given a 5:1 fallow ratio of 12,000, it is right on the K level, and with 6:2 it is well within it.

As already noted, however, the K level is useful only to indicate an upper ceiling for population and does not bear any necessary relation (except as an upper limit) to actual population at any one period. The mistake of many archaeologists in the past has been to assume demographic growth to carrying capacity as a "natural" tendency of human populations and give this as a population estimate.

Step 6. Calculation of the average labor input per productive person that will be required for the K population to be supported. "Productive person" will itself require definition, according to the population's assumed age and sex structure and the division of labor within it. The mean labor input (person-hours per productive person per year) is derived from the total energy output and the mean energy output per person-hour (assumed as being 1750 kcal at K): (Total Energy Output at K/Mean Energy Output per Person-hour) Number of Producers in K Population = Mean Labor Input per Producer per Year.

By noting McArthur's strictures on the importance of considering age and sex structure when estimating prehistoric populations, it is possible to break away from previously oversimplistic archaeological simulations of population. The traditional division of labor has been discussed elsewhere (Spriggs 1981, 1993). Garden preparation was a male task for untilled gardens, a mixed task for tilled gardens, and all other garden tasks (planting, weeding, and harvesting) are taken to have been female tasks. As some minor garden types, such as yam gardens, were exclusively made by males, I have probably slightly overestimated the total female labor component. The overall difference this would make to the weekly figures is probably insignificant, however. Table 14.2 includes the proportion of male to female labor in different gardening techniques, ranging for males from 13 to 40 percent and for females from 60 to 87 percent. For the total of gardening work in Models 1 and 3, however, the figures are 33 percent male labor to 67 percent female labor (Model 1a), 35 percent to 65 percent (Models 1b and 3a) and 39 percent to 61 percent (Model 3b). Given this division of labor, it is clear, as suggested earlier, that the limits to production are set by women's labor rather than men's.[4]

For the age and sex structure of the population, I have followed McArthur's simulations of Aneityumese population structure in the 1850s (1974, chap 1:105–106, table 5.1), which assume a population of 3,500. Of her four models, B*, D, E, and F, I have considered B*, D, and F in these simulations: "The model B* assumes no infanticide of males and allows only 75 per cent of female born to survive; in D, E and F five per cent of the males born are disposed of, and the rate of infanticide for females increases from 20 per cent in D to 25 per cent in E and 30 per cent in F" (121).

It is assumed in the calculations that "productive persons" are all those persons

Table 14.3. Aneityumese age and sex structure models (percentages).

Age range (years)	Population Model B*	Population Model D	Population Model E	Population Model F
Less than 15 (male and female non-workers)	40	34	32	31
Over 15 (female productive workers)	26	30	30	29
Over 15 (male productive workers)	34	36	38	40

Based on McArthur's Table 5.1 simulations for the 1850s, with figures converted to percentages of total population (McArthur 1974, table 5.1).

over the age of 15 years. Some younger persons may have taken part in gardening but would be balanced by the number of persons 50 and over who may have been too old to help in the gardens.

In order to consider populations above 3,500, the figures in McArthur's Table 5.1 have been converted to percentages of the population in broad age ranges (Table 12.3). Given the age- and sex-specific effects of epidemics on mortality patterns, this may not be a wholly appropriate procedure, but without much more elaborate and time-consuming modeling and a clearer idea of the nature of previous epidemics on the island, we can do no better. It is thus assumed that even if previous epidemics had occurred, the age and sex structure was not significantly different in the 1850s than in 1830.

For our purposes, mean energy output is not assumed to be 1,750 kcals but is as specified for each technique used (see Table 14.2).

Step 7. Calculation of mean labor inputs at lower population densities than K (e.g. 0.9K, 0.5K, 0.25K). This exercise will again require the productivity curves for each major land use discussed in Step 4. A smaller population than K will clearly not need to achieve maximum yields per hectare, and in most activities this in turn permits higher returns per person-hour. Since the proportion that each activity contributes to the total output is known (defined in Step 2), the total labor input that the various labor productivities imply can be calculated for each population density.

Step 8. Graphical portrayal of the aggregate energy yield of the island economy (E units per hectare) as a function of the aggregate labor productivity (E units per hour). This curve will require interpolation between the values established (for K, 0.9K, 0.5K, etc.) in Steps 5–7.

Step 9. Estimation, using this curve, of the impact on labor inputs of increasing output per person above the level needed for subsistence. If S = energy output per person at subsistence = 800,000 kcal, then we must calculate labor productivities and hence total and mean labor inputs at S + 10 percent, S + 100 percent, etc. By definition, such an operation will only be possible for populations smaller than K, since at K all resources are being fully utilized for subsistence and so no surplus is feasible.

Step 10. Formulation of a matrix, which gives for different levels of leisure (variable E per person-hour) and different levels of surplus (variable E per hectare) the populations that can be supported by the specified "island" and island economy. These population levels can be termed "standard populations," and represent the maximum numbers that could be supported given the levels of welfare (leisure or surplus) specified by the matrix.

As a fixed series of energy output figures is utilized in our calculations, the procedures are slightly different from Bayliss-Smith's. A range of surplus figures from 0–70 percent over subsistence needs was calculated, along with the population supportable given the surplus component and the number of hours that would have to be worked by men and women per week. These were calculated for the northern side of the island as a whole, the districts between Isei and Imkalau, the dominions of Anau-unjai, Anau-unse, and Anetcho-Ijipdav individually, and the districts of Ipijcau, Ohuul, and Epeke-Aname-Isav (Table 14.4).

In calculating the figures for Batiki, Bayliss-Smith (1980, 80) noted that "subsistence food-gaining activities in Pacific societies not unlike Batiki all seem to require work inputs in the range 10–20 hours." There are of course many other tasks to be done in any society. For Aneityum, 20 percent of energy needs came from other sources, so labor time spent in its procurement must be allowed for. Time spent building houses, cooking, looking after pigs, making mats and baskets, holding feasts, drinking, and recovering from the effects of kava (men only) must also be considered. I have also not included time spent in making the reed fences around the gardens, remarked on by early visitors (Spriggs 1981, appendix 3: items 8d, 20a, 20f). These are no longer constructed, so it is difficult to assess necessary labor inputs (although similar structures are still extant on Lifu in the Loyalty Islands). It is also unclear whether they were placed around all garden types or not. The function of the ones on Lifu that I have seen is clearly to intercept salt-laden winds off the sea, so they may have been required only in near-coastal areas.

Standard population models represent at best reasonable estimates, and additional "reasonable" assumptions have been made to narrow down the range of possibilities. Thus for each of the simulations, three further assumptions have been made: (1) All men work at least ten hours per week in gardening tasks; (2) no woman works in excess of thrity-five hours per week in gardening tasks; and (3)

Table 14.4. Population of Aneityum in 1830.

	Mean minimum population	Mean maximum population	Minimum popluation	Maximum population	Missionary census population
Whole island	4,600 (55)	5,800 (45)	3,500 (70)	12,000 (30)	3,500–3,800
Northern dominions	2,410 (55)	3,070 (45)	1,840 (70)	6,300 (30)	[1,840]–2,000
Ijipdav and Anetcho	1,455 (60)	1,895 (50)	1,150 (55)	2,410 (50)	[1,150–1,250]
Anau-unjai	580 (60)	790 (50)	450 (55)	1,513 (35)	450
Anau-unse	375 (60)	505 (45)	300 (65)	1,032 (25)	300
Isei to Imkalau	750 (55)	1,010 (40)	650 (45)	1,850 (25)	approx. 700
Aname, Epeke, Isav	235 (65)	300 (55)	175 (60)	465 (55)	120
Ohuul	80 (60)	85 (55)	80 (70)	121 (55)	80
Ipijcau	80 (60)	95 (55)	70 (70)	147 (55)	70

Note: Percentage surplus in parentheses; number obtained by subtraction in brackets.

the population in 1830 cannot have been significantly *lower* than the population figures as given in the 1850s.

This gives us a much narrower range of populations from minimum to maximum. The ranges are given in Table 14.4, together with the means of all the "minimum" figures and "maximum" figures. The minimum figures start at the population as recorded in the 1850s, showing that they could have produced the pattern of archaeological remains located during the survey. For the whole island, however, it is equally possible that the remains could have been produced by the 12,000 people postulated by Inglis if the maximum figures are used. If we take the means of the minimum figures and the means of the maximum figures, the range is considerably reduced to between 4,600 and 5,800 for the whole island (2,410 to 3,070 for the northern half). Given that we would expect some population decline because of the two epidemics postulated between 1830 and 1848, figures on the order of 17–33 percent higher than those recorded in the early 1850s are not unreasonable. In Table 14.5, these figures are translated into population densities based on total land area, land below 300 m, and documented agricultural land from the archaeological survey.

The surplus figures obtained by narrowing the ranges of standard populations with the three additional assumptions are also not unreasonable — between 30 and 70 percent surplus for the northern side of the island. When the means are taken, the range is only between 45 and 55 percent. Such surplus production would include a "normal" surplus component to allow for year-by-year production variations, and in a good year it would have been offered (and perhaps left to

Table 14.5. Population densities for Aneityum in 1830 using various measures.

Population (whole island)	Density (160.358 km²)	Density (land below 300 m: 102.018 km²)	Density (agricultural land)
3,500	21.8	34.3	unknown
3,800	23.7	37.2	unknown
4,600	28.7	45.1	unknown
5,800	36.2	56.9	unknown
12,000	74.8	117.6	unknown
20,000	124.7	196.0	unknown

Population (northern dominions only)	Density (72.976 km²)	Density (land below 300 m: 46.56 km²)	Density (agricultural land: 11.421 km²)
1,840	25.2	39.5	161.1
2,000	27.4	43.0	175.1
2,410	33.0	51.8	211.0
3,070	42.1	65.9	268.8
6,300	86.3	135.3	551.6
10,500	143.9	225.5	919.3

Note: The highest claim of 20,000 population (10,500 for the northern dominions) is included for comparison even though it is judged to be beyond the island's carrying capacity.

Source: McArthur 1974, table 5.1.

rot) in competitive feasts or as libations to the *natmas* or spirits, thus representing social production par excellence. Gifts and exchanges of taro continued to regulate social life on the island even after missionization (Spriggs 1981, appendix 8).

That taro was fed to pigs is noted in documentary sources (MR: Inglis, June 1858, 9, 186, 279; cf. MR: Geddie, January 1852, 9; MR: C. Geddie, December 1852, 186), although this would usually be only substandard or half-rotten tubers or peelings, according to informants. The historical sources suggest that the taro fed to pigs would have usually been cooked. On Moala Island in Fiji, which has low-intensity taro irrigation systems, Sahlins (1962, 58) noted of one village that "The lead of Nuku in taro cultivation is nearly matched by a lead in pig raising, which seems logical because taro scraps are a good feed for pigs." Extrapolating from Sahlins' figures, the pig:human ratio in Nuku was between 1:1 and 1.2:1 in a village of sixty-six people.[5] Pigs were specially fattened for feasts on Aneityum (Spriggs 1981, appendix 3: item 1; appendix 8: items 4, 5, 38), and the surplus taro production of the island would thus have turned up at the feasts in two guises — piles of taro and numbers of pigs — and left in another one: prestige for the feast giver.

Conclusions

The likely range of productivity and population for Aneityum in 1830 has been established using Bayliss-Smith's model. Even at population levels considerably higher than those of the 1850s, caloric requirements would not have been limiting.[6] The higher figure quoted by Inglis (20,000) as the possible population for the island exceeds the carrying capacity recorded, and even his 12,000 figure is at the limits of the possible range. It is clear that the 1842–1843 epidemic did take place, and a previous epidemic in the 1830s also seems likely. When the means of the upper and lower limits of the assumed population ranges are taken as the most likely approximations of the 1830 population, a fall in population on the order of 17 to 33 percent from 1830 to the mid-1850s seems quite possible. Surplus taro and other garden production on the order of 50 percent in an average year also seems within the bounds of possibility, part of the surplus being transformed into pigs and prestige in the competitive feasts.

In examining questions of productivity, population, and surplus for Aneityum, we have probably now reached the limits of inference. New and earlier population estimates from chance visitors to the island may turn up, but all will belong to Vigors' "third plan" rather than his first or second, as quoted at the beginning of this chapter. We have arguably found a "fourth plan," but Bayliss-Smith's own stricture should be remembered in closing: "Quantifying the unquantifiable is sometimes a necessary academic practice but it is justifiable only if the essentially artificial nature of the exercise is not forgotten" (1978, 130).

Notes

1. RPM refers to the *Reformed Presbyterian Magazine*, which was issued for many years during the middle to late nineteenth century. Text references to this theological magazine provide the year of publication, page numbers, and — where the context requires it — the author of the letter or article referred to.

2. MR refers to the *Missionary Register of the Presbyterian Church of Nova Scotia*, which was a magazine produced at various times between 1850 and 1859. As with RPM (see note 1), text references provide fuller information than author/date citations.

3. Inglis later described Ohuul as "one of our principal inland districts" (1890, 294), echoing his description of the unnamed one. As discussed in Spriggs (1981, appendix 7), the district of Itaho referred to by MacGillivray can be clearly identified as Ohuul. On his first visit to the inland in August 1853, Ohuul was wholly heathen, but he reports that sometime prior to his second visit in November 1854 it had "now received the *lotu* [Christianity], and a teacher resides there" (1852–1855). The agreement of dates with Inglis'

October 1854 account of the recent conversion of some of the population of an "important inland district" (MR: December 1855, 183) suggests that it is Ohuul to which Inglis is referring. Other candidates would be Ijipdav, Ipijcau, and Umka, but Ijipdav was not successfully missionized until 1857 (RPM: March 1858, 80), Ipijcau until late 1855 (RPM: December 1856, 408), and Umka, which was converted before December 1854, was described by Inglis at that time as "a small inland settlement" (RPM: April 1856, 132).

4. Modjeska (1977, 219–220; cf. Modjeska 1982) presents comparable figures from several New Guinea Highlands societies and notes that for mounded sweet potato gardens, "The more cycles a garden can be put through, the greater the percentage of female labor to the production process." He calculates that in the first cycle of Kapauku intensive shifting cultivation, women contribute 57 percent of total labor, but after four cycles this has risen to 78 percent. In Maring shifting agriculture, women's contribution is 76 percent, in six cycles of Duna intensive sweet potato gardens it is 77 percent, and in Raiapu Enga intensive sweet potato gardens it is 92 percent per cycle.

5. Pig censuses were carried out on Maewo Island in northern Vanuatu to establish pig:person ratios, and the ratio was 1:1 or higher. However, since the development of a copra-based plantation economy, coconuts now form the bulk of pig diet, with taro scraps as the second or third component (after pawpaw). Traditionally, pigs were much more important in the lives of the people, and they were allowed to forage in the bush in the daytime, returning to the homestead for feeding at night, being given cooked taro peelings, leftovers, and half-rotten tubers. Given the traditional economy, it seems likely that ratios of 1:1 pigs to people or higher could have been maintained this way without special plantings of irrigated taro specifically for pigs. It was a very efficient system, taro peelings making up about 20 percent by weight of harvested taro (Bayliss-Smith 1980) and being otherwise useless. In all irrigation systems, corm rot is a problem, and there would always have been available a percentage of substandard tubers for feeding to the pigs. Pigs will readily accept cooked taro as a food and will (albeit unwillingly) eat raw corms if necessary. The peelings and half-rotten tubers were usually lightly roasted on the fire before being given to the pigs, a practice that continues today. Boyd (1975, 216) reported that the Ilakia Awa of Eastern Highlands Province, Papua New Guinea, "occasionally gave their pigs raw taro," but more usually fed them cooked taro cormels. Sweet potato, however, formed the main item in the pig diet.

6. In a criticism of Bayliss-Smith's method, Pernetta and Hill (1980) pointed out that protein, salts, and trace-element availability may be the effective limiting factors on population rather than total energy requirements. They seem to assume, however, that population must relate closely to its biological carrying capacity and that by substituting more critical limiting factors, carrying capacity models will have greater predictive power. Their initial point is well taken, but they seem to have missed Bayliss-Smith's point that in most cases exceptional demands on labor are more likely to be limiting than availability of energy or other similar factors. Even if the other limiting factors they mention were taken into account, the pre-Contact population of most Pacific islands would still bear little relation to biological carrying capacity. There seems little point in substituting a protein, salt, or trace-element obsession for a caloric one when the ultimate limit to population is set by the hours one section of the population can force another to work — a function of the social relations of production.

CHRISTOPHE SAND, JACQUES BOLE,
AND A. OUETCHO

15

What Were the Real Numbers?

The Question of Pre-Contact Population Densities in New Caledonia

Byron reports that the half-blood inhabitants of Pitcairn island knew perfectly this fact: they greeted him very friendly, although they announced him that after the departure of the ship, new diseases would appear on the island, because this had happened after each visit of Europeans. . . . What is most remarkable (in the Marquesas, as witnessed by the surgeon Bourgarel), is that tuberculosis develops in islands never settled by Europeans as well as in the other islands: although this disease was everywhere very rare in the past. This phenomenon is not understandable, as it appears impossible that tuberculosis could be transmitted and spread like epidemic diseases. — *Bulletin de la Société d'Anthropologie de Paris*

 For the past century, anthropological studies have emphasized major differences between the western and the eastern Pacific. Relying on ethnographic accounts and a number of field studies, the proposed synthesis has highlighted in Polynesia a series of sophisticated political systems related to chiefdom organizations controlling large populations (Sahlins 1958), whereas Melanesian societies were supposedly structured in less hierarchical and politically looser and egalitarian "Big Man" systems, partly because of low population densities (Sahlins 1963). This "Big Man versus Chief" dichotomy proposed by Sahlins in a landmark paper, although remaining deeply influential, has been criticized through a number of arguments in different publications and papers over the years (e.g., Thomas 1989). One of the arguments put forward by archaeologists (e.g., Kirch 1994; Sand 1995) has been that the first historical accounts of indigenous population numbers in the islands of Melanesia were often made more than a century after first contact with Europeans, well after the initiation of population decline resulting from newly introduced diseases. The few case studies for our region have shown that an exclusive reliance on Western texts and censuses led to significant underestimation of probable population densities at contact and that archaeology could be a useful tool to define more precisely pre-Contact settlement patterns and their historical transformation linked to population decline, before as well as after colonization (e.g., Spriggs 1981 and chapter 14, this volume; Kirch 1994).

New Caledonia lies at the southern end of the Melanesian croissant. La Grande Terre, a remnant of Gondwanaland over 60 million years old, forms a long island of nearly 17,000 km², 450 km long by 50 km wide, surrounded by one of the longest coral reefs in the world. Endemism is high and soil diversity extreme, with about one-third of the island covered by an acidic peridotite crust. The landscape is heavily eroded, with only a few summits reaching over 1,000 m, and it exhibits old soil systems (Paris 1981). To the east of Grande Terre lie the Loyalty Islands, composed of raised limestone plateaus, those on Lifou exceeding 60 km in length.

The archipelago was first settled during Lapita times about 3,000 years ago and underwent a dynamic process of cultural diversification over time, ultimately being "put on the map" by Captain James Cook in 1774 (Sand et al. 2003a). In the mid-nineteenth century, the archipelago became a French colony and a convict settlement. Because of this unique colonial history—with the largest Western immigration for an island in Melanesia, massive land despoliation, and the imposition of a reservation system on the indigenous Kanak inhabitants for two generations, leading to regular breaking up of sometimes violent revolts claiming better rights—the question of the number of indigenous inhabitants of the archipelago has over the last 150 years been a major issue of local social history (Sand 2000a). Not surprisingly, official figures have always pointed to low numbers (Métais 1953), and it is only in the last decade that a new hypothesis, mainly stemming from archaeological surveys, has questioned this assumption (Sand 1995, 2000b). This chapter begins by presenting these two diverging sets of data, and it will then turn to a series of historical data on population decline prior to the colonization of New Caledonia by France in 1853 to document major episodes of precolonial population collapse. The last part will highlight in turn a number of examples of traditional cultural behavior that may directly affect statistical calculations used to infer pre-Contact population densities.

Kanak Demography: The Official Historical Picture

The demographic evaluations commonly accepted for New Caledonia for the Contact period range from 40,000 (Shineberg 1983) to 80,000 people (Rallu 1989), representing a density of between 2.3 and 4.7 p/km², which is unique for the region. Compared to other places in the Pacific, what characterized initial relations between the West and New Caledonia prior to annexation by France in 1853 was the length of this period. Some sixty-five years passed between 1774 — the year of Cook's first visit to the northeast coast of Grande Terre (Beaglehole 1961) — and the arrival of the protestant teachers of the London Missionary Society (LMS) in 1840 (Crocombe and Crocombe 1972), and another thirteen years would pass before the French takeover. Numerous authors have presented this early part of the post-Contact period as marked by limited contacts, without serious impact on the local Kanak communities (e.g., Doumenge 1982, 92). But when a list of known ship visits is consulted, this assumption becomes questionable, as it appears that indeed numerous contacts took place: at least ten before the end of the eighteenth century, a series of trading ships from Sydney and whalers during the first half of the nineteenth century, and beachcombers from the 1820s on. From 1840 to the late 1850s, the sandalwood trade led to over 400 voyages of Western ships to the archipelago (Sand 1995, 214–217).

Forster made the first evaluation of the indigenous population of the archipelago in 1774, after the visit of James Cook at Balade. Noting that the island appeared to be less densely populated than other parts of the Pacific, Forster evaluated the total number of people as being around 50,000, without giving any information on the method of calculation (Forster 1778, 22). This number was again cited at the beginning of the nineteenth century by Reybaud (1834). In 1847, Captain Leconte, after a stay on the northeast coast, gave a figure of around 55,000 people, once again without publishing his method of calculation (in Kasarhérou 1992, 61). A similar number is given by the first missionaries who settled in Balade in 1843 (Sand 1995, 290–291), although some proposed up to 100,000 inhabitants (Bouzet in Dauphiné 1989, 52). As early as 1852, Captain Woodin lowered the figure to 25,000 (Kasarhérou 1992, 61), while French officials stayed with numbers around 40,000–50,000 (Sand 1995, 300). At the time of the French takeover in the mid-nineteenth century, most of Grande Terre was virtually unknown, apart from the region around Balade-Pouebo in the northeast and some points in the southwest. No European had ever been into the hills and mountains of the interior.

In the early 1860s, publications again cite the number of 40,000 to 50,000 people. But it is not until the advent of a major Kanak revolt in 1878 (Saussol 1979) that colonial officials decided to undertake a census (Kasarhérou 1992). A count in 1880 gives a number around 35,000–40,000 of indigenous inhabitants. The first official census in 1887, done in a mere seventeen days, gives for the whole archipelago 41,874 indigenous persons. Today it is accepted that this number had no basis in reality, having been arrived at in order to satisfy a colonial administrator named Jean-Léon Gauharou, who had lived for over twenty-five years in Noumea and who had published a few years before a geography book estimating the indigenous population to be 40,000 people (Shineberg 1983, 38–39). In 1891 a

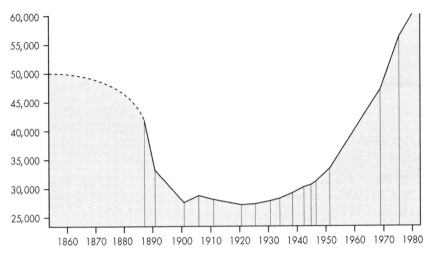

Figure 15.1. The demographic curve for New Caledonia as presented in historical publications.

second census was published, with a result of 33,000 people. Seven years later, a new census gave the number as 31,000 people. We have to await the beginning of the twentieth century to begin to have more reliable figures, with a total indigenous population of 27,768 people. The bottom of this declining curve is reached in the early 1920s with 27,000 people, before an inversion of the curve (Figure 15.1) (Sand 1995, 300–303). The total Kanak depopulation is currently estimated to be between 40 and 60 percent depending on the authors (Kasarhérou 1992). As stated by Rallu, "the less dense population and its dispersion in the landscape . . . limited the importance of the diseases. New Caledonia could be among the least important cases of depopulation in the Pacific" (1990, 280).

Prehistoric Chronology and the Archaeological Situation at Contact

As part of our efforts to understand the origins and deep historical trends of the indigenous Kanak societies of New Caledonia, our Department of Archaeology has over the last decade worked to refine the prehistoric chronology of the archipelago (e.g., Sand 1995; Sand et al. 2003a). This section aims to summarize the major phases of nearly 3,000 years of pre-European settlement by focusing especially on the dynamics that may have influenced demographic trends.

The First Millennium of Settlement

The first settlement of southern Melanesia was related to the spread of the Lapita Cultural Complex into Remote Oceania between roughly 3,100 and 2,900 BP.

The speed of this expansion over two centuries for a total distance of nearly 3,000 km is testimony to a specific social organization of "mobile founding migrant" groups, following the terminology proposed by Green (2003, 103), and certainly involved a tendency toward demographic multiplication. To fuel the colonizing front and at the same time secure permanent settlements in the newly discovered islands, the Austronesian groups needed at each generation a critical number of offspring in order to allow the community to reproduce and expand (Kirch 1997; Spriggs 1997). In New Caledonia, archaeological excavations have shown the continuous occupation of at least a dozen major Lapita settlements on Grande Terre as well as in the Loyalty Islands during the first two to three centuries after initial settlement (Sand 2001), indicating a rapid growth rate from one or several founding families. These first generations probably had an intrinsic rate of reproduction approximating that known from historical sources on Pitcairn Island (e.g., Rallu 1990) or on the Tokelau atolls (see Green and Green, chapter 12, this volume), with a tradition culturally related to a maritime colonizing process.

What the archaeological data clearly show is that this high reproduction rate rapidly shrank after first settlement, most probably in relation to a social rooting of the groups in the islands and their progressive cultural transformation. The first indications of inland movement appear at the end of the Lapita period around 800 BC, at the same time that we witness expansion of settlement into new areas on the coasts. Ceramic diversification indicates a regional differentiation in process between regions (Sand 1999c). But nowhere is any strong exponential multiplication of archaeological sites to be witnessed during the rest of the first millennium BC. The presence of sites all along the habitable coasts is testimony to a population increase, but it was probably nowhere on the order of magnitude calculated for Eastern Polynesia for its colonization period, leading to the observation that there was a considerable difference in the cultural dynamics underway between southern Melanesia and Eastern Polynesia over their respective first millennia of settlement (Sand 2002a, 292). Indirect data show that this period on Grande Terre was characterized by the initiation of major landscape disruptions, with the burning of forests, native fauna extinctions, landslides, and valley infillings mainly related to what was probably a technologically simple slash-and-burn horticultural system (Sand 1999b). Nowhere in New Caledonia — nor in the other archipelagoes of western Remote Oceania — is there indication for that time of complex agricultural techniques. Although estimates are mere speculation, it appears that with a population growth rate of under 0.5 percent for a starting number of about 100, not taking into account a first short period of higher growth at discovery, the total population after one millennium would have been at least 50,000 people for the whole of Grande Terre and easily double that number for the entire archipelago. The archaeological data fits well with a general estimate of fairly low density for Grande Terre.

The Middle Sequence

Until recently, little work had been carried out on the middle period of the cultural sequence in the region, leading in different places to a gap between the first part of the chronology and the advent of the traditional societies witnessed by the first European sailors. It appears that this period is, for Grande Terre at least, the key millennium if we want to understand the specifics of the archipelago and its cultural dynamics. The landscape studies have shown that the latter part of the first millennium BC and the first half of the first millennium AD were witness to the most severe changes in the environment, with massive infilling of some valley bottoms, probably linked to widespread development of burning in most of the cultivable areas (Sand et al. 2003b). In material culture, the beginning of the first millennium AD is marked in the north and the south of Grande Terre by a significant evolution of ceramic types, with the appearance of new vessel forms, new types of decorations, and new manufacturing techniques (Sand 1996a). The production of the large-handled Plum tradition pottery, with unique shapes, probably marks the advent of truly "indigenous" societies in the archipelago, creating new roles and social symbols around locally specific political organizations (Sand et al. 2000).

But what is probably the most important regional trend identified by archaeology over the first millennium AD is the nearly complete termination of relations between Grande Terre and the different islands of the Loyalties. In our excavations, the stratigraphic levels dating from that time show a massive if not complete reduction in the objects exchanged from Grande Terre in contrast to the previous millennium, when lithic tempered pots, stone adzes, and flakes not available in the coral islands make up most of the items recovered in the excavations (Sand 1998). Such a massive change in the archipelago-wide exchange behavior is indicative of a shift in relationships between political groups.

The change is highlighted in Maré Island by the appearance around AD 250–300 of megalithic constructions of a fortified type, with walls 10 m thick, 4 m high, and sometimes several hundreds of meters long, incorporating limestone blocks at times weighing over 5 tons and brought to the site from open-air quarries 4 km distant (Sand 1996b). The archaeological interpretation that can be made of these data is that after one millennium of human settlement, some regions of the archipelago entered into a turbulent period, probably related to interconnected factors of population growth, limitation in cultivable land, and partial soil exhaustion due to overuse of slash-and-burn cultivation techniques, all leading to a crisis in the social network and pressure on the political system. The need for new roles may have first led to the spread of warfare and in some cases the rise of more complex chiefdom systems. Cultural dynamics in more closed and isolated geographical entities certainly took directions that differed from one region and island to the other, depending on landscape characteristics as well as local situations. Although the data for Grande Terre during the first part of the millennium are less well known, it appears that it is in these problematic times that the first major use of petroglyphs developed, the signs being possibly meant as more durable marks of boundaries than natural features such as prominent stones and trees (Monnin and Sand, 2004).

The development of repetitive crises and political instability during the first millennium AD, leading to regular episodes of conflict over land to possible population displacements in Grande Terre and to the isolation of the Loyalties, must have profoundly influenced demographic growth. The indications in some Maré Island skeletons of that period of food shortage episodes leading to stress, hard labor leading to morphological trauma, as well as possible signs of cannibalism all indicate a difficult life (Valentin and Sand 2000, 53–64). The development of phenotypic differences between the regional populations of the archipelago during this millennium (Valentin and Sand 2003, 16–20) highlights the existence of far more closed systems, which probably resulted from restricted gene flow. All this tends to point to a picture of minimal population growth or even decline in population density in some areas during the first millennium AD, although once again much of this picture remains speculative.

The Intensification Process: Advent of the Traditional Kanak Cultural Complex

It is in this context of instability, with probable declines in soil fertility in some areas, that the first signs of the development of new, more structured cultivation techniques can be identified archaeologically. The first development of terraced pond-field systems for planting taro in places fairly close to water sources, as well as the structuring of high dryland mounds for yams, dates from the second half of the first millennium AD. It probably took some time to progressively spread these new cultivation techniques throughout the islands and valleys, but its massive development from the end of the first millennium on (Sand 1999b) opened a new period in the cultural trajectory of the archipelago.

Around AD 1000, a final major change in the ceramic chronology takes place, with the appearance of pottery types that were maintained up to the arrival of the European settlers in the mid-nineteenth century (Sand 1996a). In the south it is the rounded Nera pottery tradition that predominated, while in the north the ovoid Oundjo tradition pots became widely produced. The development of

Figure 15.2. Example of extensive dryland horticultural structures in the Tchamba Valley (east coast of Grande Terre).

these new ceramics went hand in hand with a massive intensification process that marks the appearance of truly Kanak cultural characteristics in an archipelago-wide "Traditional Kanak Cultural Complex" (Sand et al. 2003a). The most spectacular development was certainly in horticultural practices, with the structuring of impressive terraced taro pond-fields for wet taro on the hillsides of Grande Terre, as well as in valley bottoms. Some of these pond-fields cover hundreds of hectares, with tens of thousands of terraces stepping in rows of thirty to sometimes over eighty, one on top of the other. Water channels to supply the terraces sometimes reach lengths of over 3 km. Dryland horticulture intensification led in the thalwegs of the hills and in the valley floors to the structuring of multiple, long, raised field systems to plant predominantly yams (Figure 15.2) (Sand 1995, 171–185).

The construction of these labor-intensive and fragile structures prompted a degree of sedentism, leading to the creation of multiple hamlets of various sizes (Sand 1997). The main feature that developed in these permanent habitation sites was the raised house mound, nearly exclusively of round shape. Surveys have demonstrated the existence of a large variety of different spatial organizations of these hamlets, from the classic ethnographically described settlement along a central alley to different less-structured arrangements of house mounds. Some sites are formed by over 100 house mounds, while others comprise less than ten structures. The size of these mounds is also highly variable, ranking from low mounds less than 50 cm high and 4 m in diameter to large chiefly mounds over 2.5 m high and reaching sometimes over 20 m in diameter (Sand 2002b, 20–26).

The process of intensification underway in the second millennium AD—and now well controlled temporally by a series of radiocarbon dates—must have been driven by various restructurings of the political systems into fairly complex chiefdoms controlling large territories. The rise of these chiefdoms also led to a massive reopening of the links between Grande Terre and the Loyalty Islands, with a flow of products from the main island reappearing in the archaeological sites of the Loyalties (Sand 1998). Interestingly, the directions of exchange changed and were thus not simply a resumption of relations identified for the first millennium BC. This observation probably indicates that the opening of the different regions of the archipelago to outside influences at the beginning of the second millennium AD was made on completely new social bases. Over the succeeding centuries, alongside the regular creation of new chiefdoms by incorporation of new leaders, influences from outside the archipelago played a major role in shaping the Kanak systems in some areas. Groups from Western Polynesia, said to have come from 'Uvea, Samoa, or Tonga, managed to settle in various places (Guiart 1963). A group from Anatom (Aneityum) in southern Vanuatu had a strong influence in Lifou, Maré, the Isle of Pines, and places on the east coast of Grande Terre (Sand 1995, 204–210). It is probable that these influences went both ways, with Kanak canoes sometimes leaving for Vanuatu and Fiji.

Population Densities at Contact

No archaeological data indicates that these late prehistoric movements and settlement of people had an effect on the overall cultural structures of the indigenous societies. Pottery forms, hamlet shapes, and horticultural features show no changes over the last centuries prior to first European contact in 1774. The fossilized landscape that can still be witnessed on Grande Terre today is thus a product of the period immediately preceding first contact. Working from the limited survey data available, summarized briefly in the preceding sections, we may gain some small insight into the discrepancy between archaeological data and the demographic estimates proposed on the basis of historical sources.

The first example is from a site on the northeast coast of Grande Terre, in the lower Tiwaka Plain. This site of about 36 hectares is nearly totally structured by remains of long field systems that encircle abandoned hamlets (Sand and Ouetcho 1993; Sand 1997). Nearly every square meter of the plain was at one stage reworked (Figure 15.2). To give an idea of the extent of these man-made structures, an image might be useful here. If all the long field ridges were placed end-to-end, they would form a horticultural structure over 1 m high, between 4 and 7 m wide, and over 17 km long. If we apply the estimate of 40,000 Kanaks supposed to have lived on Grande Terre at contact to a surface of only one-third of the island, which is approximately the size of the European properties on the best soils during colonial times (Saussol 1981), we arrive at the result that this intensified area of Tiwaka was made for less than three people!

The second example that can be taken to infer local population numbers comes from the southwest coast, in the region of Païta. Ethnographic accounts have estimated the total number of the Kanak population in the region around Païta at European arrival to be around 1,200 people (Guiart 1963, 268); for our study area, we have considered a figure of around 900 people. Our survey of the terraced taro pond-fields that cover the low mountains at the front of the peridotite zone, between 50 and 400 m above sea level, has led to a minimum extent of these field systems of 1,150 hectares, which is an underrepresentation of their real extent. From that surface, we have tried to estimate the production possible and the amount of people it could feed. Expanding the low estimate of around 10 tons per hectare proposed by Barrau (1956, 82), we have used a yield of about 20 tons per hectare, to incorporate the point that a calculation made on a modern field lead in one of the systems of Païta still under cultivation arrived at a productivity of over 80,000 taro plants per hectare, and that Spriggs in the same region observed a yield of 27,800 taro plants per hectare. To content the ethnographers, we have taken as a mean a one-year plantation followed by a long fallow of six years, remembering that pond-field plantations often allow for a much shorter fallow cycle. We have used an annual consumption rate of about 400 kg of tubers per person, doubling the estimate proposed for traditional Kanak consumption by geographer Doumenge (1982, 291). It is important to highlight that all of the values we have used in these calculations are at the conservative end of the known ranges. Nonetheless, our calculation provides an estimate of 8,250 people, or 5,500 if we change the yearly consumption per person to 600 kg, only relying on the terraces. When we take into account the additional production of the extensive dryland field systems of the plains and the hills of Païta, which cover more than 10,000 hectares, as well as the potential input from fishing and shellfish gathering along the seashore and the extensive mangroves, one cannot avoid the conclusion that   even disregarding the question of surplus production   the size of the Kanak population at the end of the prehistoric period of these 30 km of coastal plains simply had to have been substantially more than the mere 900 people proposed by ethnographic accounts (Sand 1995, 218–231).

The artificial irrigation systems on Grande Terre have been identified as the most complex of Oceania (Kirch and Lepofsky 1993). Their extensive distribution over the island, compared to the other high islands of Melanesia including Fiji, must have been in response to the cycles of drought that the archipelago experiences on a regular basis. The parallel structuring of extensive walled field systems and retaining walls in the valleys, as well as massive dams to divert river courses, are testimony to a planned and organized reshaping of the environment through massive labor (Sand 2002b, 18–20). The ritualization of war in parallel to the creation of a complex and unique tradition of placing the head of the last immigrant group as the apparent leader (Bensa 2000) — but without the control over land and the associated magic — led during the second millennium AD to the rise of what must have been one of the most stable social systems in Oceania. Although nowhere in the survey data is there indication of massive habitation concentration in one single site, the fossilized landscapes still observable today clearly speak to significant population growth during the last millennium prior to European contact (Sand 2000b). A first census of what has been termed pre-Contact villages, but which are in fact sites occupied in the 1840s and onward, was conducted in the late 1970s as part of the registration of Kanak claims for land retrocession. J. C. Roux (1990) has published a synthesis of this work, counting 2,368 located and named villages, as well as 327 named villages that were not located. A study of his published maps and field notes clearly indicates that this number is dramatically too low. We cannot go into the detail of our comparisons here, but suffice it to say that our incomplete surveys in areas where Roux had listed abandoned villages increased the number of sites by as much as twelve times (Sand 1995, 170). In the synthesis maps published by Roux, numerous villages have been recorded in regions not favorable to dense occupation, and few have been recorded in large and fertile valleys (Roux 1990, 165). This is probably far more as a result of local tensions between clans during the survey leading to the witholding of information than as actual absence of sites. We are confident, however, that the number of Kanak hamlets was well over the number surveyed by Roux, with a large diversity of sizes and number of house mounds per site that do not allow a summarization of the whole picture into one simple equation of population.

To our knowledge, the only person to have proposed a density model for Grande Terre was the geographer J. P. Doumenge, who believed in a low population of about 65,000 people at contact. Nevertheless, he proposed a density of "130 to 145 inhabitants per square kilometer of used horticultural surface" (Doumenge 1982, 463, original text in French). Reducing his figures by half (i.e., seventy p/km²) to account for the vague status of the phrase "used horticultural surfaces," and again using only one-third of the surface of the island, we would arrive at 400,000 people. This result, obtained by a very simple calculation that does not take into account any of the multiple parameters we should incorporate in this type of reconstruction, is nonetheless nearly ten times higher than the low estimates proposed by historical data. Of course, such a calculation is far too crude to use as a reliable estimate; it merely underscores the improbability of the low population estimates based on post-Contact historical data.

Data Indicating Kanak Population Decline after First Contact

The exercise just presented — hinting at as many as 400,000 people with a population density of about seventy people per square kilometer over only one-third of the total surface of Grande Terre coupled with the two more specific local examples presented for Tiwaka and Païta — requires a reassessment of the population density at the end of the prehistoric period and highlights the need for a profound reconsideration of the impact of first European contact on the indigenous Kanak population of New Caledonia. The archaeological landscape is testimony to densely occupied seashores, valleys, and inner plateaus, far from the orthodox historical picture of a scarcely occupied archipelago. As already mentioned, the taro pond-field techniques of Grande Terre are known to be the most complex in the entire Pacific, and yet if we accept the orthodox population numbers, they would have been constructed in a landscape carrying a population density of a mere four persons per square kilometer. To believe — as most historians still do — that the first period of contact "did not affect the indigenous traditional society" (Doumenge 1982, 92, original text in French) appears open to major revision. Here we will try to highlight some historical data that conflict seriously with the official demographic picture.

What makes the historical figures on Kanak demography quite unique is that, over the last two centuries, no detailed study has been conducted to analyze the starting number proposed by Forster after the first visit of Cook in September 1774. Here is how Forster presented his data: "[I]f we suppose the number of souls in New Caledonia and in adjacent isles to be 50,000, the allowance, it is apprehended, can not be deemed very faulty: for though these parts be not so highly populous as some others, an extent of eighty leagues in length will justify the guess we have made concerning its state of population. . . . If any particular account should exceed the true number, it must be in New Caledonia" (1778, 22). Knowing that his stay lasted only six days, that the British were not able to circumnavigate the island and therefore had no idea of its size, and given that Balade is one of the less fertile areas of Grande Terre, the number given by Forster appears mere speculation. Nevertheless, the same general number was proposed by the missionaries in the 1840s, Bishop Douarre noting for the large Diahot plain that "in this place live less than 3000 people," although "it could feed 30,000 people if it was cultivated (and the locals less lazy): the land is so extensive that it would be possible to settle there far more people" (Kasarhérou 1992, 123, 125, original text in French). A population of 40,000 to 50,000 is also published by the first French colonial administrators (Sand 1995, 300–301), although they had never explored the island, all relying on the first number given by Forster. The evaluation finally received official confirmation in the first census at the end of the century, over a hundred years after first contact. But as early as the 1850s–1870s, some observers in the field went against these estimates, and before the first official census of 1887 we now know that the demographic collapse of the indigenous population was significant and partly calculable through local historical sources (Kasarhérou 1992), briefly presented here.

The first set of information comes from oral traditions. In the mid-nineteenth century, Kanaks explained to French settlers how the first encounters in their village or valley with Europeans a few decades before had led to the spread of devastating diseases, leading most often to the nearly complete disappearance of the local population (Garnier 1867, 195–198). On the northeast coast, people explained how the encounter with the first two boats to stop in Pouebo, probably with La Pérouse, introduced ticks and a new disease (Dubois 1989, 26). An epidemic, considered to be of magical origin, spread in Maré Island in the very first years of the nineteenth century, probably after the first visit of an Australian ship (Kasarhérou 1992, 264). When the first LMS teachers settled on Grande Terre in 1840, they noticed that the first cause of mortality was related to unknown diseases, which the people considered to have been brought by their enemies through magic, prompting war for revenge (Crocombe and Crocombe 1972).

The second set of information is linked to written documents. D'Entrecasteaux in 1793 landed in Balade at the same place where Cook had arrived nineteen years previously. He and his crew could not help but notice the massive difference between the description of friendly people made by the British captain and the fierce cannibals at war that the French encountered. During a visit to the Diahot Plain, the French observed firsthand numerous destroyed villages and abandoned fields and encountered people showing what may have been tuberculosis deformations (Pisier 1976). In the 1820s, beachcombers were responsible for introducing new diseases that "destroyed hundreds of villages" (Bernard 1894, 301, original text in French). In August 1846, the sandalwood ship *Star* was attacked at the Isle of Pines while returning to the island for an urgent repair, the local population believing that the Europeans had returned to see if the disease that had broken out just after their departure a few days before had killed the natives. The LMS teacher Ta'unga from Rarotonga wrote that "the women and the children died too, and the whole island stank because nobody was buried. Anyway, who was there to dig the holes? And who was there to carry the dead? Who was able to walk? Those who remained alive tried to bury the dead but death came upon them also. Thus they were abandoned and the ground stank. The people just left everything and did nothing at all" (Crocombe and Crocombe 1972, 49). A few

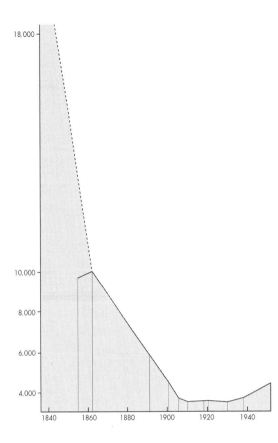

Figure 15.3. The demographic curve of the northeast coast of Grande Terre from ca. 1840 to ca. 1945, reconstructed through historical information.

months later, an epidemic broke out in the northern part of Grande Terre. The Catholic missionaries who witnessed the event considered that half of the population they knew had died (Rougeyron in Kasarhérou 1992, 136; Sand 1995, 291). They saw villages where people were lying dead close to the fire in their house, the cooking pot still with food inside.

From the early 1850s on, the data become more precise and numerous. A succession of epidemics is registered in different regions where Europeans were settled (Sand 1995, 305–307), while other regions and the inland areas remained completely unknown to the French. Taking the figure for the northern part of Grande Terre, between 1847 and the rebounding of the demographic curve in the 1920s, shows a collapse of over 80 percent of the population (see Figure 15.3) in a region that was the first to receive a Western ship in 1774 — that is, seventy-three years earlier (290–294). To conclude, it might be useful to note that during the second half of the nineteenth century, missionary letters are full of desperate complaints about the indigenous young people whom they had been trying to teach for years to send out as teachers who had died suddenly from a simple flu. Numerous other examples published in the literature could be given. They all show that the demographic curve proposed by the official history is completely unreliable, and that the numbers published for the latter part of the nineteenth century must be the low part of a demographic collapse that started at a much higher figure.

Specific Problems of Cultural Behavior in Extrapolating Numbers

The archaeological and historical data on demographic trends in the Pacific have led to conflicting views over the appropriate methods to calculate population growth and densities. Questions of carrying capacity (e.g., Bayliss-Smith 1978), rate of population growth (Rallu 1990), and rate of population decline have been central topics in these discussions. One of the parameters that scholars have had the most difficulty incorporating has been the specific behaviors of past societies as part of unique cultural traditions. The main problem in this field is that these behaviors have evolved over time. Practices observed at first contact were probably not identical one millennium earlier. In Island Melanesia, where cultural diversity is immense, traditions from one valley system cannot be applied randomly to the next part of the island.

The inclusion of cultural behaviors in our archaeological models on landscape, such as surplus amounts, are often problematic. The classic example here is the Samoan tradition of "lowland" and "upland" residences, where the entire community changed living locations between two sites on a regular basis (e.g., Davidson 1969b). As the debate from an archaeological perspective often revolves around questions of "carrying capacity," we would like to briefly take two examples here from Grande Terre in order to tackle on one side the definition of the "production yield" arrived at through the calculation of the extent of horticultural field systems and on the other side the number of people that a household calculation model can generate.

Different approaches to calculating production systems have been experimented with over the years (e.g., Spriggs 1981). The simplest models, such as the one proposed for the Païta taro pond-fields above, rely on low to median statistical figures, not taking into account parameters such as soil fertility. Kanak societies are still structured around the yam calendar, this dry tuber being the symbolic link to the ancestors (Barrau 1956; Kasarhérou 1990). A whole series of rituals highlights the hierarchical structure of the community, renews the relations between clans, and emphasizes the magic powers of the owners of the land and of particular individuals. On Grande Terre, the classic cultivation feature used to grow the long, large yams is still an artificially raised field, sometimes over 1 m high and several meters long. By reworking the entire structure and patiently breaking up the soil into fine particles, the Kanaks can obtain a very soft planting medium, in which the young tubers can easily expand and grow to their maximal size, sometimes reaching over 10 kg. The labor put into this planting technique requires a group effort and a collective sharing of the work, the men being responsible for the shoveling and reworking of the mound, while the women manage the breaking up of the soil clods (Barrau 1956). Each tuber head is separated from its neighbor by about 50 cm, allowing for a fairly dense use of the mound, with annual yields arithmetically calculable. The carrying capacity of the field systems using this type of intensified technique can be inferred from these data. Unfortunately, unique cultural traditions related to these structures may complicate terribly the typical scenario. In places like Hienghène on the northeast coast, for example, people still practice the ritual of the chief's yam. It consists of preparing a long, raised field positioned on a slope, involving a large working force, as if it was intended to be planted with numerous tubers. But in truth, only one tuber is planted on top of the mound, ritually representing the chief, which can grow alone along the entire length of the mound (B. Wedoye, pers. comm. 2000). This yam is in the end no larger than a normal yield, but it is the symbol that is of importance here. Without prior knowledge of this kind of nonproductive behavior on the intensified system — which cannot be readily quantified and varies from one chiefdom to the next — all calculations are subject to potential error.

A similar type of problem is clearly present in New Caledonia for household estimates. Although it appears today unwarranted to continue to believe that in pre-European times the Kanak villages were unoccupied most of the time, ethnographic accounts and oral traditions clearly indicate that in pre-Christian times, some hamlets were constructed specifically for feasts and special social gatherings (e.g., Boulay 1990, 57–62). These feasts were sometimes prepared for years in advance in a competitive manner, and hundreds or even thousands of people assembled for them for weeks at a time. A special place was organized for the event, with the construction of a real village at the foot of the central house, which was sometimes over 20 m in height, surrounded by numerous sleeping houses and cooking areas, dancing grounds, and so forth. In structure, the remains of these sites — occupied only for very occasional events — would look like a classic hamlet occupied for generations. The amount of activity undertaken during the gatherings was such that it might even be impossible to distinguish in archaeological excavations these short-term occupations from permanent ones. Here again, any calculation of village numbers and dwelling platforms extrapolated from archaeological surveys will potentially incorporate errors that will be difficult to correct in detail.

Analysis: How to Deal with the Long-Term Demography of Island Melanesia

The data presented in the different parts of this chapter highlight for New Caledonia a critical need for a reassessment of the prehistoric as well as post-Contact demographic history of the indigenous population. Archaeology has begun to indicate that the prehistoric chronology is not straightforward and defined by a simple cultural evolution, but rather it is marked by different episodes of transformation and crisis that preceded a period of intensification during the millennium preceding first contact. This stochastic dynamic certainly had major influences on demographic history, with periods of high population growth but probably also periods of stability, if not also of population decline. To apply to the entire span of New Caledonian prehistory a simple logistic curve is therefore unreliable and unwarranted.

In our presentation, we have also tried to show some of the multiple parameters that one would ideally have to take into account to achieve reliable estimates of population. For the archipelago, it appears that we are far from being able to assemble all these parameters. The implication of this is that it will be a long while before we are able to go beyond estimations at the local level. Although our calculation methods have been criticized by some on the grounds that there is obvious difficulty in estimating the different parameters, we believe that they are as reliable (or unreliable) as present-day examples from areas that have little in common with our archipelago. To rely on case studies from modern situations by studying environments where people are not under any kind of land stress and demographic pressure can certainly provide a set of calculation data. But their validity to infer pre-Contact situations remains questionable.[1]

Aside from narrow scientific concerns, a major topic around the question of pre-Contact population densities and the extent of Pacific population decline that is not often directly tackled concerns the repercussions of the conclusions reached by scientists for the contemporaneous indigenous communities whose past history is the object of study. Present-day people in Oceania are becoming concerned about the question of former population numbers for reasons that are linked as much to a real will to know how things were in the past as to direct political considerations (see Stannard [1989] for the Hawaiian example). Demonstrating that their ancestors achieved in prehistory a structuring of the communities allowing for numerous people to live on restricted landscapes has direct effects on the ways the future of the islands can be imagined, even if modern constraints are not the same as those of 500 years ago. But more dramatically, the massive population decline witnessed by the Pacific people in most of Oceania following first contact with Europeans had direct effects on traditional social structures, on complex political organizations, and on land ownership, not to mention on the development of wars and cannibalism. The outbreak of epidemics led to population movements within the islands, families leaving their ancestral land to escape death. Centralized chiefdom systems collapsed, and low-ranking groups managed to move into new territories and secure noncustomary political power over diminished local populations. The advent of unknown diseases was perceived as related to magic and supernatural forces for which people had no known medicine and could only blame their totemic or religious deities. It is only with time that some islanders finally perceived that the spread of new diseases was connected to contacts with the Western sailors. In places like Maré Island in the Loyalties, the subsequent arrival of the missionaries, talking about a man who had died on a cross and about the need to be baptized to be saved from hell, appeared as a response to their questions: The white men were the priests of a powerful killing spirit, *Hmakaze* ("Big," "killing," "dead body"), whose power lay in the capacity to bring diseases that killed the natives. The elders thus decided to become Christians, to worship the frightening "cannibal God" in order to be protected against epidemics (Illouz 2000).

Over the long term, the demographic collapse that hit the peoples of Oceania thus had not only an effect on population numbers, but it influenced all aspects of traditional society. The present-day indigenous organizations are a direct result of this period of massive changes, although few indigenous leaders would agree to acknowledge that part of their "traditional" organizations stemmed from such a disaster. On large islands such as Grande Terre, conflicts over land ownership between indigenous clans are becoming a central and in some cases vital issue for the stability of the entire society. Part of the peaceful resolution of the tensions may derive from a better understanding of the multiple consequences of generations of population collapse after first European contact.

Conclusions

We have tried in this chapter to present several kinds of data concerning the question of indigenous population growth during the prehistory of New Caledonia and its historical fluctuations. Over the nearly 3,000 years of prehistoric chronology, demographic trends appear to have varied. It appears that a simple model of logistic growth cannot account for the complexity of the cultural dynamics underway at different time periods. Archaeological results as well as a number of historical texts demonstrate that the very low Kanak population density usually accepted by historians at contact in 1774 is simply unreliable. Significantly, all the evidence against low population densities has still not been taken fully into account by historians; the official demographic tables in the last published graphs on

Figure 15.4. Poindi-Poweu in front of his dwelling at Nékipin in 1954, a mourning turban on his head (photo by L. Chevalier)

Kanak demography still present a depopulation curve starting at around 50,000 people at the time of the French takeover in 1853, with a low population decline of less than 8,000 people until 1887 (e.g., Angleviel 1999), even though data for that time period indicate in some areas a population drop of over 60 percent.

In concluding, it is worth quoting the observation of Rallu concerning the period of depopulation known after the middle of the nineteenth century: "The situation on Grande Terre at the end of the 19th century is similar to that of the Marquesas Islands at the same period" (1990, 277, original text in French). When it is remembered that the Marquesas Islands witnessed a population decline of at least 96 percent in the 120 years after 1800, although never being fully settled by European colonizers, the whole demographic picture of Kanak population collapse appears to diverge significantly from the official history, as we have tried to highlight here. Archaeology indicates that the archipelago had a densely structured landscape at the end of the prehistoric period. We know that James Cook and his crew introduced foreign diseases in all the islands they visited. We know that the New Caledonian archipelago was more often visited by Western ships than has often been accepted, beginning with the end of the eighteenth century. We know that epidemics started early in certain regions. We know that massive epidemics took place in the 1840s, following previous epidemics remembered in oral traditions. We know that episodes of epidemics were frequent in the decades following French takeover, aside from fertility decline related to the spread of STDs. Put into perspective, all of these data point to New Caledonia as a classic example of a malaria-free, fairly densely inhabited Pacific archipelago at contact that was massively affected from 1774 on by introduced diseases that led to a catastrophic population decline, both prior to and after the start of the harsh colonial regime.

All this being said, where do we go from here? Is there a way to evaluate precisely the Kanak population at first contact? Unfortunately, it appears that having reached this stage, we cannot go further. Any try at real numbers in the absence of more intensive archaeological surveys would yield only speculative results, open to immediate attack by colleagues who disagree with our interpretation of the data. The only certainty today is that the number of 80,000 to 100,000 people proposed by geographer J. C. Roux (1990, 172), relying on village counts, is far too low. Local-scale estimates can be made in the course of regional archaeological surveys, but the geology and natural environment of the archipelago are so diverse that any general calculation will have to incorporate multiple landscape situations, leading to countless options and in the end highly speculative results.

We would like to end this chapter on demography with a story (Chevalier 2003). In the mountains of central Grande Terre, at the very back of the valley of the Goapin tribe, there lived in the mid-1950s an old Kanak man, alone in an old tribe called Nékipin, located at an altitude of over 900 m. In this tribe, around 1895, a dispute had separated the clans, and they decided to abandon the habitation ground of their ancestors and move to the valley bottom. Soon after, an epidemic of flu appeared, killing most of the inhabitants of the former tribe. One of the younger survivors, named Poindi-Poweu (Figure 15.4), interpreted this epidemic as a punishment of the ancestors for the abandonment of the tribe. He decided to move back to Nékipin, and he lived there alone for over fifty years, spending his time speaking with invisible presences. Just before dying, he decided to become Christian and performed for his baptism a series of magical rituals in his language to chase away the old spirits, the protectors of the old times. He was the last pagan of the region, and his life had been completely molded by a tragedy that came from abroad: epidemics.

Notes

1. We can give the example here of a very nice terraced taro pond-field system in Thio, in the peridotite area of the southeast coast of Grande Terre. There, an old retired Polynesian has constructed four large irrigated terraces to plant his wet taros in red, infertile mining soil. He does it alone, at his path, because he has nothing else to do during his day, except to watch television.

PATRICK V. KIRCH

16

Concluding Remarks

Methods, Measures, and Models in Pacific Paleodemography

In the introduction (chapter 1), we canvassed some of the disagreements over estimates of Contact-era populations that have driven debates in Pacific historical demography. The fourteen intervening chapters present a diversity of Pacific Island case studies, along with a variety of theoretical models and methodological approaches aimed at bringing some empirical rigor and new insights to the vexing questions of human population numbers, rates of growth, and severity of demographic collapse following contact with the West. In this concluding chapter, I attempt to draw together some common threads in these contributions, with respect to three major themes: the *methods* used to estimate demographic parameters in pre-Contact island societies; the kinds of *measures* that have resulted; and what these results portend for our broader *models* of long-term demographic processes in the Pacific.

Methods

Traditionally, historical demography in the Pacific depended upon a single major category of evidence: documentary accounts by Western voyagers and residents and, more especially, missionary census records. As is well known — and as various contributions to this volume further elaborate — the inherent problem with depending exclusively upon this line of evidence is that one is forced to simply *assume* an arbitrary rate of Contact-period population decline for the period of time between the first reliable census data and the period of initial contact with Western voyagers and Old World diseases. Assuming that the introduction of such diseases had a relatively low impact, as did McArthur (1967), will inevitably lead one to relatively low estimates of the Contact-period population for any given island or archipelago. The method is tautological and can never yield an empirically verifiable result. This does not mean that document-based historical demography is not valid or important, for it is clearly the key method on which a historical baseline must be established for any particular island under study. Cordy's use of the extensive Mahele and related documents from early-to-mid-nineteenth-century Hawai'i (see chapter 7) demonstrates how much can still be learned of demographic patterns (such as the variation in spatial distribution of populations) through careful scrutiny of such documents. Likewise, V. Green and R. Green (chapter 12) draw upon historical accounts to derive empirical estimates of population growth and replacement rates in the small Tokelau atolls. Despite such contributions, it is incontestable that the historical documentary record will never answer our questions regarding *pre*historic island populations.

By engaging with questions of paleodemography, archaeologists contribute new methods and lines of evidence to the debate. Although by no means without its own problems and constraints, archaeological evidence is wholly independent of historical documentary evidence and thus provides a basis on which to cross-check estimates derived from backward projections of historical census data. Archaeologists in various parts of the world including the Pacific have struggled with the methodological problems of how best to estimate past populations (Hassan 1981). In chapter 1 we reviewed several main approaches, including osteological demography, settlement demography, the use of dating curves, and carrying capacity estimates. All but the first of these are applied by one or more of the contributors to this volume, but the most significant is surely that of settlement demography — specifically, the use of some form of "house-count" method. On many Pacific islands, where individual prehistoric household or residential groups can be identified on the basis of discrete clusters or sets of architectural remains (such as house platforms, enclosures, or terraces), it is feasible to carry out such prehistoric census taking by inventorying the numbers of such houses in carefully surveyed sample areas. Of course, chronological control and some means of estimating duration of house use — and whether there was reuse (see chapter 5, for example) — is essential. In the view of most of those who participated in the Mo'orea workshop, this method of house counts has the greatest potential to yield empirically grounded estimates of actual prehistoric population numbers. Not only is it possible to derive fairly accurate population numbers for discrete time periods (see chapter 6), but rates of growth or population changes over time can also be identified (see chapters 5, 6, and 8). The greatest drawback to this method, of course, is that it is time and labor intensive, requiring large infusions of research funds to carry out the necessary detailed archaeological survey, excavation, and chronological dating. In the case of Kahikinui, the population numbers estimated in chapter 6 required the efforts of a large team of archaeologists working for a decade, with major financial support for radiocarbon dating. The case studies of the 'Opunohu Valley (chapter 8) and the Hokatu Valley (chapter 9) illustrate well the difficulties and increased uncertainties of applying a house-count approach when chronological control is more limited or nonexistent. Nonetheless, the results obtained in those cases are far superior to what would be derived strictly from a McArthur-type projection based exclusively on post-Contact historical records.

A second method explored by several contributors to this volume is the use of some form of "carrying capacity" or, more often, "agricultural production capacity" estimate of potential population levels (see chapters 6, 8, 11, 13, and 14). This method — again with many variants — seeks to estimate the maximum possible number of people who might have occupied a particular area given some combination of agricultural strategies and local environmental conditions (soils, water, etc.). The role of archaeology here includes defining the nature of the agricultural production systems actually used in prehistory by applying the evidence from field system walls, irrigation terraces, and so forth. But whereas house counts yield what in theory are one-to-one relationships between population and material remains, the agricultural production capacity methods yield only theoretically possible maximum numbers. Not surprisingly, therefore, in cases where it has been possible to apply both house counts and an estimate of agricultural production (as in Kahikinui and the 'Opunohu Valley), the production capacity approach typically yields numbers significantly higher. One reason for this "disconnect" between numbers obtained from house counts and those estimated by carrying capacity calculations is that the latter generally do not account for annual variations in production occasioned by various kinds of risk (see chapter 3). These results provide a major caveat to archaeological methods of population estimation: Numbers based solely on carrying capacity estimates are likely to always significantly *overestimate* prehistoric population sizes.

Yet another methodological approach to paleodemography is to construct and examine curves of radiocarbon dates derived from archaeological contexts as proxy indicators of long-term population trends. Dye and Komori (1992b; Dye 1994) pioneered this approach in Hawai'i, and in this volume I use it (Kirch, chapter 6) as one of several methods for examining Kahikinui population trends, while Athens (chapter 13) assesses the method for Kosrae. Given a large corpus of radiocarbon dates, this method can yield useful data regarding the overall shape or general trends of population growth curves — but converting such curves to "real numbers" is highly problematic. Moreover, as discussed in chapter 4, several problems inherent in radiocarbon dating make interpretation of such curves difficult and often enigmatic.

As in any scientific endeavor, the best approach to the problem of prehistoric population numbers is doubtless to bring multiple lines of evidence and multiple methods to bear, each as a cross-check on the others. Within the spectrum of

Pacific Island cases considered in this volume, our understanding of pre-Contact population trends is certainly now the strongest for the Hawaiian Islands, where a number of regional case studies have been carried out (chapters 5, 6, and 7) and where a combination of house-count, carrying capacity, and dating curve methods have been applied, along with continued use of a rich post-Contact documentary record. Even for Hawai'i, however, the vexing question of just how many people occupied the archipelago on the eve of contact with the West is not yet satisfactorily resolved. But the error bars on our estimates are getting tighter, and continued research should in time converge on an acceptable answer.

Measures

Beyond the matter of *how* we go about tracking demographic change in the deep past, there is the question of *what* measures we hope to derive. Fundamentally, we would like to know the actual population sizes of particular valleys, regions, islands, or archipelagoes at given points in time. The whole debate over the population of Hawai'i prior to Western contact revolves around the question of how many people actually occupied the archipelago in 1778–1779. Absolute numbers such as this—still an elusive figure for Hawai'i—are the first kind of measure that we seek. But from a broader, comparative perspective, such absolute population counts—even when we can achieve them—are perhaps of less interest than a relative measure of population *density*. The relationships between populations, their natural environments and resources, their agricultural production systems, and their sociopolitical organizations, are all in some ways constrained by population density levels and by the ratio of population to these resources and production capacities. Size and density are both static measures that must be expressed for any given point in history, so in addition to these we also want to know about *rates* of change. Ideally, to write a truly nuanced account of the dynamics of any population over time, we should also be able to specify key rates of birth (fertility) and death (mortality), but these pose methodological and evidential issues that can only be addressed—perhaps!—with the use of osteological demographic methods. Since we have not considered osteological demography in this volume—and as current political trends in Hawai'i and the Pacific increasingly preclude access to human skeletal remains—these last measures are not likely to be addressed in Pacific paleodemography.

Several contributors to this volume have tackled the question of maximum pre-Contact population levels for particular regions, islands, or archipelagoes. Kirch (for Kahikinui) and Cordy (for three districts in the Hawaiian Islands) derive estimates of total population. Kahikinui, one of twelve *moku* or districts into which the island of Maui was territorially divided in late prehistory and arguably its most marginal in terms of agricultural production, probably had a population of between 3,000 and 4,000 people on the eve of Western contact. Waiʻanae, a district on the leeward side of Oʻahu, had between 4,600 and 6,100 according to Cordy's estimates. Hāmākua District on the windward side of Hawaiʻi Island is estimated by Cordy to have supported about 10,500 persons, almost double that of a leeward district. These figures are extremely important in the continuing debate on Hawaiian population, for they provide carefully argued and evidentially based estimates for district-level populations on three different islands, two in leeward, dryland ecological contexts and one in a windward context. In the Maui case, we would expect that other districts would have had populations at least as large as that of Kahikinui and, for certain districts where irrigation was feasible, probably significantly larger. This means that the total population of Maui would have to have been — at an absolute minimum — between 36,000 and 48,000 persons in 1778, and very likely it was a good deal higher. In light of this archaeologically based figure for the marginal parts of the island, Lt. King's rough 1779 estimate for Maui of 65,400 (Stannard 1989, 12) seems entirely plausible. Of course, we need similar evidentially based estimates of maximum populations for more than these few districts before the larger question of Hawaiian population at contact will be resolved to anyone's satisfaction. But these case studies demonstrate that it is possible, with time and effort, to derive archaeologically based estimates that are independent of missionary censuses and the like and that can eventually move the debates over Hawaiian population into a less polemic and more empirical context.

For other islands or archipelagoes, the quest for absolute population numbers will be harder or take longer to achieve. For Samoa, R. Green's work (chapter 11) — so long deferred after the strident critiques of McArthur — still suggests that the maximum population of that high-island archipelago must have been considerably larger than the roughly 42,000 figure estimated for the 1830s. But how much larger? Green, following early work by Pirie (1963), hints that 70,000 persons may not be an extravagant estimate, although that would yield a density of only 22 p/km^2, quite low by comparative standards. For New Caledonia (see chapter 15), all we can possibly say at this point is that the standard estimates of Contact-era population of between 40,000 and 80,000 for La Grande Terre are hopelessly low. But to begin to estimate the actual Kanak population that was dispersed over this vast and highly varied landscape on the eve of European contact will take many decades of hard archaeological and paleodemographic research.

Measures of population density, as noted above, are especially useful for comparative purposes, particularly when — as in the case of Polynesia or even Remote Oceania as a whole — one is comparing populations that were all based on similar social and economic systems but in often highly varied ecological contexts. Questions arise, however, about how to express even such a seemingly simple measure as density. Should we simply report overall density of estimated population per total land area of the island under consideration, even when in the case of large high islands this may incorporate large tracts of steep, mountainous terrain? Should density figures be calibrated to area of arable land or to the lowland zones of high islands that were the most frequented and exploited?

Empirically, the high extremes of population density for Polynesian high-island societies are probably set by the Polynesian outlier societies of Tikopia and Anuta, which have ethnographically documented densities of 242 and 432 p/km², respectively (Kirch and Yen 1982, 56; Yen et al. 1973, 4). In both of these cases, the high density levels are maintained by intensive agricultural production systems and relatively rich marine resources; population size is also closely regulated by a variety of cultural controls (Firth 1957; Kirch 1984, 116–120). Of the archaeological cases considered in this volume, that of the Kohala field system on Hawai‘i Island (chapter 5) probably rivaled Tikopia and Anuta with respect to population density in its final phase immediately prior to European contact, if the estimates of Ladefoged and Graves are correct. Over a period from about AD 1400 to the late 1700s, they see local population densities in their detailed study area rising from about 60 p/km² to a maximum of around 272 p/km². Whether this high value was sustainable over the long term is a serious question for paleodemographic research, for reasons explicated by Tuljapurkar and his colleagues in chapter 3.

A few other highly productive ecological zones in Polynesia might have achieved similar density levels. Hamilton and Kahn (chapter 8) suggest that "pockets" within the ‘Opunohu Valley on Mo‘orea had local population density levels around 220 p/km², while the high estimates of Conte and Maric (chapter 9) for Hokatu Valley in the Marquesas also range from 225 to 337 p/km². But it must be kept in mind that these are *local* density levels, not estimates for entire island surfaces. Nonetheless, there is a certainly consistency emerging from these quantitative exercises, suggesting that when environmental and production conditions were conducive, Polynesian populations often achieved local density levels exceeding 200 p/km².

On the other hand, population densities on many other islands in Polynesia and Remote Oceania seem never to have risen to such high levels. In arid Kahikinui on Maui, maximum densities are estimated at between 43 and 57 p/km². And while parts of the ‘Opunohu Valley certainly had density levels rivaling that of Tikopia, the overall density of the entire valley is estimated by Hamilton and Kahn at 52–53 p/km² (chapter 8). If Green's tentative suggestion that the pre-Contact population of Samoa was somewhere in the "ballpark" of Pirie's estimate of 70,000, then an archipelago-wide density of about 22 p/km² ensues. And for Kosrae, Athens (chapter 13) presents a great deal of evidence to suggest an island-wide density value of around 32 p/km².

The third kind of measure we are interested in is that of *rates* of population growth over long time spans. Assuming that we had accurate knowledge of the maximum population of a given island at the time of European contact, also assuming a small founding population (e.g., <100 persons), and given archaeological data on the date of initial settlement, the simplest method of estimating the rate of population growth leading to that population would be to apply the standard demographic equation

$$r = \ln (P_2/P_1) / t,$$

where P_2 is the maximum population and P_1 the founding population, and t represents the elapsed time. Rallu (chapter 2) applies such a method to ask the theoretical question of what ranges of rates would account for the growth of various Polynesian populations. In the case of Hawai'i, for example, a founding population of around 100 persons (in AD 700) could readily have given rise to a maximum population of around 400,000 by AD 1400 with a growth rate of about 1.2 percent.

The problem, of course, is that such a simple model assumes that growth rates were constant over the prehistoric sequence on any given island — an assumption that archaeological knowledge increasingly indicates is unwarranted in case after case. In the Hawaiian Islands, for example (chapter 4), there is now abundant evidence that while the archipelago-wide population grew rapidly from initial settlement until around AD 1400–1500, it quickly stabilized after that date (even as the populations of the leeward regions such as Kahikinui and Kohala continued to rise). Similarly, Burley (chapter 10) presents settlement evidence from Tonga that the population there reached a maximum density level by early in the first millennium AD. It seems increasingly evident that the sequences of population growth on islands were not constant over time and that episodes of rapid growth were often followed by periods of relative stability or, in some cases, by population declines.

Rates of population growth in the early colonization phase of Remote Oceanic islands, where most Old World diseases including malaria were absent, are likely to have been quite high. The best empirical evidence for such high growth rates on Pacific islands is the famous case of Pitcairn, where the population founded by the *Bounty* mutineers and their Tahitian wives grew at an annual rate of around 3.7 percent (Birdsell 1957; Kirch 1984, 96). The careful historical work of V. Green and R. Green for Tokelau (chapter 12) now adds additional cases where population growth and replacement occurred at rates from 2.1 up to 4 percent. Such data suggest that the population growth rates for early populations on islands (those within the first few centuries following initial colonization) are indeed likely to have been quite high, with the implication that for islands with relatively small land areas, high population density levels might have been achieved relatively quickly. This is certainly the kind of scenario suggested by Burley for the Haʻapai Group in Tonga, where the archaeological settlement data suggest a much higher rate (estimated at 0.8 percent) for the initial Lapita phase than for the subsequent and longer Polynesian Plainware period (estimated at 0.3 percent).

For the Kohala and Kahikinui regions of the Hawaiian Islands (chapters 5 and 6), close temporal control provided by large radiocarbon date spans combined with detailed archaeological surveys of residential features allow us to estimate population growth rates within these two dryland agricultural zones in late prehistory (in both cases, from about AD 1400 until European contact ca. AD 1800). In Kahikinui, if we assume that initial settlement was by just a few family groups and grew to a maximum districtwide population of between 3,000 and 4,000 by contact, an intrinsic growth rate of between about 1.42 and 1.45 percent is indicated. Based on the data for Kohala, a growth rate of 1.02 percent is suggested. More detailed work of this kind throughout other regions of the islands (especially in the windward zones where irrigated agriculture provided the possibility of higher population density) has the potential to yield information on changing rates of population growth over time.

Models

Ultimately, the methods we develop for estimating prehistoric populations and the specific measures of size, density, and rates that we derive from such methods contribute to the refinement of *models* of long-term demographic change. Understanding long-term demographic processes on islands requires feedback between model construction and the testing of models (or of case-specific hypotheses derived from general models) on empirical data. As the chapters in this volume demonstrate, we are now at a point where — thanks to the increasing attention being paid by archaeologists to paleodemographic problems — the feedback loop between models and data is an active one. Moreover, the gains in understanding to be made through the study of island cases have much potential to inform us about long-term demographic processes in general, particularly the interactions among populations, their environments and resource bases, and the economic as well as sociopolitical systems within which these populations were historically enmeshed. This is because, as many have argued, islands have the capacity to stand as "model systems" (Vitousek 2004), not only for natural but also for cultural processes. In the continuing debate over whether Malthusian population dynamics pose ultimate constraints on world economic growth (Ehrlich and Ehrlich 1991; Diamond 2005), understanding the population histories of Pacific islands and how these have interacted with changing technological and socioeconomic trends may indeed have considerable relevance.

The simplest kind of model of demographic change is that in which the population grows exponentially as a direct function of the intrinsic rate of increase *(r)*, according to the equation

$$dN/dt = rN.$$

This is in fact just the sort of unrestrained growth process evidenced by the Pitcairn Island case and seemingly by the replacement scenarios described for Tokelau in chapter 12. Exponential growth may well have characterized the early phases of population expansion on many Remote Oceanic islands, although the specific rate may have varied considerably. Moreover, the population growth curves generated by radiocarbon and site-count methods for Hawai'i, 'Opunohu Valley, and Kosrae (chapters 4, 8, and 13) are all suggestive of exponential processes over at least significant portions of the demographic histories of these islands.

At the same time, archaeological as well as ethnohistoric and ethnographic evidence suggests that by the time of European contact, most island populations were no longer growing exponentially and, if not wholly stable, were at least fluctuating around a maximum size. In some cases, population decline (as has been proposed for Rapa Nui) and even extinction (as in the cases of Henderson, Pitcairn, Nīhoa, Necker, and some other small Polynesian islands) is indicated by the archaeological records. As noted earlier, these Late Prehistoric and Contact-era populations were often at relatively high density levels, and population growth was held in check by a variety of controls and checks on both fertility and on mortality. The classic ethnographic case is, once again, that of Tikopia (Firth 1957), where celibacy, abortion, infanticide, suicide voyaging, increased mortality in times of famine, and ultimately war all combined to reduce the birthrate and increase the death rate (see also Bayliss-Smith 1974). Similar sorts of cultural controls on population are abundantly indicated in the ethnohistoric literature for many Polynesian and Remote Oceanic islands. Archaeological evidence from Hawai'i, Mo'orea, Tonga, Samoa, New Caledonia, and Kosrae is all indicative of a similar situation, where the Late Prehistoric and Contact-era populations were at relatively high density levels, no longer growing exponentially (except perhaps in certain local regions of a large archipelago such as Hawai'i). In short, the evidence leads us to the conclusion that our models of long-term demographic change on Remote Oceanic islands must account for a shift from density-independent, exponential growth to a phase of density-dependent regulation of populations. Here the key variable is no longer so much *r* per se but its constituents, birth *(b)* and death *(d)*, recalling that absent significant emigration and immigration, $r = b - d$. Moreover, K, the theoretical "carrying capacity" of an island, now also comes into play (Kirch 1984, 101–104), along with all the problems inherent in that difficult concept (Dewar 1984).

The simplest model for natural population growth in which the rate of growth decreases as population size (N) approaches carrying capacity (K) is that in which there is a linear relationship between *r* and N, as given by the well-known Verhulst-Pearl logistic equation:

$$dN/dt = rN (K - N/K).$$

This equation describes an S-shaped or sigmoidal curve, so that as N begins to approach K the intrinsic rate of growth declines asymptotically until, in theory, an equilibrium is achieved. I have suggested (Kirch 1984) that some modified form of logistic population growth may have been characteristic of the long-term demographic histories of many Polynesian islands. There are several problems with applying a strictly logistic model, however, one of which is that the true logistic assumes some degree of density damping of *r* from the beginning of the sequence. As we are beginning to realize from both historical and archaeological cases, this assumption seems increasingly unlikely. Rather, it appears that the early phases of population growth on islands may have had no density-dependent effects at all, with exponential growth being typical. Moreover, rather than a gradual and monotonically increasing application of density-dependent "brakes" on the rate of population growth, it may be that the transitions from density-independent to density-dependent controls occurred quite rapidly over the course of island histories. This certainly seems to be the story emerging for the Hawaiian Islands, where the population growth curves generated by several methods (see chapter 4) are perhaps not best modeled by a logistic curve but by an exponential curve quite rapidly replaced with a phase of severe constraints on further population growth. If such a scenario is borne out in other island cases, it will have major implications for how populations respond to density conditions.

What is especially intriguing in the Hawaiian case is that the period corresponding to the steepest part of the exponential growth curve — and that immediately preceding the transition to a phase of population stability — is marked by a number of major changes in settlement pattern, land use, agricultural technology, and sociopolitical organization (Kirch 1985, 1994). Between about AD 1200 and 1500, settlement began to expand into leeward, dryland areas of the islands, large-scale irrigation complexes were constructed wherever topography and water supply permitted, and a territorial pattern of land organization appeared. Moreover, just as the archipelago-wide population seems to have peaked and the phase of exponential growth had ended, the political systems in the islands underwent what appears to be a rapid transition from complex chiefdoms to an "archaic state" form of organization, marked by divine kingship. This is archaeologically manifested by the rapid imposition of a temple system through which the systematic collection of tribute was organized (Kolb 1991; Kirch and Sharp 2005). It is difficult to escape the conclusion that these various technological and sociopolitical developments were in some fundamental way linked to the demographic changes taking place at the same time. The challenge for paleodemography is to unpack the nature of these linkages, which were doubtless complex and not a simple matter of unilinear causation (in one direction or the other).

In chapter 3, Tuljapurkar and his colleagues point to some innovative research directions that may help us to understand these complex linkages between Late Prehistoric, high-density populations and the agricultural and economic systems to which they so closely coupled (see also Lee et al. forthcoming). New evidence from Hawai'i suggests that in the three or four centuries prior to European contact, populations were not only expanding geographically into increasingly marginal zones for agriculture but into zones where the level of risk due to high levels of stochasticity in rainfall and drought may have severely damped r through both heightened mortality and depressed fertility (Vitousek et al. 2004; Kirch et al. 2004). In these zones, evidence is also emerging that intensive dryland agriculture carried out over long periods led to measurable declines in soil nutrients (Hartshorn et al. 2006). It is through continued interdisciplinary research of this type — research that requires dynamical nonlinear models as well as empirical studies from archaeology, soil science, and demography to provide the necessary model parameters — that we may hope to make real advances in our understanding of just how island populations and their agroecosystems interacted.

Finally, there is the issue of modeling the collapse of island populations following the "fatal impact" of Western contact. Rallu (chapter 2) again provides some simple but instructive exercises to suggest that the rates of decline in many populations may have indeed been much steeper than recognized in the classic work of historical demographers such as McArthur. Stannard's claim that the effects of contact with Western explorers, merchants, and missionaries was much greater than has been admitted may prove to be true for more islands and archipelagoes than Hawai'i alone. But here again, resolution of this problem rests ultimately on our ability to determine with some accuracy and precision the actual population sizes present at the moment of first contact. Models of population collapse are of only theoretical interest unless they can be tested and verified on empirical evidence, such as that provided by archaeology. Only then do they become the basis for historical understanding.

A Final Word

Three decades ago, historical demography in the Pacific had settled into a phase of "normal science" (to invoke the Kuhnian paradigm), epitomized by the views of Norma McArthur. Fledging efforts by archaeologists such as Roger Green to suggest that pre-Contact population sizes might have been larger than those predicted by McArthur's retrodictions from the missionary censuses were met by scorn and derision (not to mention any backsliding on the part of young demographers themselves, as Rallu recounts in chapter 2). Yet as Ernst Mayr (1997) has so eloquently argued, science ultimately is a self-correcting knowledge system. As archaeologists expanded their studies of settlement patterns across the ancient landscapes of various Pacific islands, it became increasingly difficult to ignore the evidence for high levels of population density prior to contact with Western voyagers. David Stannard threw down a gauntlet of some proportions with his deconstruction of the historical demography of Hawai'i, further suggesting that the "real" population history of the islands could depend not on the same old historical documents but on new kinds of evidence, especially that to be gained through archaeology. The gradual accumulation of archaeological evidence coupled with efforts to sharpen the methods of paleodemography have now made it possible to begin to trace — however dimly — the long-term demographic histories of a number of Pacific Island societies. The fruits of some of these efforts are summarized in this volume. To be clear, we have a long way yet to travel on the road to comprehending in detail how Pacific Island populations grew, expanded, regulated themselves, occasionally went extinct prior to European contact, and after contact underwent often sickening rates of decline and collapse. This story is an essential and integral part of the larger fabric of Pacific history, and it is our hope that this book inspires others to join us on that road.

REFERENCES

Adams, H. [1901] 1976. *Tahiti: Memoirs of ariʻi Taimai e Marama of Eimeo . . . , Memoirs of Marau Taaroa, last queen of Tahiti.* R. E. Spiller, ed. New York: Scholar, Facsimiles, and Reprints.

———. 1964. *Mémoires d'arii Taimai.* Paris: Publications de la Société des Océanistes.

Agren, G., and E. Bosatta. 1996. *Theoretical ecosystem ecology: Understanding elemental cycles.* Cambridge: Cambridge University Press.

AJHR. 1951. Appendices, journals of the House of Representatives, New Zealand: Annual report, Tokelau Islands. Department of Island Territories. Wellington: Government Printer.

———. 1966. Appendices, journals of the House of Representatives, New Zealand: Reports on the Cook Islands, Niue and Tokelau Islands. Department of Island Territories. Wellington: Government Printer.

———. 1971. Appendices, journals of the House of Representatives, New Zealand: Reports on the Cook Islands, Niue and Tokelau Islands. Department of Maori and Island Affairs. Wellington: Government Printer.

Allen, J. 1987. *Five upland ʻili: Archaeological and historical investigations in the Kāneʻohe Interchange, Interstate Highway H-3, Island of Oʻahu.* Hawaii Historic Preservation Report 87-1. Honolulu: Bishop Museum.

———. 1992. Farming in Hawaiʻi from colonization to contact: Radiocarbon chronology and implications for cultural change. *New Zealand Journal of Archaeology* 14:45–66.

Ammerman, A. J., L. L. Cavalli-Sforza, and D. K. Wagener. 1976. Toward the estimation of population growth in Old World prehistory. In E. B. Zubrow, ed., *Demographic anthropology: Quantitative approaches*, 27–62. Albuquerque: University of New Mexico Press.

Anderson, A. 1980. Towards an explanation of protohistoric social organisation and settlement patterns amongst the Southern Ngai Tahu. *New Zealand Journal of Archaeology* 2:3–23.

———. 1995. Current approaches in East Polynesian colonization research. *Journal of the Polynesian Society* 104:110–132.

———. 2001. Mobility models of Lapita migration. In G. Clark, A. Anderson, and T. Vunidilo, eds., *The archaeology of Lapita dispersal in Oceania,* 23–31. Terra Australis 17. Canberra: Australian National University.

———. 2003. Initial human dispersal in Remote Oceana: Pattern and explanation. In C. Sand, ed., *Pacific archaeology assessments and prospects*, 71–84. Cahiers de l'Archéologie en Nouvelle-Calédonie 15. Nouméa: Service de la Culture et du Patrimoine.

Anderson, A., E. Conte, P. V. Kirch, and M. Weisler. 2003. Cultural chronology in Mangareva (Gambier Islands), French Polynesia: Evidence from recent radiocarbon dating. *Journal of the Polynesian Society* 112:119–140.

Angel, J. L. 1969. The bases of paleodemography. *American Journal of Physical Anthropology* 30:427–438.

———. 1972. Ecology and population in the Eastern Mediterranean. *World Archaeology* 4:88–105.

Angelo, A. H., H. Kirifi, and A. Fong Toy. 1989. Law and Tokelau. *Pacific Studies* 12:29–52.

Angleviel, F. 1999. Un nouveau regard sur la démographie Kanak. In G. Bladinières, ed., *Chroniques du pays Kanak*, vol. 1, 32–37. Nouméa: Planète Mémo.

Annual Report. 1967. *American Samoa annual report to Secretary of the Interior/Office of Samoan Information*. Pago Pago, American Samoa: The Office.

Anon. 1841. The Australasian Islands: Annatom. *Colonial Magazine and Commercial Maritime Journal* 4:335–336.

Aswani, S., and M. Graves. 1998. The Tongan maritime expansion: A case in the evolutionary ecology of social complexity. *Asian Perspectives* 37:135–164.

Athens, J. S. 1977. Theory building and the study of evolutionary process in complex societies. In L. R. Binford, ed., *For theory building in archaeology: Essays on faunal remains, aquatic resources, spatial analysis, and systemic modeling*, 353–384. New York: Academic Press.

———. 1978. Evolutionary process in complex societies and the Late period–Cara occupation of northern highland Ecuador. Unpublished Ph.D. dissertation, Dept. of Anthropology, Univ. of New Mexico. Ann Arbor, MI: University Microfilms.

———. 1990. Kosrae pottery, clay, and early settlement. *Micronesica* Supplement 2:171–186.

———. 1992. Ethnicity and adaptation: The Late period–Cara occupation in northern highland Ecuador. In E. M. Schortman and P. A. Urban, eds., *Resources, power, and interregional interaction*, 193–219. New York: Plenum.

———. 1995. *Landscape archaeology: Prehistoric settlement, subsistence, and environment of Kosrae, eastern Caroline Islands, Micronesia*. Report prepared for the Kosrae State government, Federated States of Micronesia. Honolulu: International Archaeological Research Institute, Inc.

———. 1997. Hawaiian native lowland vegetation in prehistory. In P. V. Kirch and T. L. Hunt, eds., *Historical ecology in the Pacific Islands: Prehistoric environmental and landscape change*, 248–270. New Haven: Yale University Press.

Athens, J. S., J. V. Ward, and G. M. Murakami. 1996. Development of an agroforest on a Micronesian high island: Prehistoric Kosraean agriculture. *Antiquity* 70:834–846.

Awards Books. n.d. *Awards Books*. (Contain maps of each LCA parcel.) Handwritten copy, on file, Lands Division, Department of Land and Natural Resources, State of Hawai'i, Honolulu.

Ayres, W. 1970. *Archaeological survey and excavations, Kamana-nui Valley, Moanalua Ahupua'a, south Halawa Valley, Halawa Ahupua'a*. Department of Anthropology Report Series 70–8. Honolulu: Bishop Musuem.

Bailey, M. 1989. The concept of the margin in Medieval English economy. *Economic History Review* 42:1–17.

Bailleul, M. 1995. Recensement de la population de l'île de Ua Huka le 27 décembre 1867. *Bulletin de la Société des Etudes Océaniennes* 268:82–88.

———. 2001. *Les Îles Marquises: Histoire de la Terre des Hommes du XVIIIème siècle à nos jours.* Cahiers du Patrimoine (Histoire). Papeʻete: Ministère de la Culture de la Polynésie Française.

Baisden, W. T., and R. Amundson. 2003. An analytical approach to ecosystem biogeochemistry modeling. *Ecological Applications* 13:649–663.

Barratt, G. 1990. *Russia and the South Pacific 1696–1840.* Vol. 3: *Melanesia and the Western Polynesian fringe.* Vancouver: University of British Columbia Press.

Barrau, J. 1956. *L'agriculture vivrière autochtone de la Nouvelle-Calédonie.* Nouméa: Commission du Pacifique Sud.

———. 1961. *Subsistence agriculture in Polynesia and Micronesia.* Bernice P. Bishop Museum Bulletin 223. Honolulu: Bishop Museum Press.

Barrère, D. 1971. Historical survey: Pualaa, Puna, Hawaii. In S. N. Crozier and D. Barrère, *Archaeological and historical survey of the Ahupuaa of Pualaa, Puna District, island of Hawaii,* 7–21. Department of Anthropology Report Series 71–1. Honolulu: Bishop Museum.

Bayliss-Smith, T. P. 1974. Constraints on population growth: The case of the Polynesian outlier atolls in the precontact period. *Human Ecology* 2:259–295.

———. 1978. Maximum populations and standard populations: The carrying capacity question. In D. Green, C. Haselgrove, and M. Spriggs, eds., *Social organisation and settlement,* vol. 1, 129–151. Oxford: British Archaeological Reports. BAR International Series (Supplementary) 47.

———. 1980. Population pressure, resources and welfare: Towards a more realistic measure of carrying capacity. In H. C. Brookfield, ed., *Population-environment relations in tropical islands: The case of eastern Fiji,* 61–93. MAB Technical Notes 13. Paris: UNESCO.

Beaglehole, E., and P. Beaglehole. 1941. *Pangai: A village in Tonga.* Polynesian Society Memoir 18. Wellington: Polynesian Society.

Beaglehole, J. C., ed. 1955. *The journals of Captain James Cook on his voyage of discovery.* Cambridge: Cambridge University Press for the Hakluyt Society.

———. 1961. *The journals of Captain James Cook.* Vol. 2: *The Voyage of the* Resolution *and* Adventure, *1772–1775.* Cambridge: Cambridge University Press for the Hakluyt Society.

———. 1962. *The* Endeavour *journal of Joseph Banks: 1768–1771.* 2 vols. Sydney: Angus & Robertson Ltd.

———. 1967. *The journals of Captain James Cook on his voyages of discovery.* Vol. 2: *The voyage of the* Endeavor, *1768–1771.* Cambridge: Cambridge University Press for the Hakluyt Society.

———. 1968. *The journals of Captain James Cook on his voyages of discovery: The voyage of the* Resolution *and* Discovery, *1776–1780.* Cambridge: Cambridge University Press for the Hakluyt Society.

———. 1969. *The journals of Captain James Cook on his voyages of discovery: The Voyage of the* Resolution *and* Adventure, *1772–1775.* Vol. 2. Cambridge: Cambridge University Press for the Hakluyt Society.

Bellwood, P. S. 1971. Varieties of ecological adaptations in the Southern Cook Islands. *Archaeology and Physical Anthropology in Oceania* 6:145–169.

———. 1972. *A settlement pattern survey, Hanatekua Valley, Hiva Oa, Marquesas Islands.* Pacific Anthropological Records 17. Honolulu: Bishop Museum Press.

Bengtsson, T., and O. Saito, eds. 2000. *Population and economy: From hunger to modern economic growth.* Oxford: Oxford University Press.

Bennett, G. 1831. A recent visit to several Polynesian islands. *United Services Journal* 3:188–193.

Bensa, A. 2000. Le chef kanak: Les modèles et l'histoire. In A. Bensa and I. Leblic, eds., *En pays Kanak: Ethnologie, Linguistique, Archéologie, Histoire de la Nouvelle-Calédonie,* 9–48. Collection Ethnologie de la France 14. Paris: Éditions de la Maison des Sciences de l'Homme.

Bernard, A. 1894. *L'Archipel de la Nouvelle-Calédonie.* Paris: Hachette.

Bernart, L. 1977. *The book of Luelen.* Translated by J. L. Fischer, S. H. Riesenberg, and M. G. Whiting. Pacific History Series No. 8. Canberra: Australian National University Press.

Best, S. 1988. Tokelau archaeology: A preliminary report of an initial survey and excavations. *Indo-Pacific Prehistory Bulletin* 8:104–118. Canberra: Indo-Pacific Prehistory Association.

Bicknell, H., and W. H. Bicknell. 1805. *Journal, 22 January–11 February 1805* (South Seas, Journals 2). Printed in part in *Trans. Missionary Soc.* (1795–1817), vol. 3.

Birdsell, J. B. 1957. Some population problems involving Pleistocene man. *Cold Spring Harbor Symposia on Quantitative Biology* 22:47–69.

Bishop, A. 1838. An inquiry into the causes of decrease in the population of the Sandwich Islands. *Hawaiian Spectator* 1:52–66.

Bishop Museum. Forthcoming. Imu, adzes, and upland agriculture: Inventory survey archaeology in north Halawa Valley. Draft manuscript on file, Hawai'i Historic Preservation Division, Kapolei.

Black, S. 1978. Polynesian outliers: A study in the survival of small populations. In I. Hodder, ed., *Simulation Studies in Archaeology,* 63–76. Cambridge: Cambridge University Press.

———. 1980. Demographic models and island colonisation in the Pacific. *New Zealand Journal of Archaeology* 2:51–64.

Bligh, W. 1937. *The Log of the Bounty.* 2 vols. Ed. O. Rutter. London: Golden Cockerell Press.

Bocquet-Appel, J.-P. 1985. Small populations: Demography and paleoanthropological inferences. *Journal of Human Evolution* 14:683–691.

Bocquet-Appel, J.-P., and C. Masset. 1982. Farewell to paleodemography. *Journal of Human Evolution* 11:321–333.

Bolker, B. M., S. W. Pacala, and W. J. Parton. 1998. Linear analysis of soil decomposition: Insights from the CENTURY model. *Ecological Applications* 8:425–439.

Boserup, E. 1965. *The conditions of agricultural growth: The economics of agrarian change under population pressure.* Chicago: Aldine.

———. 1981. *Population and technological change: A study of long-term trends.* Chicago: University of Chicago Press.

Bott, E. 1982. *Tongan society at the time of Captain Cook's visits: Discussion with Her Majesty Queen Salote Tupou.* Wellington: Polynesian Society.

Bougainville, L. A. [1772] 1967. *A voyage around the world. . . .* Ridgewood, NJ: Gregg Press. (Facsimile of original ed., London, 1772, trans. from French by J. R. Forster).

Boulay, R. 1990. *La maison Kanak*. Collection Architectures Traditionnelles. Paris: Editions Parenthèses–ADCK–ORSTOM.

Boyd, D. 1975. Crops, kiaps and currencies: Flexible behavioral strategies among the Ilakia Awa in PNG. Ph.D. thesis, University of California, Los Angeles. Ann Arbor: University Microfilms.

Brady, N. C., and R. R. Weil. 2002. *The nature and properties of soils*. 13th ed. Upper Saddle River, NJ: Prentice Hall.

Brenchley, J. L. 1873. *Jottings during the cruise of HMS* Curaçoa *among the South Sea Islands in 1865*. London: Longmans Green.

Brewis, A. A. 1993. Toward a more vital palaeodemography: Fertility, homology and analogy in Pacific paleodemography. Population Studies and Training Center, Brown University: Working Paper 93-06. Providence.

———. 1994. Reproductive ethnophysiology and contraceptive use in a rural Micronesian population. *Journal of the Polynesian Society* 103:53–74.

Brewis, A. A., and J. S. Allen. 1994. Biological anthropological research in the Pacific. *Journal of the Polynesian Society* 103:7–10.

Brewis, A. A., M. Molloy, and D. G. Sutton. 1990. Modeling the prehistoric Maori population. *American Journal of Physical Anthropology* 81:343–356.

Brookfield, H. C. 1972. Intensification and disintensification in Pacific agriculture: A theoretical approach. *Pacific Viewpoint* 13:30–48.

———. 1984. Intensification revisited. *Pacific Viewpoint* 25:15–44.

Brown, B. M. 1987. Population estimation from floor area: A restudy of "Naroll's Constant." *Behavior Science Research* 21:1–49.

Buikstra, J. E., L. W. Konigsberg, and J. Bullington. 1986. Fertility and the development of agriculture in the prehistoric Midwest. *American Antiquity* 51:528–546.

Buist, A. G. 1969. Field archaeology on Savai'i. In R. C. Green and J. M. Davidson, eds., *Archaeology in Western Samoa*, vol. 1, 34–54. Bulletin No. 7. Auckland: Auckland Institute and Museum.

Bulletin de la Société d'Anthropologie de Paris. 1860. Discussion sur le dépérissement des races. Séances du 19 avril et du 24 mai 1860.

Burley, D. V. 1994. Settlement pattern and Tongan prehistory: Reconsiderations from Ha'apai. *Journal of the Polynesian Society* 102: 379–411.

———. 1995. Mata'uvave and 15th century Ha'apai: Archaeological and historical landscapes in the validation of traditional Tongan history. *Journal of Pacific History* 30:154–172.

———. 1996. Report on the 1995 Lapita Project, Ha'apai Islands, Kingdom of Tonga. Unpublished report on file with the author and Prime Minister's Office, Nuku'alofa, Tonga.

———. 1998. Tongan archaeology and the Tongan past: 2850–150 BP. *Journal of World Prehistory* 12:337–392.

———. 1999. Lapita settlements to the east: New data and changing perspectives from Ha'apai (Tonga) prehistory. In J. C. Galipaud and I. Lilley, eds., *The Pacific from 5000 to 2000 BP: Colonisation and transformations*, 189–200. Paris: ORSTOM Editions.

Burley, D. V., and A. Barton. 2004. Archaeological survey and test excavations in the

Vava'u Group and on Tongatapu, 2003 field season, Kingdom of Tonga. Unpublished report on file, Tongan Traditions Committee, Nuku'alofa.

Burley, D. V., and J. Clark. 2003. The archaeology of Fiji/Western Polynesia in the post-Lapita era. In C. Sand, ed., *Pacific archaeology assessments and prospects,* 235–254. Le Cahiers de l'Archeologie en Nouvelle-Caledonie 15. Nouméa: Service de la Culture et du Patrimoine.

Burley, D. V., and W. R. Dickinson. 2001. Origin and significance of a founding settlement in Oceania. *Proceedings of the National Academy of Sciences (U.S.A.)* 98:11,829–11,831.

Burley, D. V., W. R. Dickinson, A. Barton, and R. Shutler Jr. 2001. Lapita on the periphery: New data on old problems in the Kingdom of Tonga. *Archaeology in Oceania* 36:89–104.

Burley, D. V., D. W. Steadman, and A. Anderson. 2003. The volcanic outlier of 'Ata in Tongan prehistory: Reconsideration of its role and settlement chronology. *Journal of New Zealand Archaeology* 25:89–106.

Burley, D. V., A. Storey, and J. Witt. 2002. On the definition and implications of eastern Lapita ceramics in Tonga. In S. Bedford, C. Sand, and D. V. Burley, eds., *Fifty Years in the Field: Essays in Honour of Richard Shutler Jr's Archaeological Career,* 213–226. New Zealand Archaeological Association Monograph 25. Auckland.

Burrows, W. 1923. Some notes and legends of a South Sea island: Fakaofo of the Tokelau or Union Group. *Journal of the Polynesian Society* 32:143–173.

Burtchard, G. 1996. Population and land use on the Keauhou coast, the Mauka Land Inventory Survey, Keauhou, North Kona, Hawai'i Island. International Archaeological Institute manuscript on file, State Historic Preservation Division Library, Kapolei.

Bushnell, O. A. 1993. "The Horror" reconsidered: An evaluation of the historical evidence for population decline in Hawai'i, 1778–1803. *Pacific Studies* 16:115–161.

———. 1993. *The Gifts of Civilization: Germs and Genocide in Hawai'i.* Honolulu: University of Hawai'i Press.

Buzacott, A. 1836–1837. Journal of a voyage from Rarotonga to the Navigators' Islands and tour round Savai'i. Manuscript, London Missionary Society, South Seas Letters and Journals 113, Box 8.

Campbell, A. 1967 [1822]. *A voyage round the world (1806–1812).* Honolulu: University of Hawai'i Press.

Campbell, M. 2003. Productivity, production and settlement in precontact Rarotonga, Cook Islands. *Archaeology in Oceania* 38:9–22.

Carlquist, S. 1970. *Hawaii: A natural history.* Garden City, NY: Natural History Press.

Carneiro, R. L. 1970. A theory on the origin of the state. *Science* 169:733–738.

Cartwright, F., and M. Biddiss. 1972. *Disease and History.* New York: Dorset Press.

Casselberry, S. E. 1974. Further refinement of formulae for determining population from floor area. *World Archaeology* 6:117–122.

Chamberlain, L. 1826. Journals of Levi Chamberlain 1822–1849, Chapters 1–39. Manuscript, Bishop Museum Library, Honolulu.

Chapman, J. 1999. Archaeological proxy-data for demographic reconstruction: Facts, factoids or fiction. In J. Bintliff and K. Sbonias, eds., *Reconstructing past population trends in Mediterranean Europe,* 65–76. Oxford: Oxbow Books.

Chevalier, L. 2003. L'hermite de Nekipin. *Palabre Coutumier* 9:8–11.

Childe, V. G. 1951. [1936]. *Man makes himself.* New York: New American Library.

Chung, H. L. 1923. The sweet potato in Hawaii. Hawaiian Agricultural Experiment Station Bulletin 50. Honolulu.

Clark, G. 1992. The economics of exhaustion, the Postan thesis, and the agricultural revolution. *Journal of Economic History* 52:61–84.

Clark, J. T. 1981. Archaeological survey of the proposed Lalamilo Agricultural Park, South Kohala, Island of Hawaii. Bishop Museum manuscript on file, State Historic Preservation Division Library, Kapolei.

———. 1987. Waimea-Kawaihae: A Leeward Hawaii settlement system. Unpublished Ph.D. thesis, Department of Anthropology, University of Illinois at Urbana-Champaign.

———. 1988. Paleodemography in leeward Hawaii. *Archaeology in Oceania* 23:22–30.

Clark, J., and P. V. Kirch, eds. 1983. *Archaeological investigation of the Mudlane-Waimea-Kawaihae Road corridor, Island of Hawaii: An interdisciplinary study of an environmental transect.* Department of Anthropology Report 83-1. Honolulu: Bishop Museum.

Cohen, J. E. 1995. *How many people can the earth support?* New York: W. W. Norton & Company.

Cohen, M. N. 1977. *The food crisis in prehistory: Overpopulation and the origins of agriculture.* New Haven: Yale University Press.

Coil, J., and P. V. Kirch. 2005. An Ipomoean landscape: Archaeology and the sweet potato in Kahikinui, Maui, Hawaiian Islands. In C. Ballard, P. Brown, R. M. Bourke, and T. Harwood, eds., *The sweet potato in the Pacific: A reappraisal,* 71–84. Oceania Monograph 56 and Ethnology Monograph 19. Sydney and Pittsburgh.

Collins, S. L. 1986. Osteological studies of human skeletal remains from the Keopu burial site. In T. L. Han, S. L. Collins, S. D. Clark, and A. Garland, *Moe kau a ho'oilo: Hawaiian mortuary practices at Keopu, Kona, Hawai'i,* 165–250. Department of Anthropology Report 86–1. Honolulu: Bishop Museum.

Conte, E., and P. Kirch, eds. 2004. Archaeological investigations in the Mangareva Islands (Gambier Archipelago), French Polynesia. Archaeological Research Facility Contribution No. 62. Berkeley: University of California.

Conte, E., A. Noury, and N. Tartinville. 2001. *Recherches ethnoarchéologiques à Ua Huka (Marquises, Polynésie Française). Campagne 1998–99.* Faaa, Tahiti: Université de la Polynésie Française.

Cook, J., and J. King. 1784. *A voyage to the Pacific Ocean in the years 1776, 1777, 1778, 1779 and 1780.* 3 vols. London: Nicol and Cadell.

Cook, S. F. 1972. *Prehistoric demography.* Reading, MA: Addison-Wesley Modular Publications, Module 16.

Cordy, R. H. 1974. Complex rank cultural systems in the Hawaiian Islands: Suggested explanations for their origins. *Archaeology and Physical Anthropology in Oceania* 9:89–109.

———. 1981. *A study of prehistoric social change: The development of complex societies in the Hawaiian Islands.* New York: Academic Press.

———. 1985a. Investigations of Leluh's stone ruins. *National Geographic Research* 1:255–263.

————. 1985b. Settlement patterns of complex societies in the Pacific. *New Zealand Journal of Archaeology* 7:159–182.

————. 1986. Relationships between the extent of social stratification and population in Micronesian polities at European contact. *American Anthropologist* 88:136–142.

————. 1987. An overview of Ka'u District and some thoughts on island-wide settlement patterns. Paper presented at the First Annual Society for Hawaiian Archaeology Conference, Hawai'i Volcanoes National Park. Manuscript, State Historic Preservation Division, Honolulu.

————. 1993. *The Lelu stone ruins, Kosrae, Micronesia.* Asian and Pacific Archaeology Series. Honolulu: Social Science Research Institute, University of Hawai'i.

————. 1994. *A regional synthesis of Hamakua District, Island of Hawai'i.* Honolulu: State Historic Preservation Division.

————. 1995. Central Kona archaeological settlement patterns. Manuscript on file, State Historic Preservation Division Library, Kapolei.

————. 1996a. The rise and fall of the O'ahu Kingdom: A brief overview of O'ahu's history. In J. Davidson, G. Irwin, B. F. Leach, A. Pawley, and D. Brown, eds., *Oceanic culture history: Essays in honour of Roger Green,* 591–613. New Zealand Journal of Archaeology Special Publication. Wellington.

————. 1996b. Settlement patterns of Wailuku Ahupua'a from Mahele records. Paper presented at 9th Society for Hawaiian Archaeology Conference, Wailea, Maui.

————. 2000. *Exalted sits the chief: The ancient history of Hawai'i Island.* Honolulu: Mutual Publishing.

————. 2001a. Life in 1820–1850 in Kamaile 'Ili, Wai'anae Ahupua'a: A review of the Mahele records. On file, Hawai'i Historic Preservation Division Library, Kapolei.

————. 2001b. Wai'anae Valley Ranch archaeological survey, Wai'anae Ahupua'a, Moku o Wai'anae, O'ahu. On file, Hawai'i Historic Preservation Division Library, Kapolei.

————. 2002a. *An ancient history of Wai'anae: Ka moku o Wai'anae: He mo'olelo o ka wa kahiko.* Honolulu: Mutual Publishing.

————. 2002b. Studying the history of Wai'anae District on O'ahu: The 1997–2000 Wai'anae Valley archaeological field projects of the Wai'anae High School Hawaiian Studies Program, the University of Hawai'i at West O'ahu, and the Hawai'i Historic Preservation Division. In *Proceedings of Easter Island Foundation Conference on Pacific Archaeology, Waimea, Hawai'i, 2000.* Easter Island Foundation.

————. 2003. Houses and intensive cultivation (irrigated and dryland): Archaeological work in Wai'anae Valley. Presented at Society for Hawaiian Archaeology 2003 meetings, Kāne'ohe.

Cordy, R., N. Pak, C. Johnson, M. J. Lee, and M. McFadden. Forthcoming. Nanakuli: A Leeward O'ahu Valley. Draft manuscript, Hawai'i Historic Preservation Division Library, Kapolei.

Cordy, R., A. Sinoto, D. Naboa, and M. Ortega. 2003. Large heiau and power: Major heiau in Wai'anae Valley. Presented at Society for Hawaiian Archaeology 2003 meetings, Kāne'ohe.

Cordy, R., J. Tainter, R. Renger, and R. Hitchcock. 1991. *An ahupua'a study: The 1971 archaeological work at Kaloko Ahupua'a, North Kona, Hawai'i.* Western Archaeological and Conservation Center Publications in Anthropology 58. Honolulu: National Park Service.

Corney, B. G., ed. 1913. *The quest and occupation of Tahiti by emissaries of Spain during the Years 1772–1776*. Vol. 1. London: Hakluyt Society.

Coulter, J. W. 1941. *Land utilization in American Samoa*. Bernice P. Bishop Museum Bulletin 170. Honolulu: Bishop Museum Press.

Cowgill, G. 1975. Population pressure as non-explanation. *American Antiquity* 40(2):127–131.

Cowling, W. 1990. Motivations for contemporary Tongan migration. In P. Herda, J. Terrell, and N. Gunson, eds., *Tongan culture and history*, 187–205. Canberra: Australian National University Press.

Crane, W. 1992. *The environment of Tonga: A geography resource*. Nuku'alofa: Wendy Crane Books.

Crocombe, R. G. 1964. *Land tenure in the Cook Islands*. Melbourne: Oxford University Press.

———. 1979. *The new South Pacific*. Canberra: Australian National University Press.

Crocombe, R. G., and M. Crocombe. 1972. *The works of Ta'unga. Records of a Polynesian Traveller in the South Seas, 1833–1896*. Canberra: Australian National University Press.

Crosby, A. 1986. *Ecological imperialism: The biological expansion of Europe, A.D. 900–1900*. Cambridge: Cambridge University Press.

Culbert, T. P., and D. S. Rice, eds. 1990. *Precolumbian population history in the Maya lowlands*. Albuquerque: University of New Mexico Press.

Cumberland, K. B. 1962. Conclusion: The problem reviewed and restated. In J. W. Fox and K. B. Cumberland, eds., *Western Samoa: Land, life and agriculture in tropical Polynesia*, 310–330. Christchurch: Whitcombe and Tombs.

Dauphiné, J. 1989. *Les spoliations foncières en Nouvelle-Calédonie*. Paris: L'Harmattan.

Davidson, J. M. 1967. Excavations of two round-ended house sites in the eastern portion of the 'Opunohu Valley. In R. C. Green, K. Green, R. A. Rappaport, A. Rappaport, and J. Davidson, eds., *Archaeology of the island of Mo'orea, French Polynesia*, 119–140. Anthropological Papers of the American Museum of Natural History 51 (pt. 2). New York: American Museum of Natural History.

———. 1969a. Archaeological excavations in two burial mounds at 'Atele, Tongatapu. *Records of the Auckland Institute and Museum* 6:251–286.

———. 1969b. Settlement patterns in Samoa before 1840. *Journal of the Polynesian Society* 78:44–82.

———. 1971. Preliminary report on archaeological survey of the Vava'u Group, Tonga. *Royal Society of New Zealand Bulletin* 8:29–40.

———. 1974a. Samoan structural remains and settlement patterns. In R. C. Green and J. M. Davidson, eds., *Archaeology in Western Samoa*, vol. 2, 225–244. Bulletin No. 7. Auckland: Auckland Institute and Museum.

———. 1974b. Site surveys on 'Upolu. In R. C. Green and J. M. Davidson, eds., *Archaeology in Western Samoa*, vol. 2, 181–204. Bulletin No. 7. Auckland: Auckland Institute and Museum.

———. 1974c. The Upper Falefa Valley project: Summaries and conclusions. In R. C.

Green and J. M. Davidson, eds., *Archaeology in Western Samoa*, vol. 2, 155–162. Bulletin No. 7. Auckland: Auckland Institute and Museum.

———. 1977. Western Polynesia and Fiji: Prehistoric contact, diffusion and differentiation in adjacent archipelagoes. *World Archaeology* 9:82–94.

———. 1979. Tonga and Samoa. In J. D. Jennings, ed., *The prehistory of Polynesia*, 82–109. Cambridge, MA: Harvard University Press.

———. 1984. *The prehistory of New Zealand*. Auckland: Longman Paul.

Davies, J., and D. Darling. 1851. *A Tahitian and English dictionary with introductory remarks on the Polynesian language and a short grammar of the Tahitian dialect.* Papeete: London Missionary Society.

Dening, G. 1974. *The Marquesan journal of Edward Robarts*. Canberra: Australian National University Press.

———. 1986. Possessing Tahiti. *Archaeology in Oceania* 21:103–118.

Descantes, C. 1990. Symbolic stone structures: Proto-historic and early historic settlement patterns in the ʻOpunohu Valley, Moʻorea. Unpublished M.A. thesis, Department of Anthropology, University of Auckland.

Devaney, D., M. Kelly, P. J. Lee, and L. S. Motteler. 1976. *Kāneʻohe: A History of Change.* Honolulu: Bishop Museum Press.

Dewar, R. E. 1984. Environmental productivity, population regulation, and carrying capacity. *American Anthropologist* 86:601–614.

Diamond, J. 2005. *Collapse: How societies choose to fail or succeed*. New York: Viking.

Dickinson, W. R. 2003. Impact of mid-Holocene hydro-isostatic highstand in regional sea level on habitability of islands in the Pacific Ocean. *Journal of Coastal Research* 19:489–503.

Dixon, B., P. J. Conte, V. Nagahara, and W. K. Hodgins. 1999. Risk minimization and the traditional *ahupuaʻa* in Kahikinui, Island of Maui, Hawaiʻi. *Asian Perspectives* 38:229–255.

———. 2000. Kahikinui Mauka: Archaeological research in the lowland dry forest of leeward East Maui. Manuscript in 3 vols., Hawaiʻi Historic Preservation Division. On file, Hawaiʻi Historic Preservation Division Library, Kapolei.

Dixon, B., D. Gosser, S. Williams, J. Robins, C. Oʻhare, L. Gilda, and S. Clark. 2003. Final report: Cultural resources survey of selected lands, Naval Magazine Pearl Harbor, Lualualei Branch, Island of Oʻahu, Hawaiʻi. AMEC manuscript.

Dixon, G. 1789. *A voyage round the world, but more particularly to the North-West Coast of America*. London: George Goulding.

Djindjian, F. 1991. *Méthodes pour l'archéologie*. Paris: Armand Colin.

Dobyns, H. F. 1966. Estimating aboriginal American population: An appraisal of techniques with a new hemispheric estimate. *Current Anthropology* 7:395–416.

———. 1983. *Their number become thinned: Native American population dynamics in eastern North America*. Knoxville: University of Tennessee Press.

Donham, T. 1987. Archaeological reconnaissance survey: Proposed Awakee Resort Development Project Area, land of Awakee, North Kona, island of Hawaii. PHRI manuscript. On file, Hawaiʻi Historic Preservation Division Library, Kapolei.

———. 1996. A summary of archaeological finds in Wailuku showing settlement patterns. Paper presented at the 9th Annual Conference of the Society for Hawaiian Archaeology, Wailea, Maui.

———. 2002. Data recovery excavations at the Honokahua burial site: Land of Hono-kahu, Lahaina District, island of Maui. PHRI manuscript. On file, Hawai'i Historic Preservation Division Library, Kapolei.

Doumenge, J. P. 1982. *Du terroir . . . à la ville: Les Mélanésiens et leurs espaces en Nou-velle-Calédonie.* Bordeaux: Centre d'Etudes de Géographie Tropicale.

Drennan, R. D. 1987. Regional demography in chiefdoms. In R. D. Drennan and C. A. Uribe, eds., *Chiefdoms in the Americas,* 307–324. Lanham, MD: University Press of America.

Dubois, M. J. 1989. Lapérouse en Nouvelle-Calédonie. *Bulletin de la Société d'Etudes Historiques de la Nouvelle-Calédonie* 79:24–27.

Dunmore, J., ed. 1994. *The journal of Jean-François de Galaup de la Pérouse, 1785–1788.* Hakluyt Society, Second Series No. 179. London: The Hakluyt Society.

Dye, T. S. 1988. Appendix C: Archaeological investigations on Tafahi Island. In P. V. Kirch, *Niuatoputapu: The prehistory of a Polynesian chiefdom,* 278–287. Burke Mu-seum Monograph 5. Seattle: Burke Museum.

———. 1994. Population trends in Hawai'i before 1778. *Hawaiian Journal of History* 28:1–20.

———. 1996. Early eastern Lapita to Polynesian Plainware at Tongatapu and Lifuka: An exploratory data analysis and comparison. In J. M. Davidson, G. Irwin, B. F. Leach, A. Pawley and D. Brown, eds., *Oceanic culture history: Essays in honour of Roger Green,* 461–473. Auckland: New Zealand Journal of Archaeology Special Publication.

Dye, T., and E. Komori. 1992a. Computer programs for creating cumulative probability curves and annual frequency distribution diagrams with radiocarbon dates. *New Zealand Journal of Archaeology* 14:35–43.

———. 1992b. A pre-censal population history of Hawai'i. *New Zealand Journal of Ar-chaeology* 14:113–128.

Dye, T. S., and D. W. Steadman. 1990. Polynesian ancestors and their animal world. *American Scientist* 78:207–215.

Earle, T. 1978. *Economic and social organization of a complex chiefdom: The Halele'a District, Kauai, Hawaii.* Anthropological Papers of the Museum of Anthropology, University of Michigan 63. Ann Arbor: University of Michigan.

Edmond, R. 1999. Missionaries on Tahiti, 1797–1840. In A. Calder, J. Lamb, and B. Orr, eds., *Voyages and beaches: Pacific encounters, 1769–1840,* 226–240. Honolulu: Univer-sity of Hawai'i Press.

Edwards, E. 1915 [1790–1791]. Captain Edwards' reports. In E. Edwards and G. Hamil-ton, with B. Thomsen, *Voyage of HMS "Pandora," 1790–1791,* 27–89. London: Francis Edwards.

Ehrlich, P. R., and A. H. Ehrlich. 1991. *Healing the planet: Strategies for resolving the en-vironmental crisis.* Reading, MA: Addison–Wesley.

Ehrlich, P. R., A. H. Ehrlich, and J. P. Holdren. 1977. *Ecoscience: Population, resources, environment.* San Francisco: W. H. Freeman and Co.

Elder, J., and J. Youl. 1805. *L.M.S. journal round Eimeo, 11 Oct.–1 Nov.* Tahiti.

Ellis, W. 1829. *Polynesian researches.* 2 vols. London: Fischer, Son & Jackson.

———. 1831. *Polynesian researches during a residence of nearly eight years in the Society and Sandwich Islands.* 4 vols. London: Fisher, Son & Jackson.

———. 1963 [1827]. *Narrative of a tour of Hawaii, or Owhyhee.* Honolulu: Advertiser Publishing.

Emory, K. P. 1924. *The island of Lanai: A survey of native culture.* Bernice P. Bishop Museum Bulletin 12. Honolulu: Bishop Museum Press.

———. 1928. *Archaeology of Nihoa and Necker Islands.* Bernice P. Bishop Museum Bulletin 53. Honolulu: Bishop Museum Press.

Erskine, J. E. 1853. *Journal of a cruise among the islands of the western Pacific in Her Majesty's Ship* Havannah. London: John Murray.

Evans, M. 2001. *Persistence of the gift: Tongan tradition in transnational context.* Toronto: Wilfred Laurier University Press.

Farrell, B. H., and R. G. Ward. 1962. The village and its agriculture. In J. W. Fox and K. B. Cumberland, eds., *Western Samoa: Land, life and agriculture in tropical Polynesia,* 177–238. Christchurch: Whitcombe and Tombs.

Firth, R. 1957. *We, the Tikopia.* 2d ed. London: Allen and Unwin.

Fischer, J. L., S. H. Riesenberg, and M. G. Whiting. 1977. *Annotations to the Book of Luelen.* Canberra: Australian National University Press.

Fornander, A. 1880. *An account of the Polynesian race, its origins and migrations, and the ancient history of the Polynesian people to the times of Kamehameha I.* Vol. 2. London: Trubner.

Forster, G. A. 1777. *A Voyage round the world in His Brittanic Majesty's Sloop,* Resolution, *commanded by Captain James Cook, during the years 1772, 3, 4 and 5.* 2 vols. London: B. White, J. Robson, P. Elmsly, and G. Robinson.

Forster, J. R. 1778. *Observations made during a voyage around the world in physical geography, natural history, and ethic philosophy.* London: G. Robinson.

———. 1996 [1778]. *Observations made during a voyage round the world.* Ed. N. Thomas, H. Guest, and M. Bettlebach. Honolulu: University of Hawai'i Press.

Fosberg, F. R. 1991. Polynesian plant environment. In P. A. Cox and S. A. Banack, eds., *Islands, plants and Polynesians: An introduction to Polynesian ethnobotany,* 11–23. Portland, OR: Dioscorides Press.

Fox, J. W., and K. B. Cumberland, eds. 1962. *Western Samoa: Land, life and agriculture in tropical Polynesia.* Christchurch, New Zealand: Whitcombe and Tombs.

Freeman, D. 1964. Some observations on kinship and political authority in Samoa. *American Anthropologist* 66:553–568.

Gallagher, R. E., ed. 1964. *Byron's journal of his circumnavigation, 1764–1766.* London: Hakluyt Society.

Garnier, J. 1867. *Voyage à la Nouvelle-Calédonie.* Paris: Le Tour du Monde.

Gibbs, H. S. 1976. *Soils of Tongatapu, Tonga.* New Zealand Soil Survey Report 35. Wellington.

Gifford, E. W. 1929. *Tongan society.* Bernice P. Bishop Museum Bulletin 61. Honolulu: Bishop Museum Press.

Gill, W. 1856. *Gems from the coral islands.* 2 vols. London: Ward.

Gilson, R. P. 1970. *Samoa 1830 to 1900.* Melbourne: Oxford University Press.

Glassow, M. A. 1978. The concept of carrying capacity in the study of culture process. *Advances in Archaeological Method and Theory* 1:31–48.

———. 1999. Measurement of population growth and decline during California prehistory. *Journal of California and Great Basin Anthropology* 21:45–66.

Goldman, I. 1970. *Ancient Polynesian society.* Chicago: University of Chicago Press.

Goldsmith, M. 1974. Ethnic organization of Tokelauans in Western Samoa. Unpublished manuscript, Department of Anthropology, University of Illinois at Urbana-Champaign.

———. 1975. Tokelau ethnic organizations in Western and American Samoa. Unpublished manuscript, Department of Anthropology, University of Illinois at Urbana-Champaign.

Graves, M. W., B. V. O'Connor, and T. N. Ladefoged. 2002. Tracking changes in community-scaled organization in Kohala and Kona, Hawai'i Island. In T. N. Ladefoged and M. W. Graves, eds., *Pacific landscapes: Archaeological approaches,* 231–254. Los Osos, CA: Easter Island Foundation.

Green, R. C. 1961. Moorean archaeology: A preliminary report. *Man* 61:169–173.

———. 1967. Settlement patterns: Four case studies from Polynesia. In W. G. Solheim, ed., *Archaeology at the eleventh Pacific Science Congress,* 101–132. Asian and Pacific Archaeology Series No. 1. Honolulu: Social Science Research Institute, University of Hawai'i.

———. 1969a. Archaeological investigation of Western Samoan prehistory. In R. C. Green and J. M. Davidson, eds., *Archaeology in Western Samoa,* vol. 1:3–11. Auckland Institute and Museum Bulletin No. 7.

———. 1969b. A lava tube refuge at Mulifanua. In R. C. Green and J. M. Davidson, eds., *Archaeology in Western Samoa,* vol. 1:267–270. Auckland Institute and Museum Bulletin No. 7.

———. 1972. Revision of the Tongan sequence. *Journal of the Polynesian Society* 81:79–86.

———. 1973. Tonga's prehistoric population. *Pacific Viewpoint* 14:61–74.

———. 1974. A review of portable artifacts from Western Samoa. In R. Green and J. Davidson, eds., *Archaeology in Western Samoa,* vol. 2:108–154. Auckland Institute and Museum Bulletin 7.

———. 1980. *Makaha before 1880 A.D.: Makaha Valley Historical Project summary report 5.* Pacific Anthropological Records 31. Honolulu: Bishop Museum Press.

———. 1993. Tropical Polynesian prehistory: Where are we now? In M. Spriggs, D. Yen, W. Ambrose, R. Jones, A. Thorne, and A. Andrews, eds., *A community of culture: The people and prehistory of the Pacific,* 218–238. Canberra: Australian National University.

———. 1996. Settlement patterns and complex society in the windward Society Islands: Retrospective commentary from the 'Opunohu Valley, Mo'orea. In M. Julien, M. Orliac, and C. Orliac, eds., *Mémoire de Pierre, mémoire d'homme: Tradition et archéologie en Océanie,* 209–227. Paris: Publications de la Sorbonne.

———. 2002. A retrospective view of settlement pattern studies in Samoa. In T. N. Ladefoged and M. Graves, eds., *Pacific landscapes: Archaeological approaches,* 125–152. Los Osos, CA: Easter Island Foundation.

———. 2003. The Lapita horizon and tradition: Signature for one set of Oceanic migrations. In C. Sand, ed., *Pacific archaeology: Assessments and prospects,* 99–124. Les cahiers de l'Archéologie en Nouvelle-Calédonie 15. Nouméa: Service de la Culture et du Patrimoine.

Green R. C., and J. M. Davidson. 1974. Conclusion. In R. C. Green and J. M. Davidson, eds., *Archaeology in Western Samoa,* vol. 2:278–282. Auckland Institute and Museum Bulletin No. 7.

Green, R. C., and C. Descantes. 1989. Site records of the 'Opunohu Valley, Mo'orea. Typescript report. Auckland: Green Foundation for Polynesian Research.

Green, R. C., and K. Green. 1967. Interpretation of round-ended house sites of the 'Opunohu Valley based on excavation of an example in the western portion of the valley. In R. C. Green, K. Green, R. A. Rappaport, A. Rappaport, and J. Davidson, eds., *Archaeology of the island of Mo'orea, French Polynesia,* 162–176. Anthropological Papers of the American Museum of Natural History 51 (pt. 2). New York: American Museum of Natural History.

Green, R. C., K. Green, R. A. Rappaport, A. Rappaport, and J. Davidson. 1967. *Archaeology of the island of Mo'orea, French Polynesia.* Anthropological Papers of the American Museum of Natural History 51 (pt. 2). New York: American Museum of Natural History.

Green, R. C., and V. J. Green. 2002. Ma(q)oli — across space, through time: Towards an understanding of migration to, from and within Polynesia over three millennia. Research Fellowship Seminar Paper, University of Otago. Dunedin, New Zealand.

Groube, L. M. 1970. The origin and development of earthwork fortifications in the Pacific. In R. C. Green and M. Kelly, eds., *Studies in Oceanic culture history,* vol. 1:133–164. Pacific Anthropological Records No. 11. Honolulu: Bishop Museum Press.

———. 1971. Tonga, Lapita pottery and Polynesian origins. *Journal of the Polynesian Society* 80:278–316.

Guiart, J. 1963. *Structure de la chefferie en Mélanésie du sud.* Paris: Institut d'Ethnologie, Musée de l'Homme.

Gunson, N. 1993. Understanding Polynesian traditional history. *Journal of the Polynesian Society* 28:139–158.

Hale, Horatio. 1981 [1846]. *United States Exploring Expedition during the years 1838, 1839, 1840, 1841, 1842, under the command of Charles Wilkes, USN: Ethnology and philology.* Reprinted in ko na fakamatalaga Tuhia a ni Papalagi e uiga ki Tokelau 1765–1925 (Papalagi documents on Tokelau 1765–1925). Apia and Auckland: Office for Tokelau Affairs, 38–55. [Philadelphia: Lea and Blanchard; excerpts 149–161, 358–364.]

Hammel, G. 1996. Demographic constraints on population growth of early humans: Emphasis on the probable role of females in overcoming such constraints. *Human Nature: An Interdisciplinary Biosocial Perspective* 7:217–255.

Handy, E. S. C. 1923. *The native culture in the Marquesas.* Bernice P. Bishop Museum Bulletin 9. Honolulu: Bishop Museum Press.

———. 1932. *Houses, boats, and fishing in the Society Islands.* Bernice P. Bishop Museum Bulletin 90. Honolulu: Bishop Museum Press.

———. 1940. *The Hawaiian planter. Vol. 1: His plants, methods and areas of cultivation.* Bernice P. Bishop Museum Bulletin 161. Honolulu: Bishop Museum Press.

Handy, E. S. C., and M. K. Pukui. 1958. *The Polynesian family system in Ka'u, Hawai'i.* Wellington: Polynesian Society.

Harre, J. 1968. A model for the analysis of island emigration. *Journal of the Polynesian Society* 77:177–186.

Harris, P. M. G. 2001. *The history of human populations.* Vol. 1: *Forms of growth and decline.* Westport, CT: Praeger.

Hartshorn, A. S., O. A. Chadwick, P. M. Vitousek, and P. V. Kirch. 2006. Prehistoric agricultural depletion of soil nutrients in Hawai'i. *Proceedings of the National Academy of Sciences (USA)* 103:11,092–11,097.

Hassan, F. A. 1979. Demography and archaeology. *Annual Review of Anthropology* 8:137–160.

———. 1981. *Demographic archaeology.* New York: Academic Press.

Hatcher, J., and M. Bailey. 2001. *Modeling the Middle Ages: The history and theory of England's economic development.* Oxford: Oxford University Press.

Hawkesworth, J., ed. 1789. *An account of the voyages undertaken by the order of his present Majesty for making discoveries in the Southern Hemisphere and successively performed by Commodore Byron, Captain Wallis, Captain Carteret and Captain Cook, in the* Dolphin, *the* Swallow, *and the* Endeavour; *drawn up from the journals which were kept by several commanders and from the papers of Sir Joseph Banks.* 3 vols. Perth: R. Morison, Jr.

Heath, T. 1838a. Letter from Manono dated April 16, 1838. Manuscript, London Missionary Society, South Seas Letters and Journals, Box 11, Folder 8, Jacket A.

———. 1838b. The war of A'ana: A Samoan tale. Enclosed with letter dated April 16, 1838. Manuscript, London Missionary Society, South Seas Letters and Journals, Box 11, Folder 8, Jacket A.

———. 1840a. The Navigator's or Samoa Islands: Their manners, customs and superstitions. *The Polynesian* 1(15), September 19.

———. 1840b. The Navigator's or Samoa Islands: Their manners, customs and superstitions cont'd. *The Polynesian* 1(16), September 26.

Henry, T. 1928. *Ancient Tahiti.* Bernice P. Bishop Museum Bulletin 48. Honolulu: Bishop Museum Press.

Hill, J. B., J. J. Clark, W. H. Doelle, and P D. Lyons. 2004. Prehistoric demography in the Southwest: Migration, coalescence and Hohokam population decline. *American Antiquity* 69:689–716.

Holmes, L. D. 1974. *Samoan village.* New York: Holt, Rinehart and Winston.

Home, Sir E. 1844. Visit of *North Star.* Admiralty records, accounts of visits to Samoa of British naval vessels. Adm. 1/5548. London: The Admiralty.

Hommon, R. J. 1976. The formation of primitive states in pre-Contact Hawaii. Unpublished Ph.D. dissertation, University of Arizona, Tucson. Ann Arbor: University Microfilms.

———. 1980. Historic resources of Kaho'olawe. National Register of Historic Places Inventory Nomination. Manuscript on file, State Historic Preservation Division Library, Kapolei.

———. 1986. Social evolution in ancient Hawai'i. In P. V. Kirch, ed., *Island societies: Archaeological approaches to evolution and transformation,* 55–68. Cambridge: Cambridge University Press.

———. 1992. The view from out on a limb, or confessions of a generalist. *New Zealand Journal of Archaeology* 14:151–158.

Hooker, J. D. 1896. *Journal of the Right Hon. Sir Joseph Banks.* London: MacMillan and Co.

Hooper, A. 1975. A Tokelau account of Olosega. *Journal of Pacific History* 10:89–93.

———. 1982. Aid and dependency in a small Pacific territory. Working Paper No. 62. Department of Anthropology, University of Auckland.

———. 1994. Ghosts of hierarchy I: The transformation of chiefly authority on Fakaofo, Tokelau. In M. Jolly and M. S. Mosko, eds., *Transformations of hierarchy: Structure, history and horizon in the Austronesian world. History and Anthropology* special issue 7(1–4): 307–320. Basel: Harwood Academic Publishers GmbH.

Hooper, A., and J. Huntsman. 1973. A demographic history of the Tokelau Islands. *Journal of the Polynesian Society* 82:366–411.

Houghton, P. 1980. *The first New Zealanders.* Auckland: Hodder & Stoughton.

———. 1996. *People of the Great Ocean: Aspects of the human biology of the early Pacific.* Cambridge: Cambridge University Press.

Hudson, W. L. 1981 [1846]. Excerpts from United States Exploring Expedition during the years 1838, 1839, 1840, 1841, 1842, under the command of Charles Wilkes, USN: Ethnology and philology. Reprinted in ko na fakamatalaga Tuhia a ni Papalagi e uiga ki Tokelau 1765–1925 (Papalagi documents on Tokelau 1765–1925). Apia and Auckland: Office for Tokelau Affairs, 57–78. [Philadelphia: Lea and Blanchard; August 1840–February 1842.]

Hunter-Anderson, R. 1991. A review of traditional Micronesian high island horticulture in Belau, Yap, Chuuk, Pohnpei, and Kosrae. *Micronesica* 24:1–56.

Huntsman, J. 1971. Concepts of kinship and categories of kinsmen in the Tokelau Islands. *Journal of the Polynesian Society* 80:317–354.

———. 1975. The impact of cultural exchange on health and disease patterns: The Tokelau Island Migrant Study. In Y. Chang and P. J. Donaldson, eds., *Population change in the Pacific region*, 183–192. Vancouver, BC: Proceedings of the 13th Pacific Science Congress.

———. 1994. Ghosts of hierarchy II: Transformations of the wider Tokelau polity. In M. Jolly and M. S. Mosko, eds., *Transformations of hierarchy: Structure, history and horizon in the Austronesian world. History and Anthropology* special issue 7(1–4):321–338. Basel: Harwood Academic Publishers GmbH.

Huntsman, J., and A. Hooper. 1976. The desecration of Tokelau kinship. *Journal of the Polynesian Society* 85:257–273.

———. 1985. Structures of Tokelau history. In A. Hooper and J. Huntsman, eds., *Transformations of Polynesian culture*, 133–149. Memoir 45. Auckland: Polynesian Society.

———. 1996. *Tokelau.* Auckland: Auckland University Press.

Huntsman, J., A. Hooper, and R. Ward. 1986. Genealogies as culture and biology: A Tokelau case study. *Mankind* 16:13–30.

'I'i, J. P. 1959. *Fragments of Hawaiian history.* Bishop Museum Special Publication 70. Honolulu: Bishop Museum Press.

Illouz, C. 2000. Chronique meurtrière d'une mutation théologique: Maré (Îles Loyauté).

In A. Bensa and I. Leblic, eds., *En pays Kanak: Ethnologie, linguistique, archéologie, histoire de la Nouvelle-Calédonie,* 195–215. Collection Ethnologie de la France 14. Paris: Éditions de la Maison des Sciences de l'Homme.

Inglis, J. 1887. *In the New Hebrides: Reminiscences of missionary life and work, especially on the island of Aneityum, from 1850 till 1877.* London: Nelson and Sons.

———. 1890. *Bible illustrations from the New Hebrides.* London: Nelson and Sons.

Irwin, G. 1992. *The prehistoric exploration and colonisation of the Pacific.* Cambridge: Cambridge University Press.

Jackes, M. 1994. Birth rates and bones. In A. Heming and L. Chan, eds., *Strength in diversity: A reader in physical anthropology,* 155–185. Toronto: Canadian Scholars' Press.

Jackmond, G., and R. N. Holmer. 1980. Appendix: Sapapali'i settlement. In J. D. Jennings and R. N. Holmer, eds., *Archaeological investigations in Western Samoa,* 147–152. Pacific Anthropological Records 32. Honolulu: Bishop Museum Press.

Jamet, R. 2000. *Les sols de Moorea et des Îles Sous-le-Vent.* Collection Notice Explicative No. 113. Paris: Éditions de l'IRD.

Jenkinson, D. S. 1990. The turnover of organic carbon and nitrogen in soil. *Philosophical Transactions of the Royal Society of London, Series B* 329:361–368.

Jennings, J. D., and R. Holmer, eds. 1980. *Archaeological investigations in Western Samoa.* Pacific Anthropological Records 32. Honolulu: Bishop Museum Press.

Jennings, J. D., R. Holmer, and G. Jackmond. 1982. Samoan village patterns: Four examples. *Journal of the Polynesian Society* 91:81–102.

Johansson, S. R., and S. Horowitz. 1986. Estimating mortality in skeletal populations: Influence of the growth rate on the interpretation of levels and trends during the transition to agriculture. *American Journal of Physical Anthropology* 71:233–250.

Johnson, A., and T. Earle. 1987. *The evolution of human societies: From foraging group to agrarian state.* Stanford: Stanford University Press.

Joppien, R., and B. Smith, eds. 1985. *The art of Captain Cook's voyages.* Vol. 1: *The voyage of the* Endeavour, *1768–1771.* New Haven: Yale University Press.

———. 1985. *The art of Captain Cook's voyages.* Vol. 2: *The voyage of the* Resolution *and* Adventure, *1772–1775.* New Haven: Yale University Press.

———. 1988a. *The art of Captain Cook's voyages.* Vol. 3 catalogue: *The voyage of the* Resolution *and* Discovery, *1776–1780.* New Haven: Yale University Press.

———. 1988b. *The art of Captain Cook's voyages.* Vol. 3 text: *The voyage of the* Resolution *and* Discovery, *1776–1780.* New Haven: Yale University Press.

Kaeppler, A. 1978. Exchange patterns in goods and spouses: Fiji, Tonga and Samoa. *Mankind* 11:246–252.

Kahn, J. G. 2003. Ma'ohi social organization at the micro-scale: Household archaeology in the 'Opunohu Valley, Mo'orea, Society Islands (French Polynesia). In C. Sand, ed., *Pacific archaeology: Assessments and prospects,* 353–467. Le Cahiers de l'Archéologie en Nouvelle-Calédonie 15. Nouméa.

Kahn, J. G., and P. V. Kirch. 2001. Preliminary report of archaeological research activities carried out in the 'Opunohu Valley, Mo'orea, between July 7–August 30, 2001. Unpublished research report. Berkeley: University of California.

———. 2003. The ancient "House society" of the 'Opunohu Valley, Mo'orea: Overview of an archaeological project, 2000–2002. In H. Marchesi, ed., *Bilan de la recherche archéologique en Polynésie Française 2001–2002*, 21–34. Punaauia, Tahiti: Service de la Culture et du Patrimoine.

———. 2004. Ethnographie préhistorique d'une "société à maisons" dans la vallée de 'Opunohu (Mo'orea, Îles de la Société). *Journal de la Société des Océanistes* 119:229–256.

Kamakau, S. M. 1961. *Ruling Chiefs of Hawaii*. Honolulu: Kamehameha Schools Press.

———. 1964. *Ka po'e kahiko: The people of old*. Trans. Mary Kawena Pukui, ed. Dorothy B. Barrère. Bishop Museum Special Publication 51. Honolulu: Bishop Museum Press.

———. 1976. *The works of the people of old: Na hana a ka po'e kahiko*. Bishop Museum Special Publication 61. Honolulu: Bishop Museum Press.

———. 1991. *Tales and traditions of the people of old: Na mo'olelo a ka po'e kahiko*. Honolulu: Bishop Museum Press.

Kasarhérou, C. 1992. Histoire démographique de la population Mélanésienne de la Nouvelle-Calédonie entre 1840 et 1950. Unpublished thèse de doctorat, Université Paris I.

Kasarhérou, E. 1990. Les saisons et les jardins. *De jade et de nacre: Patrimoine artistique Kanak,* 50–67. Paris: Réunion des Musées Nationaux.

Keating, B. H., D. P. Mattey, J. Naughton, C. E. Helsley, D. Epp, A. Lararwicz, and D. Schwank. 1984. Evidence for a hot spot origin of the Caroline Islands. *Journal of Geophysical Research* 89:9,937–9,948.

Kellum-Ottino, M. 1971. *Archéologie d'une vallée des Îles Marquises*. Paris: Publications de la Société des Océanistes.

Kelly, J., and B. Marshall. 1996. *Atlas of New Zealand boundaries*. Auckland: Auckland University Press.

Kelly, R. L. 1995. *The foraging spectrum: Diversity in hunter gatherer lifeways*. Washington, DC: Smithsonian Institution Press.

Kikuchi, W. K. 1963. Archaeological surface ruins in American Samoa. Unpublished M.A. thesis, University of Hawai'i, Honolulu.

Kingsland, S. E. 1985. *Modeling nature: Episodes in the history of population ecology*. Chicago: University of Chicago Press.

Kirch, P. V. 1980. Polynesian prehistory: Cultural adaptation in island ecosystems. *American Scientist* 68:39–48.

———. 1982. The impact of the prehistoric Polynesians on the Hawaiian ecosystem. *Pacific Science* 36:1–14.

———. 1984. *The evolution of the Polynesian chiefdoms*. Cambridge: Cambridge University Press.

———. 1985. *Feathered gods and fishhooks: An introduction to Hawaiian archaeology and prehistory*. Honolulu: University of Hawai'i Press.

———. 1986. Rethinking East Polynesian prehistory. *Journal of the Polynesian Society* 95:9–40.

———. 1988a. Long-distance exchange and island colonisation: The Lapita case. *Norwegian Archaeological Review* 21:103–117.

———. 1988b. *Niuatoputapu: The prehistory of a Polynesian chiefdom*. Burke Museum Monograph 5. Seattle: Burke Museum.

———. 1991. Polynesian agricultural systems. In P. A. Cox and S. A. Banack, eds., *Is-*

lands, plants and Polynesians: An introduction to Polynesian ethnobotany, 113–133. Portland, OR: Dioscorides Press.

———. 1992. *The archaeology of history.* Vol. 2 of *Anahulu: The anthropology of history in the Kingdom of Hawaii,* by P. V. Kirch and M. D. Sahlins. Chicago: University of Chicago Press.

———.1994. *The wet and the dry: Irrigation and agricultural intensification in Polynesia.* Chicago: University of Chicago Press.

———. 1997a. Introduction: The environmental history of Oceanic islands. In P. V. Kirch and T. L. Hunt, eds., *Historical ecology in the Pacific Islands: Prehistoric environmental and landscape change,* 1–21. New Haven: Yale University Press.

———. 1997b. Kahikinui: An introduction. In P. V. Kirch, ed., *Na mea kahiko o Kahikinui: Studies in the archaeology of Kahikinui, Maui,* 1–11. Berkeley: Oceanic Archaeology Laboratory, Special Publication No. 1.

———. 1997c. *The Lapita peoples: Ancestors of the Oceanic world.* Oxford: Blackwell Publishers.

———. 1998. Landscapes of power: Late prehistoric settlement and land use of marginal environments in the Hawaiian Islands. In P. Vargas, ed., *Easter Island and East Polynesian prehistory,* 59–72. Proceedings of the Second International Congress on Easter Island and East Polynesian Archaeology. Santiago: Instituto de Estudios Isla de Pascua, Universidad de Chile.

———. 2000. *On the road of the winds: An archaeological history of the Pacific Islands before European contact.* Berkeley: University of California Press.

Kirch, P. V., ed. 1997. *Na mea kahiko o Kahikinui: Studies in the archaeology of Kahikinui, Maui.* Berkeley: Oceanic Archaeology Laboratory, Special Publication No. 1.

Kirch, P. V., O. Chadwick, M. Graves, S. Hotchkiss, T. Ladefoged, S. Tuljapurkar, and P. M. Vitousek. 2001. Human ecodynamics in the Hawaiian ecosystem, from 1200–200 yr B.P. Grant proposal submitted to the National Science Foundation.

Kirch, P. V., and R. C. Green. 2001. *Hawaiki, ancestral Polynesia: An essay in historical anthropology.* Cambridge: Cambridge University Press.

Kirch, P. V., A. S. Hartshorn, O. A. Chadwick, P. M. Vitousek, D. R. Sherrod, J. Coil, L. Holm, and W. D. Sharp. 2004. Environment, agriculture, and settlement patterns in a marginal Polynesian landscape. *Proceedings National Academy of Sciences, USA* 101:9,936–9,941.

Kirch, P. V., and M. Kelly, eds. 1975. *Prehistory and ecology in a windward Hawaiian valley: Halawa Valley, Molokai.* Pacific Anthropological Records 24. Honolulu: Bishop Museum Press.

Kirch, P.V., and D. Lepofsky. 1993. Polynesian irrigation: Archaeological and linguistic evidence for origins and development. *Asian Perspectives* 32:183–204.

Kirch, P. V., and S. O'Day. 2003. New archaeological insights into food and status: A case study from pre-Contact Hawaii. *World Archaeology* 34:484–497.

Kirch, P. V., and M. Sahlins. 1992. *Anahulu: The anthropology of history in the Kingdom of Hawaii.* 2 vols. Chicago: University of Chicago Press.

Kirch, P. V., and W. D. Sharp. 2005. Coral [230]Th dating of the imposition of a ritual control hierarchy in precontact Hawaii. *Science* 307:102–104.

Kirch, P. V., and D. E. Yen. 1982. *Tikopia: The prehistory and ecology of a Polynesian outlier.* Bernice P. Bishop Museum Bulletin 238. Honolulu: Bishop Museum Press.

Kolb, M. 1991. Social power, chiefly authority, and ceremonial architecture in an island polity, Maui, Hawaii. Unpublished Ph.D. thesis, Department of Anthropology, UCLA.

Kolb, M., P. J. Conte, and R. Cordy. 1997. Kula: The archaeology of upcountry Maui in Waiohuli and Keokea. Manuscript on file, Hawai'i Historic Preservation Division Library, Kapolei.

Kramer, A. 1902. *Die Samoa-Inseln.* Vol. 1. Stuttgart: E. Schweizerbartsche Verlagsbuchhandlung (E. Nagele).

Ladefoged, T. N. 1991. Hawaiian architectural transformations during the early historic era. *Asian Perspectives* 30(1):57–69.

Ladefoged, T. N., and M. W. Graves. 2000. Evolutionary theory and the historical development of dry-land agriculture in North Kohala, Hawai'i. *American Antiquity* 65:423–448.

———. 2005. Modeling the human ecodynamics of Kohala, Hawai'i. In C. M. Stevenson, J. M. Ramirez Aliaga, F. J. Morin, and N. Barbacci, eds., *The Reñaca Papers.* Sixth International Conference on Rapa Nui and the Pacific, 155–160. Los Osos, CA: Easter Island Foundation.

———. 2006. The formation of Hawaiian territories. In I. Lilley, ed., *Archaeology of Oceania,* 259–283. London: Blackwell Press.

———. Forthcoming. Radiocarbon dates from the southern *ahupua'a* of the Kohala fieldsystem. Manuscript on file, Department of Anthropology, University of Auckland.

Ladefoged, T. N., M. W. Graves, and J. Coil. 2005. The introduction of sweet potato in Polynesia: Early remains in Hawai'i. *Journal of the Polynesian Society* 114(4):359–373.

Ladefoged, T. N., M. W. Graves, and R. P. Jennings. 1996. Dryland agricultural expansion and intensification in Kohala, Hawai'i Island. *Antiquity* 70:861–880.

Ladefoged, T. N., M. W. Graves, and M. McCoy. 2003. Archaeological evidence for agricultural development in Kohala, Island of Hawai'i. *Journal of Archaeological Science* 30:923–940.

Lal, R. 1997. Degradation and resilience of soils. *Philosophical Transactions: Biological Sciences* 352:997–1,008.

Lamb, J., V. Smith, and N. Thomas, eds. 2000. *Exploration and exchange: A South Seas anthology, 1680–1900.* Chicago: University of Chicago Press.

Law, R. G. 1977. Genesis in Oceania. *New Zealand Archaeological Association Newsletter* 20:86–106.

Lay, T. E. 1959. A study of certain aspects of human ecology in the Polynesian high islands during the pre-contact period. Unpublished Ph.D. dissertation, University of California.

Lea, D. A. M. 1969. Some non-nutritive functions of food in New Guinea. In F. Gale and G. H. Lawton, eds., *Settlement and encounter,* 173–184. Melbourne: Oxford University Press.

LeBlanc, S. 1971. An addition to Naroll's suggested floor area and settlement population relationship. *American Antiquity* 36:210–211.

Lee, C., S. Tuljapurkar, and P. Vitousek. Forthcoming. Risky business: Temporal and spatial variation in preindustrial dryland agriculture. *Human Ecology.*

Lee, R. D. 1987. Population dynamics of humans and other animals. *Demography* 24:443–465.

Lepofsky, D. 1994. Prehistoric agricultural intensification in the Society Islands, French Polynesia. Unpublished Ph.D. dissertation, University of California, Berkeley.

———. 1995. A radiocarbon chronology for prehistoric agriculture in the Society Islands, French Polynesia. *Radiocarbon* 37:917–930.

———. 1999. Gardens of Eden? An ethnohistoric reconstruction of Ma'ohi (Tahitian) cultivation. *Ethnohistory* 46:1–29.

Lepofsky, D., H. C. Carries, and M. M. Kellum. 1992. Early coconuts on Mo'orea Island, French Polynesia. *Journal of the Polynesian Society* 101:299–308.

Lepofsky, D., P. V. Kirch, and K. P. Lertzman. 1996. Stratigraphic and paleobotanical evidence for prehistoric human-induced environmental disturbance on Mo'orea, French Polynesia. *Pacific Science* 50:253–273.

Lesson, P. A. 1981 [1844]. Note sur les maladies des indigènes des Iles Marquises en 1844. *Bulletin de la Société des Etudes Océaniennes* 18 (216):915–943.

Lightfoot, K. 1995. Culture contact studies: Redefining the relationship between prehistoric and historical archaeology. *American Antiquity* 60:199–217.

Lightfoot, K. G., and W. S. Simmons. 1998. Culture contact in protohistoric California: Social contexts of native and European encounters. *Journal of California and Great Basin Anthropology* 20:138–170.

Lisiansky, U. 1814. *Voyage round the World, 1803–1806, in the ship "Neva."* London: Longmans.

Long, W. H. 1979. The low yields of corn in Medieval England. *The Economic History Review, New Series* 32:459–469.

Lowenthal, D. 1985. *The past is a foreign country.* Cambridge: Cambridge University Press.

Lummis, T. 1997. *Pitcairn Island: Life and death in Eden.* Burlington, VT: Ashgate Publishing Co.

Lütke, F. P. 1835. *Voyage autour du monde, exécuté par ordre de sa Majesté l'Empereur Nicolas 1er sur la Corvette Le Seniavine, dans les anneés 1826, 1827, 1828, et 1829.* Paris: Didot Frères.

Lyons, L. 1842. Statisticks book. Manuscript on file, Hawaiian Mission Children's Society Library, Honolulu.

MacArthur, R. H., and E. O.Wilson. 1967. *The theory of island biogeography.* Princeton: Princeton University Press.

MacDaniels, L. H. 1947. *A study of the fe'i banana and its distribution with reference to Polynesian migrations.* Bernice P. Bishop Museum Bulletin 190. Honolulu: Bishop Museum Press.

MacGillivray, J. 1852–1855. Voyage of HMS *Herald* under the command of Captain H. Mangles Denham, RN, being a private journal kept by John MacGillivray, naturalist, 1852–5. Manuscript held in the Admiralty, London.

Macgregor, G. 1937. *Ethnology of Tokelau Islands.* Bernice P. Bishop Museum Bulletin 146. Honolulu: Bishop Museum Press.

Malo, D. 1839. On the decrease of the population on the Hawaiian Islands. *Hawaiian Spectator* 2:121–130.

———. 1951. *Hawaiian Antiquities.* Bernice P. Bishop Museum Special Publication 2. Honolulu: Bishop Museum Press.

Marck, J. 1999. Revising Polynesian linguistic subgrouping and its culture history implications. In R. Blench and M. Spriggs, eds., *Archaeology and language IV: Language change and cultural transformation,* 95–122. London and New York: Routledge.

———. 2000. *Topics in Polynesian language and culture history.* Pacific Linguistics 504, Research School of Pacific and Asian Studies. Canberra: Australian National University.

Maric, T. 2002. Les vestiges archéologiques du Plateau de Vaikivi, Ua Huka, Marquises. Etude préliminaire. Mémoire de D.E.A. (unpublished master's thesis), Université de la Polynésie Française, Tahiti.

Maric, T., and A. Noury. 2002. Prospection archéologique du Plateau de Vaikivi, Ua Huka, Archipel des Marquises. Campagne 2000. Rapport de Mission. Punaauia, Tahiti: Service de la Culture et du Patrimoine.

Massal, E., and J. Barrau. 1956. *Food plants of the South Sea Islands.* Technical Paper No. 94. Nouméa: South Pacific Commission.

Matagi Tokelau. 1991. *Matagi Tokelau: History and traditions of Tokelau.* English ed. Apia and Suva: Office of Tokelau Affairs and Institute of Pacific Studies.

Mattey, D. P. 1982. The minor and trace element geochemistry of volcanic rocks from Truk, Ponape, and Kusaie, eastern Caroline Islands: The evolution of a young hot spot trace across old Pacific Ocean crust. *Contributions to Mineralogy and Petrology* 80:1–13.

Maude, A. 1965. Population, land and livelihood in Tonga. Unpublished Ph.D. dissertation, Australian National University, Canberra.

———. 1970. Shifting cultivation and population growth in Tonga. *Journal of Tropical Geography* 31:51–64.

———. 1973. Landscape shortage and population pressure in Tonga. In H. C. Brookfield, ed., *The Pacific in transition: Geographical perspectives on adaptation and change,* 721–986. Canberra: Australian National University Press.

Maude, H. E. 1968. *Of islands and men.* Melbourne: Oxford University Press.

———. 1981. *Slavers in paradise: The Peruvian labour trade in Polynesia, 1862–1864.* Stanford: Stanford University Press.

Maxwell, Capt. 1848. Visit of *Dido.* Accounts of visits to Samoa of British Naval Vessels. Adm. 1/5590. London: The Admiralty.

Mayr, E. 1997. *This is biology: The science of the living world.* Cambridge, MA: Harvard University Press.

McAllister, J. G. 1933. *Archaeology of Oahu.* Bernice P. Bishop Museum Bulletin 104. Honolulu: Bishop Museum Press.

McArthur, N. 1967. *Island populations of the Pacific.* Canberra: Australian National University Press.

———. 1970. The demography of primitive populations. *Science* 167:1,097–1,101.

———. 1974. Population and prehistory: The Late Phase on Aneityum. Unpublished Ph.D. thesis, Australian National University, Canberra.

————. 1978. "And, behold, the plague was begun among the people." In N. Gunson, ed., *The changing Pacific: Essays in honour of H. E. Maude,* 273–284. Oxford: Oxford University Press.

————. 1981. *New Hebrides population 1840–1967: A re-interpretation.* SPC Occasional Paper 18. Nouméa: South Pacific Commission.

McArthur, N., I. W. Saunders, and R. L. Tweedie. 1976. Small population isolates: A micro-simulation study. *Journal of the Polynesian Society* 85:307–326.

McArthur, N., and J. F. Yaxley. 1968. *New Hebrides: A report on the first census, 1967.* Sydney: New South Wales Government Printer.

McCarthy, D. D., and D. G. Carter. 1967. Report on filariasis in the Tokelau Islands. Unpublished report to the Medical Research Council of New Zealand, Auckland.

McCoy, M. 2000. Agricultural intensification and land tenure in prehistoric Hawai'i. Unpublished M.A. thesis, University of Auckland, New Zealand.

McFadgen, B. G., F. B. Knox, and T. R. L. Cole. 1994. Radiocarbon calibration curve variations and their implications for the interpretation of New Zealand prehistory. *Radiocarbon* 36:221–236.

McKern, W. C. 1929. *The archaeology of Tonga.* Bernice P. Bishop Museum Bulletin 60. Honolulu: Bishop Museum Press.

McMurtrie, R. E., and H. N. Comins. 1996. The temporal response of forest ecosystems to doubled atmospheric CO_2 concentration. *Global Change Biology* 2:49–57.

Meggitt, M. 1962. Growth and decline of agnatic descent groups among the Mae Enga of the New Guinea Highlands. *Ethnology* 1:158–165.

Meindl, R. S., and K. F. Russell. 1998. Recent advances in method and theory in paleodemography. *Annual Review of Anthropology* 27:375–399.

Métais, P. 1953. Démographie des néo-calédoniens. *Journal de la Société des Océanistes* 3:99–128.

Miller, R. S. 1975. *Misi Gete: John Geddie, pioneer missionary to the New Hebrides.* Launceston: Presbyterian Church of Tasmania.

Millerstrom, S., and P. V. Kirch. 2005. Petroglyphs of Kahikinui, Maui, Hawaiian Islands: Rock images within a Polynesian settlement landscape. *Proceedings of the Prehistoric Society* 70:107–128.

Mills, P. R. 2002. *Hawai'i's Russian adventure: A new look at old history.* Honolulu: University of Hawai'i Press.

Mills, W. 1838. Letter from Apia, dated August 15, enclosing list of schools in his district. Manuscript, London Missionary Society, South Seas Letters and Journals, Box 11, Folder 8, Jacket B.

Missionary Herald. 1823. Mission at the Sandwich Islands; joint letter of the missionaries. *Missionary Herald* 19(10). Boston.

Modjeska, N. 1977. Production among the Duna. Unpublished Ph.D. thesis, Australian National University, Canberra.

————. 1982. Production and inequality: Perspectives from central New Guinea. In A. Strathern, ed., *Inequality in New Guinea Highlands societies,* 50–108. Cambridge: Cambridge University Press.

Molloy, M., and J. Huntsman, 1996. Population regeneration in Tokelau: The case of Nukunonu. *Journal of the Polynesian Society* 105:41–61.

Monfat, A. 1981 [1890]. Les Samoa ou Archipel des Navigateurs: Etude historique et re-ligieuse. Reprinted in translation, in *Ko na fakamatalaga Tuhia a ni Papalagi e uiga ki Tokelau 1765–1925* (Papalagi documents on Tokelau 1765–1925). Apia and Auckland: Office for Tokelau Affairs, 90–93 [304–310].

Monnin, J., and C. Sand. 2004. *Kibo, le serment gravé: Essai de synthèse sur les pétro-glyphes Calédoniens.* Les Cahiers de l'Archéologie en Nouvelle-Calédonie 16. Nou-méa: Service de la Culture et du Patrimoine.

Moore, J., A. Swedlund, and G. Armelagos. 1975. The use of life tables in paleodemogra-phy. *American Antiquity Memoir* 30:57–70.

Morgan, W. N. 1988. *Prehistoric architecture in Micronesia.* Austin: University of Texas Press.

Morrison, J. 1935. *The journal of James Morrison, boatswain's mate of the* Bounty, *de-scribing the mutiny and subsequent misfortunes of the mutineers, together with an ac-count of the Island of Tahiti.* Ed. O. Rutter. London: Golden Cockerel Press.

Morrison, K. D. 1994. The intensification of production: Archaeological approaches. *Journal of Archaeological Method and Theory* 1:111–160.

Mortimer, G. 1791. *Observation and remarks made during a voyage to the islands of Teneriffe, Amsterdam, Maria's Island near Van Diemen's Land, Otaheite, Sandwich Islands, Owhyhee, the Fox Islands on the north west coast of America, Tinian, and from thence to Canton in the brig* Mercury *commanded by John Henry Cox.* London: T. Cadell, R. Robson, and J. Sewell.

Moyle, R. M., ed. 1984. *The Samoan journals of John Williams, 1830 and 1832.* Pacific History Series No. 11. Canberra: Australian National University Press.

MR. 1850–1859. *The Missionary Register of the Presbyterian Church of Nova Scotia.*

Mulrooney, M. A., and T. N. Ladefoged. 2005. Hawaiian *heiau* and agricultural produc-tion in the Kohala dryland field system. *Journal of the Polynesian Society* 114:45–67.

Mulrooney, M. A., T. N. Ladefoged, R. Gibb, and D. McCurdy. 2005. Eight million points per day: Archaeological implications of laser scanning and three-dimensional modeling of Puʻukoholā Heiau, Hawaiʻi Island. *Hawaiian Archaeology* 10:18–28.

Munford, J. K., ed. 1963. *John Ledyard's journal of Captain Cook's last voyage.* Corvallis: Oregon State University Press.

Murai, M., F. Pen, and C. D. Miller. 1958. *Some tropical South Pacific Island foods.* Hono-lulu: University of Hawaiʻi Press.

Murray, A. W. 1840. Journal, Pagopago, January 4–June 30. Manuscript, London Missionary Society, South Seas Letters and Journals 124, Box 9.

Naroll, R. 1962. Floor area and settlement population. *American Antiquity* 27:587–589.

Native Register. n.d. (ca. 1848–1849). Native register of kuleana claims recorded by the Board of Commissioners to Quiet Land Titles in the Hawaiian Islands. Manuscript (translation) on file, Archives of the State of Hawaiʻi, Honolulu.

Native Testimony. n.d. (ca. 1849). Native testimony recorded by the Board of Commis-sioners to Quiet Land Titles in the Hawaiian Islands. Manuscript (translation) on file, Archives of the State of Hawaiʻi, Honolulu.

Newbury, C. 1980. *Tahiti Nui: Change and survival in French Polynesia, 1767–1945.* Ho-nolulu: University of Hawaiʻi Press.

Newbury, C. W., ed. 1961. *The history of the Tahitian mission, 1799–1830, written by John Davies, missionary to the South Sea Islands.* Cambridge: Cambridge University Press for the Hakluyt Society.

Newman, T. S. 1970. *Hawaiian fishing and farming on the island of Hawaii in A.D. 1778.* Honolulu: Division of State Parks, State of Hawaii.

———. 1974. Kona field system. Hawaii register of historic places nomination form. Site 10-37-6601. On file, State Historic Preservation Division, Kapolei.

Nordyke, E. C. 1989. *The peopling of Hawai'i.* 2d edition. Honolulu: University of Hawai'i Press.

Nunn, P., R. Kumar, and S. Matararaba. 2003. Recent research relating to Lapita settlement in Fiji. In C. Sand, ed., *Pacific archaeology: Assessments and prospects,* 183–186. Le Cahiers de l'Archéologie en Nouvelle-Calédonie 15. Nouméa: Service de la Culture et du Patrimoine.

Oakes, N. 1994. Household space and organization in Society Islands, French Polynesia. Unpublished M.A. thesis, Simon Fraser University, Burnaby, BC.

O'Day, S. 2004. Marine resource exploitation and diversity in Kahikinui, Maui, Hawaii: Bringing together multiple lines of evidence to interpret the past. *Archaeofauna* 13:97–108.

Oliver, D. 1974. *Ancient Tahitian society.* 3 vols. Honolulu: University of Hawai'i Press.

———. 1988. *Return to Tahiti: Bligh's second breadfruit voyage.* Honolulu: University of Hawai'i Press.

———. 1989. *Oceania: The native cultures of Australia and the Pacific Islands.* 2 vols. Honolulu: University of Hawai'i Press.

Orbell, G. E., W. C. Rijkse, M. D. Laffan, and L. C. Blakemore. 1985. Soils of part of the Vava'u Group, Kingdom of Tonga. New Zealand Soil Survey Report 66. Wellington.

Orliac, C. 1982. Materiaux pour l'etude des habitations protohistoriques à Tahiti (Polynésie Française). Unpublished Ph.D. dissertation, Université de Paris.

———. 2000. *Fare et habitat à Tahiti.* Marseille: Editions Parenthèses.

Ottino, P. 1990. L'habitat des anciens Marquisiens: Architecture des maisons, évolution et symbolisme des formes. *Journal de la Société des Océanistes* 90:3–15.

Ottino, P. R., and M.-N. de Bergh. 1990. *Hakao'hoka: Etude d'une vallée Marquisienne.* ORSTOM, Collection Travaux et Documents Microédités No. 66. Paris.

Pacific Islands Yearbook. 1972. 11th edition. Judy Tudor, ed. Sydney: Pacific Publications.

Paine, R. R. 1997. The need for a multidisciplinary approach to prehistoric demography. In R. R. Paine, ed., *Integrating archaeological demography: Multidisciplinary approaches to prehistoric population,* 1–20. Center for Archaeological Investigations Occasional Paper No. 24. Carbondale: Southern Illinois University.

Papy, H. 1954. *Tahiti et les îles voisines: La végétation des Îles de la Société et de Makatea.* Travaux du Laboratoire Forestier de Toulouse 5(1:3). Toulouse, France.

Paris, J. P. 1981. *Géologie de la Nouvelle-Calédonie.* Mémoire BRGM 113. Paris: Bureau de Recherches Géologiques et Minières.

Parkes, A. 1997. Environmental change and the impact of Polynesian colonization: Sedimentary records from central Polynesia. In P. V. Kirch and T. L. Hunt, eds., *Historical ecology in the Pacific Islands: Prehistoric environmental and landscape change,* 166–199. New Haven: Yale University Press.

Parkinson, S. 1784. *A journal of a voyage to the South Seas, in His Majesty's Ship, the En-deavour.* London: Charles Dilly and James Phillips.

Parton, W. J., D. S. Schimel, C. V. Cole, and D. S. Ojima. 1987. Analysis of factors controlling soil organic matter levels in Great Plains grasslands. *Soil Science Society of America Journal* 51:1,173–1,179.

Parton, W. J., J. W. B. Stewart, and C. V. Cole. 1988. Dynamics of C, N, P, and S in grassland soils: A model. *Biogeochemistry* 5:109–131.

Patterson, G. 1882. *Missionary life among the cannibals: Being the life of the Rev. John Geddie, D.D., first missionary to the New Hebrides.* Toronto: Campbell.

Pernetta, J., and L. Hill. 1980. Carrying capacity: A biological view of a geographer's nightmare. Unpublished manuscript, University of Papua New Guinea, Port Moresby.

Petard, P. 1986. *Quelques plantes utiles de Polynesie et raau Tahiti.* Papeʻete: Editions Haere Po No Tahiti.

Petersen, W. 1975. A demographer's view of prehistoric demography. *Current Anthropology* 16:227–245.

Pietrusewsky, M. 1969. An osteological study of cranial and infracranial remains from Tonga. *Records of the Auckland Institute and Museum* 6:287–402.

———. 1976. *Prehistoric human skeletal remains from Papua New Guinea and the Marquesas.* Asian and Pacific Archaeology Series 7. Honolulu: Social Science Research Institute, University of Hawaiʻi.

Pirie, P. 1963. Geography of population in Western Samoa. Unpublished Ph.D. thesis, Australian National University, Canberra.

———. 1968. Polynesian populations. *Australian Geographical Studies* 6:175–182.

———. 1971. The effect of treponematoses and gonorrhea on the population of the Pacific Islands. *Human Biology in Oceania* 1:187–206.

———. 1972. Population growth in the Pacific Islands. In R. G. Ward, ed., *Man in the Pacific Islands,* 189–218. Oxford: Clarendon Press.

Pisier, G. 1976. *D'Entrecasteaux en Nouvelle-Calédonie, 1792–1793.* Nouméa: Publication de la Société d'Etudes Historiques de Nouvelle-Calédonie 13.

Platt, A. G., 1835–1836a. Raiatea to Hervey and Samoa groups. LMS Journals, 27 March 1836, ms. read in microfilm at Alexander Turnbull Library, Wellington.

———. 1835–1836b. Raiatea to Hervey and Samoa groups. LMS Journals, 28 March 1836, ms. read in microfilm at Alexander Turnbull Library, Wellington.

Pollack, N. J. 1992. *These roots remain: Food habits in islands of the central and eastern Pacific since Western contact.* Lāʻie, HI: Institute for Polynesian Studies.

Pool, D. I. 1973. The effects of the 1918 pandemic of influenza upon the Maori population of New Zealand. *Bulletin of the History of Medicine* 47(3):273–281.

———. 1977. *The Maori population of New Zealand, 1769–1971.* Auckland and Oxford: Auckland University Press and Oxford University Press.

———. 1991. *Te iwi Maori: A New Zealand population past, present and projected.* Auckland: Auckland University Press.

Postan, M. M. 1966. *The Cambridge economic history of Europe.* 2d ed., vol. 1: *The agrarian life of the Middle Ages.* Cambridge: Cambridge University Press.

Poulsen, J. 1987. *Early Tongan prehistory: The Lapita period on Tongatapu and its relationships.* Terra Australis 12. Canberra: Australian National University.

Pratt, G. 1842. 25th May, stationed at Matautu. Manuscript, Box 15, Folder 5, Jacket C, Reel 31, Alexander Turnbull Library.

Prior, I. A. M., A. Hooper, J. Huntsman, J. Stanhope, and C. Salmond. 1977. The Tokelau Island migrant study. In G. A. Harrison, ed., *International biological programme,* vol. 2. Cambridge: Cambridge University Press.

Pritchard, G. 1845. British Consulate in Samoa records. Foreign Office Records (F.O.): 58/38, 31.12.1845.

Quantin, P. 1979. *Archipel des Nouvelles-Hébrides: Sols et quelques données du milieu naturel: Erromango, Tanna, Aniwa, Anatom, Foutouna.* Paris: ORSTOM.

Raich, J. W., W. J. Parton, A. E. Russell, R. L. Sanford, Jr., and P. M. Vitousek. 2000. Analysis of factors regulating ecosystem development on Mauna Loa using the CENTURY model. *Biogeochemistry* 51:161–191.

Rallu, J.-L. 1989. Position de thèse. *Journal de la Société des Océanistes* 88-89:129–132.

———. 1990. *Les populations Oceaniennes aux 19e et 20e Siecles.* Institute National d'Etudes Demographiques. Paris: Presses Universitaires de France.

———. 1991. Population of the French overseas territories in the Pacific: Past, present and projected. *Journal of Pacific History* 26:169–186.

———. 1992. Mortality transition in the Marquesas Islands (French Polynesia). *Health Transition Review* 2:177–194.

Ramenofsky, A. F. 1987. *Vectors of death: The archaeology of European contact.* Albuquerque: University of New Mexico Press.

Rappaport, R., and A. Rappaport. 1967. Description of test excavations in coastal sites. In K. Green, R. A. Green, A. Rappaport, R. Rappaport, and J. Davidson, eds., *Archaeology of the island of Moʻorea, French Polynesia.* Anthropological Papers of the Museum of Natural History 51 (pt 2). New York.

Raspe, P. D. 1973. Analysis of the breeding structure of a Polynesian isolate. Unpublished M.A. thesis, University of Auckland.

Raynor, W. C. 1989. Structure, production, and seasonality in an indigenous Pacific Island agroforestry system: A case example on Pohnpei Island, F.S.M. Unpublished M.A. thesis in agronomy and soil science, University of Hawaiʻi, Honolulu.

Read, D. W., and S. A. LeBlanc. 2003. Population growth, carrying capacity, and conflict. *Current Anthropology* 44:59–85.

Reybaud, L. 1834. *Voyage pittoresque autour du monde.* Paris: Tenré.

Ricardo, D. 1817. *On the principles of political economy and taxation.* London: Murray.

Rice, G. 1983. Maori mortality in the 1918 influenza epidemic. *New Zealand Population Review* 9-1 (April).

Richardson, G. W. 1925. Memorandum to minister for external affairs, 21 October. NZNA A.O.35/14/-[EX83/20].

Rick, J. W. 1987. Dates as data: An examination of the Peruvian preceramic radiocarbon record. *American Antiquity* 52:55–73.

Rickman, J. 1966 [1781]. *Journal of Captain Cook's last voyage to the Pacific Ocean on Discovery; performed in the years 1776, 1777, 1778, 1779.* Facsimile reprint edition by Readex Microprint [1781: London: E. Newberry].

Ritter, L. T., and P. L. Ritter, 1981. *The European discovery of Kosrae Island: Accounts by Louis Isidore Duperrey, Jules Sébastien César Dumont D'Urville, René Primevère Lesson, Fyedor Lütke, and Friedrich Heinrich von Kittlitz.* Micronesian Archaeological Survey Report No. 13. Saipan: Historic Preservation Office, Trust Territory of the Pacific Islands.

Ritter, P. L. 1981. The population of Kosrae at contact. *Micronesica* 17:11–28.

Robertson, G. 1948. *The discovery of Tahiti: A journal of the second voyage of H.M.S. Dolphin round the world, under the command of Captain Wallis, R.N., in the years 1766, 1767, and 1768, by George Robertson.* Ed. H. Carrington. London: Hakluyt Society.

Robins, J., and R. Spear 1997. Research design for a cultural resources inventory survey of the Schofield Barracks training areas and the preparation of a historic preservation plan for U.S. Army training ranges and areas, Oʻahu Island, Hawaiʻi. Manuscript on file, Hawaiʻi Historic Preservation Division Library, Kapolei.

Rogers, G. 1969. Some comments on the "Report on the results of the 1966 census," Kingdom of Tonga, 1968. *Journal of the Polynesian Society* 78:212–222.

Rosendahl, P. H. 1972. Aboriginal agriculture and residence patterns in upland Lapakahi, Island of Hawaii. Unpublished Ph.D. dissertation, University of Hawaiʻi.

———. 1994. Aboriginal Hawaiian structural remains and settlement patterns in the upland agricultural zone at Lapakahi, Island of Hawaiʻi. *Hawaiian Archaeology* 3:14–70.

Rosendahl, P. H., A. Haun, J. Halbig, M. Kaschko, and M. S. Allen. 1988. Kahoʻolawe excavations, 1982–3 Data Recovery Project: Island of Kahoʻolawe, Hawaiʻi. PHRI ms. on file, State Historic Preservation Division Library, Kapolei.

Roux, J. C. 1990. Traditional Melanesian agriculture in New Caledonia and pre-Contact population distribution. In D. Yen and J. M. J. Mummery, eds., *Pacific Production Systems,* 161–173. Occasional Papers in Prehistory 18. Canberra: Australian National University.

Roy, P. 1997. The morphology and surface geology of the islands of Tongatapu and Vavaʻu, Kingdom of Tonga. In A. M. Sherwood, ed., *Coastal and environmental geoscience studies of the southwest Pacific Islands,* 153–173. SOPAC Technical Bulletin 9.

RPM. Various dates (nineteenth century). *Reformed Presbyterian Magazine.*

Sahlins, M. 1958. *Social stratification in Polynesia.* Seattle: American Ethnological Society.

———. 1962. *Moala: Culture and nature on a Fijian island.* Ann Arbor: University of Michigan Press.

———. 1963. Poor man, rich man, big-man, chief: Political types in Melanesia and Polynesia. *Comparative Studies in Society and History* 5:285–303.

———. 1973. Historical anthropology of the Hawaiian Kingdom. Proposal to the National Science Foundation. On file, State Historic Preservation Division Library, Kapolei.

———. 1985. *Islands of history.* Chicago: University of Chicago Press.

———. 1992. *Historical ethnography.* Vol. 1 of *Anahulu: the anthropology of history in the Kingdom of Hawaii,* by P. V. Kirch and M. S. Sahlins. Chicago: University of Chicago Press.

Salmond, A. 2003. *The trial of the cannibal dog: The remarkable story of Captain Cook's encounters in the South Seas.* New Haven: Yale University Press.

The Samoan Reporter. 1853. No. 14.

Sand, C. 1995. *Le temps d'avant: La préhistoire de la Nouvelle-Calédonie*. Paris: l'Harmattan.

———. 1996a. Recent developments in the study of New Caledonia's prehistory. *Archaeology in Oceania* 31:45–71.

———. 1996b. Structural remains as markers of complex societies in southern Melanesia during prehistory: The case of the monumental forts of Maré Island, New Caledonia. In I. C. Glover and P. Bellwood, eds., *Indo-Pacific prehistory: The Chiang Mai papers*, 37–44. Bulletin of the Indo-Pacific Prehistory Association 15. Canberra.

———. 1997. Variété de l'habitat ancien en Nouvelle-Calédonie: Etude de cas sur des vestiges archéologiques du Centre-Nord de la Grande Terre. *Journal de la Société des Océanistes* 104:39–66.

———. 1998. Recent archaeological research in the Loyalty Islands of New Caledonia. *Asian Perspectives* 37:194–223.

———. 1999a. Empires maritimes préhistorique dans le Pacifique: Ga'asialili et la mise en place d'une colonie tongienne à Uvea. *Journal de la Société des Océanistes* 108:103–124.

———. 1999a. From the swamp to the terrace: Intensification of the horticultural practices in New Caledonia from first settlement to European contact. In C. Gosden and J. Hather, eds., *The prehistory of food*, 252–269. One World Archaeology Series 32. London: Routledge.

———. 1999b. Lapita and non-Lapita ware during New Caledonia's first millenium of Austronesian settlement. In J. C. Galipaud and J. Lilley, eds., *The western Pacific, 5000 to 2000 BP: Colonisations and transformations*, 139–159. Paris: IRD Editions.

———. 2000a. Archaeology as a way to a shared future in New Caledonia? In I. Lilley, ed., *Native title and the transformation of archaeology in the postcolonial world*, 164–180. Oceania Monograph 50. Sydney: Oceania Publications.

———. 2000b. Reconstructing "traditional" Kanak society in New Caledonia: The role of archaeology in the study of European contact. In R. Torrence and A. Clarke, eds., *The archaeology of difference*, 51–78. One World Archaeology Series 38. London: Routledge.

———. 2001. Evolutions in the Lapita Cultural Complex: A view from the Southern Lapita Province. *Archaeology in Oceania* 36:65–76.

———. 2002a. Creations and transformations of prehistoric landscapes in New Caledonia, the southernmost Melanesian Islands. In T. Ladefoged and M. Graves, eds., *Pacific landscapes: Archaeological approaches*, 11–34. Los Osos, CA: Easter Island Foundation.

———. 2002b. Melanesian tribes vs. Polynesian chiefdoms: Recent archaeological assessment of a classic model of sociopolitical types in Oceania. *Asian Perspectives* 41:284–296.

Sand, C., J. Bolé, and A. Ouetcho. 2000. Les sociétés préeuropéennes de Nouvelle-Calédonie et leur transformation historique: L'apport de l'archéologie. In A. Bensa et I. Leblic, eds., *En pays Kanak: Ethnologie, linguistique, archéologie, histoire de la Nouvelle-Calédonie*, 171–194. Collection Ethnologie de la France 14. Paris: Éditions de la Maison des Sciences de l'Homme.

———. 2003a. Prehistory and its perception in a Melanesian archipelago: The New Caledonia example. *Antiquity* 77:505–519.

———. 2003b. Transformations et aménagements des espaces insulaires océaniens par l'homme durant la préhistoire: Des traits régionaux aux spécificités de l'exemple calédonien. In H. Mokaddem, ed., *Approches autour de culture et nature dans le Pacifique Sud,* 233–252. Nouméa: Expressions.

Sand, C., and A. Ouetcho. 1993. *Etude d'impact de la transversale Koné-Tiwaka sur le patrimoine archéologique.* Les Cahiers de l'Archéologie en Nouvelle-Calédonie 2. Nouméa.

Santley, R. S. 1990. Demographic archaeology in the Maya lowlands. In T. P. Culbert and D. S. Rice, eds., *Precolumbian population history in the Maya lowlands,* 325–344. Albuquerque: University of New Mexico Press.

Sarfati, Jonathan. n.d. How did we get so many people in such a short time? http://www.answersingenesis.org/docs/537.asp.

Sattenspiel, L., and H. C. Harpending. 1983. Stable populations and skeletal age. *American Antiquity* 48:489–498.

Saussol, A. 1979. *L'héritage: Essai sur le problème foncier Mélanésien en Nouvelle-Calédonie.* Publication de la Société des Océanistes 40. Paris.

———. 1981. L'espace rural européen: Cadre foncier. Plate 36 in *Atlas de la Nouvelle-Calédonie et Dépendances.* Paris: ORSTOM.

Schacht, R. M. 1981. Estimating past population trends. *Annual Review of Anthropology* 10:119–140.

Schimel, D. S., VEMAP participants, and B. H. Braswell. 1997. Continental scale variability in ecosystem processes: Models, data, and the role of disturbance. *Ecological Monographs* 67:251–271.

Schmitt, R. C. 1968. *Demographic statistics of Hawaii, 1778–1965.* Honolulu: University of Hawai'i Press.

———. 1971. New estimates of the pre-censal population of Hawaii. *Journal of the Polynesian Society* 80:237–243.

———. 1973. *The missionary censuses of Hawaii.* Pacific Anthropological Records 20. Honolulu: Bishop Museum Press.

———. 1977. *Historical statistics of Hawaii.* Honolulu: University of Hawai'i Press.

———. 1998. Population. In S. P. Juvik and J. O. Juvik, eds., *Atlas of Hawai'i,* 3d ed., 183–197. Honolulu: University of Hawai'i Press.

Scott, S. D. 1969. Reconnaissance and some detailed site plans of major monuments of Savai'i. In R. C. Green and J. M. Davidson, eds., *Archaeology in Western Samoa,* vol. 1:69–90. Auckland Institute and Museum Bulletin No. 7.

Shapiro, H. L. 1968. *The Pitcairn Islanders.* New York: Simon and Schuster.

Shawcross, W. 1970. Ethnographic economics and the study of population in prehistoric New Zealand: Viewed through archaeology. *Mankind* 7:279–291.

Shineberg, D. 1967. *They came for sandalwood.* Melbourne: Melbourne University Press.

———. 1983. Un nouveau regard sur la démographie historique de la Nouvelle-Calédonie. *Journal de la Société des Océanistes* 76:33–43.

Simmonds, N. W. 1962. *The evolution of the bananas.* London: Longmans.

Skaggs, J. M. 1994. *The great guano rush: Entrepreneurs and American overseas expansion.* New York: St. Martin's Griffin.

Smith, H. M. 1975. The introduction of venereal disease into Tahiti: A re-examination. *Journal of Pacific History* 10:38–45.

Smith, P., J. U. Smith, D. S. Powlson, W. B. McGill, J. R. M. Arah, O. G. Chertov, K. Coleman, U. Franko, S. Frolking, D. S. Jenkinson, L. S. Jensen, R. H. Kelly, H. Klein-Gunnewiek, A. S. Komarov, C. Li, J. A. E. Molina, T. Mueller, W. J. Parton, J. H. M. Thornley, and A. P. Whitmore. 1997. A comparison of the performance of nine soil organic matter models using datasets from seven long-term experiments. *Geoderma* 81:153–225.

Smith, V. 2000. William Ellis: Unutterable practices. In J. Lamb, V. Smith, and N. Thomas, eds., *Exploration and exchange: A South Seas anthology, 1680–1900,* 203–217. Chicago: University of Chicago Press.

Smith, W. 1813. *Journal of a voyage in the missionary ship* Duff, *to the Pacific Ocean in the years 1796. . . .* New York: Collins and Co.

Snow, C. 1974. *Early Hawaiians: An initial study of skeletal remains from Mokapu, Oahu.* Lexington: University of Kentucky Press.

Soudsky, B. 1962. The Neolithic site of Bylany. *Antiquity* 36:190–200.

Sparrman, A. 1944. *A voyage round the world with Captain James Cook in H.M.S.* Resolution (Cook's second voyage). Waltham St. Lawrence, UK: Golden Cockerel Press.

Spear, R. L. 1992. Settlement and expansion in an Hawaiian valley: The archaeological record from North Halawa, Oʻahu. *New Zealand Journal of Archaeology* 14:79–88.

Spenneman, D. H. R. 1986. *Archaeological fieldwork in Tonga, 1985–1986.* Tongan Dark Ages Research Programme Report No. 7. Canberra: Australian National University.

———. 1987. Availability of shellfish resources on prehistoric Tongatapu, Tonga: Effects of human predation and changing environment. *Archaeology in Oceania* 22:81–96.

———. 1989. ʻAta ʻa Tonga mo ʻata ʻo Tonga: Early and later prehistory of the Tongan Islands. Unpublished Ph.D. dissertation, Australian National University, Canberra.

———. 2002. Late Lapita colonization of a high island in Western Polynesia: The case of ʻEua Island, Tonga. *The Artefact* 25:26–32.

Spooner, B., ed. 1972. *Population growth: Anthroplogical implications.* Cambridge, MA: MIT Press.

Spriggs, M. 1981. Vegetable kingdoms: Taro irrigation and Pacific prehistory. Unpublished Ph.D. thesis, Australian National University, Canberra.

———. 1984. Taro irrigation techniques in the Pacific. In S. Chandra, ed., *Edible aroids,* 123–135. Oxford: Clarendon Press.

———. 1986. Landscape, land use and political transformation in southern Melanesia. In P. Kirch, ed., *Island societies: Archaeological approaches to evolution and transformation,* 6–19. Cambridge: Cambridge University Press.

———. 1993. Quantifying women's oppression in prehistory: The Aneityum (Vanuatu) case. In H. du Cros and L. Smith, eds., *Women in archaeology: A feminist critique,* 143–150. Occasional Papers in Prehistory 23. Canberra: Department of Prehistory, Australian National University.

———. 1997. *The Island Melanesians.* Oxford: Blackwell.

Spriggs, M., and P. V. Kirch, 1992. 'Auwai, kanawai, and waiwai: Irrigation in Kawailoa-Uka. In P. V. Kirch and M. Sahlins, Anahulu: The anthropology of history in the Kingdom of Hawaii, vol. 2:118–164. Chicago: University of Chicago Press.

Stair, J. B. 1897. Old Samoa. London: Religious Tract Society.

Stannard, D. E. 1989. Before the horror: The population of Hawai'i on the eve of Western contact. Honolulu: Social Science Research Institute, University of Hawai'i.

———. 1992. American holocaust: The conquest of the New World. New York: Oxford University Press.

Steadman, D. W., A. Plourde, and D. Burley. 2002a. Prehistoric butchery and consumption of birds in the Kingdom of Tonga. Journal of Archaeological Science 29:571–584.

Steadman, D. W., G. Pregill, and D. Burley. 2002b. Rapid prehistoric extinction of iguanas and birds in Polynesia. Proceedings of the National Academy of Sciences, USA 99:3,673–3,677.

Sterner, R. W., and J. J. Elser. 2002. Ecological stoichiometry: The biology of elements from molecules to the biosphere. Princeton: Princeton University Press.

Stock, J., J. Coil, and P. V. Kirch. 2003. Paleohydrology of arid southeastern Maui, Hawaiian Islands, and its implication for prehistoric human settlement. Quaternary Research 59:12–24.

Stokes, J. F. G. 1919. Heiaus of Hawaii. Bishop Museum manuscript on file, State Historic Preservation Division Library, Honolulu.

Stuiver, M., and G. W. Pearson. 1993. High-precision bidecadal calibration of the radiocarbon time scale, AD 1950–500 BC and 2500–6000 BC. Radiocarbon 35:1–23.

Stuiver, M., and H. Polach. 1977. Discussion: Reporting of ^{14}C data. Radiocarbon 19:355–363.

Suggs, R. C. 1961. The archaeology of Nuku Hiva, Marquesas Islands, French Polynesia. Anthropological Papers of the American Museum of Natural History 49 (pt 1). New York.

Sutton, D. G., and M. A. Molloy. 1989. Deconstructing Pacific paleodemography: A critique of density dependent causality. Archaeology in Oceania 24:31–36.

Swinbourne, C. A. 1925. Report of district officer, Ellice and Union Islands, for administrator of Western Samoa, 15 July 1925. NZNA Union Islands [EX 94/1] IT 1 EX 94/1/1.

Tanner, J. T. 1975. Population limitation today and in ancient Polynesia. BioScience 25:513–516.

Taylor, P. 2003. A preliminary report of volcanic ash falls in the Kingdom of Tonga: A probable effect on developing communities. Unpublished paper presented at the Tonga History Association Conference, Nuku'alofa.

Taylor, R. E. 1987. Radiocarbon dating: An archaeological perspective. New York: Academic Press.

Thaman, R. 1978. The Tongan agricultural system with special emphasis on plan assemblages. Unpublished Ph.D. dissertation, University of California at Los Angeles.

Thisted, R. A. 1988. Elements of statistical computing: Numerical computation. New York: Chapman and Hall.

Thomas, N. 1989. The force of ethnology: Origins and significance of the Melanesia/Polynesia division. Current Anthropology 30:27–41.

———. 2003. *Cook: The extraordinary voyages of Captain James Cook.* New York: Walker & Company.

Tinielu, I. 1972. The Tokelau Islands Medical Service: A historical review. Report prepared for TIMS and New Zealand Department of Health. Fakaofo, Wellington: Epidemiology Unit, Wellington Hospital Board.

Tomonari-Tuggle, M. 1988. North Kohala: Perception of a changing community, a cultural resources study. State Parks ms. on file, State Historic Preservation Division Library, Kapolei.

Townsend, A. R., P. M. Vitousek, and S. E. Trumbore. 1995. Soil organic matter dynamics along gradients in temperature and land use on the island of Hawai'i. *Ecology* 76:721–733.

Tuggle, H. D. 2004. Methodological problems in the archaeology of Kona. Paper presented at the Society for Hawaiian Archaeology meetings, Kāne'ohe, O'ahu.

Tuggle, H. D., and P. B. Griffin, eds. 1973. *Lapakahi, Hawaii: Archaeological studies.* Asian and Pacific Archaeological Series 5. Honolulu: Social Science Research Institute, University of Hawaii at Manoa.

Tuggle, H. D., and M. Tomonari-Tuggle. 1997. Synthesis of the cultural resources of the 'Ewa Plain. International Archaeological Research Institute ms. on file, Hawai'i Historic Preservation Division Library, Kapolei.

Turchin, P. 2003. *Complex population dynamics: A theoretical/empirical synthesis.* Monographs in Population Biology 35. Princeton: Princeton University Press.

Turner, B. L., II. 1990. Population reconstruction for the central Maya lowlands: 1000 B.C. to A.D. 1500. In T. P. Culbert and D. S. Rice, eds., *Precolumbian population history in the Maya lowlands,* 301–324. Albuquerque: University of New Mexico Press.

Turner, P. 1835. Letters from Satupa'itea dated October 8–10, 1835, containing extracts from journal. Manuscript, Methodist Missionary Society, Correspondence in Samoa 1834–1870, Nos. 49, 50.

———. 1836. Letters from Matautu dated February 10, 1836, containing journal entries. Manuscript, Methodist Missionary Society, Correspondence in Samoa 1834–1870, No. 54.

———. 1837–1839. Journal, vol. 5. Manuscript, read in microfilm, CY REEL 268; B304 at Mitchell Library, Sydney.

Underwood, J. 1969. *Human skeletal remains from sand dune site (H1), South Point, Hawaii.* Pacific Anthropological Records 9. Honolulu: Bishop Museum Press.

———. 1973. Population history of Guam: Context of microevolution. *Micronesica* 9:11–44.

Valentin, F., and C. Sand. 2000. *Archéologie des morts: Etudes anthropologiques de squelettes préhistoriques de Nouvelle-Calédonie.* Les Cahiers de l'Archéologie en Nouvelle-Calédonie 11. Nouméa.

———. 2003. Squelettes de Nouvelle-Calédonie et sociétés préhistoriques océaniennes. In C. Orliac, ed., *Archéologie en Océanie insulaire: Peuplement, sociétés et paysages,* 10–27. Paris: Editions Artcom.

Valenziani, C. 1940. *Renaissance démographique en Océanie Française.* Rome: Tipografia Conzortio Nazionale.

Vigors, P. D. 1850. A private journal of a four months cruise through some of the South Sea Islands and New Zealand in HMS *Havannah*. Manuscript. Typescript copy in the Auckland Institute and Museum.

Vitousek, P. M. 2004. *Nutrient cycling and limitation: Hawai'i as a model system*. Princeton: Princeton University Press.

Vitousek, P. M., O. A. Chadwick, T. E. Crews, J. H. Fownes, D. M. Hendricks, and D. Herbert. 1997. Soil and ecosystem development across the Hawaiian Islands. *GSA Today* 7:1–8.

Vitousek, P. M., T. N. Ladefoged, P. V. Kirch, A. S. Hartshorn, M. W. Graves, S. C. Hotchkiss, S. Tuljapurkar, and O. A. Chadwick. 2004. Soils, agriculture, and society in precontact Hawai'i. *Science* 305:1,665–1,669.

Waimea Station Reports. 1832–1851. On file, Hawaiian Mission Children's Society Library, Honolulu.

Walsh, A. C. 1970. Population changes in Tonga: An historical overview and modern commentary. *Pacific Viewpoint* 11:27–47.

Ward, R. G., 1997. Land tenure. In D. Denoon, ed., *Pacific Edens? Myths and realities of primitive affluence*, 90–96 (*The Cambridge History of the Pacific Islanders*). Cambridge: Cambridge University Press.

Watters, R. F. 1958. Settlement in old Samoa, 1840. *New Zealand Geographer* 14:1–18.

Weisler, M., and P. V. Kirch. 1985. The structure of settlement space in a Polynesian chiefdom: Kawela, Moloka'i, Hawaiian Islands. *New Zealand Journal of Archaeology* 7:129–158.

Weiss, K. M. 1973. *Demographic models for anthropology*. Memoir 27, Society for American Archaeology. *American Antiquity* 38:2 (pt 2).

Wessen, A. F., A. Hooper, J. Huntsman, I. A. M. Prior, and C. E. Salmond. 1992. *Migration and health in a small society: The case of Tokelau*. Oxford: Clarendon Press.

Whistler, W. A. 1991. Polynesian plant introductions. In P. A. Cox and S. A. Banack, eds., *Islands, plants and Polynesians: An introduction to Polynesian ethnobotany*, 41–66. Portland, OR: Dioscorides Press.

Whitesell, C. D., C. D. Maclean, M. C. Falanruw, T. G. Cole, and A. H. Ambacher. 1986. *Vegetation survey of Kosrae, Federated States of Micronesia*. Resource Bulletin PSW–17. U.S. Dept. of Agriculture, Forest Service, Pacific Southwest Forest and Range Experiment Station, Berkeley, CA.

Whitney, M. 1923. The yield of wheat in England during seven centuries. *Science* 58:320–324.

Wilder, G. P. 1928. *The breadfruit of Tahiti*. Bernice P. Bishop Museum Bulletin 50. Honolulu: Bishop Museum Press.

Wilkes, C. 1845. *Narrative of the United States Exploring Expedition during the years 1838, 1839, 1840, 1841, 1842*. 5 vols. Philadelphia: Lea and Blanchard.

———. 1981 [1845]. *Narrative of the United States Exploring Expedition during the years 1838, 1839, 1840, 1841, 1842*. Vol. 5. Reprinted in Ko na fakamatalaga Tuhia a ni Papalagi e uiga ki Tokelau 1765–1925 (Papalagi documents on Tokelau 1765–1925). Apia and Auckland: Office for Tokelau Affairs, 25–37. [London: Wiley and Putnam, 5–18.]

Williams, J. 1832. Narrative of a voyage performed in the missionary schooner *Olive*

Branch, and observations on the navigators. Manuscript, London Missionary Society, South Seas Letters and Journals, 101, Box 7.

———. 1837. *A narrative of a missionary.* London: J. Snow.

Williams, S. 1992. Early inland settlement expansion and the effect of geomorphological change on the archaeological record in Kaneʻohe, Oʻahu. *New Zealand Journal of Archaeology* 14:67–78.

———. 2003. The archaeology of the Makua Military Reservation. Paper presented at 2003 Society for Hawaiian Archaeology Meetings, Kāneʻohe.

Williamson, M. 1981. *Island populations.* Oxford: Oxford University Press.

Wilson, A., and F. Beecroft. 1983. *Soils of the Haʻapai Group, Kingdom of Tonga.* New Zealand Soil Survey Report 67. Lower Hutt: New Zealand Soil Bureau.

Wilson, E. O., and W. H. Bossert. 1971. *A primer of population biology.* Sunderland, MA: Sinauer Associates.

Wilson, W. 1799. *A missionary voyage to the Southern Pacific Ocean, performed in the years 1796, 1797, 1798, in the ship* Duff, *commanded by Captain James Wilson. Compiled from journals of the officers and the missionaries . . . by a committee appointed for the purposes by the directors of the Missionary Society.* London: T. Gillet.

———. 1805. First [and second] missionary voyage[s] to the South-Sea, performed in the years 1796, 1797 and 1798 in the ship *Duff,* commanded of the Missionary society. In *The universal navigator and the modern tourist: Comprehending authentic and circumstantial narratives of the most interesting voyages and travels, which have, at various periods, been undertaken to all parts of the world, by popular navigators, circumnavigators, commanders, and distinguished tourists.* London: J. Cundee.

Wolforth, T., W. Wulzen, and S. Goodfellow. 1998. Archaeological data recovery at West Loch Estates, Residential Increment 1, and Golf Course and Shoreline Park, Land of Honoliuli, ʻEwa District, Island of Oʻahu. PHRI manuscript on file, Hawaiʻi Historic Preservation Division Library, Kapolei (O–1317).

Wood, A. H. 1943. *A history and geography of Tonga.* Nukuʻalofa: Government Printer.

Wood, J. W., G. R. Milner, H. C. Harpending, and K. M. Weiss. 1992. The osteological paradox: Problems of inferring prehistoric health from skeletal samples. *Current Anthropology* 33:343–370.

Yaldwyn, J. C., and K. Wodzicki. 1979. Systematics and ecology of the land crabs *(Decapoda, Grapsidae* and *Gecarcinidae)* of the Tokelau Islands, central Pacific. *Atoll Research Bulletin* 235. Washington, DC: Smithsonian Institution.

Yen, D. E. 1974. *The sweet potato and Oceania: An essay in ethnobotany.* Bernice P. Bishop Museum Bulletin 236. Honolulu: Bishop Museum Press.

Yen, D. E., P. V. Kirch, and P. Rosendahl. 1973. Anuta: An introduction. In D. E. Yen and J. Gordon, eds., *Anuta: A Polynesian outlier in the Solomon Islands,* 1–8. Pacific Anthropological Records 21. Honolulu: Bishop Museum Press.

J. Stephen Athens, International Archaeological Research Institute, Inc., 2081 Young St., Honolulu, Hawai'i, 96826, USA. jsathens@iarii.org

Jacques Bole, Department of Archaeology, New Caledonia Museum, BP 2393, 98846 Nouméa Cedex, New Caledonia

David V. Burley, Department of Archaeology, Simon Fraser University, 8888 University Drive, Burnaby, British Columbia, Canada V5A 1S6. burley@sfu.ca

Eric Conte, Université de la Polynésie Française, BP 6570, 98702, Faa'a, Tahiti, French Polynesia. Eric.Conte@upf.pf

Ross Cordy, West O'ahu College, University of Hawai'i. rcordy@hawaii.edu

Michelle Figgs, Biological Sciences, Stanford University, Stanford, CA 94305, USA

Michael W. Graves, Department of Anthropology, University of Hawai'i, Honolulu, HI, 96822, USA. mgraves@hawaii.edu

Roger C. Green, Research Associates (Pacifica) Ltd., P.O. Box 60 054, Titirangi, Auckland 1230, New Zealand. pounamu@ihug.co.nz

Valerie J. Green, Research Associates (Pacifica) Ltd., P.O. Box 60 054, Titirangi, Auckland 1230, New Zealand. pounamu@ihug.co.nz

Brenda K. Hamilton, Department of Anthropology, University of California, Berkeley, CA, 94720, USA. bhamilt@berkeley.edu

Jennifer G. Kahn, Department of Anthropology, University of California, Berkeley, CA, 94720, USA. jkahn@sscl.berkeley.edu

Patrick V. Kirch, Department of Anthropology, University of California, Berkeley, CA, 94720, USA. kirch@berkeley.edu

Thegn N. Ladefoged, Department of Anthropology, University of Auckland, Auckland, New Zealand. t.ladefoged@auckland.ac.nz

Charlotte Lee, Biological Sciences, Stanford University, Stanford, CA 94305, USA. charlotte.lee@stanford.edu

Tamara Maric, Service de la Culture et du Patrimoine, Ministere de la Culture, Punaauia, Tahiti, French Polynesia. tamaramaric1@yahoo.fr

A. Ouetcho, Department of Archaeology, New Caledonia Museum, BP 2393, 98846 Nouméa Cedex, New Caledonia

Jean-Louis Rallu, INED, 133, Boulevard Davout, 75980 Paris Cedex 20, France. rallu@ined.fr

Christophe Sand, Department. of Archaeology, New Caledonia Museum, BP 2393, 98846 Nouméa Cedex, New Caledonia. sand.smp@gouv.nc

Matthew Spriggs, Archaeology and Anthropology, AD Hope Bldg., Australian National University, Canberra, ACT 0200, Australia. matthew.spriggs@anu.edu.au

Shripad Tuljapurkar, Department of Biological Sciences, Herrin Labs 454, Stanford University, Stanford, CA 94305-5020, USA. tulja@stanford.edu

Note: Page numbers in **bold** indicate illustrations and tables

abortions, 239, 250, 334
Adams, H., 130, 134, 155
agriculture, 10; Aneityum, 282, 289, 292–304, **297**; chronology of development in, 76–80, **77**, 87; demography and, 12, 35–51, 70–89, **72–87**, 103–104, 156, 181–182, 331–333; expansion, 38, 49, 55–57, 78–88, 294; harvesting, 44–50, **45–48**; Hawaiian Islands, 56–57, 70–92, 94, 102–104, 107, 114–119; Kosrae, 13, 262–267, 273–274; Maʻohi, 129–130; marginal areas, 38–39, 65, 91; model of plant-soil dynamics, 42–45, **44**, **45**; New Caledonia, 310; ʻOpunohu Valley, 138–139, 144–157, **147–150**, **152**, **154**; Samoa, 213–216, 218–219, 223, 230; seasonality, 50; soil nutrient status, 42–50, 336; surplus production, 9, 61, 86–88; sustainability, 38–46, 49, 264, 331; technology, 37, 39; temporal stochasticity, 50; Tonga, 181–182, 184–186, **186**, 191–197, 291. *See also* carrying capacity; food; horticulture; intensification, agricultural; irrigation systems
ahupuaʻa, 111
alcohol consumption, health effects, 11, 27, 30, 31
Allen, J. S., 234
American Samoa, **204**, 208, 210, 212–216, **215**, 235
Anahulu Valley, Oʻahu, 9, 60–61, 157, 281
Aneityum/Anatom, Vanuatu, 9, 13, 32, 278–305, 314; age and sex structure models, 299–300, **300**; agriculture, 282, 289, 292–304, **297**; pre-Contact population, 283–304, **302**
Anuta, population density, 331
Apolima, population estimates, 208
archaeology: cultural systems theory, 55–56, 257; dark age, 196; and ethnohistory, 13, 60–61, 129–176; paleodemography and, 2, 5–9, 54–65, 83–107, 327, 333, 334, 337; processualist, 55, 57; reexcavation of sites, 17. *See also* ceramics; dating; demographic archaeology; skeletal remains
Atafu, **204**, 234–235, **237**, 240–250, **242**, **245**, 255
ʻAtele burial mounds, Tonga, 6, 198–199
Athens, J. Stephen, 13, 257–277, 328, 332
atolls, **204**, 232–256, 259; Tuvalu, **204**, 235. *See also* Tokelau atolls

Bailey, M., 38
Bailleul, M., 173
bananas: Hawaiian Islands, 103, 119, 123; Kosrae, 263, 264, 265, 266; Society Islands, 145, 146, 149, 150
Banks, Joseph, 16
Barrau, J., 103, 149, 315
Bayliss-Smith, T. P., 9, 156, 291–304, 305
Beaglehole, E., 101
Beaglehole, P., 101
Bellwood, P. S., 9, 102, 156, 160, 166
Best, S., 240
Bicknell, H., 145
Bicknell, W. H., 145
"biocomplexity" project, 92
birthrates, 18–19, 234, 336; demographic reconstruction, 39–40, **41**, **43**; Kosrae, 266; Malthusian view, 36; post-

Contact, where?, 112; Samoa, 218; sexu-
ally transmitted (STDs) and, 18, 112, 218,
325; social regulation of, 239, 244, 250–
251, 334–335; Tokelau atolls, 239–240,
250, 251. *See also* infant mortality
Black, S., 277
Bligh, William, 1, 53
Bocquet-Appel, J.-P., 269
Boenechea, 15, 25, 32, 33
Bole, Jacques, 13, 306–325
Bolker, B. M., 43
Bora-Bora, population density, 31
Boserup, Ester, 5
Bougainville, L. A., 1
Bounty, 18, 33, 332; Bligh, 1, 53
breadfruit: Aneityum, 295–296; Hokatu
Valley, 175; Kosrae, 13, 260, 262–266;
Samoa, 213; Society Islands, 3, 137, 144–
145, 146, 150; Tokelau atolls, 252; Tonga,
182
Brenchley, J. L., 286, 287
Brewis, A. A., 190, 234, 250, 272
Brown, B. M., 141–142, 248
Buck, Peter, 54
burials, 6, 177; Aneityum, 281; Kosrae,
262, 269; Tonga, 6, 196, 198–199. *See also*
skeletal remains
Burley, David V., 13, 177–202, 333
Buzacott, A., 207

"calibration stochastic distortion (CSD)
effect," 96, **97**
canoes, voyaging, 33, 68, 267, 276; Hawaiian Islands, 52, 90; Tahitian war, 130;
Tokelau atolls, 235, 236, 246, 247, 254,
255
Carneiro's formula, 186
Caroline Islands, Micronesia. *See* Kosrae,
Caroline Islands
carrying capacity, 3, 6, 8–10, 36–38, 108,
196, 289–290, 335; defined, 36; Hanatekua Valley, 166; Hawaiian Islands
(post-Contact), 61; Hawaiian Islands
(pre-Contact), 59, 68, 94, 102; Kosrae,
264–266; New Caledonia, 320–321;

'Opunohu Valley, 129–130, 143–157;
standard and maximum, 156; Tonga
(pre-Contact), 182–185, 194, 199, 201,
290; "welfare" approach, 291–304
Casselberry, S. E., 164
celibacy, 250, 283, 334
censuses, 12, 110, 111, 233; 'Ewa, 110, **120**,
121; Mo'orea, 132; New Caledonia, 308;
pig, 305; Tonga, 181, **181**, 184, 198; Vigors
on, 278, 283. *See also* house counts; missionary censuses
CENTURY simulation model, 42–45, **44**,
45
ceramics: New Caledonia, 310, 311, 312–313;
Tonga, 187–189, 191–195, **195**, 196, 200
chiefs/chiefdoms, 35, 258, 306; Aneityum,
281; Hawaiian, 88, 121, 125, 126, 127, 157,
335–336; Hokatu Valley, 162; Kosrae,
260–261, **261**, 262, 268, 275; Ma'ohi, 132,
136, 137; New Caledonia, 312, 314, 321,
323; Samoa, 220–221; Society Islands,
156, 158; Tonga, 178, 180, 196–199, 202
Childe, V. Gordon, 5
China, early population growth rates, 18
Chung, H. L., 103
Clark, Jeffrey, 60, 127, 128
climate: Aneityum, 278–279; Kahikinui,
91, 107; Kohala, 88, 111, 122; Kosrae, 259–
260; Wai'anae, 113. *See also* weather
coconuts, 11; Aneityum, 295, 305; Kosrae,
260, 263, 264, 266; Samoa, 213, 225; Society Islands, 137, 144, 145, 146; Tokelau
atolls, 252, 255; Tonga, 182
Cohen, J., 37, 272, 277
colonization. *See* explorers; founding
populations
"colonizer's complex," 16
Contact era: atolls, 236; dating, 110. *See
also* Contact-era population; diseases;
explorers; missionaries; "pericontact"
period; post-Contact depopulation;
pre-Contact population
Contact-era population, 10–12, 15, 233–234,
326, 334; Aneityum, 278–305; "colonizer's complex," 16; Forster-McArthur-

Stannard divergences, 2–5, 9, 14, 130, 155, 336, 337; Hawaiian Islands, 4, 14, 52–54, 108–128, 233, 329; Kosrae, 262, 263–264, 265–266; New Caledonia, 309–317, 330; Tahiti, 2–4, 16, 29–34, **30**, 130–132, 155. *See also* methods (population estimation)

Conte, Eric, 13, 160–176, 331

Cook, James, 1, 32, 70, 164; Aneityum, 279; death, 53; diseases brought by, 1, 324; Hawaiian Islands, 4, 24, 52–53, 67, 90, 106–107, 112; house dwelling, 139; New Caledonia, 307, 308, 318; Tahiti, 2, 15–16, 130. *See also* King, Lt. James, Hawaiian population estimates

Cook Islands, population density, **31**, 32

Copeland, J., 279, 289

la Coquille, 262, 263

Cordy, Ross, 12; Hawaiian Contact-era population, 100–101, 108–128, 327, 329, 330; Kosrae, 262; Mahele land records, 12, 109–128, 327; models for estimating population, 57–60, **58**, 62

Coulter, J. W., 213

cultural systems theory, 55–56, 257

Cumberland, K. B., 225

curve, population growth. *See* population growth curves

Cusack-Smith, 247

cyclones, Tokelau atolls, 235, 240, 254

dating: house sites, 109–110; volcanic-glass, 57, 59, 60, 68, 69, 110. *See also* radiocarbon dating

Davidson, Janet, 193, 198, 206, 217, 224, 227–230, 248

death rates, 25–28, **26**, 33, 112, 336; demographic reconstruction, 39–40, **41**, **43**; Gompertz model of mortality, 39; infant, 18, 112, 205; Kosrae, 266; Malthusian view, 36; Pitcairn, 18; Tikopia, 334; Tokelau atolls, 239, 251. *See also* burials; epidemics

demographic archaeology, 5–9, 17–25, 68, 257, 327, 334, 337; Aneityum, 289–291;

Hawaiian Islands, 12, 52–128, 333; Hokatu Valley, 160–176; Kosrae, 266–275; New Caledonia, 309–317, 320–321; Samoa, 206; Tonga, 177–202. *See also* carrying capacity; dating; osteological demography; paleodemography; settlement demography

demographic reconstruction, 6; Aneityum, 281; Hawaiian Islands, 12, 40, 60, 67, 71–73, 91–93, 108–128; Hokatu Valley, 162; New Caledonia, 316, **319**; prehistoric, 35, 39–41, **41**, **43**; Samoa, 205, 210, 224, 230, 233; Society Islands, 129, 133, 158; Tokelau atolls, 13, 237, 240

demography, 176, 177; agriculture and, 12, 35–51, 70–89, **72–87**, 103–104, 156, 181–182, 331–333. *See also* demographic archaeology; demographic reconstruction; historical demography; migrations; osteological demography; paleodemography; population; settlement demography; social demography

density. *See* population density

D'Entrecasteaux, B., 1, 318

depopulation: Aneityum, 289; Kosrae, 268. *See also* disasters, natural; diseases; migrations; population regulation; post-Contact depopulation; warfare

Descantes, C., 139

development models, population growth rate, 17–25, 32–33, 190, 332

de Vries effect, 64

disasters, natural, 19, 235; cyclones, 235, 240, 254; hurricanes, 19; typhoons, 260, 266; volcanic eruption, 182, **220**. *See also* drought; famine

diseases, 1–2, 11, 15, 25 34, 326–327; dysentery, 25, 27, 29, 236, 244, 246–247, 255, 287; Hawaiian Islands, 1, 53–54, 112, 285; hepatitis, 236; infant, 27, 112; New Caledonia, 318–320, 322, 323, 324–325; respiratory, 27; Samoa, 211, 218, 246, 255; sexually transmitted (STDs), 1, 18, 112, 218, 325; skin, 236; Society Islands, 18, 27, 29, 32, 132, 158; Tokelau atolls,

235–236, 244, 246–247, 254, 255; Tonga, 181, 211, 218; tuberculosis, 27, 236. *See also* epidemics

"dispersal" model, 251–252

Diuturnal Settlement Model, 253

Dixon, George, 67, 98

Djindjian, F., 166

documents. *See* literature; records

Dolphin, 2, 3, 130; Commodore Byron, 235, 240, 306; Shipmaster Robertson, 2, 15, 130; Captain Wallis, 1, 15, 145

Doumenge, J. P., 315, 317

drought, 336; Marquesas, 33; New Caledonia, 315–316; Tokelau atolls, 235. *See also* famine

Duff, 134; Captain James Wilson, 1, 3, 28, 137

Duperrey, Louis, 263

Du Petit-Thouars, A., 173

dwelling-area approach, 98, 141–143, 247–250. *See also* residential structures

Dye, Tom, 5, 8, 61–69, **62**, 328

dysentery, 25, 27, 29; Aneityum, 287; Tokelau atolls, 236, 244, 246–247, 255

Easter Island (Rapa Nui), 21–22, 33

ecodynamics, human, 73

ecology: atoll, 251; "ecological imperialism," 1–2; "ecologically marginal" regions, 60, 65, 91, 107; ecological niches for land tenure arrangements, 228–229; population, 12, 36, 164, 166, 257, 290. *See also* ecosystem

economics, 333–334; economic rent, 38; Polynesian, 107, 330–331; Vanuatu, 292, 296, 300, 301, 305; Waipi'o, 123. *See also* agriculture

ecosystem: Hawaiian pre-Contact modifications, 68; plants and soils, 35, 42–50; Polynesian variety, 330–331; tropical island, 107. *See also* agriculture; ecology; environment; land use; marginal areas; volcanic islands

Edwards, E., 236, 240–241

Ehrlich, P. R., 277

Ellis, William, 110, 124, 127, 129

Emory, Kenneth, 54–55, 68, 134

England, 36, 38, 39. *See also* London Missionary Society (LMS)

environment: Aneityum, 278; atolls, **237**; Kahikinui, 92–98, 102; Kosrae, 259–262, **260**; New Caledonia, 307; 'Opunohu Valley, 132–133. *See also* agriculture; climate; ecosystem; land use; soil; water; wild food

epidemics, 15, 16–17, 25–34, **26**; Aneityum, 283, **284**, 285–291, 304; dysentery, 25, 27, 29, 287; flu, 25, 26, 27, 32, 211, 325; Hawaiian Islands, 53–54, 112, 285; measles, 25, 26, 27, 29; New Caledonia, 318–320, 322, 324–325; pre-Contact, 32, 285–291; scarlet fever, 27, 29–30; smallpox, 25–26, 27, 29, 30; "virgin soil," 1–4, 10, 28, 53–54; whooping cough, 25, 27. *See also* diseases

Erskine, J. E., 207, 210

ethnohistory, 13; archaeology and, 13, 60–61, 129–176; dwelling-area approach, 98, 141–143, 247–250; Nukunonu, 237; sources, 133–134, 232–233. *See also* explorers; missionaries; records; settlement demography; social demography

European contact. *See* Contact era; explorers; missionaries

evolution: ceramic, 311; cultural, 35, 57–58, 59; human, 257, 258–259; nonhuman natural organisms, 257; in structures used, 168. *See also* long-term population trends

'Ewa, O'ahu, 110, 118–121, **119–120**, 125, 126

expansion, 23, 35; agricultural and demographic, 38, 49, 55–57, 78–88, 294; Hawaiian Islands Expansion Period (AD 1100–1650), 60, 65–66; Hawaiian Islands inland expansion, 55–57, 60, 97–98, 105–106; Kohala DSA, 75, 78–88, **80, 84**; Kosrae, 261; Lapita, 193, 253, 309–310; Tokelau atolls, 235, 251, 253, 254; Tonga, 178, 180, 182, 193, 196–201. *See also* migrations explorers, 133–134; Aneityum, 279–280; *Bounty*/Bligh, 1, 18, 33, 53, 332; *la Coquille*, 262, 263; New Caledonia, 308; *Senyavin*, **261**, 262, 263; United States Exploring Expedition (USEE), 235, 236, 243, 244, 246, 247. *See also* Cook, James; *Dolphin*; *Duff*; Forster, Johann Reinhold; migrations

exponential population growth, 10, 17, 35–36, 310, 334; Hawaiian Islands, 20, **21**, 65–66, 70–71, 97, 106, 334, 335; Kahikinui, 95, 97, 106; Tonga, 186, 194, 200–201

extinction, 10, 193, 269, 276, 334

Fakaofo, **204**, 234–252, **237**

famine, 334; Marquesas, 30, 33; Tokelau atolls, 244, 247. *See also* drought

Fanga 'Uta Lagoon, 187, 189, 190, **192**, 193, 196–198

feedback loops, 50, 58, 333; Malthusian, 36–37

fertility: soil, 38–39, 153. *See also* birthrates

Figgs, Michelle, 12, 35–51

Fiji: ceramics, 187–189; diet needs, 295; Lakeba, 218, 229, 296

fish and shellfish: Aneityum, 295; Hawaiian Islands, 94, 119, 121; Kosrae, 263; New Caledonia, 315; Tokelau atolls, 252, 255; Tonga, 180, 189

flu epidemics, 25, 26, 27, 32, 211, 325

food: Aneityum, 279, 295–304; food stress, 199; harvest and supply of, 49–50; New Caledonia, 312; "non-nutritive functions," 291; population size and, 35–51, 103–104, 156; Tokelau atolls, 235, 251–252. *See also* agriculture; bananas; breadfruit; coconut; famine; fish and shellfish; horticulture; wild food

Forster, Johann Reinhold: New Caledonia, 308, 317; Tahiti, 2–3, 15, 130, 137, 141, 155

founding populations, 19, 35, 55, 68, 185–186, 310; Hawaiian Islands, 68, 332; Kosrae, 269–272, **270**, **271**; New Caledonia, 310; Tokelau atolls, 232, 237–238, 240–244, 247, 250–254; Tonga, 186, 187, 190–191, 200

Fox, J. W., 225

Freeman, Derek, 217, 229

frequency distributions, radiocarbon dates, 108; Kahikinui, Maui, 95–96, **95–96**, 100, **100**. *See also* site-frequency histograms

Gambier Archipelago, pre-Contact population, 21–22

gardens: Aneityum, 282, 292, 294–298, **297**, 299–300, 301–302, 304; Kahikinui, 103; New Guinea Highlands, 305; Samoa, 225, 228; Tonga, 182, 189, 194. *See also* horticulture

Geddie, Charlotte, 289

Geddie, John, 280, 283–288, 289

genealogies: Hawaiian islands, 121, 123; Tokelau atolls, 238, 241, 243, 254–255

geography: Kosrae, 259–262, **260**. *See also* environment

Gifford, E. W., 177, 180

Gill, W., 286

Gompertz model of mortality, 39

La Grande Terre, 13, 233, 307–325, **313**, **319**, 330

Graves, Michael W., 12, 70–89, 331

Green, Roger C., 13, 337; atolls, 232–256, 327, 332; carrying capacity, 184, 289–291; "mobile founding migrant" groups, 310; Samoa, 191, 203–231, 330, 331–332; Society Islands, 133, 144, 158; Tonga, 184, 189, 230, 290; Wai'anae, 128

Green, Valerie, 232–256, 327, 332

Guiart, J., 197

Ha'apai, Tonga, 180–185, **188**, **190**, 192–195, **194**, 198, 333

Hale, Horatio, 236, 247

Hāmākua, Hawai'i, 110, 121–125, **122**, **124**, **125**, 126

Hamilton, Brenda K., 13, 37, 102, 129–159, 331

Hanatekua Valley, 166, 167

Handy, Edward S. C., 107, 161
Hardie, 286–287
Hassan, F. A., 143–144, 156, 190, 272–273, 274
Hatcher, J., 38
Hawai'i, 10, 233; Hāmākua, 110, 121–125, **122**, **124**, **125**, 126. *See also* Kohala, Hawai'i
Hawaiian Islands, 52–128, 329, 335; agriculture, 56–57, 70–92, 94, 102–104, 107, 114, 115, 118–119; Contact-era population, 4, 14, 52–54, 108–128, 233, 329; Cook arrival, 4, 24, 52–53, 67, 90, 106–107, 112; demographic reconstruction, 12, 40, 60, 67, 71–73, 91–93, 108–128; Expansion Period (AD 1100–1650), 60, 65–66; exponential population growth, 20, **21**, 65–66, 70–71, 97, 106, 334, 335; founding populations, 68, 332; Hommon model for "primitive states" in, 55–56; house counts, 54–55, 57, 68, 85–86, 91–92, 98–105, 108–111, 114–117, 124, 127; inland expansion, 55–57, 60, 97–98, 105–106; missionary census (1932), 53, 62, 64, 65, 104–105, 124, 220; Native American Graves Protection and Repatriation Act (NAGPRA), 7; paleodemography, 6, 12, 54–69, 70–107, 327, 329–333; politics of skeletal remains, 7, 329; population density, 54, 58, 65, 66–67, 331; post-Contact depopulation, 31, 104–105, 112; pre-Contact population, 4–5, 8, 20, 22, 52–108, 328. *See also* Hawai'i; Kahikinui, Maui; Kealakekua; O'ahu
health services, 11, 28, 205. *See also* diseases
Heath, T., 207–208
Henry, T., 134, 145
hepatitis, 236
Hill, L., 305
historical demography, 11, 18–21, 233; debates in, 2–5, 9, 12–13, 14, 53–54, 66, 233–234, 326, 336–337; New Caledonia, 307–309, **309**; Western, 21, 32, 54. *See also* archaeology; censuses; Contact era;

dating; ethnohistory; literature; oral histories; prehistory; records
Hokatu Valley, Ua Huka Island, 13, 160–176, **161–164**, **169–173**, 331
Holmer, R., 223
Holmes, L. D., 214
Home, Sir E., 207, 208, 210
Hommon, Robert, 55–61, **56**, 91, 97
Hooper, A., 247, 248, 249
horticulture, 91; Kahikinui, 92; Marquesas, 162, 175; New Caledonia, 310, 313, **313**, 314–315, 316, 320; Samoa, 223. *See also* agriculture; gardens; *kalo*; soil; sweet potatoes; taro; yams
house counts, 127–128, 327, 328; Hawaiian Islands, 54–55, 57, 68, 85–86, 91–92, 98–105, 108–111, 114–117, 124, 127; Hokatu Valley, 162, 327–328; 'Opunohu Valley, 13, 135–143, 153–156, 159, 327–328. *See also* residential structures; sleeping areas
Hudson, W. L., 235, 236
human sacrifice, 19, 32, 157–158
Huntsman, J., 234, 237–244, 247–249
hurricanes, 19

infant diseases, 27, 112. *See also* infant mortality
infanticide, 16, 19, 32, 239, 250, 334; gender-selective, 18, 283, 299; Ma'ohi, 157–158
infant mortality, 18, 112, 205. *See also* infanticide
Inglis, John, 280, 283–289, 298, 304–305
Ingraham, Captain Joseph, 173
intensification, agricultural, 5, 55–57, 67, 331, 336; Aneityum, 290, 294, 296; Hawaiian Islands, 75, 78–88, **80**, **84**, 108, 111, 115–116, 121, 331; Kosrae, 264, 267; New Caledonia, 312–315, 321–322; Samoa, 215, 216, 230; Tokelau atolls, 253; Tonga, 191–196, 201
irrigation systems, 49–50, 305; Aneityum, 282, 292, 294; Fiji, 303; Grande Terre, 315–316, 325; Hawaiian Islands, 9, 60–61, 91, 93, 112, 114–121, 123, 128, 330, 333, 335;

Hokatu Valley, 175; 'Opunohu Valley, 145–149

Jamet, R., 153
Jennings, J. D., 223, 228, 244–245
Jouan, H., 173

Kahikinui, Maui, 12, 90–107, **92, 99–102**, 126, 327, 329–333; radiocarbon dating, 91–92, 94–98, **95–97**, 100, 328; residential structures, 91–92, 98–105, **99–101**
Kahikinui Archaeological Project (KAP), 91–92
Kahn, Jennifer G., 13, 37, 102, 129–159, 331
kalo: Hawai'i, 123; O'ahu, 112, 114–121, 128
Kamakau, S. M., 127
Kanak culture, New Caledonia, 307–325, 330
Kealakekua, 52–53, 90, 125–128; King's population estimates, 53, 106, 111–112, 118, 126, 127
Kellum-Ottino, Marimari, 160, 166, 167, 170–174
King, Lt. James, Hawaiian population estimates, 4, 52–54, 57, 62–63, 67–68, 110; Kaua'i, 128; Kealakekua, 53, 106, 111–112, 118, 126, 127; Maui, 100–101, 106, 330
Kirch, Patrick V., 1–14, 234; agricultural yields, 146, 150; Anahulu Valley, 60–61, 157; Kahikinui, 12, 90–107, 329; marginal areas, 38, 65, 91, 93–94, 101, 106, 107; models of long-term demographic change, 10, **11**, 35, 37, 57–60, 177, 326, 333–336; paleodemography, 5–9, 37, 54–69, 90–107, 326–337; Tonga, 181–201, **190**
Kittlitz, Friedrich, 263
Kohala, Hawai'i: agricultural development and demography, 12, 70–89, **72–87**, 331–333; chronology of wall and trail construction, 76–80, **77**, 87; climate, 88, 111, 122; C-shaped structures, 71, 81–88, **82**, **84**; detailed study area (DSA), 73–88; domestic archaeological features, 71, 81–88, **82–86**, 127; expansion areas,

75, 78–88, **80, 84**; intensification areas, 75, 78–88, **80, 84**, 331; southern *ahupua'a*, 83–87
Komori, Eric, 8, 61–69, **62**, 328
Kosrae, Caroline Islands, 13, 257–277, **258**, 332; breadfruit, 13, 260, 262–266; radiocarbon dating, 267–268, **268**, 277, 328

Ladefoged, Thegn N., 12, 70–89, 331
Lakeba, 218, 229, 296
land unit of analysis, *ahupua'a*, 111
land use: Aneityum, 291–294, **293–294**; Kosrae, 264–266; Samoa, 212–216, **215**, **217**, 218–219, **219**, **220**, 223–229. *See also* agriculture; residential structures; soil
La Pérouse, Jean-François de Galaup de, 1, 90, 211, 318
Lapita culture, 252, 253; Melanesia, 309 310; New Caledonia, 307; Tonga, 178, 180, 186–201, **187**, **188**, **190**, 333
Lawson, 173
Lay, T. E., 213–216
LeBlanc, S., 57
Lee, Charlotte, 12, 35–51
Lelu, 260–261, **261**, 277
Lepofsky, D., 138–139, 159
Lesson, René, 30, 262–263, 264
life expectancy, Polynesia, 19
life tables, 6–7, 39–40, 68, 198. *See also* birthrates; death rates
literature: ethnohistoric sources, 133–134, 232–233. *See also* explorers; missionaries; oral histories; records
logistic population growth, 10, 17, 58–60; Dye/Komori model, 62; Kosrae, 267–268, 274; Malthusian view and, 36; modified, 10, 59, 60, 66, 201, 335; New Caledonia, 322, 323; Tonga, 200–201; Verhulst equation, 267, 335; west Hawai'i, 10, 59–60
London Missionary Society (LMS): Aneityum, 279–281; New Caledonia, 308, 318; Samoa, 207–209, 222, 279; Society Islands, 3, 134; Tokelau atolls, 242, 243

Long, W. H., 39
long-term population trends, 1–14, 19–20, 36, 175–176, 234, 322, 337; dating curves as proxy indicators, 5–8, 13, 56, 61–67, **62**, 69, 134, 267, 328; Hawaiian Islands, 55, 66, 67, 105; Kirch models, 10, **11**, 35, 37, 57–60, 177, 326, 333–336; Melanesia, 322–323; ʻOpunohu Valley, 134–135; Tonga, 178. *See also* depopulation; population growth; pre-Contact population; radiocarbon dating
Loomis, 128
Loyalty Islands, 301, 307, 310, 311, 312, 314, 323
Lütke, Fyedor, **261**, 263

MacArthur, R. H., 10
Macgregor, G., 241–242, 255
Mahele land records, 12, 109–128, 327
Malthusian population dynamics, 36–39, 333–334
Mangareva, 21–22
Manono, 207, 208
Manuʻa, 208, 214, 216, 218
Maʻohi people, 129–158, **131**
Maori population, 23
Maré Island, 311–312, 314, 318, 323
marginal areas, 38–39, 65; ecologically, 60, 65, 91, 107; Kahikinui, 91, 93–94, 101, 106, 107, 126
Maric, Tamara, 13, 160–176, 331
Marquesas: first European contact, 173; Hokatu Valley, Ua Huka Island, 13, 160–176, **161–164, 169–173**, 331; monumental structures, 162–170, **164, 165, 169–170**; post-Contact depopulation, 27–32, **28**, 173, 324; pre-Contact population, 20, 24, 160–176
marriage: Aneityum, 281, 283; endogamy, 283; exogamy, 244; Kosrae, 270; polygamy, 281; polygyny, 242; Tokelau atolls, 239, 242–244; Tonga, 198. *See also* sexuality
Massal, E., 103, 149

Maude, A., 181, 184–185, 194, 238, 239, 244, 246, 247
Maui. *See* Kahikinui, Maui
Maupiti, 31
Maxwell, Capt., 207, 210
Mayr, Ernst, 337
McArthur, Norma, 3–4, 14, 233, 272–273, 291, 326–327, 336–337; Aneityum, 283, 285–290, 299–300; Samoa, 205, 217, 229, 330; Stannard challenge, 4–5, 9, 14, 336, 337; Tahiti population, 3–4, 16, 29–30, 130, 155; Tonga, 217
McFadgen, B. G., 96
measles, 25, 26, 27, 29
measures (population estimation), 70, 108, 326, 329–333. *See also* dating; population density; population dynamics; population growth
Meindl, R. S., 39
Melanesia, 320; ceramics, 187; Lapita culture, 309–310; long-term demography, 322–323; social structure, 306. *See also* New Caledonia; Vanuatu
Melville, Herman, 166
methods (population estimation), 5–10, 24, 60–65, 160, 199–200, 320–322, 326–329; archaeological, 108–112, 126, 164–174, 175–176, 289; based on modern data, 39, 50; dwelling-area approach, 98, 141–143, 247–250; Forster's, 3, 308; Kellum-Ottino's, 160, 166, 167, 170–174; Lay's, 213–216; population and agricultural development tracked together, 71–73, 75; projections, 15, 18, 26–27, 32, 98, 327. *See also* carrying capacity; censuses; dating; demographic reconstruction; ethnohistory; house counts; literature; missionaries; models; osteological demography; population growth curves; proxy data; retrodictions; settlement demography
Micronesia. *See* Kosrae
migrations, 269; Diuturnal Settlement Model, 253; Kosrae, 267, 269–272, **270**,

271; Marquesas, 33; population control through, 239, 250; and population development, 17–18, 23–24, 33; Tokelau atolls, 235, 240–243, 246–247, 254–256; Tonga, 190, 197–198. *See also* expansion; explorers; founding populations

Mills, W., 207–208, **209**

missionaries: Aneityum, 279–281, 283–286; atoll migration coerced by, 235, 246–247; New Caledonia, 308, 318–320, 323; Proto-Historic period before, 70; Samoa, 205, 206–211, **209**, **211**, 219–223; Society Islands, 132, 134; Tonga, 221. *See also* London Missionary Society (LMS)

missionary censuses, 326; Aneityum, 283–285; Hawaiian Islands (1932), 53, 62, 64, 65, 104–105, 124, 220; Samoa, 205, 206–211, **209**, **211**

models: Aneityum age and sex structure, 299–300, **300**; Bayliss-Smith, 9, 156, 291–304, 305; CENTURY simulation model, 42–45, **44**, **45**; "dispersal," 251–252; Diuturnal Settlement Model, 253; Dye/Komori, 5, 6, 8, 61–67, **62**, 328; Gompertz model of mortality, 39; Hommon/Cordy/Kirch, 55–61; islands as "model systems," 333–334; Kirch models of long-term population trends, 10, **11**, 35, 37, 57–60, 177, 326, 333–336; Kohala detailed study area (DSA), 73–88; "Pacific model," 272; plant-soil dynamics, 42–45, **44**, **45**; Rallu demographic growth model, 17–33, 65, 190, 332; social production, 61; stepped, 201

moku (districts), 112

Molloy, M., 234, 237, 238, 239, 240, 243–244, 247

monumental structures: Marquesas, 162–170, **164**, **165**, **169–170**; New Caledonia, 311–312. *See also* residential structures; stone structures

Mo'orea, 129–159, **152**, **155**, 327; population

density, 130–131, 153–155, 331. *See also* 'Opunohu Valley

mortality. *See* death rates

Naroll, R., 7, 57, 141, 164, 166, 247–248

National Science Foundation, 92

Native American Graves Protection and Repatriation Act (NAGPRA), 7

Nera pottery tradition, 312–313

New Caledonia, 13, **280**, 306–325; Catholic Marists fleeing from, 281; Contact-era population, 309–317, 330; post-Contact depopulation, 31, 308–309, **309**, 317–325; pre-Contact population, 5, 233, 306–325, 330

Newell, 247

New Zealand, **204**, 233; and atolls, 235, 255–256; post-Contact population, 26, 31; pre-Contact population, 22–23, 24

Niuatoputapu, 178, 180, 187, 189, **190**, 191, 197

Nordyke, Eleanor, 4, 54, 62–63, 66, 106

Nukuleka, 187–189

Nukunonu, **204**, 234–240, **237**, 246, 248–250, 254

nu'u, Samoa, 224

O'ahu: Anahulu Valley, 9, 60–61, 157, 281; 'Ewa, 110, 118–121, **119–120**, 125, 126; Wai'anae, 110, 112–118, **113**, **118**, 125–126, 128, 330

Ohuul, 285, 304–305

Oliver, Douglas, 3, 130, 137, 155

Olohega, **204**, 235, 244–246, 247

'Opunohu Valley, Mo'orea, 13, 129–159; agriculture, 138–139, 144–157, **147–150**, **152**, **154**; carrying capacity, 129–130, 143–157; radiocarbon dating, 134–135, **135**; residential structures, 13, 135–143, **138**, **140**, **143**, 153–156, 159, 327–328

oral histories: New Caledonia, 318, 324–325; Tahitian, 134; Tokelau atolls, 240

oscillating population, 10, 60

osteological demography, 6–7, 327, 329. *See also* burials; skeletal remains

Ouetcho, A., 13, 306–325

Oundjo tradition pots, 312–313

overshoot, 10, 59–60

Païta, 315, 317, 320

Palauli Bay, 220–222, **221**, 223, 228

paleodemography, 7, 13, 176, 326–337; archaeology and, 2, 5–9, 54–65, 83–107, 327, 333, 334, 337; Hawaiian Islands, 6, 12, 54–69, 70–107, 327, 329–333. *See also* demographic archaeology; life tables; measures; methods; models; pre-Contact population

Parton, W. J., 43

"pericontact" period, 234–236, 245–251

Pernetta, J., 305

petroglyphs, 312

Pietrusewsky, M., 198

pigs, Aneityum, 303–304, 305

Pirie, P., 205–211, 217, 218, 229, 230, 330, 331–332

Pitcairn, 234, 306; population growth, 18, 21–22, 33, 240, 272, 310, 332, 334

Platt, A. G., 220

Plum tradition pottery, 311

Poindi-Poweu, **324**, 325

politics, 306; Kosrae, 261–262, 268–269, 274; Melanesia/New Caledonia, 306, 311–312, 314, 322, 323; Samoa, 224–225, 227; Tokelau, 246. *See also* chiefs/chiefdoms; warfare

Polynesian Plainware phase (700 BC to AD 400), Tonga, 178, 191–196, **192**, **194**, **195**, 198, 201, 333

Pool, D. I., 233

population: Bayliss-Smith model, 9, 156, 291–304, 305; oscillating, 10, 60; projections, 15, 18, 26–27, 32, 98, 327–328; redistribution, 203; stabilization, 12, 17–25, 33, 66, 97, 106, 197–200, 332; "standard," 9, 156, 290–291, 301–302. *See also* Contact-era population; demography; depopulation; founding

populations; measures; methods; pre-Contact population

population density, 10, 20, 25, 37, 320–321, 329–337; Aneityum, **303**; Cook Islands, **31**, 32; Hawaiian Islands, 54, 58, 65, 66–67, 331; Hokatu Valley, 174–175, 331; Kahikinui, 102, 106, 331; Mo'orea, 130–131, 153–155, 331; New Caledonia, 13, 306–325; Samoa, 224; Society Islands, 2, 31, **31**, 174; Tokelau atolls, 256; Tonga, 178, 180–184, 190, 193–202. *See also under* population growth

population dynamics, 35–37, 176, 257–258; Hawaiian Islands, 57–69, 94–98, 105; Kosrae, 257–277; Malthusian, 36–39, 333–334. *See also* long-term population trends; population growth

population growth, 10, 320–321; density-dependent, 10, 37, 58, 66–67, 178, 190, 197–202, 258, 267–269, 274–276, 334–335; density-independent, 10, 18, 58, 66, 334–335; dependent variable, 70; development models, 17–25, 32–33, 190, 332; Hawaiian Islands, 10, 20, **21**, 55–71, **56**, **58**, **62**, 97, 106, 332, 333, 334, 335; independent variable, 55–56, 57, 58, 70; Kosrae prehistoric, 257–277; New Caledonia, 310–311, 320–321; nonlinear, 56; 'Opunohu Valley, 134–135, 157–158; "Pacific model," 272; Pitcairn, 18, 21–22, 33, 240, 272, 310, 332, 334; population pressure, 57, 157–158, 197, 289; stepped models, 201; Tokelau atolls, 240, 244, 247, 252–253, 310, 327, 332, 334; Tonga, 177–202, **186**, 230, 333; United States (1670s–1850s), 272; world (AD 1–1650), 272. *See also* depopulation; expansion; exponential population growth; logistic population growth; long-term population trends; population growth curves

population growth curves, 4–5, 56; radiocarbon dating curves as proxy models, 5–8, 13, 56, 61–67, **62**, 69, 134, 328; site-count, 56–60, **56**, **59**, 69, 100, 334. *See also* exponential population growth;

logistic population growth; long-term population trends

population regulation, 10, **11**, 12, 19, 32, 58, 157–158, 250, 334; atolls, 251; and food availability, 35–51; human sacrifice, 19, 32, 157–158; Kosrae, 267–268; reproductive, 198, 239, 244, 250–251, 334–335; Tahiti, 21; Tikopia and Anuta, 331; Tonga, 198, 199. *See also* famine; infanticide; migrations; stabilization; warfare

Postan, M., 38

post-Contact depopulation, 2–4, 10–12, 17, 25–34, **28**, **30**, 336; Hawaiian Islands, 31, 104–105, 112; Marquesas, 27–32, **28**, 173, 324; Moʻorea, 132, 158; New Caledonia, 31, 308–309, **309**, 317–325; Tokelau atolls, 235, 236, 238–240, 243–247, 255; Tonga, 211. *See also* death rates; diseases; "pericontact" period

Postels, Alexander, **261**, 262

pre-Contact population, 4–9, 11, 12, 15, 17–25, 32, 337; Aneityum, 283–304, **302**; Hawaiian Islands, 4–5, 8, 20, 22, 52–108, 328; "Hawaiian-specific model," 57; Marquesas, 20, 24, 160–176; New Caledonia, 5, 233, 306–325; Proto-Historic period (AD 1650–1795), 60, 67, 70, 203–231; Samoa, 203–231, **206**, **209**, **211**, **212**, 330, 331–332; Society Islands, 21, 129–159; Tonga, 177–202, **186**, 230, 290, 333. *See also* paleodemography; "pericontact" period; prehistory

prehistory: demographic reconstruction, 35, 39–41, **41**, **43**; food and population, 35–51, 103–104, 156; Kohala, 12, 70–89; Kosrae, 257–277. *See also* archaeology; founding populations; paleodemography; pre-Contact population

Pritchard, W. T., 209

"processualist" approach, 55

productivity. *See* carrying capacity

projections, demographic, 15, 18, 26–27, 32, 98, 327–328

Proto-Historic period (AD 1650–1795), 60, 67, 70, 203–231

proxy data, 70, 177–178, 233–234; ceramics and archaeological sites, 178, 199–200; dwelling areas, 98, 242, 247–249; radiocarbon dating curves, 5–8, 13, 56, 61–67, **62**, 69, 134, 267, 328; "sitepopulation growth sequences," 56, **56**

Pukapuka, **204**

radiocarbon dating, 68, 98, 328, 334; dating curves as proxy models, 5–8, 13, 56, 61–67, **62**, 69, 134, 267, 328; Dye/Komori model, 5, 6, 8, 61–67, **62**, 328; frequency distributions, 95–96, **95–96**, 100, **100**, 108; Hawaiian Islands, 59–60, **59**, 69, 73, 91–92, 94–98, **95–97**, 100, **100**, 108, 110, 328; Hokatu Valley, 170; Kosrae, 13, 267–268, **268**, 277, 328; ʻOpunohu Valley, 134–135, **135**, 141, 158; Tonga, 187, 189

rainfall, 336; Hāmākua, 123; Kahikinui, 93, 94; Kosrae, 259–260

Rallu, Jean-Louis, 1–34, 233, 336; demographic growth model, 17–33, 65, 190, 332; Marquesas, 173, 324; New Caledonia, 309, 324; Society Islands, 130, 132, 155

Rapa Nui (Easter Island), 21–22, 33

Raspe, P. D., 241, 242, 243, 255

real case studies, 234, 250

reconstruction: agricultural systems, 144–145, **152**, 153, 223–224. *See also* demographic reconstruction

records, 111, 232–233; Mahele land records, 12, 109–128, 327; Samoa historical, 205–212. *See also* censuses; explorers; literature; missionaries; oral histories

regulation/controls. *See* population regulation

reproductive regulation, 198, 239, 244, 250–251, 334–335. *See also* birthrates; infanticide

residential structures, 7–8, 127, 162–164; contemporaneity, 141, 168–170, 176; dwelling-area approach, 98, 141–143, 247–250; ʻEwa, 119–121; Kahikinui, 91–92, 98–105, **99–101**; Kohala, 71,

81–88, **82, 84, 85,** 127; Kosrae, **261,** 262; Marquesas/Hokatu Valley, 162–173, **165,** 327–328; New Caledonia, 313–314, 316–317, 320–321; ʻOpunohu Valley, 13, 135–143, **138, 140, 143,** 153–156, 159, 327–328; permanent, 7–8, 109, 127; Samoa, 222, 224–228, **226,** 248; size of Polynesian households, 101, 127–128, 136–137; specialized activity areas, 139–141; temporary, 109, 127, 245–246; terraces, 138–139, 142; Tokelau atolls, **245,** 247–250, **249,** 256; Tonga, 190, 198. *See also* house counts; sleeping areas

respiratory diseases, 27

retrodictions, 11, 15, 25, 29–32; Hawaiian Islands, 54, 106; McArthur's, 337; Society Islands, 29–30, **30,** 32, 130

Reybaud, L., 308

Ricardo, D., 38

Rick, John, 8, 61

Ritter, P. L., 263, 265, 266

Robertson, George, 2, 15, 130

Rodriguez, G., 33

Rogers, G., 181, 198

Rosendahl, P. H., 71, 73, 75, 127

Rothamsted experiment, 39

Roux, J. C., 316, 325

Russell, K. F., 39

Sahlins, M., 60, 228, 303, 306

Samoa, **179,** 187, 203–231, **204;** American, **204,** 208, 210, 212–216, **215,** 235; diseases, 211, 218, 246, 255; land use, 212–216, **215, 217,** 218–219, **219, 220,** 223–229; pre-Contact population, 203–231, **206, 209, 211, 212,** 330, 331–332; residential structures, 222, 224–228, **226,** 248; Tokelau atoll population and, 246, 247, 255–256

Sand, Christophe, 5, 13, 233, 306–325

sandalwood trade, 279–280, 308, 318

Savaiʻi, Samoa, 207–208, 216, 218–226, **220, 226,** 229, 230, 247

scarlet fever, 27, 29–30

Schmitt, R. C., 54, 62–63, 66–68, 111–112, 124, 233

Senyavin, **261,** 262, 263

settlement demography, 6, 7–8, 12, 327. *See also* ceramics; expansion; migrations; residential structures; sleeping areas

sexuality: celibacy, 250, 283, 334; permissiveness, 18–19, 23; sexually transmitted diseases (STDs), 1, 18, 112, 218, 325. *See also* marriage; reproductive regulation

Simeona, 286, 287, 288

site-frequency histograms: west Hawaiʻi, 59–60, **59,** 69. *See also* frequency distributions

"site-population growth sequences," 56, **56**

skeletal remains, 6–7, 68, 269, 312, 329. *See also* burials

"skimming" mode, 251

slave ships, atoll recruitment raids, 236, 238–240, 243–247, 255

sleeping areas: Marquesa, 164, 166–167, 170, 171, 175; North Kona, 57. *See also* house counts

smallpox, 25–26, 27, 29, 30

social demography, 19–20, 177; Aneityum, 281–283, 299, 301–303; Hawaiian Islands, 335–336; Kosrae, 262–263, 268–269; New Caledonia, 307–309, **309,** 311–312, 314, 320–321; ʻOpunohu Valley, 157–158; Society Islands, 156; Tokelau atoll, 251. *See also* chiefs/chiefdoms; disease; economics; ethnohistory; life tables; marriage; population regulation; residential structures

social production models, 61

Society Islands: population density, 2, 31, **31,** 174; post-Contact flu death rates, 26; pre-Contact population, 21, 129–159. *See also* Moʻorea; Tahiti

soil: Aneityum, 278–279, 292–294; degradation, 39, 43; fertility, 38–39, 153; model of plant-soil dynamics, 42–45, **44, 45;** moisture, 50; Moʻorea, 150–153, **151, 155;** New Caledonia, 307, 312, 320–321; nutrient status, 42–50, 336; Samoa, 223; soil organic matter (SOM), 43; Tonga, 182, **183**. *See also* agriculture

Soudsky, B., 164

South Pacific, **204**

Spennemann, D. H. R., 191, **192**, 193

Spriggs, Matthew, 5, 9, 13, 157, 278–305

stabilization, population, 12, 17–25, 33, 66, 97, 106, 197–200, 332

Stair, J. B., 207, 209, 222–223

Stannard, David: Hawaiian population, 14, 29, 53–54, 62, 66, 104, 106, 111–112, 128, 337; McArthur challenged by, 4–5, 9, 14, 336, 337

stepped models, 201

stochasticity, 37, 50, 96, **97**, 322, 336

Stock, J., 93

stone structures, Hokatu Valley, 162, **164**, 168, **169–170**

Suess effect, 63–64

sugarcane: Hawaiian Islands, 94, 114, 118, 121; Kosrae, 263

sustainability, 37–46, 49, 264, 331

Swains Island, **204**, 214, 235

sweet potatoes, 305; Hawaiian Islands, 68, 73, 91, 94, 103, 107, 119, 123; Society Islands, 145, 146; Tonga, 182

Swinbourne, C. A., 244

Tahiti, 15–16, 21; agriculture, 145; Contact-era population, 2–4, 16, 29–34, **30**, 130–132, 155; Cook, 2, 15–16, 130; diseases, 18, 27, 29, 32; European arrival, 1, 24, 130; food, 156; Forster, 2–3, 15, 130, 137, 141, 155; Green survey, 133; as Otaheite, 1, 2–4, 53; residential structures, 139, 142–143

Tahiti Nui, 28

Taiarapu, 28, 32, 33

taro, 291; Aneityum, 282, 292, 295, 297, 298, 303–304, 305; Atiu, 214; Hawaiian Islands, 60–61, 103, 112, 119, 123; Kosrae, 263, 264–265; New Caledonia, 313, 315, 317, 325; Society Islands, 145–150; Tonga, 182

Tartinville, Nathalie, 161

technology, agricultural, 37, 39

terraces: agricultural/horticultural, 138, 144, 150, **150**, 294, 313, 325; residential, 138–139, 142

Tikopia, 157, 248, 250, 331, 334

Tinielu, I., 236

Tiraoou, wars, 32

Tiwaka, 314, 315, 317

Tofua volcanic arc, 178–180, 192–193

Tokelau atolls, 13, **204**, 232–256, **237**; population growth, 240, 244, 247, 252–253, 310, 327, 332, 334; residential structures, **245**, 247–250, **249**, 256. *See also* Atafu; Fakaofo; Nukunonu; Olohega

Tokelau Islands Migrant Study (TIMS), 241, 254–255

Tonga, 13, 177–202, **179**, 217–218; diseases, 181, 211, 218; maritime chiefdom, 196–199; missionaries, 221; pre-Contact carrying capacity, 182–185, 194, 199, 201, 290; pre-Contact population growth, 177–202, **186**, 230, 333; Samoa and, 211, 217–218, 221, 230. *See also* Tongatapu

Tongatapu, 180–186, **187**, **190**, **192**, 230; agriculture, 181–182, 184–186, 191–197, 291; soil, 182, **183**

Tuamotus, 22, 253

tuberculosis, 27, 236

Tu'i Tonga, 197

Tuljapurkar, Shripad, 12, 35–51, 331, 336

Tupaia, 16

Turner, B. L., II, 7

Turner, Peter, 207, 208, 220–221

Tutuila, 208, 213–214, 215, 216, 247

Tuvalu, **204**, 235

typhoons, 260, 266

Ua Huka Island, Marquesas, Hokatu Valley, 13, 160–176, **161–164**, **169–173**, 331

United States Exploring Expedition (USEE), 235, 236, 243, 244, 246, 247

'Upolu, Samoa, 207–210, 216, 218–219, **219**, 224–225, 229, 230

'Uvea, **179**, 235, 246

Vanuatu, 252, 278, **280**, 283, 305; Ane-
ityum/Anatom, 9, 32, 278–305, **297**, **300**,
302, 314
Vava'u, 180–186, **183**, **188**, **190**, 192–196, **195**
Vigors, P. D., 278, 283, 289, 304
Vincendon-Dumoulin, C. A., 173
"virgin soil epidemics," 1–4, 10, 28, 53–54.
See also diseases
volcanic eruption, 182, **220**
volcanic-glass dating, 57, 59, 60, 68, 69, 110
volcanic islands, 228–229, 252; Aneityum,
278; Kosrae, 260; Samoa, **220**, 223;
Tofua arc, 178, 180, 192; Tonga, 196
voyagers. *See* explorers; migration

Wai'anae, O'ahu, 110, 112–118, **113**, **118**,
125–126, 128, 330
Waimanu, 122–123
Waimea, 127
Waipi'o, Hawai'i, 120–125, 126
Walsh, A. C., 183–184
Ward, R. G., 229
warfare, 19, 32; Aneityum, 283; Hokatu
Valley, 161, 174; New Caledonia, 318;
Society Islands, 132, 157–158; Tonga, 181,
199
water: 'Ewa, 118–119, 120; Hāmākua, 121–
123; Kahikinui, 93, 94; 'Opunohu Valley,
144, 145, 146–149; Tonga, 182; Wai'anae,
113, 115–118, 128. *See also* drought; irriga-
tion systems; rainfall
Watters, R. F., 225, 229, 230
weather: and food supply, 36–37. *See also*
climate; disasters, natural; drought
Weiss, K. M., 39–40
Whitesell, C. D., 259, 264
Whitney, M., 39
whooping cough, 25, 27
wild food: Aneityum, 278, 295–296; Kahikinui, 93–94, 102; Kosrae, 263–265;
'Opunohu Valley, 156; Tokelau atolls,
252; Tonga, 189, 193. *See also* fish and
shellfish
Wilkes, C., 207, 208, 209, 215, 216
Williams, John, 207, 208, 219–223
Williamu, 286–288
Wilson, E. O., 10
Wilson, James, 1, 3, 28, 137
Wood, A. H., 180
Wood, J. W., 39

yams: Aneityum, 297, 299; Hawaiian
Islands, 94; Kosrae, 263, 265; New Caledonia, 312, 313, 320–321; Society Islands,
145, 146; Tonga, 182, 214
Yen, D. E., 103

HAWAI'I Production Notes for Kirch | THE GROWTH AND COLLAPSE
OF PACIFIC ISLAND SOCIETIES

Cover and interior designed by April Leidig-Higgins in Minion

Composition by Copperline Book Services, Inc.

Printing and binding by The Maple-Vail Book Manufacturing Group

Printed on 60# Text White Opaque, 426 ppi